UBUNTU

UBUNTU

GEORGE M. HOUSER AND THE STRUGGLE FOR
PEACE AND FREEDOM ON TWO CONTINENTS

Sheila D. Collins

OHIO UNIVERSITY PRESS • ATHENS

Ohio University Press, Athens, Ohio 45701
ohioswallow.com
© 2020 by Ohio University Press
All rights reserved

Printed in the United States of America
Ohio University Press books are printed on acid-free paper ⊗ ™

31 30 29 28 27 26 25 24 23 22 21   5 4 3 2 1

Library of Congress Cataloging-in-Publication Data
Names: Collins, Sheila D., author.
Title: Ubuntu : George M. Houser and the struggle for peace and freedom on two conti-
nents / Sheila D. Collins.
Other titles: George M. Houser and the struggle for peace and freedom on two continents
Description: Athens : Ohio University Press, [2020] | Includes bibliographical references and
index.
Identifiers: LCCN 2020027055 (print) | LCCN 2020027056 (ebook) | ISBN 9780821424247
(hardcover) | ISBN 9780821446959 (pdf)
Subjects: LCSH: Houser, George M. | Houser, George M.--Friends and associates. | Ameri-
can Committee on Africa--History. | Africa--Relations--United States. | United States--Rela-
tions--Africa. | Political activists--Africa--Biography. | Congress of Racial Equality--History.
| National liberation movements--Africa--History--20th century. | Africa--Politics and
government--20th century. | Nonviolence--Religious aspects. | Civil rights workers--United
States--Biography.
Classification: LCC DT38.1 .C65 2020 (print) | LCC DT38.1 (ebook) | DDC 323.092 [B]--dc23
LC record available at https://lccn.loc.gov/2020027055
LC ebook record available at https://lccn.loc.gov/2020027056

For my husband, John,

lifelong champion in the struggle

for peace with justice

Ubuntu (Zulu/Xhosa)—a southern African philosophy that speaks about the essence of being human. Archbishop Desmond Tutu explained it in these words: "A person with Ubuntu is open and available to others, affirming of others, does not feel threatened that others are able and good, based from a proper self-assurance that comes from knowing that he or she belongs in a greater whole and is diminished when others are humiliated or diminished, when others are tortured or oppressed."

—*No Future without Forgiveness*,
Doubleday/Random House, 1999

Contents

Illustrations

Acknowledgments

Many people have helped to make this book possible, not least George and Jean Houser and their children, to whom I owe an incalculable debt for opening their home, their lives, their memories and their personal papers so that a fuller, more intimate story could be told of a life that was lived mostly through the organizations he led. I am especially indebted to Steven Houser and Martha (Martie) Leys for providing me with important details about their father's life and legacy that he was too modest to convey. Although many people I had hoped to interview for this book had already passed away, I am grateful to those who were still around and had worked with or knew George and took the time to plumb their memories for insights into the man, his times, and his work. In addition to Steven and Martie, these include Jean Houser, David Houser, Thomas Houser, Meghan Houser, Richard Lapchick, Tilden LeMelle, Peter Weiss, Cora Weiss, Gail Hovey, Matt Meyer, Bernard Rivers, Karen Rothmyer, Evelyn Rich, Marvin Rich, Richard Knight, Prexy Nesbitt, Janet Hooper, and the late Donald Benedict.

This book could not have been written without Steven Houser's encouragement, deep historical knowledge, and invaluable editorial suggestions on both content and style, not to mention his corrective insights into his father's character. Prexy Nesbitt was especially helpful in suggesting other people and resources I should consult and in clarifying some dynamics around a controversy that arose within the ACOA while he was on staff. Gail Hovey gave me valuable insights on George's work style and character, as well as suggesting other people I should interview. Peter and Cora Weiss graciously fed me lunch in their home, suggested resources and contacts, and were most helpful in bringing a number of Houser's friends together for a gathering at their apartment. And I thank Cora for enlightening me about the "Airlift to America" in which she had played such a prominent role. Much of my acquaintance with the heyday of the antiapartheid movement and its intersection with other movements during the late 1970s and early 1980s came from attending the regular gatherings of movement activists at the home of the late Carole Bernstein Ferry and Ping Ferry in Scarsdale, New York. The lively discussions there ranged from how to deal with the latest atrocities in South Africa to plans for challenging the US deployment of Pershing II and cruise missiles in Europe and campaigns to limit the proliferation of nuclear weapons.

I am also grateful for the research support I received from several people, not to mention institutional archives. My research for this book was greatly aided by the marvelous collection of documents that Richard Knight digitized for the online African Activist Archive at Michigan State University as well as for his own writings on some of the ACOA history. Knight was also helpful in suggesting people I should interview and in pointing me to several documents he thought I should look at. I must thank Gail Gerhart, a consummate African scholar, for steering me to several important sources of information on southern African history and Sheila Michaels for pointing me to her oral history collection at Columbia University. I also benefitted from conversations about Houser and the ACOA with two men whose own lives touched many of the same chords as those of Houser: the late Reverend William Wipfler, former human rights director of the National Council of Churches and Reverend William Howard, civil and human rights activist and former president of the National Council of Churches and moderator of the WCC's Programme to Combat Racism, among other roles.

Christopher Harter and his staff at the Amistad Research Center provided me with access to the voluminous ACOA archives and were helpful in miraculously locating in record time a crucial document in those files whose box number and folder I had failed to record on my last visit to the archives. I also want to thank Wendy Chmielewski at the Swarthmore College Peace Collection for providing me with the relevant boxes. Carolyn Bratnober, Elizabeth Call, and Betty Bolden at the Burke Library of Union Theological Seminary helped me to locate the correspondence between Houser and Roger Shinn as well as Houser's "Diary" in the *Union Review* and material on the seminary's history.

I owe a deep debt of gratitude to two graduate students who were willing to share their research and expertise on Africa with me while working on their own dissertations relating to parts of the story in this book. Zac Peterson generously provided me with digitized copies of many of the original source documents from the CORE Papers and Amistad archives, shortening the time and expense involved in my travel to these archives, as well as sharing recordings of his own interviews with Houser, Jennifer Davis, and Prexy Nesbitt. Zeb Larson read the chapters that cover Houser's work with the ACOA and provided corrective comments. Zeb also suggested several recent sources of scholarship on Africa that I was unfamiliar with.

I am grateful to the two anonymous reviewers for their careful, thoughtful review of the manuscript. Their suggestions for contextualizing certain parts of the story, as well as pointing me toward resources I had overlooked and correcting some inaccuracies have made this a better book. Houser's story would not have seen the light of day without my acquisitions editor, Rick Huard, who believed in its potential and gave me several deadline extensions to get it finished.

Two grants, one from the Samuel Rubin foundation and the other from the General Commission on Archives and History of the United Methodist Church, enabled me to travel to the archives where parts of Houser's story are housed. I also want to express my appreciation to the Schoff Fund at the University Seminars at Columbia University for the grant I received to help with indexing. Material in this work was presented to the University Seminar on Full Employment, Social Welfare and Equity. Thanks go to the Fellowship of Reconciliation for providing me with fiscal sponsorship and especially to Ethan Vesely-Flad, FOR's director of national organizing, for his enthusiastic support of this project and for sharing several photos of Houser with me.

Finally, I owe a deep debt of gratitude to my husband, John, for his loving encouragement and patience with me as I fretted through the several years it has taken me to complete this manuscript.

Introduction

IT WAS DAWN ON THE MORNING OF NOVEMBER 4, 1979. The shimmering sun was just beginning to crest over the horizon of the Western Sahara when the small caravan of captured Spanish Santanas stopped after having traveled across the desert. About a dozen guerrilla fighters laid down their rifles, hopped from the cabs, got down on their knees facing Mecca, and began to pray. The two men left sitting in the cab, a Spanish journalist and an American named George Mills Houser, were both wrapped in the traditional Berber *shesh*, which protected them from both the chilly night air and the blistering daylight heat. They were guests of the POLISARIO Front, a nationalist movement that had been fighting Morocco's occupation of the Western Sahara since early 1976. Driving west over a roadless track through the desert, they had come upon the town of Mahbes, which had been the site of a recent battle. The town was deserted except for a few scrawny dogs, burned-out trucks, empty ammunition cases, spent bullets, and abandoned detritus of about fifty Moroccan corpses in various stages of decomposition. Later in the day, left to contemplate his own role in this strange tableau, Houser thought to himself, "What in the world is an ordained Christian clergyman and a lifelong pacifist doing in the middle of the Sahara Desert with a bunch of armed, Muslim guerrillas fighting for the independence of their country? Why wasn't I preaching a sermon on this Christian Sabbath back somewhere in Colorado?"[1]

Why, indeed, wasn't he back in Colorado, living the comfortable life of a Midwestern Protestant clergyman? After all, this is what his father, a Methodist Episcopal minister, had always envisioned for him. Instead, Houser's path had taken him to turbulent centers of the struggles for peace, racial justice, and self-determination in radical resistance to the "war machine" during World War II; to nonviolent civil disobedience campaigns challenging racial segregation in the United States; and to efforts supporting anticolonial movements throughout Africa during the Cold War. During the course of a life that stretched just a year shy of a century, he would come to know and work with most of the leading figures of the twentieth century's major movements for peace, human rights, and self-determination, as well as almost every leader of the major independence movements—many of whom would become heads of state—in the struggle for self-determination in Africa.

Asked toward the end of his life how he would sum up his life's work, Houser thought for a moment and then answered with characteristic understatement: "Well, I had an interesting life. I saw a lot of history."[2] But he also helped to make some of that history, not as one of the "great men" of schoolbook history texts but as a behind-the-scenes organizer and pioneer in modeling many of the strategies and tactics adopted by movement activists later in the century.

In his seminal work on the origins of the civil rights movement, Aldon D. Morris pointed out that movements responsible for historical change do not spring up spontaneously but are the work of unsung organizers who prepare the soil ahead of time.[3] Twenty-five years before a draft resistance movement against the Vietnam War emerged, Houser refused to register for the World War II draft. Seventeen years before the Greensboro sit-ins riveted the nation's attention on the long festering wound of racial segregation, Houser led sit-ins and other forms of civil disobedience in northern and border states in support of desegregation in public accommodations. Twenty-five years before passage of the Fair Housing Act of 1968, Houser challenged racially restrictive housing covenants. Fourteen years before the famous "Freedom Rides" into the South made national headlines in 1961, Houser and Bayard Rustin organized the first "Freedom Ride" into the upper South. Twenty years before a large-scale solidarity movement with victims caught up in the wars in Central America emerged in the 1970s, Houser was pioneering a model of transnational activism with the victims of colonialism and imperialism in Africa.

Houser not only helped to make history but had a front row seat at several historic landmarks. He was an invited guest at most of the pivotal political events associated with African independence, attended many independence celebrations, all three of the All-African People's Conferences, and the founding conference of the Organization for African Unity (OAU). He also served as an observer of the first free elections in Zimbabwe and Namibia.

Few people recognize Houser's name outside those familiar with the scholarship on the civil rights or African anticolonial movements. Perhaps this is because he was a white man whose life's work supported the liberation of those oppressed by racism and colonialism; he was also an unassuming man who saw himself as part of the larger movement of collective history. Yet Houser was more than just a bit player. He was central to that early civil rights movement. Without his steady shepherding of the Congress of Racial Equality (CORE) as its executive secretary for over a decade—at a time when funding was almost nonexistent and agitation for racial justice did not always make for front-page national news like it eventually would—the organization might have folded, making its resurrection later as one of the major civil rights organizations of the 1960s revolution unlikely.

Scholarship on Africa, with some exceptions, has largely downplayed Houser's role, yet his most far-ranging contribution to the struggle for justice in the latter half of the twentieth century was his role in founding and leading the American Committee on Africa (ACOA). According to Dumisani Kumalo, postapartheid South Africa's first ambassador to the UN, "Their [Houser's and ACOA's] efforts have yet to be properly memorialized or even properly recognized. The truth is that many Americans came to know about Nelson Mandela and apartheid through the efforts of George and his comrades."[4] From the 1950s through to the end of South African apartheid in 1994, this small organization played a disproportionate role in introducing the leaders of emerging African independence movements to the world. ACOA also secured their international legitimacy by helping to build support for their causes and in serving as a liaison between the civil rights movement at home and the cause of African liberation abroad.

Although movements are never the work of one person, Houser had a single-minded dedication to the networking that bridged cultures and two continents. His extraordinary administrative, organizational, and strategic mind and his sheer persistence (some would say stubbornness) in midwifing two landmark organizations were essential in laying the groundwork for ending not only institutionalized racial segregation in the United States but also the apartheid state in South Africa and colonialism throughout Africa.

1

A Man of Many Parts, 1916–38

GEORGE HOUSER WAS A MAN OF SEEMINGLY CONTRADICTORY PARTS. He was a deeply committed pacifist who went to prison rather than support the war machine; yet he later supported those engaged in armed struggle in Africa. He was a white man who dedicated his life to the liberation of peoples of color. He was a devout Christian who worked with people of different faiths (or no faith), as well as with those who had different ideological commitments, seeing his work for freedom and self-determination as his ministry. He was an internationalist long before the world was connected by the internet. He was a man who took the long view of history and was a fulcrum of progressive change years before the changes he helped set in motion were recognized by the wider society. He was a gentle man who was nevertheless drawn to risk and adventure. He was a fearless man who rarely talked about the courage it took to back unpopular causes, build organizations with no funding, and risk one's life in serving others. He was also a man who liked to be at the center of the action yet remained in the background, rarely seeking prominence.

The third of four children, George Mills Houser was born to Otto H. and Ethel Mills Houser on June 2, 1916, in Cleveland, Ohio. Otto was a Methodist Episcopal clergyman, and his mother was the daughter of a Methodist clergyman in upstate New York. Otto Houser was an old-school pietist who believed in individual salvation through grace, personal rectitude, and Prohibition. Yet he had a restless, adventurous spirit that would eventually rub off on his son. The family moved every few years, which was an unusual pattern for a Methodist clergyman. Under the Methodist Episcopal system, clergy were assigned to churches by a bishop who presided over a regional jurisdiction. While clergy were expected to move about within that jurisdiction, it was unusual for them to move between states or even across

4

the country. And it was still less likely that clergy would move to another country to do missionary work.

In 1919, when Houser was only three, his family pulled up stakes and moved from Lisbon, Ohio, where Otto was serving a church, to the Philippines, then a US colony. Otto assumed a post as pastor at a Methodist Episcopal church in Manila close to the University of the Philippines campus. Later, the family would move to Buffalo and Troy, New York; Berkeley, California; and Denver, Colorado. Houser's lifelong interest in travel, his sense of adventure, and his ability to successfully operate across different cultures was shaped by this early peripatetic experience.

In an interview later in life, Houser said that he did not remember being conscious of race, and his parents seemed to keep it that way. They maintained long-lasting relationships with their Filipino parishioners and neighbors, while their home in the United States was always filled with African Americans and other non-Caucasians. This cross-racial amity was unusual in a time of strict racial segregation.[1]

THE INTERWAR YEARS: THE MAKING OF A PACIFIST

Born just as America was entering World War I and coming of age just as the country entered World War II, Houser's pacifist calling was to be shaped by these two great cataclysmic bookends. Horrified by the terrific loss of lives and treasure caused by World War I, Americans were in no mood for another war. Houser recalled as a child seeing gruesome photos of the death and destruction wrought by that war and feeling that this was "unthinkable."[2] Isolationism was part of the zeitgeist in America and had been fed by a series of books and articles published in the 1920s and 1930s arguing that arms merchants had tricked the United States into entering World War I.[3] Between 1935 and 1939 Congress sought to codify this isolationism, passing a series of five neutrality acts that repudiated all US involvement in foreign conflicts, including economic engagement with belligerents, even as hostilities were heating up in Europe and Asia.

Existing in tandem with isolationist sentiment was a large and active pacifist movement, which was mostly Christian in orientation. Deriving its inspiration from Jesus's ethical teachings, the pacifist movement held that war violated Christian ethics and that Christians should not involve themselves in war or engage in any kind of violence. The general idea that emerged in the pacifist movements of the 1920s and 1930s was that of noncompliance with the war system.[4] The organizations that exemplified this orientation included the Fellowship of Reconciliation (FOR), founded in Cambridge, England, in 1914 at the outbreak of World War I; the historic "peace" churches—the Mennonites, the Quakers, and the Brethren; the Catholic Worker Movement, founded in 1933; and the secular War Resisters League, founded in 1923. All of these groups shared an optimistic egalitarian vision of social change that included work for civil rights and civil liberties (the FOR had been one of the organizers of the National Civil Liberties Bureau, now the American Civil Liberties Union), cooperative economics, and an anti-imperialist outlook.

No individual exemplified this combination of the abhorrence of war with a commitment to socialist-leaning politics more than the Reverend A. J. Muste. Dubbed the "American Gandhi," he would become the most influential mentor in Houser's life.[5] Although the pacifist organizations were independent of the mainstream religious bodies, Muste wrote that by 1924 "there was a great upsurge of pacifism in the churches": "It came to be recognized as something which had a rightful place—even an indispensable function—in the Christian churches, and not only in the peace churches. The right of conscientious objection was recognized and the duty of the church to give moral backing to its COs."[6]

THE SOCIAL GOSPEL AND AMERICAN RADICALISM

The optimistic social outlook expressed in the pacifist movements drew from a larger cultural influence—that of the Progressive Era, a term generally applied to the period between 1890 and 1920. Though the term refers to a wide range of political tendencies and beliefs, Progressives were generally reformers who repudiated social Darwinism and believed that these conditions could be overcome through the provision of social services for the poor, government regulation of business, electoral reform, public education, and conservation of natural resources. While the Progressive Era was thought to have ended with World War I, its optimistic view of human nature and social change continued to live on in a movement within the mainstream Protestant denominations known as the Social Gospel movement. Originating in the late nineteenth and early twentieth centuries, this movement had its most significant impact on American churches in the 1920s and 1930s; the movement was also instrumental in steering Protestant Christianity away from individualistic notions of sin and salvation and toward the struggle for a more humane social order.

Social Gospelers took their reading of Jesus's ethical teachings into the streets, the labor halls, the settlement houses, and sometimes politics in an effort to reform American society and establish the "Kingdom of God" in the structures of the socioeconomic-political order. In concert with its secular counterparts, the Social Gospel movement called attention to poverty, urban distress, and the harsh conditions of working people and immigrants: the movement generated support for reforms similar to those enacted in New Deal legislation. Indeed, several New Dealers had been brought up in families imbued with the Social Gospel.[7] Early Social Gospelers were also among the leaders of the Women's Christian Temperance Union, the American Civil Liberties Union, and the NAACP. By 1932 a "Social Creed" was adopted as the official statement of the Federal Council of Churches, which represented most of the mainline Protestant denominations.[8]

THE GREAT DEPRESSION: A LESSON IN DISSENT

The interwar years were characterized not only by isolationism and abhorrence of war but also by the Great Depression and the social turbulence it engendered.[9] Young people between the ages of sixteen and twenty-four were perhaps hardest hit by the Depression. An estimated 20 to 30 percent of youth were unemployed. Youth from lower-income families had few educational opportunities, and of course for African American youth such socioeconomic problems were exacerbated. Even college-educated youth had trouble finding work. And as the Depression deepened, increasing numbers of those who could have gone to college saw their student loan funds and parental support dry up. As a clergy family enjoying a guaranteed appointment by the church, the Housers escaped unemployment in the 1930s. George's father had to take a cut in salary but somehow managed to send his son to college. Nevertheless, Houser's lifelong frugality probably stemmed from this experience as it did for so many others who lived through the Depression.

The economic crisis led students like Houser and many others of his generation to question both the logic and value of American capitalism and its connection with the war machine. The result was the growth of the first mass student movement in the United States.[10] According to one of its biographers, "The student rebels of the Depression era rank among the most effective radical organizers in the history of American student politics."[11] Unlike their counterparts in Germany, they appealed to the better angels of our nature, encouraging students to identify with the working class, to value a more just distribution of income and wealth, and to oppose racism. Knowing that their generation would be called on to fight the next war, these activist students became more intensely involved than any other segment of the population with foreign policy and with the need to avoid foreign military entanglements.[12]

In its broadest form the movement was composed of several different factions: a democratic-socialist faction that tended to be more liberal than socialist, a socialist faction that was aligned with the Socialist Party, a Communist faction, and a Student Christian Movement (SCM) that had grown out of the Young Men's Christian Association (YMCA) and Young Women's Christian Association (YWCA).

Three influences from abroad were also at work on Houser's generation. In 1933 Oxford University students had created the "Oxford Pledge," committing students to refuse to fight "for King and country." The pledge received immediate headlines on both sides of the Atlantic, and soon American students had their own version of the Oxford Pledge, in which students would "refuse to support the government of the United States in any war it might undertake." By autumn 1933, this pledge had been taken by students at anti-war conferences across the United States. During its peak years, from spring 1936 to spring 1939, the student movement mobilized at least five hundred thousand collegians (about half of the American student body) in annual one-hour strikes against war. It was the first mass student protest movement in American history. The movement also organized students on behalf of an extensive reform agenda, which included federal aid to education, government job programs for youth, abolition of the compulsory Reserve Officers' Training Corps (ROTC), academic freedom, racial equality, and collective bargaining rights.

A second foreign influence on some students in the 1930s was the example of the Communist experiment in the Soviet Union. Here they had a living demonstration of an alternative to capitalism. Some of the most effective student leaders were either in the Communist Party or were sympathetic to its causes, although probably only a minority of students gravitated to the Communist Left.[13] A less radical alternative was available in the Socialist Party and its youth arm: the Young People's Socialist League (YPSL). Even if one were not a card-carrying member of the YPSL, socialism as the vision of a more democratic, self-governing society was in the air. Houser and other students freely used the term "socialist" to describe themselves.

Finally, a third influence from abroad on students of the 1930s was the example of Mohandas Gandhi, who demonstrated that nonviolent civil disobedience could be an effective method for bringing about positive social change. During the early 1930s, articles about the Gandhian movement in India appeared almost daily in the major newspapers, and in 1934 Richard Gregg, the son of a Congregationalist minister and a lawyer who had spent seven months in Gandhi's ashram in India, published *The Power of Non-violence*, a systematic discussion of Gandhian nonviolent direct action techniques showing how they were an effective and practical method of social change.

The Student Christian Movement (SCM) shared many similarities with the Social Gospel movement and was made up of mainline Protestant campus ministries and organizations that were linked to one another and to their partners overseas through the World Student Christian Federation (WSCF), which was one of the earliest manifestations of the ecumenical movement and the oldest international student organization.[14] As early as 1913 race relations emerged as an issue within the SCM. Following World War I, pacifism and economic justice emerged along with concerns about racism. With its emphasis on student leadership in the service of a peaceful and just human community, the SCM would groom many young people for leadership roles in progressive movements worldwide. Among those who received this training were Houser and several people he would work with over the coming years.

Similar to the ecumenical SCM, and in some cases loosely associated with it, were denominational student movements that had been established by the mainline denominations. The Methodist Student Movement (MSM) was the most radical. As the son of a Methodist Episcopal clergyman, Houser became deeply immersed in the MSM, attending institutes in his high school and college years where Social Gospel evangelists like Sherwood Eddy and his secretary, United Church of Christ clergyman Kirby Page, were invited speakers. Both Eddy and Page had founded the Fellowship for a Christian Social Order in 1921, a Christian socialist organization with a strong pacifist orientation. Both were prolific writers and lecturers whose reputation spread well beyond the United States.

Sherwood Eddy was also the interwar era's foremost exponent of a new kind of Christian internationalism. Early in the century, Eddy had been an itinerant missionary working for the YMCA among social outcasts and the poor in India. Later, as traveling secretary of the YMCA, he worked with students in Asia, South Asia, and Russia. During the 1920s and 1930s he was one of the most influential international leaders in American Protestantism. Eddy wrote thirty-seven books and numerous articles that were widely read by young people in the ecumenical movements, and he spoke to students across the world. He also brought to his American audiences an awareness of the larger world, albeit a world that needed the "modernizing" influences of the West.[15] He affirmed the *"legal* right of the state to declare war and to pass a law conscripting the man power and the money power of the nation against war"—but only until war was abolished. Nevertheless, Eddy upheld the "ultimate moral right to refuse conscription on a fundamental moral issue. . . . I must render to God the things that are God's; and nothing is more his than the moral sphere of the conscience. If the secular government is supreme here we have displaced God from the holy of holies of religion and have enthroned instead the idolatry of the state."[16] This was the message the young Houser took to heart.

Like other Social Gospelers, Eddy also spoke against racism. His international experience had enabled him to see racism in the United States for what it was: the hypocrisy lurking within American exceptionalism. "How could Americans claim to be of a 'superior' race when we still lead the world in our record of lynchings, in race and color prejudices?" he would ask.[17] In addition to other Social Gospel themes like the need for a fairer economic order, Eddy carried an anti-imperialist message to his audiences. His global experiences had led him to conclude that the Anglo-Saxon democracies had conquered or exploited over half of Asia and all but one-thirtieth of Africa; together they spent more on naval armaments than the rest of the world combined.[18]

Michael G. Thompson has argued that the Christian internationalism preached by Eddy was a distinctively new phenomenon in the interwar years, as it "rejected outright the notion that God's universal cause could be seen as immanent within the nation's cause." Rather it "was to be a check against the tendencies to make falsely religious claims."[19] Pacifism, socialism, antiracism, and this new critical internationalism were early influences on Houser that would stay with him for the rest of his life.

A YEAR ABROAD: THE FORMATION OF AN INTERNATIONALIST

After graduating from Berkeley High School in 1934, Houser entered the College of the Pacific in Stockton, California (now the University of the Pacific). As a freshman, he came under the influence of Glenn Young, a senior and president of the SCM on campus. Young had gone to Hawaii as an exchange student the year before and persuaded Houser that he should consider doing a year abroad.

The following year, Houser excitedly joined twenty-four other exchange students from all over the United States, sailing from Seattle to Japan en route to Lingnan University, which was then situated on Honan Island in the Pearl River, three miles off the coast of Canton, China. Perhaps realizing what he was leaving behind, Houser wrote a shipboard letter to his parents, thanking them for "doing an awful lot for me by sending me to China and I will try to make good on all you have invested in me. There are no other parents in this world as nice as mine and there are no other families as nice as ours."[20]

The crossing from Seattle to Japan had taken the ship far north, very near the Aleutian Islands. The weather had been cold and foggy and the seas rough, "bordering on a gale for several days," and Houser boasted to his parents that despite the weather, he "wasn't the least bit seasick"—evidence of the physical stamina that would later carry him trekking through African jungles with hardly an episode of illness.[21]

Houser's natural curiosity about other cultures and peoples, his basic trust in them (however naïve at this point in his life), and his lifelong ability to see past the political propaganda of his own country are revealed in a series of letters he sent home to his parents.

Throughout the early 1930s, as Japan occupied Manchuria, withdrew from the League of Nations, and built up its military, articles had appeared in the American press hinting ominously that Japan represented a potential threat to Western powers. No doubt in American public opinion there was a good deal of racial animosity, as racial discrimination against the Japanese had poisoned Japanese-Western relations since the forced opening of the country in the 1800s. But for the young man out to discover the world, the nightmares of politicians and journalists were not to be taken for the whole of reality. Traveling for two weeks in Japan en route to China, Houser wrote to his parents: "I can assure you that I have had some splendid experiences and my opinion of the Japanese people has changed greatly. It has risen far above what the American newspaper would allow a loyal citizen of the U.S. to believe."[22]

In his letters home, Houser also reveals a discernible pride in getting by on little money, but his boastfulness about frugality is not without a tinge of the standard American arrogance and racial prejudices of the time. "Our main objective [while traveling around Tokyo] in all cases was to save money. It is great fun to see how far down it is possible to make a salesman or taxi driver come from his original price. When I get back to the U.S. I'm afraid my instinct will be to 'Jew' everybody down."[23] Houser would spend the rest of his life fighting against such attitudes.

After two weeks in Japan, the students boarded a smaller ship and set sail across the Inland Sea for the Chinese mainland. During the passage from Kobe to Shanghai, the ship got caught in a typhoon. Houser described in some detail the rocking and pitching of the ship. As most of the other passengers started turning green, Houser boasted that he was glad to have inherited his father's ability to travel on the sea "because I didn't get seasick at all. . . . I felt quite proud of myself to take every meal when there were only about four well members in our party and only about ten in the entire dining room for dinner that night."[24] Like the small child back in the Philippines in a washtub riding the waves in his backyard during a typhoon, Houser found the experience of being caught in this typhoon exhilarating.[25]

Before the ship had landed in Shanghai, Houser had already planned out how he would see the city during the seven-hour layover. Characteristic of a cocky young man who thinks he can understand an entire country in a few hours, Houser tells his parents:

> During that time I became fairly well acquainted with Shanghai. I saw the three sections of the city, . . . I also saw enough to know that China is in a horrible position in many ways. They have no feeling of brotherhood for their fellow men at all and no concern whatever for the plight of other men. They think that that is life and they will never get anything better. They also have no feeling as a nation. During the year I am going to try and learn much more about poor China. At any rate I could see with hardly a glance that China can't begin to compare with Japan in anything.[26]

Yet another side of the young Houser was revealed on this trip. In addition to the adventurer thrilled by danger and the cocksure anthropologist convinced he could fully absorb a foreign culture in one day, we also see a deeply thoughtful young man beginning to seriously contemplate his place in the world.

After a month of travel, the students arrived at Lingnan University in Guangzhou on September 14, 1935. Houser wrote that he is thrilled to be in China at "the storm center of world politics."[27] Lingnan was a Christian liberal arts university that had evolved from its beginnings as a college established by the Presbyterian Church in 1888. But by the time Houser and his fellow students had arrived, the university was governed by a Chinese board. The students lived in campus dormitories with no heat or hot water. In his letters home, Houser commented at length about having to wear several layers of sweaters and overcoats to class during the cold, damp winter months. Travel both on and off campus was by bicycle.

As he settled in at Lingnan, Houser began reading Chinese history and speaking with more Chinese people. He also began attending lectures by famous scholars and exploring surrounding areas outside the campus. Soon his naïve idea of China as a backward country with no sense of its own history and the Chinese as having no feeling for others began to change. He described his Chinese roommate as a quiet, thoughtful, ambitious student "in search of knowledge so that he might help the whole world, not his own country alone." "I am sure," says Houser, "that during the course of the year I will be able to learn much from him." He noticed that the Chinese students treated the exchange students better than Chinese students would have been treated in the United States: "It really makes me blush to think," he says, "that there are people in America calling these people 'chinks.'"[28] He realizes that the high level of "superstition" he has encountered in the Chinese people stems mainly from the high illiteracy rate and is embedded in ancient religious practices that date back before Christ. Instead of a people who have no feeling of brotherhood and no nationalist solidarity (as he had earlier described the Chinese), he came to see a country that had been largely misunderstood and much abused by foreign powers:

> The people throughout the world blame the Chinese for backward
> civilization, for uncleanliness, for lack of administration, for
> banditry, for corrupt officials, . . . But it seems to me that, under
> the circumstances, China has done remarkably well to maintain
> herself at all, with foreign imperialism continuously hounding her
> and a dozen different powers telling her what she ought to do, and
> unmercifully scoring her if she doesn't do it. If the other powers
> would only give China a chance to think about her own problem
> of education, administration and so forth, by quietly withdrawing
> from the scene, the Chinese would ultimately show themselves to be
> thoroughly able to manage their own problems.[29]

The seeds of Houser's lifelong commitment to the self-determination of peoples may be revealed in those last lines.

Yet as the political turmoil in China began to heat up, Houser also found himself wrestling with questions of violent revolution versus gradual reformism and Chinese nationalism versus Westernization. Commenting on the rising prospect of Sino-Japanese confrontation, he reveals a struggle in his own mind that was then beginning to take shape about the lengths to which a commitment to pacifism can be taken:

> I have always believed pacifism was the only means whereby a
> Christian might carry his doctrines to the complete end, but I have
> changed my mind. I can justify a war between Japan and China, not
> on patriotic or nationalistic grounds or from the point of view of
> business, etc., but for the people. The only alternative to war is to
> allow the Japanese to march down the coast spreading corruption,
> probable cruelty, and above all demoralizing the people for their
> own gain. The Chinese would never be subjects of the Japanese
> but would be little short of slaves. . . . In talking with the students
> I find that the Chinese to a man want war because they can't see

the gradual loss of land and home. Yet when I concentrate upon
the hatred of war, the famine, death, and destruction, which is
absolutely inevitable. I don't know where I stand.[30]

This early conflict between his pacifist convictions and his acceptance of the
occasional necessity of armed resistance would play out later in his life when
wrestling with his feelings about armed struggle in Africa.

Houser's personal conviction about pacificism, however, would be reinforced by one particular speaker who visited the campus. Muriel Lester,
a British citizen, was at the time the traveling secretary for the International Fellowship of Reconciliation (FOR), the most famous pacifist organization in the world and the organization through which Houser would
later find his life's calling. Lester was a nonconformist who during World
War I had declared that war was as outmoded as "cannibalism, chattel slavery, blood feuds and dueling."[31] She had accompanied Gandhi on his tour
of earthquake-shaken regions in Bihar while on his anti-untouchability tour
during 1934. When Houser first met Lester, she was on a world tour promoting international peace and social justice along the lines of the Social
Gospel. Lester's presence and message seemed to have a profound effect on
the still-evolving Houser.

At a dinner party with Dr. Hume, another visitor to the Lingnan campus
and a famous medical doctor, the question arose as to whether China would
adopt the Western way of science and democracy, embrace the best attri-
butes of East and West, or remain thoroughly Chinese. Houser expressed the
hope that China would adopt Western science and democracy. "It seems to
be the opinion of the intelligent people in China," he averred. Then, arguing
with himself, he said, "People say that this would cause the loss of Chinese
culture, but it couldn't with their cultural background; anything they adopt
will naturally become Chinese."[32]

As Houser becomes more acquainted with Chinese religion, he begins
to assess his own faith in contrast:

> I tried to contrast each of them [Confucianism, Buddhism and
> Taoism] with Christianity as I was reading their doctrines, ethics
> and modes of action. None of them have the dynamic force of
> Christianity in meeting problems, in living a life not ascetically, but
> mingling freely with sin and conquering it, and the force of One
> behind all movements who is personal and loving. One becomes
> more and more sure of the Christian way of life by just doing this
> sort of contrasting.[33]

During his year in China, Houser's faith in his Social Gospel Christianity would be tested by more than mere bookish learning. The numbing cold the students experienced during the winter was minor compared with what he saw in the streets of Canton. He witnessed "poor people attempting to sleep on the wet, hard sidewalk wrapped in a piece of burlap or canvas . . . little children whose heads are literally covered with open and festered sores, either playing half naked in the streets or sleeping on the backs of their toiling mothers."[34] And there was the thief he watched being caught in Canton, who was "just a poor coolie, dirty and dressed in rags. His captors, well dressed Cantonese, had his hands probably numb with cold tied behind his back. They searched him thoroughly to find any stolen articles, but only found an empty tin can. Every once in a while a man would step up and beat his back brutally. Then after an interval someone would pound his stomach and back both."[35]

Testing his optimistic faith in Christianity's ability to speak to social injustice against the argument of well-known philosopher Dr. Hu Shih—that Chinese nationalism would arise and banish Christianity as a symbol of Western imperialism[36]—Houser wistfully concluded: "Christianity wouldn't do China any good? To be sure our religion is not Chinese in origin. It may be contrary to the quietive philosophy of Taoism, the conservative doctrine of Confucianism, or the desireless attitude of Buddhism, but it does have something to cure the evils in China today."[37] At other times, however, Houser expressed less confidence in his own opinions, revealing that the year abroad had generated an inner struggle in him. We hear in his letters the rather lonely, poignant voice of an earnest, idealistic young man fighting his inner imperfections.

By the end of December, the exchange year was halfway over, and Houser's letters began to reveal his desire to see more of China when school let out in the spring. He told his parents that if they could afford it, he would like to travel in northern China, ride across Manchukuo through Korea and then to Japan, Hawaii, and San Francisco. Throughout his correspondence to his parents, Houser was continually trying to figure out how to pay for the things he wanted to do. It is apparent that Houser is less financially well off than many of the other exchange students and must continually write home requesting even small amounts of money. At one point he is forced to borrow money to pay for his daily needs. He does not complain, however, but takes pride in seeing how frugally he can live and travel. However, one detects that under the bravado there are regrets that he had to live so close to the bone.

The winter holidays in January offered the opportunity for travel. Houser had considered traveling to Hunan province where the Communists were then engaged in fierce fighting. "It might be exciting for me to get up there," he opines,[38] but instead he decides to go to the Philippines to visit his childhood haunts and friends of the family, a more expensive trip made possible by a loan from two of his fellow exchange students. On returning, he reflects on the Filipinos he met and stayed with, who were "kind, generous, polite and above all were so complimentary of my parents. That made a deep impression on me and made me see that friendships are one thing in life which are really worth living for."[39] This would be an important lesson: Houser maintained many friendships throughout his life that spanned decades and continents.

One letter, dated in March, reveals Houser's developing attitude toward organized religion. Discussing some enmity between two factions in churches in the Philippines his father had been associated with, he states that "the church as itself means very little to me but what the church apparently stands for means a lot. In some respects the church seems to be only a big machine and some men seem to be caught in that machine but I refuse to be, at any time in my life."[40] That affirmation would turn out to be prophetic:

Toward the end of the school year, Houser begins to sum up of his experiences abroad:

> Such things as eating Chinese food with chopsticks at the student "fan tong" (mess hall) and enduring cold weather without heat in the buildings are lighter experiences, yet ones which will not soon be forgotten. More than this, however, we are awakening to the vastness of Chinese culture and civilization, the attractiveness of which is imbedded deep in the three religions of China. . . . Of most importance to the Exchange Students, however, is the constant touch we have with the Chinese students—with their friendship and their point of view. This is truly the great value of the Exchange Student plan. If there is ever to be a perfect understanding between nations in our world, it will be stimulated by students. We are beginning to appreciate more and more "the other side of the question." When the spirit of understanding and friendship has permeated the entire world, the real value of students will be appreciated and the real importance of Exchange Students will be known.[41]

Houser's parents had written presuming he would come back from his year abroad a different person. In response, Houser tells them that he still has the same personality as when he left. What he discovered during the year abroad is that he liked working with people. However, Houser chastised himself for not being a better exchange student. He expressed regrets that he had not yet found his place in the world, and he found fault with his temperament and felt that his ambition was "too pronounced." "The only reason it bothers me," he says, "is that it is against my principles. . . . It very often makes me feel jealous, makes me a little uncooperative although I am willing to go more than half way with anyone providing they give me a chance, produces in me what you [his parents] once told me was a negative reaction. I blame many of my faults on this one evil of self-ambition." "Some people," he continued, "would not recognize the fault in them and would let it drive them to their natural inclinations and thoughts. I have Christianity as my standard and don't believe in this. I believe it is possible to get along with everyone. I don't believe in disliking anyone and I believe in being satisfied with the powers which are naturally one's own."[42] What the youthful Houser could not see then was that the two sides warring within him, including the side he had the most negative feelings about—his ambition—would be just that combination of qualities that would impel him to lead some of the twentieth century's great movements for justice and peace.

At the end of the year at Lingnan, Houser set off with his good friend Curtis Smith, who was also the son of a clergyman, to travel north by train to the capital of Hunan province, Changsha. It was 1936, and the political situation in China was heating up. After the Long March, Mao was consolidating his forces in the north to move south, and Chiang Kai-Shek was attempting to unify the eighteen provinces of China under the Kuomintang. Halfway to their destination the two young men were deterred when the train was commandeered by Chiang Kai-Shek's troops. Houser and his friend then had to decide whether to return to Canton or take a riverboat to Nanjing. Determined to see more of China, they decided to take the riverboat.

The three- to four-day trip was an adventurous one. Houser suffered a severe sunburn, was badly bitten by bugs, drank tea made from the river water, and ate any food that could be found along the route. Nights were spent camping out with missionaries in villages along the way. Houser's formidable constitution finally met its match. He fell ill and had to spend two days in a hospital. The two men finally reached Nanjing and from there went on to Peking (Beijing) and then to Korea as they had planned. Then they returned to Canton, where they boarded a ship to Japan. After three more weeks of travel in Japan, the two friends headed back to the United States, landing in San Francisco. It had been a momentous year.

Before Houser left China, he had gotten word that his parents would be moving once again, this time to Denver, Colorado. His father had accepted an appointment to a large church in downtown Denver. During the year abroad, Houser had been contemplating not returning to College of the Pacific but transferring elsewhere. His parents' move eventually prompted an application to the University of Denver, where he was to major in social science with a focus on international relations.

Houser lived at home, commuting by bus to the college, which at the time had a Methodist affiliation. By now, Houser's curiosity about other cultures was well established: between classes he would walk down to one of Father Divine's churches, the Pillar of Fire, to experience this charismatic brand of Christianity as a kind of sociological phenomenon. Father Divine, a black evangelical preacher whose followers claimed he was God incarnate, had a genius for responding to economic need during the Great Depression. By the late 1930s he had established a vast empire of churches, clothing shops, and restaurants, and his interracial followers numbered in the tens of thousands.

While finishing his college education in Denver, Houser became president of the Cosmopolitan Club on campus, an interracial organization that ran programs on international issues. He also resumed his interest in the SCM, attending, as he had previously, numerous regional and national gatherings that were held at Estes Park, Colorado, and conducting, along with other SCM members, Sunday services for young men working for Roosevelt's Civilian Conservation Corps in the Rocky Mountains.

In August 1936 the chancellor of the university sent Houser to Evanston, Illinois, to represent the university at a meeting of the National Conference of Methodist Youth. There he heard Charles Webber, a left-wing Methodist minister and labor organizer who had been on the faculty of Union Theological Seminary. Houser also learned about two professors at Union whom he would later study under: Harry F. Ward, a radical Social Gospeler, and Reinhold Niebuhr, one of the most famous theologians of the day.[43] He also met several young men who would become lifelong friends and colleagues, each making their own significant contributions to the struggle for peace and social justice. Among these was a young African American student named James Farmer, who would later cofound the Congress of Racial Equality with Houser. Another was John M. Swomley Jr., who would later join Houser at Union Theological Seminary. A Methodist minister and theologian, Swomley would go on to serve as national secretary of the FOR and director of the National Council Against Conscription, which was instrumental in opposing a plan for national peacetime conscription. As an activist and author of several books on militarism and the Cold War, Swomley was among the community of FOR leaders who helped shape Dr. Martin Luther King Jr.'s understandings of active nonviolence.[44] Franklin Littell, another of Houser's new friends, would spend nearly ten years in postwar Germany as chief Protestant religious adviser in the high command assigned especially to the task of de-Nazification during the occupation. He was deeply affected by World War II atrocities and dedicated his life to researching the Holocaust and bringing its lessons in human rights to widespread public attention.[45] Finally, Herman Will, who also attended the conference, became a lifelong friend and colleague: like Houser, he would eventually work for the FOR, mostly in racial justice, and hold several positions related to peace and social justice in the hierarchy of the Methodist Church.

As his college years drew to a close, Houser made the decision to apply to Union Theological Seminary in New York City, an interdenominational institution that trained people for careers in the Protestant ministry and academia. Otto Houser had graduated from Boston University School of Theology, a Methodist school, and had assumed that his son would go there too. But at one of the SCM meetings in Estes Park, Houser had met and talked with Union faculty member Henry Pitney Van Dusen. Since Reinhold Niebuhr and Harry Ward both taught at Union, Boston was out of the question for Houser. The decision of fellow Denver classmate Francis Hall to go to Union was another incentive, as was Union's reputation as a center of intellectual ferment and social activism. The two years Houser spent at Union would prove to be a pivotal period in his life.

2

No Turning Back, 1938–41

IN SEPTEMBER 1938, GEORGE HOUSER STEPPED OFF THE BUS
at the Greyhound terminal outside New York City's old Beaux-Arts-style
Penn Station. Houser had the erect bearing and serious demeanor of a young
Prussian military recruit. The straitlaced son of a preacher, he had come to
New York to attend theological seminary and follow in his father's footsteps;
but from this year on, Houser's life would be anything but conventional.

For a young man eager to engage the world, New York City on the brink
of World War II was the place to be, and Union Theological Seminary, a
gothic hulk dominating four square blocks between West 120th and West
122nd Streets on Manhattan's Upper West Side, was an ideal location from
which to test one's antiracist and pacifist beliefs and to immerse oneself in the
intellectual and theological currents of the time. At Union many of the traditional orthodoxies of reformed Protestantism were challenged. Just three
blocks north lay 125th Street, Harlem's major east-west thoroughfare. Union
Seminary existed in a rich cultural milieu. Nearby were the Jewish Theological
Seminary, the Juilliard School of Music, Columbia University, and the interdenominational Riverside Church. Built with Rockefeller money, the large
neogothic church structure was the premier Protestant pulpit. It was here
that Harry Emerson Fosdick, the epitome of liberal Protestantism, preached
to a congregation of thousands and spoke by radio to millions more, while
his books became best sellers. Fosdick had become prominent in the 1920s
and 1930s for challenging the fundamentalist trend within Protestantism
with his brand of socially committed Christianity.[1]

During his first year at the seminary, Houser attended classes with theologians like Reinhold Niebuhr—who, much to the disappointment of some
of his students, had shed his Social Gospel optimism and had become the
proponent of "Christian realism," the philosophy that human society could

20

not be perfected and that ethical compromises had to be made in an imperfect world.[2] But Houser soon gravitated to the seminary's chapter of the Religion and Labor Foundation, whose purpose was to support labor unions and advocate for civil rights and racial equality.[3] He also joined the seminary's Social Action Committee and ended up heading it. Between classes Houser, always more interested in the sociology of the streets than in the theology of the classroom, would often walk a few blocks north to the streets of Harlem. He would take in the sights and sounds and, occasionally, as he had done in Colorado, drop in at Father Divine's Kingdom at 152 West 126th Street for their fifteen-cent chicken dinners.

Harlem was the black mecca of the world, the northern terminus for the Great Migration from the southern cotton and tobacco fields. Known for its jazz and swing dancing, its vibrant nightlife at places like the Savoy Ballroom and Small's Paradise, its fiery preachers thundering from pulpits in grand old stone and brick structures that were cheek by jowl with barbershops, beauty schools, fish-fry joints, and pawnshops—Harlem was brimming with life. But it had been hit hard by the Depression and suffered from appalling poverty. Street hustlers like the young Malcolm X hung out on street corners and in poolrooms and bars; homeless alcoholics clutching brown paper bags roamed the streets; latch-key children, their keys on strings draped around their necks, went home to empty apartments, their mothers out working and their fathers absent. For Houser, this was all grist for the mill.

Houser also walked six blocks south to 114th Street and Broadway to the offices of the FOR, where he signed the Statement of Purpose, which committed its signers to "identify with those of every nation, race, gender and religion who are the victims of injustice and exploitation, and seek to develop resources of active nonviolence to transform such circumstances; and refuse to participate in any war or to sanction military preparations; work to abolish war and promote good will among races, nations and classes."[4] He would also join the Norman Thomas wing of the Socialist Party as a member of the Young People's Socialist League (YPSL). The first of many picket lines he was to join was in support of A. Philip Randolph's Brotherhood of Sleeping Car Porters. He was now, more than ever, an official renegade.

Those training for the ministry at Union were required to do part-time fieldwork at a local church—a kind of in-service training program. By this time, Houser had decided he did not want to work in a traditional suburban church. Several of his friends, who also held socialist and pacifist convictions, felt that the cloistered world of the seminary did not represent the real world outside its doors and that if their studies were to have meaning they should be working among the poor. Some chose to do their fieldwork at settlement houses in East Harlem and Newark. Houser chose the Church of All Nations on New York's Lower East Side. The large brick edifice was described by the *New York Times* as "a splendid place, with a gym, an assembly hall, classrooms, dorms, a swimming pool and a rooftop playing field." During the Great Depression government food tickets were handed out in the church's halls, and on hot summer days, boys played baseball on the caged-in roof.[5]

Located on the southern and eastern side of Manhattan, close to the East River and Port of New York, the Lower East Side was New York's quintessential melting pot, the most populous, most "old-world" district in the city and a mecca for newly arrived immigrants from Eastern and Southern Europe. In 1938, the area bustled with old law tenement buildings—so called because they were built between the Tenement House Act of 1879 and before the New York State Tenement House Act of 1901 (new law). In such neighborhoods on stifling summer days women in housedresses and men in shirtsleeves lounged and gossiped on their front stoops. In pocket parks old men played boccie while others sat at makeshift sidewalk tables playing dominoes. On Italian feast days the Virgin would be paraded through the streets on a pallet held aloft by several men. Sidewalk pushcart markets, barber colleges, tattoo shops, flophouses where the infamous "Bowery Bums" slept off a night's carousing, secondhand clothing exchanges, and gangs of Italian and Jewish kids who played stickball in the streets and occasionally engaged in petty crime: all of this made for a colorful cultural stew for a young man eager to experience city life.

TO PUT HIS CONVICTIONS more fully to work, Houser decided in his second year at Union to leave the comfortable seminary quarters where "professors are getting much too comfortable salaries and students slowly lose their social insight because they are in an ivory tower"[6] and move into a roach- and bedbug-infested tenement apartment on First Street, a half block from the church. Houser recalled being eaten alive by the bugs. He shared the apartment with four other young men. His job was to work with local gangs—mostly Italian youth—and get them to come into the church as "clubs" where they would be in a more wholesome environment and not as likely to engage in criminal activities. This didn't always work, however. Houser later recalled that occasionally the gangs would engage in a riot, throwing furniture around and otherwise creating bedlam.[7]

While living on the Lower East Side, Houser attended a sermon by the Reverend A. J. Muste, at the Presbyterian Labor Temple on Second Avenue and

14th Street, where Muste was then serving as minister. Known as the "most radical church" in New York, the Labor Temple served not only as a church but also as a union hiring hall and school. Houser was immediately drawn to the gaunt Muste, who appeared to have the characteristics that Houser was striving for: a progressive conscience and the willingness to take risks for one's pacifist convictions. It would turn out to be a consequential meeting.

During the spring of his second year in seminary, Houser was chosen to represent Methodist youth at the first general conference of the new Methodist Church, a merger of three branches of Methodism into one large eight-million-member denomination. The meeting, held in Atlantic City in April, was seized with tension when Houser rose to challenge the church's guest speaker, Texas Representative Martin Dies, head of the House Committee to Investigate Un-American Activities (HUAC). In the buildup to World War II, HUAC had been established to investigate alleged subversive and disloyal activities, including organizations suspected of having Communist ties. Dies had spoken that day on the theme that "what we needed was old time religion." Addressing the eight thousand delegates, Houser argued, "Yes, let's get back to old time religion—to Amos and Hosea and Jeremiah"— the Old Testament prophets who had thundered against the corrupt rulers of their day. Following the talk, some people questioned how he could represent Methodist youth, threatening that "they ought to do something with you." Others, however, told him they loved his remarks.[8] It was the first but certainly not the last time Houser would find himself at the center of controversy.

That summer Houser would try out still another cultural milieu, taking a temporary job as pastor of a small rural church in Norwood, Colorado, in the western reaches of the Rocky Mountains near the Utah border. Norwood, with a population of four hundred, was home to a sheepherding industry and at the opposite planetary pole from the teeming cosmopolitan atmosphere he had left behind in New York City. Houser's father had asked him to take the position. By this time Otto had become a district superintendent of the Methodist Church in Colorado, supervising the work of churches across the state. The church in Norwood needed a pastor for the summer and Otto—perhaps sensing that his son was drifting away from the vocation he had long envisioned for him—thought he might be enticed back by having this experience. Norwood, however, was to have the opposite effect on Houser.

Houser's work at Norwood consisted of preaching on Sundays, leading prayer meetings, and making house calls—all traditional duties of a parish minister. What was perhaps not traditional was his decision to accompany some of the farmers as they drove their sheep herds to the nearest railroad. The overland hike took several days, during which Houser enjoyed eating mutton and fishing for trout in the streams they passed. He would also hang out at the local pool hall. Since his days as a student in China, table games like Ping-Pong and pool had been favorite pastimes. He was to scandalize some of the church women, however, when they found out that he had frequented the poolhall that also served as a bar. The Methodist Church had a tradition dating back to the nineteenth-century temperance movement of prohibiting alcohol. Although Houser was a teetotaler at the time, for these pious church ladies, even to be found inside a bar was taboo.

As a well-traveled and educated young man, Houser was troubled by the parochialism of the community he was serving. As he related to his diary: "There was hardly anybody in town, with whom I felt in the same league," and, "The active world is a dim reality here in the mountains." Realizing this, he concluded that the rural ministry was not for him.[9] The decision to disappoint his father, however, did not come easily. He had not yet decided against going into the parish ministry and had been admitted as a probationary minister by the Colorado Annual Conference that summer, but he was bothered by the fact that he did not feel comfortable in this setting. Methodist ministers—part of an itinerant tradition—were supposed to adjust to wherever they were sent. With the end of the summer and his return to Union, Houser was temporarily saved from having to wrestle further with his filial disloyalty.

WAR CLOUDS

As Europe was heading to war, President Roosevelt came to feel that the United States would have to make its weight felt in a conflict it had sought to avoid.[10] Following Hitler's invasion of Poland and declarations of war by Britain and France, the president, in a fireside chat on September 3, 1939, sought to prepare the American public for its eventual involvement in war even while reiterating his fervent hope for peace and his commitment to neutrality.[11] On September 23 he went before Congress explaining that the Neutrality Acts might give passive aid to an aggressor country. After a fierce debate, Congress passed the last of the Neutrality Acts on November 4, which again reiterated the US desire for neutrality but allowed for arms trade with friendly belligerents provided the belligerent paid cash and carried away the materiel in their own ships, thus in effect ending the arms embargo.

When World War II broke out in Europe in September 1939, Houser was attending a national Methodist youth conference in Warrenton, Missouri.

Hitler's aggression and the beginning of the war had a sobering effect on the young people. They rejected the totalitarianism, militarism, and anti-Semitism of the Nazis, but having been tutored in isolationism and nonviolence, most were also convinced that a massive war was not the best way to resist this evil. Houser remembered thinking that Christians should not go to war, as that would be a violation of Christian love as taught by Jesus. "Our creed was the love ethic of the New Testament. But our faith," he admitted, "had never really been tested."[12]

As the Battle of Britain raged through summer 1940, bringing the war ever closer, the heads of the army and navy urged the president to accelerate arms production and conscription as a step toward "complete military and naval mobilization."[13] It was during the summer in Norwood that Houser heard on the radio that a bill to institute the first peacetime conscription in American history was making its way through Congress. Disturbed, he began to propagandize his parishioners against war; but, as he related to his diary, "my exhortations have made no difference."[14]

On July 1, 1940, Congress passed the Selective Training and Service Act by one vote. The act required all men between the ages of twenty-one and thirty-six to register for the draft but for the first time included a provision to allow alternative service for conscientious objectors (COs). Short of calling for all-out mobilization as the military had wanted, the terms of the act required draftees to serve for one year and then spend ten years in the reserves, subject to call-up in case of war. In Norwood, the collective indifference to the outside world that had so bothered Houser just a few weeks before had turned to active support for the war effort. "It's strange and I think tragic," Houser wrote in his diary, "that people who give little thought to world problems are nevertheless caught in the ideology of the American Legion. All over town one sees placard after placard distributed by the Legion and the Lions club with such cryptic phrases as: 'If you don't like America, you can always get a passport to the land of your choice'; 'Millions for battleships but not one cent for tribute.'"[15] To Houser, the people of Norwood seemed to be accepting conscription and all that went with it without thinking. "It seems to me that the only thing that might awaken people to their prejudices is for someone to refuse to comply with the Act. It might cause them to consider what the real nature of conscription is, and whether our democracy can be defended by force of arms."[16]

Returning to Union for his senior year, Houser was now wondering what he should do about the deeply disturbing call-up. The date for registration with Selective Service was set for October 16, 1940. He was not the only one perplexed by this moral dilemma. The draft issue, according to fellow student Don Benedict, "quickly involved practically everyone at the seminary, where we discussed it in relation to the Christian faith."[17] Those who held pacifist convictions were torn. Although seminary students were exempt from the draft, they were still required to register. Was registration itself a kind of commitment to the machinery of war? Could one in good conscience escape the draft simply by being a seminarian when everyone else was subject to call-up? Even if you took the route of conscientious objection, weren't you inevitably lending yourself to the war machine? As these discussions proceeded, Houser's conviction that he should refuse to register became more and more salient. But there was also another reason for his growing conviction, as he wrote in his diary:

> Various people have reminded me again and again that the action would inevitably lead to jail. The reason why I think I look at a jail experience partly in a selfish way is that I have so greatly feared the possibility in my later ministry of compromising with popularity. As one stays in the church year after year, it might be almost inevitable that he would compromise with the vigor of his mission . . . and look forward to being a popular minister, to big churches and big salaries. I am quite sure that if I had a jail sentence "under my belt" the way of compromise will be less a danger. People who are "popular" Christians don't usually want anything to do with a minister who has been in jail.[18]

A few sentences later, however, he wondered if it were really honest to use the penalty of refusal to register as a means of escaping compromise. But then, he confessed, "Quite aside from this, if it is valid to refuse to register, then it will be delightful to realize that bridges are burned behind, and the way of compromise with 'popular' Christianity will not be too great a danger."[19]

THE DECISION

A number of other students were coming to the same conclusion. Late during the night of October 9, 1940, Houser and his roommate were awakened by fellow students Dave Dellinger and Bill Lovell, who told them that a statement was being written announcing that a number of students would refuse to register for the draft. Houser immediately responded to the call, though he confessed some lingering uncertainty.[20]

The initial draft of the statement was written by David Dellinger, Donald Benedict, and Howard Spragg, with editing and additions by Houser and

Meredith Dallas. All five had worked together on the seminary's Social Action Committee headed by Houser. The draft was then circulated to other seminarians. In the end, twenty students signed the statement, declaring their intention to "refuse to cooperate with the government in any way in regard to the Selective Training and Service Act of 1940."[21] The short declaration was accompanied by a two-page statement setting out the rationale they would present to the government on October 16.

Each of the drafters would go on to lead extraordinary lives, distinguishing themselves in various forms of work for peace and social justice. David Dellinger, son of a blueblood Boston lawyer, was to remain a radical pacifist, as well as an antiwar and antiracist activist, until the end of his life, being arrested for civil disobedience numerous times. In 1969 he would achieve notoriety as one of the "Chicago Eight" (later the "Chicago Seven") falsely accused by the Nixon administration of conspiracy to incite a riot and to teach the "use, application and making of incendiary devices" during the chaotic events outside the 1968 Democratic National Convention in Chicago.[22] Another draft resister, Donald Benedict, whose autobiography, *Born Again Radical*, distills his equally iconoclastic life, would go on to found several organizations that made significant contributions to the social justice ministry of the Protestant Church, including the East Harlem Protestant Parish (which, in the 1960s, became a model for urban ministry across the country), the Chicago Community Renewal Society, the Urban Training Center, and the Justice Coalition for Greater Chicago, among others.[23] Howard Spragg, Houser's roommate and the senior class president, was later instrumental in the formation of the United Church of Christ and became executive vice president of its board of homeland ministries. In this capacity he would lead denominational support for the United Farmworkers' grape and lettuce boycotts and rally support for textile workers in North Carolina and woodcutters in Mississippi. Meredith Dallas, the son of a factory foreman, would later shun the ministry for a career as a director and actor in Antioch College's world-class theater program.[24] The bonds these men developed through their shared commitment to confronting the state would remain with them throughout their lives.

The statement adopted by the twenty began by saying that they were taking this action only in light of "what we believe the will of God to be." It went on to declare that it is impossible to think of conscription without at the same time thinking of the whole war system, which "is an evil part of our social order . . . because it is a violation of the Way of Love as seen in God through Christ." There followed a description of all the "evils" that war engenders and conscription as a totalitarian act, as when the government insists that the manpower of the nation take a year of military training or when "the president is able to conscript industry to produce certain materials which are deemed necessary for national defense without considering the actual physical needs of the people."[25] It is clear that the young men had in mind the experience of World War I, with its horrific toll and dubious outcome; but they were also conscious of the totalitarian military buildup in Germany and feared that their own country might succumb to the same thing. "If it is urged that this act, however bad, has been arrived at by the democratic process," they wrote, "let us not forget that it is possible, democratically, to vote democracy out of existence. That is what has happened in Germany and is now taking place in this country."

Since the government had provided for conscientious objection from military service, the twenty students were compelled to answer the question of why they had not chosen CO status.[26] They answered that although pacifists of goodwill had undoubtedly influenced the government to make this available, "It has also been granted because of the fear of the government that, without such a provision, public opposition to war would be too great to handle. In particular, it seems to us that one of the reasons the government has granted exemption to ministers and theological students is to gain a religious sanction for its diabolical war." By refusing this alternative, they knew they could not stem the tide of war, but perhaps their action would help catalyze a nonviolent movement that would conquer war in the future.[27]

The statement was mimeographed and sent to fifteen hundred ministers, friends, other theological schools, antiwar groups, and the press. And then, as Bill Lovell later recalled, "All heaven broke loose."[28] As the Union Eight were the first of some six thousand pacifists who would go to prison rather than participate in the war effort, the story of the Eight's refusal immediately made headlines in all the major newspapers, both nationally and in the students' hometowns. The story got massive radio coverage and top billing in the newsreels that were shown in movie theaters of the time.[29] Houser's aunt Emma, while sitting in a movie theater in Florida, let out a small scream when her nephew's picture suddenly appeared on the big screen.

Until this time, the students were buoyed by the sense of camaraderie and daring that their action had evoked. But a more sobering mood set in as they learned that Colonel Arthur McDermott, director of Selective Service in New York, had warned that authorities would "crack down without delay" on them and that violation of the law carried a penalty of five years in prison and a fine of $10,000. McDermott ridiculed the students as "so-called young intellectuals who have smugly decided that their judgment and intelligence is so far superior to that of Congress and the American people that they propose to disdain the requirements of the law."[30] The students responded, "Our act may be interpreted as evading the Selective Service Act. Anyhow, they won't have any trouble apprehending us. We are walking right in. We are not taking this action in a spirit of truculence and no doubt it will be up to the law to say whether we are considered evaders."[31]

But other sobering comments began to appear in newspaper editorials, letters to the editor, and op-eds. Some called the men "un-American," expressed "pity" for "these misguided youth," and even counseled harsh punishment. After negative press began appearing, Houser admitted that he had a "mighty shaky hand" while shaving. "The emotion involved in the first experience of facing an unsympathetic army administrator or judge has caused me once again to think through the entire position. . . . The awful thought cannot be escaped that maybe—just maybe—we are refusing to budge at the wrong point."[32]

But this was only the beginning of the pressure. The seminary administration was deeply disturbed by the students' action. Enraged funders had been calling and in some cases demanding the students' expulsion. Henry Sloane Coffin, the seminary's president, was especially sensitive to the implied threats from his funders because the seminary's budget had suffered in the Depression, resulting in retrenchment. Although by 1940 the budget was slowly picking up, it was still short of its goal.[33] Coffin was also anxious not to have the seminary be seen as a center of radical controversy as it had been in the preceding decade, when groups of students, radicalized by the Social Gospel, had engaged in left-wing activities.[34] Now, faced with another example of unwanted publicity, the president was quoted as saying that he thought the students ridiculous because there was ample provision under the act for conscientious objection.[35] Reinhold Niebuhr, under whom Houser had planned to write his senior thesis, expressed "thorough disagreement," saying the students' stand "goes against any valid pacifism."[36] "I have every appreciation for the integrity of our eight young men," he wrote to a correspondent, "but I do not see how they can be helped when in effect they courted martyrdom. . . . It is one thing for a martyr to say that he will take a course of action because he can take no other. It is another thing to court martyrdom as 'an instrument of policy' in the hope that this martyrdom will have this or that effect on public opinion."[37]

The faculty published a statement for the press saying that while they recognized "that there are circumstances when individuals or groups may deem it necessary to refuse to follow the will of government because to do so would be to deny their religious convictions," this was not one of them, since the elected representatives of the nation had taken account of the rights of a minority in providing for conscientious objection. "To refuse to register and supply the government with factual information is to refuse what any government has a right to ask its citizens. No member of the faculty has advised any student to follow this course of action."[38] The Student Cabinet, however, was more affirming: "We of the Student Cabinet affirm that regardless of our disagreements and in some cases strong opposition to policies of others, we will hold in respect and reverence those who in sincerity and humility maintain their loyalty to conscience."[39]

Although Coffin refused to expel the students, he sent a telegram to each man's family asking if they could "prevent this tragedy," since he had been unable to turn them around. Though basically supportive, Houser's parents expressed anguish over his decision, his mother wishing that he could find another way. Despite getting death threats, Otto Houser defended his son's decision from the pulpit, as well as in a letter in the *Rocky Mountain News* and in interviews with reporters. "I would have done the same thing if I were in his position. I have known about my son's stand for a long time. It is no flash in the pan," he told the paper.[40] But Houser's mother, bombarded by questions from parishioners and friends, was particularly anxious for her son, confessing that she was praying for guidance and for the strength "to face this hard thing, whatever it is, with courage."[41] Other students were not so fortunate. David Dellinger's father threatened to commit suicide if David did not back down.[42] Still other students' mothers expressed the fear that their sons' actions might cause their fathers to have heart attacks. The students were also visited by representatives of various tendencies within the peace movement, among them Harry Emerson Fosdick, and members of the ACLU and the American Friends Service Committee.[43] No doubt these representatives thought that explaining the consequences of the students' actions to them and to the opportunity for conscientious objection for which these groups had lobbied might change their minds.

Additional pressure came from hundreds of letters and telegrams that began to pour in from all over the country. Most criticized the young men, but many were supportive. A. J. Muste, now newly appointed executive secretary of the FOR, and Evan Thomas, a World War I objector and brother of the socialist leader Norman Thomas, wrote: "In a moral universe great good always results when men stand unflinchingly by their convictions and act upon them. . . . We believe the time has come when it will be recognized that this [non-registration] has been a genuine service to the well-being of the nation and of the church, and to the cause of peace, democracy and true religion."[44] Others, like Roger Baldwin of the ACLU, supported them on civil liberties grounds. Houser's older sister, Margaret, although agreeing that "war never solved anything," confessed that she was personally "in favor of a strong national defense right now. . . . In a world threatened now by Hitler, . . . I don't want the fate that is now Poland's, France's, and Norway's." She said she understood the reasons for her brother's actions and that the world needed men like him "to help prepare the way to a Christian world." "I'm proud of you," she told him, "and I have cried many times because I know the sacrifice you are making in order to obey your conscience and convictions."[45] Houser's other sister, Martha, while also expressing deep pride in and support for her brother, was a bit more blunt. "I think you are right to insist on the freedom of deciding for yourself an issue like this one of conscription, but I can hardly help but wish you were like the brothers of all my friends, and that you would go to the registration places and abide by the laws!"[46] Houser's old friend and mentor, Glenn Young, wrote that "although I had left the pacifist position three years ago, I think I understand it still. When so much of Christianity means so little, it is good to have some cling so closely to it that they are willing to go to jail."[47]

On October 13, 1940, the twenty students met for several hours in anguished deliberation over the path they had set themselves on, with some beginning to have doubts about whether they were doing the right thing. In the end, twelve decided to register as conscientious objectors. Houser wrote in his diary, "No matter what the decision of each may be as to his course of action, there is no one of us who will not have come to an understanding of the meaning of prayer, of consecration, of vital fellowship, and of wrestling with truth."[48] On the evening of October 15, the day before registration, a worship service was held in James Chapel at Union Seminary attended by almost all the faculty and students. Houser recalled that James Russell Lowell's hymn "Once to Every Man and Nation Comes the Moment to Decide" was never sung more meaningfully.[49] The service was a tremendous emotional and moral boost. The next day, the eight who had stuck with their convictions met briefly for silent prayer on the sixth floor of the dormitory and then proceeded down the stairs to a classroom set aside to register seminary students. There they were met by members of the draft board to whom they handed their statement. They had appended a paragraph to this statement saying that they did not mean to evade conscription but "to face it with all sincerity and try to make clear our reasons for not complying with it." The men were immediately served with subpoenas by the US attorney to appear before a grand jury at the federal courthouse in Foley Square the next day but were told that they could change their minds until 9:00 p.m. that day.

At the federal courthouse the next day the press was out in force as Houser and others filed in to appear before the grand jury, following them as they went in and cornering them when they came out. It was a new experience for Houser, who had never known what it felt like to be hounded as a celebrity. Houser was among three of the defendants who spoke to the grand jury explaining their reasons for refusal. Although he admitted to some trepidation in appearing before the jury, he found the jurors' reactions mixed. Some seemed to try to understand the students' position, while others tried to intimidate them: "Do you realize you're imposing your will against a worthy cause?" Some jurors warned of the consequences should the seminarians persist: "Do you realize a prison sentence will be a black mark against you for the rest of your life, that you will be turned down for jobs because of your record?"[50] Of course, Houser had already anticipated this as a way to avoid becoming "popular" in the church.

A bill of indictment from the US Court for the Southern District of New York charged the men with "unlawfully, willfully and knowingly" failing and neglecting to present themselves for and submit to registration "against the peace of the United States and their dignity and contrary to the form of the statute of the United States."[51] The trial date was set for November 14. The men were released on their own recognizance but were required to report to a probation officer in the interim.

Many of the group decided to make visits home while awaiting trial. Houser returned to Colorado to visit his parents and to console his mother, who was still anxious, as well as to report to his probation officer, with whom he spoke for several hours about the reasons for his stand. Yet he still harbored misgivings about the motivation for his decision. He admitted to being embarrassed by a minister who approached him in Denver with tears in his eyes, saying, "I feel humble in your presence." "I suppose if I were a saint," wrote Houser, "I would take this kind of remark in all humility and with grace. But because I know what an imperfect creature I am, such remarks make me feel like crawling with the worms."[52]

On November 14, the date of the trial, as the war resisters approached the federal courthouse, they encountered a large supportive picket line, but there were also counterpicketers as well. A few of them shouted insults, and one spit in Don Benedict's face. Inside, the courtroom was packed to overflowing, the audience sad-faced and hushed. Kenneth E. Walser, the seminarians' Wall Street attorney, at first tried to persuade them to plead not guilty, but on realizing that they would refuse, he prepared a rather unusual argument for leniency.[53] In addition to giving the usual character references, he argued that the men had answered a call to the ministry and in so doing "interpreted the teachings of Jesus in a way in which many others do not. Perhaps it would be more accurate to say," he argued, "that they do not interpret those teachings so that they do not mean what they state, but they believe that those teachings mean what they say, and they find in those teachings an instruction to have nothing to do with this mass killing which we call war."[54]

The US attorney did not buy the argument. The seminarians had broken the law and "so far as probation goes, probation assumes as a condition for its being granted, an intention on the part of the defendants to comply with the law." It was obvious that they had been given every opportunity to comply but had refused. After the prosecution's closing argument, each of the defendants was given the opportunity to state his case. Again, they reiterated their stand. They were then given another opportunity to change their minds. None did. According to the *New York Times*, some of the girls and older women in the courtroom wept as the sentence was announced, and an older man was heard to say: "Another triumph for Hitler."[55]

Although the judge had wrestled with the kind of sentence to give the men (including the possibility of conspiracy, which could mean at least fifteen years in prison), he ended up sentencing them to a year and a day in prison. This made the act a felony. But in a goodwill gesture the judge declared that he would keep the term of the court open for the length of the sentence in case any of the men decided to change their minds.[56] If they did so, they could reduce their sentence. After the proceedings, Dr. Henry Sloane Coffin (or "Uncle Henry" as he was known around the seminary) issued a statement regretting that the eight men, "whose Christian characters and devotion we admire, had persisted in their defiance of the law." He said he hoped that "having made their position clear, they will see that no further purpose can be served by persisting in this course."[57]

The men were immediately photographed, fingerprinted, and handcuffed without even the chance to say goodbye to their relatives and friends, many of whom were crying as the bailiff led them away. The next day, major newspapers carried headlines about the sentencing and photos of the men seated in a paddy wagon on their way to a week's incarceration at the Federal Detention Center on West Street in lower Manhattan. In the paddy wagon Houser remembered the famous quote from another prisoner of conscience, the socialist Eugene V. Debs: "While there is a lower class, I am in it, while there is a criminal element I am of it, while there is a soul in prison, I am not free."[58] Inside West Street the seminary men mingled with Mafia men, bank robbers, and others who were baffled by these pacifists. "I am in jail for killing people," one Mafioso remarked, "but you are here for refusing to kill anyone. It doesn't make sense."[59]

The story made front-page news in the Denver papers with an editorial in the *Rocky Mountain News* expressing no sympathy for the resisters "in their self-imposed hair shirts." There were several angry letters to the editor. Others, however, painted a different picture. Houser was described by one Reverend Mr. Marble who knew him as a "studious and quiet boy." Marble continued: "There is nothing braggadocio about him. He is soft-voiced and not the type to attract attention. But if he felt that if a principle was being attacked, he could go into action in a way to make people open their eyes."[60] The *Rocky Mountain Churchman* headed its article "Students Reproduce New Acts of the Apostles." Houser confessed that he didn't feel much like an Apostle, but he was relieved that the ordeal was over and felt both exhilarated and apprehensive.

DANBURY: A YEAR AND A DAY

Two cars left the Federal Detention Center in downtown Manhattan on November 20, 1940, bound for a brand-new correctional facility in Danbury, Connecticut. It was a two-story rectangular structure with an inner courtyard about the size of a football field. Houser was handcuffed to two other war resisters in the back seat. In the front rode Edgar Gerlach, the warden of the new facility, and a guard. When the men in the back asked if an open front window that was sending a chilly blast of air to the back could be closed, they were met with stony silence, a taste of the arbitrary authoritarianism they would subsequently challenge inside the prison. On arrival, each was given a number—Houser's was 280—and locked up in an individual cell in a block separated from the rest of the prison. This is where the men would stay for the first thirty days of a "quarantine" period. They would only be let out to go to the mess hall, participate in recreational activity, or to have individual interviews with prison officials. During these interviews the warden tried to figure out what made the divinity students tick. Houser recalled the warden asking if he hated his father. Houser just laughed at this amateurish attempt to psychoanalyze him. This was a young man who had once told his parents that there were no other parents in the world as nice as his.

Losing no time in planning how to make the prison experience efficacious, Houser immediately set about drafting and circulating a list of common suggestions for the other war resisters: "1) We should be a force for as great a democracy as possible within this institution; 2) We should be thinking continually with one another of what we are going to do when we leave here, of our mission to build a better world, and to build a movement of vitality in the church; and 3) We should practice daily devotions, if possible at the same time."[61] It is interesting to note that Houser was using his prison experience as a kind of university and as a training ground for fighting unjust treatment and arbitrary authority, much as those South African political prisoners he would later defend would use their prison time.

Before the first month was over, the divinity students had become a force inside the prison. Not only had they challenged the Danbury softball team to a game and won 15–1 (Don Benedict was a champion pitcher with semipro ability), but as the men were integrated into the larger prison community, they began to make themselves known in other ways, challenging the petty authoritarianism and racism that pervaded the prison setting. If taking this stand were to mean something, then as pacifists they could also act out of conscience inside the prison. Like the rest of society, prisons at that time were racially segregated.[62] The young war resisters were not about to countenance white guards calling black prisoners "black nigger bastards" or accept the segregated routines of their daily life. Some in the group were given solitary for sitting among black inmates at mealtimes or at the weekly movie. In various ways they continued to protest racial segregation, sending joint communications to the warden or to the head of the Bureau of Prisons in Washington, DC. Houser, who had been given a job as the part-time prison chaplain's assistant, had access to a typewriter. And on days when the chaplain was absent, he typed such messages.

One day, as he was working alone in the chaplain's office, the warden appeared. Houser greeted him while seated. "Houser!" he bellowed, "when I come into the room, I want you to stand up." "Warden," Houser replied, "I respect you as a man, but not as the warden." At this, the warden angrily stormed from the room. Houser was called before the disciplinary committee and reassigned to work in the boiler room. All winter long he was forced to crawl into the large boilers and clean them by hand, a process that gave him a constant cold and dust in the nostrils. Perhaps the warden's anger had also been stoked by his having been upstaged by Houser at Ping-Pong. At the end of their building was an open space containing a Ping-Pong table with limited time for playing. On several occasions during that first period, the warden had come into the men's cellblock after lights out and had challenged Houser to a game of Ping-Pong. The warden, as Houser recalled, was a lousy player and Houser, a Ping-Pong champion, beat him every time. Houser had requested a transfer to the prison farm, and this was granted just in time for the spring planting season. He was glad to be outdoors and in air that he could breathe in deeply.

As the other prisoners witnessed the seminarians' defiant behavior, as well as their sports prowess, the group gained respect from the regular prison population. They were, in effect, carving out an alternative definition of masculinity and bravery.[63] Many times they were approached by illiterate men asking for help in writing letters to their families or for advice and counseling for personal or familial difficulties.

Prisoners held at Danbury were limited to a small number of correspondents. Houser's consisted of his parents; his close seminary friend, Roger Shinn; and Jean Walline, who would later become his wife. Regulations only permitted the sending of two letters per week, and visiting hours were limited to one hour a month, which could be divided into two half-hour visits. Throughout Houser's imprisonment, Shinn, who had lived across the hall from Houser and played basketball with him, carried on a correspondence with Houser as the two friends wrestled with their respective positions on the draft and war.

Shinn had his own internal battle about whether to accept the seminarians' exemption from the draft. With his wavering convictions about pacifism, he was a perfect interlocutor for Houser. They questioned and critiqued each other's positions on the best way of responding to the threat of Nazism. On December 22, 1940, Shinn wrote to Houser that he was essentially in agreement with the draft, and while he would make a "rotten soldier," he thought he ought to refuse exemption and join the draft.[64] Houser responded, "In principle—you and I agree pretty much. But the more I think about the world situation, the more I feel that I would have to become a complete defeatist and cynic in order to support one side or the other in the war. . . . The cycle has to be broken somewhere, and I think one of the important points at which to break it is at the point of the method of war."[65] In a later letter he wrote that he hated to admit it, but "if I had your opinion on the war and defense, etc., I would want to do the same thing. . . . How strange to think that I should find myself in a position of thinking it wise for a person to go in the army. . . . The hate, the disregard for life, the externally imposed fascistic discipline—all repels me terribly. But probably no more than you." Although he found himself at the opposite political pole from his friend, he concluded: "I hope that neither one of us can claim our position as final truth."[66]

In a later critique of Houser's position, Shinn argued that if they were to forgo the use of force or violence and "allow a terrible tyranny to overcome civilization and govern the world, then we make our program irrelevant to the practical goal we have in mind. . . . and we make any early approximation of the goal an impossibility."[67] Houser's answer was that he had no hope for a world order of decency after modern war: "I believe that one can take a minority group position in any political struggle quite justifiably when it is obvious the major alternatives are mutually destructive of the good in each other."[68] These early statements contain the seeds of Houser's lifelong faith in the efficacy of minority action taken in the full knowledge that whatever one does on behalf of peace and justice will always produce an indeterminant result.

Undeterred by Houser's insistence that no good could come from war, Shinn replied that although he despaired whenever he thought about war's outcome, "there are possibilities of getting something fairly just and stable; and in any case, the outcome of a victory of the democracies must be better than the domination of Nazism. . . . I think there have been wars. . . which despite their brutality. . . have made possible the working out of good which would otherwise have been impossible."[69]

As Shinn's draft number came up, he had to decide whether to take the conscientious objector route, as his professors had counseled him to do, or to enlist in a war from which some good might be possible. By late April 1941, Shinn had decided to join the army as soon as school finished for the semester, forgoing his planned graduate studies. When he made his decision, Houser was one of the first people he told. Houser wrote back disagreeing with his friend but supporting his decision to accept the consequences of supporting the war.[70] Both Shinn and Houser would remain true to their respective convictions until well after the war.

While the actions of Houser and his fellow resisters were ultimately deluged by the juggernaut of war, they had modeled an alternative that would be picked up years later by draft resisters during the Vietnam War. In 1947, Houser would join with A. J. Muste, Bayard Rustin, David Dellinger, and other radical pacifists in the nation's first draft card burning.[71] While hating war, Shinn would go on to fight as an infantryman at the Battle of the Bulge, endure 171 days of brutal interrogations and a six-hundred-mile forced march through Germany in the waning days of the war, and win a Silver Star for valor. He would later become a professor of ethics at Union Theological Seminary and write a book, *Wars and Rumors of Wars*, which reflected on the ethical, political, and personal issues involved in the war and humanity's propensity for war.[72] Despite their differences, the two men would remain lifelong friends, Shinn passing away at the age of ninety-six, just three years before his sparring partner.[73]

In mid-April the eight seminarians, along with about a dozen other COs who by this time had arrived there as well—some from Quaker backgrounds, some socialists—decided to test the prison authorities once again. This time they would go on a work strike in keeping with an annual National Student Strike against War that had grown out of the Oxford Pledge. Houser wrote a memo to the prison administration explaining what the National Student Strike was, why it was important, and why his incarceration should not deter him from participating in this event. He then explained that the men would not work on April 23 and would spend the day fasting and in meditation. Houser argued that these acts should not be seen by the prison authorities as opposition to their administration.

From the warden's perspective, however, this was indeed a challenge to his authority. Assembled for dinner, the entire inmate population was treated to a rabble-rousing speech from Gerlach who, hoping to turn the other prisoners against the war resisters, accused them of being disloyal to the government, trying to get all the prisoners to strike, and intending to take over the prison. But the warden's tactic backfired. Several of the other prisoners went out of their way to bring them extra coffee and encouraging words. But the prison authorities were not about to let the strike proceed. The day before the threatened strike, Houser and his fellow protesters were taken to isolation cells and given thirty days in solitary.

Two weeks into their isolation, however, a baseball game in which the Danbury inmates were playing a team outside the prison was in trouble. Danbury was losing. The prisoners began shouting, "We want Benedict! We want Benedict!" Knowing he had a star pitcher being held in solitary, the warden—probably to save his pride—summoned Benedict to pitch in the last part of the fourth inning of a seven-inning game. Benedict won the day for Danbury and was taken back to his isolation cell. A few days later another game was scheduled. Benedict was again summoned, but this time he refused to go unless the others were released from solitary. The warden gave in, and again Benedict was the hero. But it appeared that the war protesters' release was temporary, for they were again taken back to the isolation unit. At dinner time that evening, however, the warden gave the signal for their release. As the men entered the mess hall, a wild applause broke out: their fellow prisoners were giving them a standing ovation. Nonviolent civil disobedience had won out over the coercive power of the state. It was a lesson that would not be lost on Houser.

In early April the men received a letter from Union Theological Seminary setting forth the terms on which they would be readmitted to the institution upon their release: they must agree to comply with whatever requests the administration makes of them or quietly withdraw; and they must spend their time entirely on their studies and in a fieldwork job and do nothing that would bring further publicity to the seminary. The men reacted with disappointment and anger. In a letter to Shinn, Houser declared that he planned to tell the seminary administration that he would reenter seminary only as he had entered it originally: he would not have any restrictions that other students didn't have, he would not obey a request from the seminary unless he knew what that request would be ahead of time, and he intended to continue with the kind of organizational work he had been engaged in before going to prison. "I hope that this will allow me to re-enter, but I don't plan to compromise," he stated.[74]

As the time approached for the men's release from prison, Henry Sloane Coffin came to visit them, bringing with him the same terms for their readmittance to Union. The war resisters decided that it would be impossible to accept Union's conditions. Benedict, Dallas, and Dellinger, who had earlier worked among the poor in Newark, decided to return to that work. Houser and the four others decided to finish their theological training at Chicago Theological Seminary, where President Albert W. Palmer, himself a pacifist, had said they would be welcome.

In June 1941, Houser wrote to A. J. Muste, who by this time had become executive secretary of the FOR, that he felt it was time to build a new mass nonviolent movement "with the immediate aim of opposing the war, of preserving as much democracy as possible here at home, and of working ultimately for a more socialist society. There are literally thousands of young people throughout the country who are just waiting to line up with some such group as this." He asked his mentor "whether or not this non-violent movement is an important and realistic thing in your mind" and where he could fit in with it. Fishing for some kind of assurance from Muste but not certain of his own prospects, he concluded by asking Muste if he had any specific suggestions for work upon his release from prison "whether along the lines developed above, or along other lines which seem to be getting at the core of our problem today."[75]

In a lengthy response, Muste supported the idea but told him that a new organization was not necessary. He stated that existing organizations such as the FOR, the historic peace churches, and others needed to be strengthened and their work coordinated. There might also be recruitment possibilities in the civilian public service camps. But as an older and more experienced pacifist, Muste was quick to curb Houser's overly optimistic assessment of the youth potential, pointing out that the small minority of young people who had signed up as COs reflected the peace movement's state of mind and stage of development. Muste also noted the fact that few young people had experience in applying nonviolent techniques in industrial and racial situations. Muste suggested that Houser complete his seminary work and offered him a part-time job with the FOR in Chicago, hinting that he could turn this into full-time work upon completion of his seminary degree. This part-time job could also serve as his Chicago Theological Seminary fieldwork.[76] Seeing an opportunity to work with his mentor and to do the kind of peace organizing he had dreamed of, Houser gladly accepted the offer.

On September 3, 1941, Houser and his fellow inmates received a commutation for good conduct and were released on conditional parole seventy-two days before the end of their sentence expired. Before their release, each inmate was called into the warden's office, presumably for an official goodbye. But then they were all handed a draft card to sign. Each man, not knowing the others had been handed the same thing until they compared notes later, refused to sign. The prison warden, however, had orders from Washington to register the men anyway. A year later, Houser received a letter from the Selective Service Board in Denver asking him to fill out an occupational questionnaire. Once again, he refused to comply with the order.

The prison experience had been a testing ground for Houser. It had validated the necessity to act on one's conscience regardless of the cost. Emerging from the experience he felt stronger and more confident than ever in the life course he had chosen. His bridges had been burned. There would be no turning back. As Marian Mollin has observed, the prison experience of war resisters like Houser had turned the image of the pacifist as weak and effeminate into a manly rite of passage.[77] He and his comrades had also demonstrated that one could act on humane values even in the absence of freedom. Word of the seminarians' protests against Jim Crow conditions inside the prison spread quickly to other prisons through the CO grapevine and was transmitted to the public by organizations like the FOR, the War Resisters League, and the NAACP, as well as through journals like *Fellowship* magazine, the *Conscientious Objector, The People's Voice* (an African American newspaper published by Adam Clayton Powell), the *Pittsburgh Courier*, and the *Christian Century.* Letters began flowing into the Federal Bureau of Prisons in Washington from outside groups. Within a year after the Union Eight had walked out into the sunshine, segregation had been abolished in the Danbury assembly hall. And by 1943, a full-fledged campaign had been organized by inmates to end segregation at the prison. Similar protests involving work stoppages and hunger strikes ran rampant throughout the prison system, especially in places that housed conscientious objectors. Protestors often faced solitary confinement, and not all the protests resulted in complete desegregation. But prison officials and the public had been warned: they were harboring a caged tiger.[78]

AN EPISTOLARY COURTSHIP

It was shortly before the Statement of Conscience was written that Houser met Jean Walline. She was the oldest of three children born to Edwin and Ruth Walline, who were serving as Presbyterian missionaries in South China. Young Jean grew up in a missionary community on the banks of the Pearl River south of Canton where she went to elementary school. While Edwin was known to be a stern Calvinist, his frequent trips to outlying parishes allowed Jean a great deal of freedom. At fourteen she was sent to Shanghai to attend the Shanghai American School. Graduating in 1936, she traveled by herself to the United States, where she enrolled at the College of Wooster in Ohio, training as a classical pianist. Two years later, when the senior Wallines came to New York on furlough, Jean decided to follow her music professor to Barnard College, where she would eventually receive her bachelor's degree. When she met Houser, Jean was a student in Union's School of Sacred Music and living in the women's dormitory at Union.

In September 1940, while working in the seminary library, Jean's attention became riveted on a handsome young man who had come into the library. He was of average height with wide, deep-set brown eyes framed by thick dark lashes, a straight nose that flared slightly at the bottom, and a healthy crop of dark brown hair brushed straight back from a wide forehead. This is someone I'd like to get to know, she thought. Although she lived across the street from Houser, the two did not meet until the evening of October 10, 1940, when they both happened to attend an event at a Chinese restaurant to commemorate Sun Yat-sen Day. Houser had been asked to speak at the event, and Jean naturally had an interest in all things Chinese. After hearing the man who had grabbed her attention in the library, she became even more intrigued. On the subway headed back to Union, Houser noticed an attractive blonde woman hanging on to a subway strap, realized she had been at the restaurant, and asked her where she was going. She told him she was getting off at 116th Street, the subway stop closest to Union Seminary. He told her that he was also getting off there. The two walked back to the seminary together and made a date for the following Saturday to go to a Chinese opera. They were to meet downtown at a drug store in

Times Square. Arriving half an hour late, Houser apologized, explaining that he had been working on the Statement of Resistance the entire day. It was only then that Jean Walline learned that Houser would refuse to register for the draft on the following Monday and would likely be facing prison.

For the next month, Houser was not a part of Jean's life. He had gone back to Colorado. Upon his return to New York, however, he contacted her again, and the couple had a few dates that consisted of walking through the Cloisters hand in hand, riding the Staten Island Ferry, and walking across the George Washington Bridge. Jean didn't know much about pacifism, so partly as a come on, she asked Houser for some literature to read up on it. As she read, she became more and more interested in pacifism. But she also began taking a keen interest in Houser. On the day of the trial, she managed to slip him a note asking if there was any way she could be of help to him. Because of that offer, Houser put her on his prison correspondence and visiting list.

Jean wasted no time in writing to Houser and thence began twice-monthly visits, traveling with the wives and sweethearts of the other war resisters to face their loved ones for a half-hour conversation across a table. On November 18, Houser wrote his first letter to his new pen pal, telling her that he had been thinking of her a great deal. Despite the comradeship in the prison and the daily routines, there was an aching in his heart at the separation from the outside world. Jean was his lifeline to that world. For the next nine months he would pour out his soul to her in letters that began formally but became more ardent as the months progressed.

Through letters and twice-monthly half-hour prison visits sitting apart, unable to touch, an enduring love that would last for over seventy years would slowly blossom.

By the end of his first week in Danbury, Houser was asking Jean for personal favors but still in the rather formal language of people who were but acquaintances. By early December, Houser's letters discussed books he was reading or wanted her to send. His correspondence also described his daily routines, his thoughts about pacifism and God's place in the universe, and his ruminations on what it means to try to approximate the will of a loving God. But they were still signed, "Very sincerely yours." Now, however, he had a new request—for her picture—which he said "would brighten up my room immeasurably." Jean's letters to Houser were filled with updates about friends, description of events in the seminary, and news about the war (now a constant); they were signed, "bye for now," or "as ever." By the end of December, Houser was writing about how wonderful Jean's letters were and the thrill her picture gave him. He was now beginning to broach the subject that had been the elephant in the room between these two platonic pen pals. Typically, for Houser, it was phrased as a self-scrutinizing dilemma:

> There are so many things that come into play in the relationship of a fellow to a girl. There is the intellectual friendship which must be of the most creative type. And then there is the physical attraction. . . . I guess when the two elements are blended together in real love, one knows by intuition. But the process of becoming blended is an arduous one. The mind says one thing; the heart says another. Therefore, it is unsafe to trust either. I say this simply because there is the deep urge within me to say things to you which I know I must not say. Because of the somewhat unnatural social life of this institution, one does not always have his emotions under perfect control. Therefore, my mind says, "take it easy," but my heart says: "let yourself go." I am a believer in listening to the mind above the heart in most situations of this type and that is why I am analyzing my thoughts rather than expressing my heart.[79]

By the beginning of January, the salutations on the letters had become, "Dearest Jean" and "Dearest George," and the discussion of what had been building between them was a bit more direct:

> I often wonder if I ever ought to think about a love between myself and any girl. If I am true to what I see as my purpose in life, my days of hardship have just begun. Not only do I expect to see the inside of a prison some more, but even when I am outside there will not be much ease. I never want to compromise my purpose in life to accept large positions in institutions such as the church. Furthermore I have committed myself to a life of voluntary poverty. . . . Also I will always be part of minority groups in both the church and society. So you see, there might be lots of what may seem like insecurity in my life. To me it is the only true security however. Love, for me, will develop to the fullest when someone wants to travel down this path with me. . . . And yet I am sure that I feel love in its initial form towards you. How far it can develop it is impossible to say.[80]

The letter was signed, "with love, George."

MORE LETTERS NOW SIGNED "lot's of love, George," were to follow in which the two continued to test each other's faith and the values that Houser had laid out for his own life. Details about their life histories were now pouring out. By January 27, 1941, they realized that they had been in Canton, China, at the same time in 1935 and had known some of the same people. They discovered that their respective paths took similar routes in 1924 when the Wallines were returning to China from a furlough via Europe, and the Housers were returning to the United States via Europe from the Philippines. But there was also to be more reflection on the nature of pacifism and the need to put it into real-world action.

By February, a less formal tone had crept into the relationship, and the letters were now signed, "with a great deal of love." By this time the letters also reveal a level of give-and-take that moves toward greater trust and intimacy. In one of the missives, Houser confessed: "I think you might find me rather difficult to get along with in some ways, my tactlessness at times, my absolutistic attitude (which really isn't absolutistic), but even personality adjustment will be interesting." Jean now felt confident in criticizing some of Houser's behavior and he in advising her not to switch her focus to religious education, which she had been contemplating: "It seems so cold, intellectual and middle class. . . . The need of this day is for something revolutionary and urgent."[81]

By the third week in April, the salutations in the letters had been shortened to the most intimate term of all: "Dearest." And Houser was now probing for more direct responses to some of the lifestyle challenges he had been raising in his letters. In a previous letter Jean had expressed some doubt about whether she had the "necessary complementing capabilities to make for a really creative and mutually effective life" [with Houser].[82] Now Houser responded, "I have a feeling that you were somewhat confused by that part of our conversation Sunday in which I was trying to find out what your attitude toward me and my life work is. I don't suppose my approach is very good. Unfortunately I can't see myself in too objective a fashion. Perhaps I made a mistake in bringing it up. . . . I just want to know what the score is at this moment."[83]

By the end of April, Houser had his answer. "I guess we feel pretty much the same in all respects," he wrote her. "The only thing to do is to wait and see how we appear to one another in a position different from that posed by a table between." But a few lines later he writes, "I hope it isn't a case of over idealizing the future. Only three possible barriers loom: 1) if the country is at war, it might be difficult to take even a short time out from activity; 2) I have seventy-two days in which I am not completely free and may have to be somewhat under the surveillance of a probation officer; 3) money—I'll be broke. I think there are ways of meeting these difficulties, and the best way is to start making definite plans as soon as feasible."[84] With such barriers to decision making, however, it was difficult for the two of them to make definite plans.

In August, Houser relayed the disappointing news to Jean that they would not be able to get together for at least two weeks upon his release from prison. As a condition of his parole he was to be shipped home to Colorado and might only manage a short stopover in New York. On his release on September 3, Houser took the train to New York. For two days the couple walked and talked but had to part again as Houser was given forty-eight hours to report to his parole officer in Denver. Houser's decision to go from there to Chicago, once he had permission from his parole officer, meant that the couple would have to wait once again to formalize their relationship.

During the next year they would see each other only four times, once at Thanksgiving when Houser returned to New York and then at Christmas when Jean went to Chicago. Houser returned to New York around Easter 1942, bringing with him his grandmother's diamond ring. Taking the ring out of his pocket, Houser awkwardly handed it to Jean. "You have to do better than that!" was her reaction. Houser admitted later to being "darn new at this love business."[85] The fourth visit was later in April when the two attended a FOR conference in Cincinnati. Jean was disappointed; she thought this would be another opportunity to steal some intimacy with Houser. After returning to New York she wrote him a letter expressing her frustration in having only a few minutes together on a Saturday night. With another year of correspondence between them, there was time to raise and settle many other issues that Houser's commitment to a life of public asceticism would engender: issues such as living communally as a married couple, raising children in a low-income neighborhood, living without a lot of material benefits, and so on. Their life together for the next seventy years would be a testament to having weathered these early trials.

They Wrote a New Page in the
History of America, 1941–49

ON SEPTEMBER 25, 1941, GEORGE HOUSER BOARDED A TRAIN
for the Windy City to begin the next phase of his life. Arriving in Chicago,
he joined his fellow war resisters at the Chicago Theological Seminary. But
soon Houser and the four other Union Seminary war resisters, along with
another young man, decided the atmosphere was too arid. Hoping to also
save money, they took an apartment in an old building at 4257 Cottage Grove
Avenue on Chicago's South Side where they kept house with resident mice
and cockroaches. Forming the eastern border of the Black Belt (one side of
the street was all white, the other all black), Cottage Grove and its milieu
would be a particularly ripe setting for the kind of organizing that Houser
was about to engage in.

Chicago was not only one of the major destination cities for the Great
Migration of southern blacks to the North following the Civil War, but from
the early part of the twentieth century it bore the distinction of being one
of the most segregated cities in the nation. Blacks were squeezed into a narrow strip of real estate on Chicago's South Side. The Great Depression saw
a slackening of black migration to the city, but with the onset of World War
II, migration picked up as new jobs became available in the defense industry.
In the North they faced a more subtle form of discrimination than the legalized apartheid of the South. Although blacks could find work and housing in
the city and were courted by the Democratic Party for their votes, they still
lived in segregated neighborhoods, were often refused service at restaurants,
denied access to a range of public accommodations, and faced employment
discrimination. Kept out of white neighborhoods by deed restrictions and
restrictive covenants in which property owners signed agreements not to sell

or rent to blacks, they lived in increasingly crowded conditions, fleeced by unscrupulous landlords and block-busting realtors.[1] Northern segregation and discrimination, often referred to as "de facto" segregation, was not just a product of custom but also a combination of individual choices and government policies: some of these were blatant, others were, on the surface, technically neutral. Many New Deal policies that had been shaped by southern Democrats and northern Republicans had contributed to this.[2]

In the 1940s African Americans began pushing against the de facto borders of the Black Belt.[3] As blacks from the South and returning veterans moved into these areas, they were often set upon by white mobs, and black homes were stoned and often set afire with Molotov cocktails.[4] Working-class whites, many of whom had also moved from the South with their racial prejudices intact, fled to the near suburbs and beyond.

On the national level, race relations in the early 1940s were becoming more politically charged. Entering the fight against racial discrimination in Europe, the United States could no longer hide the hypocrisy of its own continuing racial discrimination. Moreover, the armed forces were strictly segregated, and blacks faced discrimination in the defense industry. On January 25, 1941, A. Philip Randolph, president of the Brotherhood of Sleeping Car Porters, proposed the idea of a national, black-led march on the capital in Washington, DC, to demand desegregation of the armed forces and an end to discrimination in the defense industries. The call had a galvanizing effect on the black community, as grassroots organizations and churches began organizing chapters and securing buses for the march scheduled for July 1, 1941. Under the threat of up to a hundred thousand protesters in the streets of the capital, President Roosevelt signed Executive Order 8802 a week before the scheduled march, establishing the first Fair Employment Practices Committee (FEPC) outlawing racial discrimination in any defense industry receiving federal contracts. In return, Randolph cancelled the march but established the March on Washington Movement (MOWM) to hold the FEPC to its mission and to continue agitating for civil rights.

After war was declared on December 8, 1941, spontaneous and individual acts of resistance to segregation sprouted across the country but especially in the South. Black soldiers demanded service in train dining cars and protested the abusive treatment they often experienced in military camps. Throughout summer 1942, the MOWM organized popular mass rallies. Although the MOWM was one of the two most important civil rights movements of the early 1940s (the movement lasted until 1947), it failed to build the grassroots infrastructure for a concerted attack on centuries of racial discrimination and bigotry. That work remained to be taken up by other organizations such as the Fellowship of Reconciliation.

Fired by his enthusiasm for Gandhian-style nonviolent direct action that might be applied to social justice issues like racism, A. J. Muste had hoped that the FOR might become a vehicle for such activity. For Muste, pacifism meant a commitment to active, nonviolent resistance to evil. The FOR's governing body, the National Council, however, was filled with genteel old-style pacifists who were wary of direct action that might challenge traditional political arrangements and appeared to engage in coercion. To create a counterbalance to the National Council, Muste began hiring a group of young men several of whom, like Houser, had cut their teeth in the militant Methodist Student Movement of the 1930s.[5] Two of these men, James Farmer and Bayard Rustin, would become Houser's closest associates and lifelong friends. Historian and Rustin biographer Jervis Anderson commented that the hiring of Farmer, Rustin, and Houser (along with Reverend Glenn Smiley) "were probably the finest staff appointments Muste ever made" and constituted his "gifts to the future movement for racial and social reform in America."[6]

Like Houser, Farmer was a Methodist minister's son and the product of the Methodist Student Movement.[7] The two had previously met as college students at the National Council of Methodist Youth in August 1936, in Evanston, Illinois. Upon graduation in fall 1941 from Howard University, he accepted a full-time position with the FOR as race relations secretary. Headquartered in Chicago as a central location from which to move around the country, Farmer's role was to travel for the FOR with a schedule arranged by the New York office. He gave talks that explained the racial situation to groups of pacifists and sympathizers wherever he could get an audience, inspiring them to take up the cause of combatting racial discrimination through nonviolent direct action. Farmer would later achieve prominence in the 1960s as head of the Congress of Racial Equality (CORE) and architect of the 1961 Freedom Rides.

Raised by his Quaker grandparents who were active in civic affairs and whose friends included African American leaders like W. E. B. Du Bois and James Weldon Johnson, Rustin grew up with a deep commitment to racial integration.[8] For a three-year period he had flirted with Communism because of its progressive stance on racial justice, joining the Young Communist League but becoming disillusioned when Stalin decided that racial justice work would have to take a back seat to winning the war against Hitler.[9]

After briefly working with Randolph's MOWM, Rustin was hired by Muste in 1941 as a youth field organizer. Operating out of the New York headquarters, he traveled the country speaking to youths in civilian service work camps, on college campuses, at denominational youth conferences, and at church summer camps about the necessity for nonviolent direct action against racism and war.[10] He would, of course, make frequent visits to Chicago where he met Houser, the two becoming fast comrades. Rustin would later become the foremost (if mostly behind-the-scenes) strategist of the modern civil rights movement, educating Martin Luther King Jr. on the practice of nonviolent direct action and organizing the famous 1963 March on Washington. Unfortunately, Rustin's unabashed homosexuality and early Communist ties would haunt him throughout his work in the civil rights movement and force him to remain in the background as others achieved more public prominence.

Houser, Rustin, and Farmer all looked to Muste as their mentor and role model. Rustin and Farmer were not particularly close and would compete for the attention and approval of the older man. Although Houser recalled that A. J. reminded him of an Old Testament prophet,[11] it's unlikely that he tried to emulate his prophetic character as Rustin did, nor did he crave Muste's approval as Farmer did (and when he didn't get it, he became angry).[12] Houser would frequently seek out Muste as a sounding board for his developing ideas on pacifism and nonviolent direct action and advice on the action projects he was continually dreaming up. While Muste encouraged Houser's proposals he also sought to curb the young man's sometimes overly ambitious ideas with a more realistic assessment of their possibilities for success. Recognizing the tension that existed between Rustin and Farmer, who both competed for Muste's mantle, Houser nevertheless maintained deep friendships with both. This ability to stay on good terms with competing personalities and factions in the struggle for freedom would be a signature characteristic of Houser's modus operandi.

As youth fieldworker for the Chicago FOR, Houser's job was to organize groups of college students into discussion groups, or cells: an idea Muste had picked up from a brief flirtation with Trotskyism. According to a set of guidelines Houser developed, a "well-rounded cell" was to include four components: growth in the life of the spirit, study, action, and the organizational life of the cell, which meant attention to recruitment and organizational maintenance.[13] The students were to meet regularly to study nonviolent strategy and develop campaigns to utilize what they had learned. Their texts were Gandhi's autobiography, Richard Bartlett Gregg's *The Power of Nonviolence* and Krishnalal Shridharani's *War without Violence*, the first systematic explanation of Gandhi's method of *satyagraha* (truth force), the philosophy and practice of nonviolent direct action. In between classes at the seminary, Houser traveled to area campuses, securing opportunities to speak, to hand out the organization's newsletter, FORward, and to organize the cells. Within a few months seventeen cells were operating throughout the greater Chicago area.

Among the early activities cell members engaged in were picketing theaters that showed films depicting the Japanese as mongrels. Houser recalled one theater on State Street in the downtown Chicago Loop area. In front of the theater was a picture of a bucktoothed Japanese on a board that rotated on a pedestal. A sign on the sidewalk said, "Kick Me," and people would go by and kick the picture, which would then twirl around.[14] The young activists also campaigned against the Red Cross policy of excluding African Americans from their blood drives, organizing their own drives and donating the blood to hospitals rather than the military. Houser remembered picketing the British consulate in support of Indian independence and participating in so-called poster walks, a now outmoded term signifying something similar to a picket line in which marchers carried signs protesting the draft.

Back in New York, Jean had decided to switch her degree from sacred music to a joint master's program in religious education from Union Theological Seminary and Columbia University's Teachers College from which she graduated in May 1942. Houser finished his seminary coursework and comprehensive exams at about the same time.[15] The two were now free to marry. Jean traveled to Chicago, and the two of them were married by Otto Houser in a small wedding on June 26, 1942, in the chapel at the University of Chicago's Divinity School.

After a weekend honeymoon at a Unitarian camp that had not yet opened for the summer at Lake Geneva, Wisconsin, the couple returned to Houser's apartment in Chicago. By this time, his roommates had left, leaving the newlyweds to set up house in what Jean recalled was "frankly, a dump." When Jean's mother visited she was shocked to see her daughter living in such conditions.[16] Very soon, however, the couple were sharing the apartment with another young, recently married couple as well as with one of the black men who had served time in prison when the Union Eight were there.

While Jean tried to make their apartment more livable, Houser lost no time in getting back to the work he had cut his teeth on. With school behind him, he was now able to put all his energy into the FOR. As "executive secretary" of the Chicago branch he opened an office on Rush Street next to the Midwest office of the FOR. Although Houser was now working full time, he was still getting part-time pay. By this time, an executive committee of the Chicago FOR was formed, and plans were made to hold annual conferences that would bring representatives of the cells together. Houser's work was to facilitate this network as well as to assist imprisoned war resisters with their grievances and help COs both in work camps and upon release.

During the next year, Houser's focus began to shift from antiwar work and support for COs to racial injustice. Looking back years later on his war resistance, Houser admitted some guilt in having played no role in directly challenging the evils of Nazism: "If I had been in Europe I could have joined other pacifists in the underground railroad to help rescue Jews and opponents of Hitler. But from my vantage point in the United States, this was impossible."[17] It was partly this realization that now led him to turn his attention to fighting racial segregation in the United States. While protesting the war was bearing witness to one's own belief in nonviolence, it was not going to change the wider political situation any time soon. On the other hand, using nonviolent direct action to tackle racial injustice provided the opportunity to be nonviolent, relevant, and perhaps even effective in changing local conditions.[18] The efficacy of that optimism, however, had yet to be tested.

Spearheading the FOR's foray into using Gandhian methods to combat racism was a mixed-race cell Houser had organized at the University of Chicago. Its dominant personalities were Bernice Fisher, a fiery young religious education student at the university who would later become a labor organizer, and James (Jimmy) Robinson, a graduate student in English and a member of the Catholic Worker Movement. Robinson would later serve time as a CO. He would take the reins of CORE after Houser's resignation in 1954 and later join Houser at the ACOA as its fundraiser. Both Fisher and Robinson were white. Other key members of the cell who, in addition to Farmer and Houser, were most influential in founding CORE were Homer Jack and Joe Guinn. Jack, the son of Eastern European radicals, had traveled to Stalin's Russia, Hitler's Germany, and Mussolini's Italy on the tail end of a year spent in Europe doing research for his doctoral dissertation in biology. Convinced of the need to work for peace and racial justice after visiting these totalitarian countries, he left science to study for the ministry at the Unitarian Meadville Theological School. He would later follow Houser into the ACOA, working from 1959 to 1960 as its associate director, and still later help to establish the Committee for a Sane Nuclear Policy.[19] Joe Guinn, an African American from Chicago, was head of the local NAACP Youth Council.[20]

Meeting on Saturday afternoons to study and discuss *War without Violence*, the dozen pacifist cell members began to deliberate over how to apply Gandhian direct action techniques to racial problems. Black students at the University of Chicago found it almost impossible to obtain housing in the immediate neighborhood. Learning about the restrictive covenant system from an adviser to the group, they decided to challenge that system by forming an interracial men's Fellowship House modeled after the Gandhian cooperative communities known as "ashrams." The idea was that they could generate a public protest over restrictive covenants by refusing to be evicted when and if such an order were issued, and they might even get national publicity if the eviction were to take place.[21]

Farmer had drafted a memo, with some editing by Houser and a few others, to A. J. Muste on the need for a large, semiautonomous, "Brotherhood Mobilization" on a national scale. Farmer felt that neither the NAACP nor the Urban League were able to deal effectively with a problem as comprehensive as that of race.[22] Initially impressed with the memo, Muste sent it to the National Council for discussion but had misgivings about the prospect of a semiautonomous organization not under the control of the FOR. The National Council, with its all-white membership, opposed the program's plan of using coercion and confrontation. Farmer and Houser were disappointed with the outcome. But Muste, still hoping that the FOR might play a role in initiating nonviolent direct action, fashioned a plan to keep the idea on the table. Farmer was authorized to continue, with the thought that a convention to launch such a movement might take place sometime in the future.[23]

While the organization described in the memo was never formally endorsed by the FOR, it had fired the imaginations of these idealistic students who, with guidance from Houser and Farmer, began to embody the idea in concrete form.[24] Despite the FOR's rejection of a formal endorsement, Muste continued to keep Houser and Farmer on the payroll, thus subsidizing the birth of a new organization by default.

After several weeks of investigation and preparation, Fellowship House was about to become a reality. Jimmy Robinson and another white seminarian had secured a lease on a house in the all-white Hyde Park–Kenwood section near the university. In January 1942 a group of ten men moved into the house. Most were white, but among them were Farmer and another African American. During the summer months, members of the Fellowship House entertained mixed groups of young black and white women on their front porch and on Sundays held interracial picnics in neighborhood parks in open defiance of racial patterns.[25] Backed by their Saturday afternoon cell group and the promise of help from attorneys, the group was ready to resist any eviction the real estate company might impose. Their plans were thwarted, however, when after six months their lease ran out. By this time, however, they had already made plans to form another interracial house.[26]

BIRTH OF THE CONGRESS OF RACIAL EQUALITY (CORE)

In March 1942 a preliminary organizing committee consisting of Houser and several others met to discuss the organization of an interracial non-violent direct action group. Farmer was out of town at the time.[27] Having reached out beyond the small pacifist community attached to the university, the group was emboldened to think in broader terms. The new group, which decided in June 1942 to call itself the Chicago Committee of Racial Equality, met at a settlement house inside the Black Belt, rapidly attracting both new black members from the surrounding community and nonstudent whites from the area around the university.[28]

Buoyed by their experiment in challenging restrictive housing covenants, the group decided to tackle discrimination in public accommodations. Although Illinois law did not allow any public establishment to refuse service to blacks, this law was widely ignored. The group's first target was Jack Spratt's, a coffee shop near the Fellowship House that had refused service to Farmer when he had gone there on a couple of occasions with Jimmy Robinson. In keeping with the steps outlined in Shridharani's book, the group first wrote to Jack Spratt's asking to discuss the policy. When that didn't work, they phoned to try to talk with the owner but got no satisfaction. Then they went in person to the coffee shop intending to have a discussion with management.[29] After these efforts failed, both black and white testers went in, but the restaurant continued to refuse blacks. Moving to the next step in Shridharani's manual, they spread the word on campus, informed the *Chicago Defender* (the black newspaper of record), and apprised the NAACP Youth Group of their intention to challenge the discriminatory policy at Jack Spratt's. They then wrote Jack Spratt's directly, informing management that unless they changed their policy, action would be taken against them.

Training sessions in nonviolent civil disobedience commenced on Saturday mornings. Although scattered efforts at civil disobedience had previously been undertaken by the NAACP and other groups,[30] Houser later recalled that "we felt we were really plowing new ground. If other experiences had taken place, we had heard about them only from a distance. So when we got together and planned our strategy . . . we felt that this was something that we were doing for the first time."[31] Support came from labor, the NAACP, and some churches. Recruits were told that they did not have to be a pacifist to participate, but they did have to pledge to remain polite and nonviolent no matter what happened. The action was to be a sit-down strike, modeled loosely after the successful autoworkers' sit-down strike in Flint, Michigan, in 1937.

The restaurant finally changed its policy. But the strike was only the first of a series of actions following a similar pattern that would eventually result in the formation of the Congress of Racial Equality. As Jimmy Robinson later recalled, "One of the reasons CORE generated so much enthusiasm was the sudden exposure of well-meaning but privileged whites to the kind of routine abuse blacks were used to. Whites in a sit-in were radicalized by treatment they saw and sometimes received treatment they never dreamed existed outside the South."[32]

Shortly after their success at Jack Spratt's, the group learned of another opportunity to test the racial waters. The White City Roller Rink, in the heart of a district that had shifted from white to predominantly black, was found to be discriminating against blacks under the ruse that it was a private club. Suspecting that the alleged "club" was fictitious, the members of the Chicago Committee decided to test that suspicion. On the appointed day, around seventy-five to a hundred people turned out for the project, which was enough to scatter the participants throughout the line of those waiting to get into the rink.[33] When whites tried to enter, there was no mention of it being a private club. After several unsuccessful attempts by blacks to enter, the manager came out and tried to persuade them to leave. The police were called but made no arrests. Members of the Chicago Committee subsequently arranged a visit to the manager who continued to maintain the ruse.

Feeling they were running up against a stone wall, the Chicago Committee decided to take the case to court.[34] That was the one instance, Houser recalled later, in which the group had violated its principle of sticking to direct action.[35] Delaying tactics employed by the defendants dragged the case on for eight months. When the case finally went to court, an assistant state's attorney suddenly appeared, declaring that he was taking over the prosecution from the lawyers who had been working with the interracial complainants. As James Farmer recalled, "Throughout the trial, the assistant state's attorney seemed to be defending the defendants rather than prosecuting them."[36] The trial ended with the state's attorney calling for the acquittal of the White City Roller Rink. By this time, however, most of those who witnessed the discriminatory acts had either graduated from school or been drafted; so despite his sympathy for the complainants, the judge felt he was obliged to find the defendants not guilty, much to the dismay of Houser, Farmer, and others who had been active from the beginning.

The effort, however, had not been entirely in vain. The young people had learned a lesson about the legal complications involved in cases of public discrimination. More importantly, the case had generated enthusiasm among those who knew about it. Several articles had appeared in the *Chicago Defender*, and from this publicity a stronger group of about fifty young enthusiasts was recruited. In April 1942 this newfound enthusiasm culminated in the formation of a permanent organization to carry on the nonviolent work against racial discrimination. This marked the birth of what later came to be known as the Congress of Racial Equality. "Charter members" willing to accept the nonviolent discipline were named, and a steering committee was chosen.[37] By June 1942, after rejecting the moniker "Committee on Racial Democracy," the group settled on "Congress of Racial Equality of Chicago."[38]

Houser was soon churning out mimeographed disciplinary guidelines for the charter members. The CORE Action Discipline began with a description of the newly formed organization's purpose and stipulated that members "must agree to follow to the best of their ability" a set of nineteen rules from which they were not to deviate for any reason, including "personal, family or other considerations." Members were to follow "cheerfully" the decisions of the authorized leadership or spokesperson for the project. Individuals who did not agree with these decisions could not participate in the specific project but could still have a voice in the discussion surrounding it.[39]

On July 1, 1942, a second Fellowship House was begun in a large apartment a few blocks east of Cottage Grove. Through connections they had made with the Urban League, NAACP, and other leaders in the black community, members of the first Fellowship House were able to attract young black men who were not university students but who found it amusing to defy the restrictive covenant.[40] After a month of occupancy, a letter came from the realty company threatening eviction. Defying the order, the group began ringing the doorbells of their neighbors asking whether they objected to their presence and requesting their signatures in a letter of support. Most said they had been good neighbors, but some were reluctant to sign for fear of retaliation by the landlord. Surprised by the signatures, the realty company asked for a continuance of the case, which was eventually dropped for lack of prosecution witnesses.[41] Shortly after the second men's house was begun, a mixed-race housing unit was also established for women. It, too, was successful in breaking the restrictive covenant.

During the next year, Chicago CORE took on many projects. The lengthiest was an action to desegregate Stoner's Restaurant, a spacious so-called white tablecloth establishment in the Chicago Loop. Houser made several test visits to the restaurant and found the owner extremely hostile, claiming that he would lose his clientele if "colored people" came to his restaurant: the owner also complained that allowing two races to eat in the same restaurant would lead to interracial marriage. After six weeks of fruit-less negotiations, CORE groups passed out leaflets in front of the restaurant asking patrons to protest as they paid their bills. Test groups were then sent in. After a considerable wait, some were finally served but received insulting treatment. One group got meatballs mixed with eggshells on their plate, another got a plate of food so salty that it was inedible. On one visit, a tray of hot food was dumped over the head of one of the blacks in the party. On yet another occasion, a black busboy rushed out to keep the delegation from eating sandwiches he said had been made by Mr. Stoner from garbage.[42] After a survey of all the restaurants in the Loop revealed that Stoner's was the only place flagrantly violating Illinois law, CORE published a leaflet entitled "50 Loop Restaurants Which Do Not Discriminate," circulating it widely. Mr. Stoner was informed of the survey results; but when further un-successful attempts were made at being served, the group decided to stage a sit-in. In a memoir of his Chicago CORE days, Jimmy Robinson reflected on the amount of time and energy this group of unsung and unpaid foot sol-diers had committed to righting this social wrong: "Hundreds and hundreds of test visits, scores of time-consuming negotiations by letter, by phone, and by personal visit, went into this significant project. And the publicity needed to get Negroes to use the restaurants which had been opened was another daunting task."[43]

While the Chicago CORE was getting its feet wet, Farmer and Rustin were traveling the country as staff for the new Department of Race Rela-tions, which Muste had created within the FOR.[44] Bringing news of the Chi-cago groups' activities to other cities, Farmer and Rustin helped to stimulate similar local committees and to link with established groups. By summer 1943, enough interest from disparate places inspired members of Chicago CORE to consider forming a national federation of such groups.

On the first weekend of June 1943, a conference that representatives of these groups had been invited to was held in Chicago at the Woodlawn African Methodist Episcopal Church. The church's pastor, a Chicago alder-man, offered office space in his church basement, the use of a mimeograph machine, and money from church collections if the collection plates at the meetings ran a little dry. About thirty delegates came—from Baltimore, New York City, Syracuse, Detroit, Colorado Springs, Columbus, Philadelphia, In-dianapolis, and, of course, Chicago.[45] The guest speaker at this conference was Krishnalal Shridharani, the man whose work the group had been study-ing. Shridharani encouraged the group to go forward but advised them that Gandhi's methods could not be lifted intact from India to the United States as the Hebraic-Christian culture was not identical to that of Hinduism.[46] They would have to work out their own application of nonviolent direct action.

After a heated debate between Bernice Fisher who argued for a tight national structure, and leaders of the Columbus and Baltimore groups who advocated for preserving local autonomy, a compromise was urged by Houser and Farmer who had received a letter from Muste warning the group not to jump ahead with a tight national structure. He felt there were too many organizational and funding difficulties attendant to forming a new organization.[47] The result was a National Federation of Committees of Racial Equality with a statement of purpose, a constitution, and an *Action Discipline* pamphlet, largely based on the Chicago model. Local groups were to be given a great deal of autonomy, but the emphasis was to be on action.

The committee working out the *Action Discipline* had been headed by Houser, and the guidelines issued to the group were mostly his handiwork. The discussion of the proposed *Action Discipline*, however, revealed the extent to which some members of the group were uncomfortable with its rigid requirements, believing that many of the new groups were too disorganized to adhere to them. The proposed *Action Discipline* was thus accepted as an ideal the groups would work toward.[48] Houser also recommended the establishment of a periodic newsletter, a central headquarters, a financial arrangement whereby local groups would contribute to the national office, a national conference to be held the following year, and the election of a chairman and secretary to work on getting new groups started. Houser was clearly worried that a national federation would flounder without the funds to support a national coordinator. The participants, however, were clearly not ready for a tight national structure. Thus, a continuations committee composed of Chicagoans and representatives of local groups was approved to receive feedback from local groups on unresolved issues and was tasked with developing new groups. Farmer was elected president, and Fisher was named secretary-treasurer; these elections meant a mandate to develop new groups.[49]

To immerse the assembled delegates in the kind of direct action the Chicago group had perfected, they had decided to use the occasion of the conference to have participants engage in a sit-down strike at Stoner's. The plans for the sit-down strike had been devised by Houser in what Farmer characterized as a "masterpiece of nonviolent strategy."[50] Jean Houser, who at this time was chair of the "public places" unit of Chicago CORE, presented the group with the plans and instructions and led the discussion.[51] Sixteen blacks and forty-nine whites participated. Since the restaurant could seat up to two hundred, the plan was to send in groups of two to four that would be scattered throughout the restaurant. Between 4:30 p.m. and 5:10 p.m., white groups went in and were seated. At 5:15 p.m. the first of two interracial groups walked in. But those in the first group were ignored when they asked for seats. So they stood at the front waiting to be seated while other patrons were given seats. One of the whites in the group behind Houser asked why they weren't being seated, and others in the line told Stoner to start seating people. Stoner, who knew Houser from previous test visits, cussed him out.[52] Motioning to Houser and his friend to follow him, the now furious Stoner turned around and gave Houser a swift kick in the shin but led them to seats. "That's all right, Mr. Stoner," said Houser, "we know how you feel about it."[53] Still more interracial groups arrived and were kept waiting for an hour and a half. But by this time all eyes were on the unfolding drama, and many of the white patrons realized for the first time that the restaurant had been discriminating against blacks. Engaging in conversations with other patrons, sit-down participants elicited plenty of sympathy. Three times during the evening the police were called on the pretense that a riot was imminent but upon arrival told Stoner there was nothing they could do, as there was no sign of a riot. The police then threatened to arrest the owner if he called them again. Finally, Stoner, seeing that he was beaten, gave in. As the last four were seated at a table that Stoner claimed had been reserved, a spontaneous applause arose. Nonviolent direct action had won the day.[54] Other campaigns during this period involved a successful attack on racism in the University of Chicago barbershop and preliminary steps in a longer-range campaign against discrimination at the university's hospital and medical school.[55]

The relationship between the FOR and the new organization was still an open question. In a letter to Houser and Farmer, Muste had urged that CORE "should take time to grow organically and should maintain an experimental attitude and shape for at least a little while longer"; but he mused that work in the field of racial conflict would probably become a greater part of the FOR's work and that staff changes in the fall might allow Houser and Farmer to take on a larger share of those duties.[56] Responding to Muste, Houser expressed reservations about the FOR's "sponsoring" of direct action groups, fearing that the more conservative wing of the organization might put off certain people they had been attracting, or that they might interfere with their direct action tactics. He also feared that if the FOR took up direct action against racial discrimination it would be in competition with CORE, an organization he was beginning to feel some personal proprietorship for.[57] Rather, he said, the FOR should encourage those interested in this kind of movement to join CORE.[58] His top priority was now race relations, and he felt that by remaining independent, CORE could attract a wider following. The fledgling bird was beginning to leave its nest.

In his desire that CORE be autonomous, Houser was joined by Farmer, who argued more fervently with Muste that CORE should not be a pacifist organization but rather "it should bring pacifists and non-pacifists together under a commitment to nonviolence as a tactic, a device for fighting racism." "The masses of Negroes," he argued, "will not become pacifists. Being Negroes for them is tough enough without being pacifist too. Neither will the masses of whites." According to Farmer, Muste then asked how an autonomous organization was going to raise its money, and when Farmer suggested direct-mail fundraising, Muste put his foot down, fearing this would interfere with the FOR's fundraising. Farmer took this as a personal rebuff, and from that time on his relationship with Muste began to cool.[59] In a note to Houser long after that incident, Muste's associate, John Swomley, clarified Farmer's negative reading of Muste's argument about fundraising, saying that he and A. J. were not against direct-mail fundraising as long as CORE did not use FOR membership lists.[60] The senior administrator knew that one's turf had to be protected in the struggle to fund unpopular causes.[61]

In June 1943 Houser traveled to Denver to be ordained an elder in the Methodist Church, which traditionally meant that he was ready to be assigned to a local church by the bishop. But he had tried local church work and found it wanting. Besides, his work with CORE was much more exciting.[62] But by early December 1943, Houser was expressing concern about the still ad hoc nature of his position as a local FOR staff member. Family considerations were now beginning to influence his thinking about his vocation as he and Jean were expecting their first child the following spring. It was one thing to express the desire to live an ascetic lifestyle as a young bachelor but quite another when one was responsible for supporting a growing family. Writing to Muste, he expressed the desire for a position with some permanence well before the birth. Regional FOR positions, he observed, were full time and paid more than the job he had been in, but he admitted that handling "the organizational aspects of a fellowship of pacifists" did not excite him.[63] Muste replied that he was strongly inclined to think that Houser should join the FOR staff for a while in the field of nonviolent direct action and industrial relations. "You do have the equipment and a concern to an unusual extent," said Muste.[64]

Houser, however, was not convinced that the FOR was going to be a nonviolent direct action movement. As he had observed, "Not all pacifists

are interested in or concerned about a movement in any except the broadest
terms. . . . In general it could be said that this group sees the answer to the
problem of recurring strife in human society lying only within each individual human heart."[65] While expressing respect for the FOR's religious base, he
felt the time was ripe for a new organization composed of disciplined nonviolent activists who could take the nonviolent, direct action approach into as
many arenas of life as possible.

By early January 1944, Muste replied that while he agreed that not everyone in the FOR was ready to be a nonviolent, direct actionist, he saw
no place for such a movement to grow except within the general religious
pacifist movement: "If it does not have this spiritual connection, I am sure
that it will go wrong. One way in which it might do that would be by pro-
gressively under-emphasizing the religious basis and inspiration. Another
danger would be that such [a movement] . . . by itself would go off the deep
end on the use of violence, as a number of us did after the last war under
the stress of first-hand contact with industrial conflict."[66] Admitting that the
FOR had not made much progress with nonviolent direct action to date,
Muste was not ready to give up on the idea. "I believe," Muste continued,
"the FOR is ready to give strong encouragement to any group . . . who are
firmly attached to the fundamental Fellowship faith . . . provided that they do
not insist that this shall be the sole activity of the Fellowship or that N.V.D.A.
people shall think of themselves as grade-A pacifists, so to speak, in com-
parison with whom others are a lower grade."[67] This was meant as a gentle
rebuke to his occasionally sanctimonious young mentee. Muste concluded
by saying that if Houser were willing to function as an organizer of nonviolent direct action groups within the administrative structure of the FOR,
he would be disposed to support such a position.[68] Houser, perhaps seeing
no other way forward, replied that he was delighted with the proposal; but a
lingering misgiving remained. His father was coming to Chicago for a visit.
He felt quite sure that Otto wanted him to go into a local church and was
uncertain as to how he would react to his son's postponing that vocational
direction once again. Yet Houser went on to outline a preliminary plan for
his work, obviously having made up his mind that the role of an organizer of
nonviolent direct action campaigns was his preferred path.[69] At a meeting in
February 1944, the FOR executive committee voted unanimously to extend
a call to Houser to join the national staff as a full-time employee to start on
May 1 of that year.

During that same time, Muste transferred Farmer from Chicago to the
New York office and assigned him to work full time for the FOR. Farmer

interpreted this transfer as Muste's way of trying to rein in Farmer's free-wheeling work for CORE.[70] If, as Farmer assumed, Muste was afraid that he was spending too much time on CORE even as CORE was using the FOR's money and resources, it is curious that he did not rein in Houser, who happened to be doing the same thing. In a review of Farmer's autobiography years after these events, Houser recalled that his perception of A. J.'s role was different from Jim's. "I never had the feeling that A. J. was an organizationally jealous person," he wrote. "I never felt pressure from A. J. during the ten years I was CORE Executive Secretary, or when I spent time organizing Americans for South African Resistance which led to the formation of the American Committee on Africa. . . . A. J. was capable of being hard and tough, as Jim says, but he was not petty."[71] In fact, the FOR administration had been growing frustrated with Farmer's loose adherence to organizational protocol. He had failed to show up at a number of meetings and events he was scheduled to attend and seemed to prefer public speaking to the more mundane aspects of administrative work, which was precisely Houser's forte.[72]

At the annual conference of the National Federation of Committees of Racial Equality in June 1944, the name of the federation was changed to the Congress of Racial Equality, and an executive committee was elected in addition to three vice chairs. Farmer and Fisher were reelected to their posts, but without tight national leadership the loose federation would limp along for another year.

Shortly after the 1944 CORE conference, Houser penned a memo reviving the idea, first raised by Farmer, of building a national nonviolent, direct action mass movement that would go beyond the limited efforts already begun by CORE. In Houser's mind, neither the NAACP nor the Urban League were primarily committed to nonviolent direct action, and the MOWM did not have local grassroots organizations. Bayard Rustin had held the same opinion of the MOWM as early as 1942.[73] While black individuals would form the mass base of such an organization, the movement, Houser argued, "must not exclude white persons from membership." Such a movement has a "strategic advantage" against white bigots as "it would be impossible for race-baiters to say that they were being persecuted simply by Negroes. The fact that Negroes and whites are working together in the same organization undermines the racist theory that the two races can't mix. Finally, . . . it gives white persons who are anxious to oppose discrimination an opportunity for real action."[74]

The memo outlined the steps necessary to organize such a movement. Funding—for both a national coordinating office and for local chapters—was of critical importance to Houser. Also important was experienced local leadership. To build such leadership, Houser proposed that CORE hold a series of interracial weekend institutes in nonviolent training and two- to three-week workshops in key communities across the country with the hope that local leadership groups would emerge that could tie into a national training center where people could come "from all parts of the country for a period of a month or two to work with a project and thereby gain valuable experience."[75]

It would take the failure of the loose arrangement that had been decided on at the 1944 convention, with officers scattered geographically, to convince delegates to the 1945 annual meeting to form a more centralized structure to include a council composed of two representatives from each affiliated group empowered to make decisions between meetings.[76] Houser was elected to the unsalaried, part-time position of executive secretary. Plans also called for an advisory committee. By 1947 that committee would comprise a roster of many of the leading lights in the field of civil rights. Among them were A. Philip Randolph; A. J. Muste; Roger Baldwin, director of the American Civil Liberties Union; the philosopher John Dewey; NAACP attorney Charles Houston; Dr. E. Stanley Jones, a prominent Methodist missionary and theologian; Dorothy Maynor, the concert soprano; Lillian Smith, the author of *Dark Fruit*; and influential theologian and philosopher Dr. Howard Thurman.

By the time he was elected executive secretary of CORE, Houser had been appointed director of Special Action Projects for the FOR, and he and Jean had been assigned to move to Cleveland where he was to "make it a point to get acquainted with as many labor leaders as possible at both the national and local level" and to get himself on the mailing list of a considerable number of labor periodicals.[77] They spent the first five weeks living with friends, moving into their own four-room apartment just in time for the birth of their first child, Martha (Martie) on June 3, 1944. From his base in Cleveland, Houser would work with two different constituencies: first to coordinate the FOR's work with FOR members helping them "to witness more effectively for Christian pacifism" and secondly, to develop action projects for those FOR members who could give more time to nonviolent direct action activities. "These would deal largely with the fields of industrial relations and race, but also with anti-war and other activities," wrote Houser.[78] This was clearly Muste's attempt to curb the more ambitious visions that Houser and Farmer had each articulated for an autonomous, nonviolent mass movement and to bring Houser's work more closely within the FOR's orbit.

Since he had earlier expressed disinterest in coordinating the work of more traditional FOR members, Houser was not about to let this deter him from what had become his major passion. Although he continued to devote some time to the FOR's antiwar work, for all intents and purposes Houser's work focused more heavily on coordinating the work of local CORE affiliates.[79] In addition to starting a Cleveland chapter of CORE, Houser organized weekend workshops on nonviolence in cities such as Toledo, Ohio; Chicago and Peoria, Illinois; Fort Wayne, Indiana; Pasadena, California; and Denver, Colorado.

Houser's leadership of CORE at this point had come at a crucial time for the organization. Bernice Fisher had left Chicago to do labor organizing. Rustin received a letter from his draft board in 1943 and resisted. And because he had encouraged others to burn their draft cards, Rustin was now serving a three-year prison sentence in Kentucky. Early in the spring of 1945, A. J. had called Farmer into his office and told him that he was failing to organize or to sign up new members for the FOR. Farmer took it as a sign that his work for the FOR was no longer favored and decided to offer his resignation both from the FOR and from his role as CORE's national chairman.[80] In late 1945, Farmer took a job with the Upholsterer's Union International, but he and Houser continued to remain in touch and would remain lifelong friends.[81]

With Rustin in prison and Farmer gone, the FOR was left without its race relations staff. With still no national budget to speak of, it would be up to Houser, with a salary provided by the FOR, to carry the weight of CORE's national coordination.[82] Muste had warned him that if he continued to use FOR resources to fund work with CORE, then "he will have to shift his organizational connection as FOR is not going to put any more money and time into an effort to build a national CORE."[83] Funding for CORE was still nominal. Postage and mimeographed material were covered by small local donations, and lawyers donated their time to cases where they were needed. Over the next few years, Houser would build a list of funders—usually white liberals—that he called "Friends of CORE." But the funding base was never enough to support a full-time paid director, so Houser was forced to rely on his FOR salary.

The new job with the FOR in Cleveland had come with an increase in annual income for the Houser family. They were now living on George's salary of $2,000, little more than what would later amount to the poverty threshold for a family of four. Houser's concern about finances, however, must have been heightened when, fifteen months after the birth of their first child, Houser was forced to rush back from the summer CORE convention to welcome the birth of a second child, David, into the Houser household.

Houser's work as CORE's executive secretary consisted of editing the organization's newsletter (the *CORE-lator*), giving speeches to student groups, dreaming up new action campaigns, making suggestions on organizational management, writing endless appeals for money, strengthening the work of CORE's affiliated organizations, and conducting weekend workshops in various cities. It was, however, a daunting task. Although most of the CORE affiliate members came from middle-class backgrounds, keeping alive an interracial coalition in which whites and blacks, despite similar educational levels, experienced life in racist America in profoundly different ways was (and remains) an extremely difficult enterprise. Blacks, from life experience, were never as wedded to nonviolence "as a way of life" as were the pacifists who had come from the FOR experience. And when black activists met with sometimes brutal repression—as in a series of attacks by white mobs in Chicago from 1947 to 1951 over residential segregation—self-defense measures became more appealing than nonviolent resistance.[84]

Coordination of the organization was made more difficult by the nature of the loose federation in which each group maintained its own autonomy, the constantly revolving memberships of the affiliated groups, and the volunteers who were not always dependable. Houser's only real power was his ability to recommend and persuade. Nevertheless, by virtue of his position, he would set the organization's tone for the next ten years. That tone would include a commitment to interracialism, an emphasis on the redemptive effect of nonviolence on the wrongdoer, and the use of direct action as a last resort.[85]

In July 1945, in a report on CORE's third annual convention, Houser wrote that CORE was now reaching its maturity and beginning to find its norm.[86] CORE had amassed enough experience with interracial organizing that Houser was able to write and distribute a small booklet entitled *Erasing the Color Line* under the imprint of FOR's publishing arm. The sixty-three-page booklet described the principles of nonviolent direct action, explained why it was preferable to other possible approaches to the race question, and presented a series of case studies in which the strategy had been pursued in restaurants, barber shops, swimming pools, skating rinks, movie theaters, housing, prisons, and employment.[87] The booklet sold for forty cents and was republished in 1947 and 1950.

Midway through 1946, with Rustin now out of prison, Muste decided that he and Houser should head a new FOR Department of Racial and Industrial Relations. Houser would focus on the organizational aspect of the work, and Rustin would be on the road as a fieldworker.[88] Houser was now anxious to be located closer to the national FOR office, claiming that it was difficult to get things done without more convenient access to the national office. Accordingly, the decision was made that he should move the family to New York City. In August of 1946, the Housers relocated once again, this time to an apartment in the South Bronx. Houser then began work at the FOR's New York offices.

Pursuant to the 1944 memo Houser had written that proposed a series of training institutes, CORE now began to conduct both weekend institutes and two-month-long summer "interracial workshops" in cities around the country. Houser envisioned these institutes as having a two-fold purpose: They would serve as training centers for leaders and experienced workers in the use of non-violent techniques to combat racism. They would also provide a source of man-power for local organizations in the communities where the projects settled.[89]

Over the next nine years CORE would conduct one- or two-month-long summer workshops in Chicago, Los Angeles, St. Louis, and Washington, DC. Several week-long workshops were held in Toledo, Bloomington, and Washington, DC, among other venues. Drawing participants from many different states and Canada, including students, professionals, and housewives, these workshops were held in church-related retreat centers or camps. In addition to Chicago, Houser led summer workshops in Los Angeles in 1948 and in Washington, DC, with Bayard Rustin in 1947, 1949, and 1950. Three others were led by Wallace (Wally) Nelson, a young black man who had joined CORE in Cincinnati. The nation's capital was chosen as a major venue because, as a Jim Crow city, it held a symbolic resonance for the rest of the nation. "More and more," wrote Houser and Rustin, "men are recognizing that the United States, despite its wealth and power cannot gain and maintain a position of moral leadership in this troubled world until social, economic and political democracy have been made to work at home."[90]

The carefully planned workshops reflected Houser's keen attention to process and detail. Meticulous reports were kept on each workshop and its results, and participants engaged in lengthy evaluations of what worked and what didn't. Houser and Rustin made preliminary visits months in advance to the cities in which workshops were planned in order to gain local support and to ascertain potential targets for direct action.[91] Workshop participants were carefully vetted. They had to fill out a detailed application and get letters of reference from three people who could attest to their cooperativeness, work habits, leadership skills, and appearance. (Houser wanted to be sure that participants looked like clean-cut, "respectable" citizens.) The workshops included serious discussion of the tenets of nonviolent direct action, preparation for and participation in real-time direct action at venues found to be discriminatory (and evaluation of the action afterward), and public education in the form of leaflet distribution and mass meetings.

Various tactics short of direct action were employed before resorting to more disruptive strategies. Participants would often survey the public to demonstrate to management that they could employ principled policies without incurring public disapprobation. If unsuccessful, they would use shaming tactics, such as demonstrating that other facilities in the area did not discriminate. If shaming failed, sit-ins were employed, as was the case at two venues in the nation's capital that were supposed to be bastions of moral rectitude: the coffee shop at the YMCA and the cafeteria in the United Methodist Building, which was controlled by the Methodist Church Board of Public Temperance and Morals.[92]

The workshops were not all work. Time for participant recreation and bonding was also scheduled. Participants held picnics, went swimming, and engaged in dances, parties, musical gatherings (literature sent to participants ahead of time encouraged them to bring their musical instruments), and other forms of innocent fun. Those taking part in the longer-running workshops produced their own newsletters, illustrated with cartoonlike drawings as well as leaflets, factsheets, and even musical compositions. During the workshop held in July 1947 in Washington, DC, the participants composed, mimeographed, and distributed thirty thousand leaflets on a variety of topics from interstate transport to public accommodations. Among them were the lyrics and music to a new song, "You Don't Have to Ride Jim Crow," handed out at the Greyhound bus station. Based on the African American spiritual "There's No Hidin' Place Down Here," the lyrics had been written by Rustin, Houser, and some of the workshop participants.[93] Prominent persons in the race relations field were often brought in as guest speakers: A. Philip Randolph; the educator Mary McLeod Bethune; politician and civil rights activist Anna Arnold Hedgeman; noted sociologist E. Franklin Frazier; anthropologist Margaret Mead; Gandhi's personal physician, Dr. Shushila Nayar; Senator Hubert Humphrey; and leaders from the NAACP and the Congress of Industrial Unions, among others.

The workshops employed sociodrama in anticipating what participants might encounter. Houser recalled getting tossed out of the YMCA coffee shop in Washington, DC, by a bouncer hired by the management during the sit-in, nearly getting beaten up by a racist mob in Cleveland after trying to integrate a roller rink, and getting arrested at a cafeteria when two paddy wagons had to be called to take the protesters away.

Trouble with the public often happened at parks, where the workshop participants would often experience abusive language and rough treatment. When trying to integrate an amusement park in Cleveland, Houser was called "white scum" by a policeman who then snarled, "We don't want any of you nigger-lovers around here!" The policeman then grabbed Houser by the shirt collar, practically choking him while lifting him off his feet and then threatening to "crack him over the head" if he didn't leave the park. When Houser tried to explain that he was a Methodist minister, the policeman replied, "You're a shame to the cloth."[94] In this case, Houser was lucky. In another incident at the same park, a black man who was on the Cleveland police force and also a CORE member was shot in the leg while trying to protect his wife from racial slurs.[95] New York CORE protesters received particularly harsh treatment when they tried to integrate a swimming pool in the Palisades Amusement Park across the Hudson River in New Jersey. Fifty arrests were made between 1947 and 1948. Park guards wielding blackjacks hit protester Jim Peck so hard he was knocked out cold, suffering a fractured rib and broken jaw while police looked on.[96] At a sit-in at a Whelan's Drug Store in Washington, DC, CORE participants found counters mopped up with ammonia, hydrogen sulfide in the ventilators, and young people goaded by the store owner into throwing stones, firecrackers, and miniature torpedoes at the workshoppers as they left the building.[97] While only the workshop in Washington, DC, appeared to have evolved into a year-round project as Houser originally envisioned, such workshops and institutes would become the model for the nonviolent training sessions conducted for the later civil rights movement by Reverend James Lawson.

CORE REACTS TO THE RED SCARE

As CORE was making a name for itself, the Red Scare was overtaking the country, and the stalwart group of antiracists would once again wrestle with its implications. In March 1947 President Truman signed Executive Order 9835, which established a loyalty oath for government workers; and in June, Congress passed the Taft-Hartley Act, curbing labor's power and forcing a purge of leftists from the labor unions.

Since many who had been active in CORE had been called "Communists," CORE members were compelled to issue a statement on the Communist issue at their national convention in June 1948. A heated discussion arose over whether the group should denounce Communism. Wally Nelson argued strongly against it, and others argued that they needed to make clear that CORE was a non-Communist group. In the end, the group stated their opposition to "the undemocratic tactics that Communists and Communist front groups use in order to attain their ends."[98]

The group then voted unanimously to exclude all groups from affiliation that were known to be Communist controlled. This stance probably kept Houser from being hauled before the House Un-American Activities Committee (HUAC), although he was the subject of extensive FBI surveillance from the 1940s onward. Looking back on CORE's decision years later, Houser said that he would not have taken that position. Following his stint with CORE, he would find himself working with many Africans for whom Communism was not the threat that it appeared in the United States during the McCarthy era. The African National Congress (ANC), for example, worked closely with the South African Communist Party.[99] Despite the group's renunciation of Communism, however, Houser would not escape the Communist label in the years to come.

Until 1946, all CORE challenges to racial discrimination had taken place in northern and border cities where, even though de facto racism existed, state laws generally outlawed such discrimination, and police had to uphold the law. In 1946 a Bartlesville, Oklahoma librarian, Miss Ruth Brown, a white woman who had seen an article about CORE, wrote to Houser to request affiliation for an interracial group she had helped to organize: the Committee on the Practice of Democracy (COPD). The group hoped to address major problems in the African American community. Houser extended a welcome, and the COPD became the first and only Deep South CORE affiliate. Between 1946 and 1951, Brown and Houser kept up a correspondence, with Brown reporting on their activities and Houser offering advice and encouragement.[100] In February 1950, ten years before the Greensboro sit-ins, Brown and two young African American teachers, using CORE's guidelines, conducted a sit-in at a drugstore that served food and were refused service. But a campaign using well-honed McCarthyist tactics designed to purge the city of Brown and her sympathizers eventually ended the experiment and cost Miss Brown her job. Such boldness in the Deep South was not to be countenanced. Taking the attacks on her with aplomb, she wrote to Houser: "Don't be discouraged, for the South is changing very rapidly," but there would have to be "throes and agonies in the process."[101]

THE FIRST FREEDOM RIDE

Houser and Rustin knew, of course, that the real challenges lay in the Deep South. Houser had been concerned that although individual CORE groups were doing important work in breaking racial barriers in their local areas, CORE was not receiving the kind of national publicity and recognition necessary for the mass movement that he and Farmer had envisioned.[102]

The Irene Morgan case presented Houser and Rustin with their first opportunity to take CORE into the South and give it a dramatic national focus. Eleven years before Rosa Parks refused to give her seat to a white man, thus sparking the Montgomery, Alabama bus boycott, twenty-seven-year-old defense worker Irene Morgan, who was recovering from a miscarriage, had refused to give her seat to white passengers on a Greyhound bus headed for Baltimore from Norfolk, Virginia. The passengers had boarded after she had already been seated, and giving up her seat meant she would have to stand. The driver then called the local sheriff, and Morgan was dragged from the bus and arrested. Morgan decided to mount a legal challenge to her arrest for violating Virginia's segregation laws, vowing to take the case all the way to the Supreme Court if necessary.[103] NAACP lawyers Thurgood Marshall and William H. Hastie, who had been looking for a suitable test case, decided to take Morgan's case. On June 3, 1946, the Supreme Court, in *Morgan v. Commonwealth of Virginia,* ruled that state laws segregating interstate passengers on intrastate or interstate carriers "placed an undue burden on interstate commerce," thus violating the commerce clause of the Constitution.[104] Houser and Rustin, now working together in New York, discussed the implications of the ruling. From personal experience they had learned that laws and court decisions, however just, were only as good as their enforcement. Shortly after the Morgan decision came down, it became clear to both that officials in the Deep South were not about to heed the Supreme Court's ruling. Out of their discussions came rudimentary plans for a trip into the South to test the Court's decision.

Plans for the first Freedom Ride, also referred to by its pacifist organizers as the "Journey of Reconciliation," were further refined at a meeting of CORE's executive committee three months after the Supreme Court's opinion. Several considerations made it an appealing project. First, ever since the Court's decision in *Plessy v. Ferguson* (1896), segregation on public conveyances—which provided a backbone for black mobility across the South—had become a potent symbol of Jim Crow injustice. According to Houser, "It touched virtually every black person, was demeaning in its effect and a source of frequent conflict." Second, they felt that challenging discrimination on transportation would get public attention. Third, even though they would be challenging state laws, the project would have the force of a national Supreme Court decision behind it. Fourth, it would put CORE as a national movement on the map and hopefully act as a catalyst for funding the always impecunious CORE coffers. Houser increasingly felt that CORE's financial dependence on the FOR limited its potential. And finally, the case could be an opening wedge for CORE into the Deep South where racism was most pernicious.[105]

Since Houser and Rustin were being paid by the FOR, it was agreed that the journey would be jointly sponsored by both the FOR and CORE. The original plan for the ride called for participants to travel from Washington, DC, to New Orleans, Louisiana. However, as Houser and Rustin began to talk with those who lived in the South, such as the author Lillian Smith and members of the Fellowship of Southern Churchmen, they were reluctantly persuaded to limit the Journey of Reconciliation to the upper South where wholesale violence would be less likely to occur.[106] However, they entertained the idea that another trip into the Deep South might still be made depending on what came out of this first experiment. A second change in the original plan involved the decision to exclude women. In talking with advisers, Houser and Rustin deemed that mixing races and genders might increase the danger to participants by adding the element of sexual relations into the mix. The South was notorious for its fixation on the alleged sexual prowess of black men and their danger to white women. Houser also feared that adding this element would be a distraction from the focus on Jim Crow laws per se. Several women who had hoped to go on the trip, including black activists Ella Baker and Pauli Murray, were deeply disappointed. Wally Nelson's wife, Juanita, was enraged that she couldn't go.[107] Houser's decision to exclude women was a pragmatic one, but in reluctantly agreeing to exclude them he was, in a sense, bowing to the racist stereotypes that were central to white supremacy's hold on the South.

The organizers received support from A. Philip Randolph, Mary McLeod Bethune, Howard Thurman, well-known philosopher and theologian Bishop F. W. Alstork of the AME Zion Church, and the Fellowship of Southern Churchmen. The NAACP, however, refused to endorse the project. Thurgood Marshall was particularly outspoken in his opposition, telling a conference of NAACP youth at Dillard University in New Orleans that "a disobedience movement on the part of Negroes and their allies, if employed in the South, would result in wholesale slaughter with no good achieved." Moreover, it would result in a loss of public sympathy "from the cautious and timid—something we need badly."[108] However, NAACP-affiliated lawyers like Charles Houston, Spottswood Robinson, and Belford Lawson gave the organizers helpful suggestions and the NAACP, realizing that Houser and Rustin were not about to give up, supplied them with a key list of their branches along the planned route.

For the next several months, Houser and Rustin conducted a preliminary foray along the route the bus travelers were to follow, lining up lawyers in fourteen communities in case of arrests, contacting sympathetic local organizations, raising thousands of dollars for bail, and arranging more than thirty speaking engagements. To avoid arrest or arouse suspicion about what they were planning, the two scrupulously obeyed Jim Crow laws and customs and rode on different buses to avoid confrontation, agreeing where and when to meet.[109] The Journey of Reconciliation was to begin in Washington, DC, on two different bus lines: Greyhound and Trailways. The route was to take them through Virginia, North Carolina, Tennessee, and Kentucky with stops along the way to speak to local groups in churches and colleges. They were encouraged by the support they found among the younger and more restive elements of the NAACP in the South and were able to arrange public meetings, mostly in the black community. As Houser later wrote, "We felt our group of participants would not be isolated victims as they challenged the local and state laws."[110]

The next task for Houser and Rustin was to choose participants from the CORE and FOR lists who had already demonstrated commitment to nonviolent actions against racism. The conditions for participation were not easy. Participants had to be available for at least a two-week period, have the money to travel, be committed to nonviolence, and be willing to be arrested. In the end, sixteen volunteers were chosen, half of them white and half of them black. The majority were convinced pacifists, while the others were willing to adopt a nonviolent discipline for the duration. Among the white participants in addition to Houser were Jim Peck, a radical journalist and pacifist who had spent three years in prison as a CO and who would be the only one to participate in both the Journey of Reconciliation and the 1961 CORE Freedom Ride;[111] Homer Jack; Worth Randle, a biologist and pacifist CORE member from Cincinnati; Igal Roodenko, a member of the War Resisters League and a CO who had also spent three years in prison; and Joseph Felmet, a CO from North Carolina and a leader of the southern branch of the Workers' Defense League.[112] In addition to Rustin, black participants included Conrad Lynn, a civil rights attorney from New York City who would take up civil rights cases considered too radical by the NAACP;[113] the FOR-affiliated Methodist ministers Ernest Bromley and Louis Adams, both from North Carolina; Dennis Banks, a jazz musician from Chicago; Eugene Stanley, an agronomy instructor at North Carolina A & T College; and William Worthy, a New York journalist active with the New York Council for a Permanent Fair Employment Practice Committee, later to become one of the first black TV news correspondents. Also along for the ride was Cincinnati FOR member Nathan Wright, then a church social worker; law student Andrew Johnson, also from Cincinnati; and finally, Wallace (Wally) Nelson from Columbus. At thirty-nine, Conrad Lynn was the eldest of these young men, most of whom had no experience in the South. While the journey was officially a product of interracial, nonviolent pacifists, its participants included some who would eventually move between the two poles of inter-racialism and Black Nationalism.[114]

Houser and Rustin decided not to publicize the trip in advance, consid-ering that if they did so, the bus companies might just decide to let them ride through. They did, however, invite black journalists Lem Graves of the *Pittsburgh Courier* and Ollie Stewart of the *Baltimore Afro-American* to be ob-servers and to accompany the men for about half the journey. While these journalists openly recorded the activities of the Freedom Riders, FBI agents were also keeping notes.[115]

In late March or early April, nine of the participants met in Washington, DC, for a two-day orientation. Houser and Rustin had reluctantly accepted the fact that only about half the participants were free to participate for the whole two-week period.[116] The nonpacifists lacked training in the principles of nonviolent direct action, so Houser and Rustin led the men through a series of role plays—according to Houser, some quite violent—in order to anticipate and work through a variety of situations they might encounter.[117] Each rider was also provided with a detailed list of instructions, the first of which read, "If you are a Negro, sit in a front seat. If you are a white, sit in a rear seat." Other instructions included what to say to the bus driver if you were asked to move, what to do if the police asked you to "come along" but refused to arrest you (in which case participants were advised to stay put un-less they were arrested), what to do and whom to call if you were arrested, and what to do about bail.[118] Additional arrangements were made on the eve of departure. They included assigning special tasks to individuals who were to obey Jim Crow rules, so they could act as witnesses if a case came to court or provide bail and telephone numbers for lawyers should others be arrested. They also decided that members of the group would travel as if they were unacquainted with one another unless two men were assigned to sit together. It was important to the organizers that if arrests were made that they not be made all at once, for that would halt the trip. Thus, on each lap of the trip, assignments were to be shifted.

It was a balmy spring morning on April 9, 1947, six days before Jackie Robinson made his Major League Baseball debut, when nine men, interstate bus tickets in hand, gathered at the bus station in the nation's capital. They were excited but nervous as they boarded the buses. As planned, interracial groups of two or three sat in both the front and back of the buses. Between

Washington and Richmond, Virginia, little attention was paid to the seating arrangements except that it spurred some other passengers to violate the accepted pattern of segregation. Houser speculated that this was because there had already been so many cases in the Richmond courts testing segregation. On the Trailways bus between Richmond and Virginia, Conrad Lynn and Wally Nelson sat unmolested in the front of the bus. However, an African American sitting in the rear provided Houser and Roodenko with a sobering assessment. "A Negro," he said, "might be able to get away with riding up front here, but some bus drivers are crazy, and the farther South you go, the crazier they get."[119]

The first to be arrested was Conrad Lynn. This occurred shortly after the Trailways bus began heading from Petersburg to Raleigh, North Carolina, on April 11. When Lynn refused to move, the police were called, but getting a warrant from the bus company meant that the bus was delayed for two hours. Houser was amazed that the majority of passengers stayed calm and neutral, but a white uniformed Navy man grumbled that Lynn's behavior merited a response from the Ku Klux Klan, and a black porter named Shorty, who had boarded the bus, provided another threat. Pointing to Lynn, he said, "What's the matter with him? He's crazy. Where does he think he is? We know how to deal with him. Let's take this Nigger off." Conrad Lynn confessed to feeling "sick and sorry" for this man. "He was so demoralized and dehumanized that he would curry favor with whites by trying to be even more hostile than they were."[120] Ollie Stewart later commented that "the most vicious criticism of the young men who risked their lives by sitting in the front of the buses came from our people."[121]

The next to be arrested were Andrew Johnson, Bayard Rustin, and Jim Peck. This took place on Trailways in the Durham bus station just before departure for Chapel Hill. Although the men were released without charge, it was in the police station that they overheard a Trailways official saying to a policeman, "We know all about this. Greyhound is letting them ride. But we're not."[122] This was to be the pattern for the rest of the trip. All the arrests would occur on Trailways buses.

The most serious incident occurred in Chapel Hill, North Carolina, on a beautiful Sunday afternoon: ironically, it was the one place—a college town—where problems had not been anticipated. The group had spoken at a series of supportive meetings on the university campus and at the Presbyterian church, which was pastored by Reverend Charles Jones, a white integrationist and officer of the Fellowship of Southern Churchmen. From Chapel Hill they were scheduled to go to Greensboro, but Trailways was the only company making that run. Consequently, they divided up into two groups to take buses scheduled to leave three hours apart. Shortly after boarding the first bus, Johnson and Felmet were arrested while sitting in the front. When he didn't get up quickly enough, Felmet was physically pulled up and shoved out of the bus. Rustin and Roodenko, sensing an opportunity, then decided to move to the front seat that had been vacated by Johnson and Felmet. They, too, were arrested and released on $50 bonds.

The arrests delayed the departure for nearly two hours. Peck had been assigned to run interference between the bus and police station checking on his colleagues' bags and trying to keep tabs on the situation while waiting for Houser—who was at the Presbyterian church parsonage—to arrive with the bail money. A group of taxi drivers who were standing around the bus station became aroused at these "outside agitators." Recognizing that trouble was brewing, Peck started for the police station across the street to try to call the parsonage, but as he was doing so, one of the mob gave him a hard knock on the head, snarling, "Coming down here to stir up the niggers!" Hilton Seals, an assistant at the church happened to be passing and saw the trouble. He called Reverend Jones to come quickly to get the men. In the police station, some of the men standing around could be heard saying, "They'll never get a bus out of here tonight."

When Houser and Jones arrived with the bail, Peck warned them about what he had heard. On Reverend Jones's advice they decided to travel to Greensboro by car, the last bus having already departed. Heading to the parsonage in Jones's car for a brief stop before leaving town, they noticed two cabs filled with angry whites were speeding after them. According to Conrad Lynn, local taxi drivers had stirred up a "lynch spirit."[123] As the interracial group piled onto the front porch of the Joneses' home, ten cabs pulled up and one drove up onto the lawn of the house. Houser was afraid for a moment that it was going to crash through the door. When they saw men jumping out of the cabs brandishing sticks and rocks, the travelers quickly ran into the house, locking the doors as the hate-filled mob rushed up toward the porch, and a rock was hurled through one of the windows. When some young members of the Communist Party heard about what was being planned, they stationed themselves on the roof of Jones's house with rifles. Looking out the window, the frightened party saw that the cab drivers were being called back by one of their number. It is not clear why they decided to retreat, but Lynn surmised that it was probably their fear that they could be targets of the rooftop snipers.[124] Shortly after, the phone rang in the parsonage, and a voice on the other end warned Jones, "Get those damn niggers out of town or we'll burn your house down. We'll be around to see that they go."[125] The group decided they had better leave before it got dark. Reverend Jones then got three university students to drive the group to Greensboro by way of Durham, fearing they might be attacked on the highway if they went directly to Greensboro. He also called the police requesting an escort to the county line, which the police grudgingly provided. Houser recollected later that if Jones hadn't come along with the car, he feared they would have been attacked.[126]

Houser confessed that he had always felt guilty about this incident because they had left Reverend Jones to face the consequences. Charles Jones was already a marked man, as he had integrated his church and was always on the cutting edge of racial and social justice issues. After the group left, he received other threatening calls and moved his wife, Dorcas, and children to a friend's house for safety. He remained in the parsonage but had to face a crowd of angry white protesters in his front yard, while several callers either threatened to kill him or burn his church down. Later that evening, when he sent his preaching assistant to check on his wife and children, someone who mistook the assistant for Jones threw a brick at him. Fearing for her children's safety, Dorcas Jones took her children farther away to the mountains. Several university students volunteered to guard Jones's home and church, but the intimidation finally subsided after the university's president, Dr. Frank Porter Graham, a member of Jones's church as well as a member of President Truman's Committee on Civil Rights, engaged in a forceful consultation with the local police.[127] However, the incident may have generated a split in Jones's church, eventually causing him to seek out another pulpit.[128]

At Greensboro, their next stop, the tension that had accompanied them as they left Chapel Hill was temporarily assuaged by a rousing mass meeting at the Shiloh Baptist Church, where they told their stories to a packed sanctuary amid congratulatory handshakes and tears. This was the same church that would host the Freedom Riders in 1961.[129] Although the threat of violence in Chapel Hill was the most blatant, the tension that accompanied each violation of the Jim Crow pattern never left the participants. Ollie Stewart observed that "every member of the group, on approaching the bus station, scene of the test, was tight-lipped and grim."[130] Homer Jack, joining the group eight days after they had left Washington, found "a group of men exhibiting the somewhat taut morale of ten arrests." "The whites," he commented, "were beginning to know the terror that many Negroes have to live with all the days of their lives. All members of the party were dead-tired, not only from the constant tension, but also from participating in many meetings and conferences at every stop."[131] There were to be a few more arrests after the dramatic escape in Chapel Hill, but as Raymond Arsenault pointed out, the mass meeting at Greensboro was the emotional high of the journey, and the last ten days represented little more than an anticlimax.[132]

In Chapel Hill, Rustin and Johnson were given a fine to cover court costs and sentenced to thirty days on the chain gang, the statutory limit, while Roodenko and Felmet, both white, were given sixty days. The judge admitted that he purposely discriminated against the white men presumably to send a message to other northern whites who might want to come to the South to stir things up. At their trial in Asheville, Banks and Peck were sentenced to thirty days on the chain gang and released on $250 bonds pending appeal. In the courtroom Peck was astonished to see that even the Bibles were separated by race, one marked "white" and the other marked, "colored."[133]

Several of the riders had left the journey in Louisville on April 19. Those who remained arrived back in the nation's capital on April 23, exhausted but proud of what they had accomplished. To their disappointment, however, there was no public event and no group of reporters waiting to ask whether it was worth it and whether they would do it again.

The Journey of Reconciliation had logged twenty-six tests of compliance, twelve arrests, and one act of violent resistance. In all but one set of arrests, the charges were dropped on appeal, or small fines were assessed. NAACP lawyers appealed the Chapel Hill case to the North Carolina Supreme Court, which upheld the lower court's conviction. In 1949 Rustin, Johnson, Roodenko, and Felmet were required to return to North Carolina to serve their time on the chain gang. Johnson, then in his senior year in college, refused to go, thus forfeiting the bail. Rustin later wrote a searing account of his experience on the chain gang that was published in the *New York Post* and *Baltimore Afro-American*. The piece led to a legislative investigation of conditions in North Carolina's prison camps.[134] Accounts of the journey and the arrests and court cases received publicity in over thirty newspapers, putting CORE for the first time in the national news.[135]

After the Journey of Reconciliation, Houser and Rustin summarized the story of the journey and the lessons they thought could be learned from it in a pamphlet entitled *We Challenged Jim Crow!* "Without direct action on the part of groups and individuals," they concluded, "the Jim Crow pattern in the South cannot be broken down. We are equally certain that such direct action must be non-violent."[136]

Looking back on the journey forty-five years later, Houser wrote that "it did not, of course, end segregation in interstate travel in the South. Perhaps it was an entering wedge." Nor did it generate a mass uprising, stir any real repercussions in Congress or the White House, or lead to any landmark legal case that would have strengthened the Irene Morgan decision. The NAACP had advised against appealing the case against Rustin, Felmet, and Roodenko to the Supreme Court, believing that the technicalities of the trial in the lower courts did not make as strong a case as another that was pending. The journey's organizers accepted the NAACP's decision.[137] The project, Houser noted, was perhaps ahead of its time. "The backup machinery was not there to make it more than it was—a planned and often an audacious attack on Jim Crow before the civil rights movement was full blown."[138]

Houser's vision of a nationwide, interracial, nonviolent mass movement did not come to fruition in the 1940s. The time was not yet ripe. As Meier and Rudwick point out, the gains were modest at best, as they were for all of the racial advancement groups.[139] This might have lent credence to a rather damning memo sent to A. J. Muste eight months earlier by John Nevins Sayre, who headed the FOR with Muste until 1946. Reacting to a memo in which Houser had outlined ideas for his work as codirector of the Racial and Industrial Department, Sayre had called Houser's proposals "overly ambitious" and recommended that the FOR not invest four or five thousand dollars a year "in such a one-man attack on the fringes of the race problem, especially when we don't feel that he is able to give really experienced and qualified leadership."[140]

ASSESSING THE EARLY CORE'S EFFECTIVENESS

Yet the courage and accomplishments of these early CORE protestors should not be underestimated. Actions had been taken at roller skating rinks, restaurants, hotels, theaters, amusement parks, swimming pools, public beaches, playgrounds, barbershops, and on public transport. Not all campaigns ended in immediate victory. Campaigns against employment and housing discrimination were particularly intractable, but in a number of northern and border cities discriminatory policies in public accommodations were permanently changed, and discrimination on some interstate train lines had been banned.

By 1954, after six years of intensive applications of nonviolent direct action by CORE activists, the climate in Washington, DC, had decidedly changed. The proof was when the US Supreme Court upheld a resurrected DC statute that forbade discrimination in eating places. After restaurants lifted their restrictions, several theater chains opened on a nonsegregated basis as well as playgrounds and swimming pools.[141] Moreover, in generating press attention from the many mass meetings held and the many leaflets handed out, CORE activists served to inform and educate a wider audience about the nature of institutionalized racism. They also inspired some of those affected by racism either to question their own compliance with Jim Crow laws, or to look with sympathy on those who refused to obey these laws. During the 1940s when race in the northern and border states had become increasingly spatialized, insulating whites from the recognition of their own white privilege, the work of Houser and his comrades in exposing racist patterns served to remove a number of those blinders.[142] Chairman of the Chicago Housing Authority Robert Taylor wrote to Houser that the Chicago summer workshop in 1945 had "activated a great many Chicagoans of both races to rededicate themselves to the cause of racial equality. All over the city people interested in race relations were inspired by the uncompromising stand which your group took on the issue."[143] When controversy arose over attempts of participants in the Washington, DC, Interracial Workshop to integrate the Anacostia pool, Secretary of the Interior J. L. Krug wrote to Houser expressing his appreciation "for the cooperation which you are extending to this Department in this difficult situation" and commended the Interracial Workshop "for the splendid effort it is making to bring harmonious relationships between the white and Negro citizens of the National Capital."[144]

The historian Thomas Sugrue goes even further, pointing out that the coverage of the civil disobedience campaigns in black newspapers empowered individual blacks all over the North who had not been involved in desegregation efforts to engage in their own kinds of protest.[145] Houser admitted there was no way of measuring these responses, but he was impressed with the number of people who spoke to the group about wanting to flout segregation practices.[146] As Ollie Stewart of the *Baltimore Afro-American* wrote: "Based on what I saw, between Washington and Asheville, I think the 'Journey of Reconciliation' knocked several props from beneath the already tottering Jim Crow structure. . . . History was definitely made. White and colored persons, when the whole thing was explained to them . . . will never forget what they heard (or saw). . . . All these people now have an awareness of the problem. . . . I heard one man refer to the group as pioneers. I think he had something there. They wrote a new page in the history of America."[147]

It is fortunate that Muste did not take Sayre's advice. Two years later, Houser and Rustin were honored with the prestigious Thomas Jefferson Award for the Advancement of Democracy by the Council against Intolerance in America. In a letter to Houser announcing the award, the council noted that "you were one of the individuals in your field—Public Service— receiving the highest number of votes in the poll . . . [which] was taken of over a thousand organizations concerned with the furtherance of the democratic ideal in America, as well as 500 newspaper editors throughout the country." The letter mentioned that Houser was now in the company of Jefferson Award winners in other fields such as Jackie Robinson, Branch Rickey, Bill Mauldin, and Sinclair Lewis.[148] Sayre had clearly underestimated the unassuming young man with the overly ambitious agenda.

Indeed, the page that Houser and his comrades wrote was the prologue to a story that would find its denouement in the 1960s. For most of the CORE participants, these experiences in nonviolent direct action were life changing and would have future resonance in often unrecognized ways in other arenas of life. As one of the participants in a workshop held in 1950 wrote: "When a workshopper leaves to go back to his home or school community, he takes with him experience in putting principles of brotherhood into practice—principles which are practical not just for one month, but for all his life."[149] Many of the workshop participants would go on to join and even lead the civil rights movement that erupted in the late 1950s and early 1960s, thus vindicating Farmer and Houser's vision that only a mass nonviolent movement would break the stranglehold of Jim Crow. Taking a page from Houser and Rustin, James Farmer would return to CORE to organize the Freedom Rides of 1961 that helped awaken the nation's conscience and finally enforce the *Irene Morgan* decision. Bayard Rustin would teach Martin Luther King Jr. the lessons and strategies in nonviolent direct action that as leaders he and Houser had worked out in those early days. The restaurant sit-ins and other civil disobedience actions Houser pioneered would inspire the sit-ins and civil disobedience campaigns of the 1960s that brought an end to de jure racial segregation in the South.

Others would apply the lessons they had learned to their daily lives, helping to transform in quieter ways the communities they lived in. Frank Kajikawa, who participated in the Washington, DC, workshop, embodies the kind of personal transformation wrought by those experiences. "Despite the fact that I served in the armed forces in the last war," he said, "I have had a very great experience in the use of nonviolent direct action. I am now convinced that such methods are effective. My whole thinking pattern has changed."[150] Helen Oerkovitz, who wrote Houser to thank him for her experience in a Washington, DC, workshop in the 1940s, put her training to work in a lifetime of social justice activism.[151] Houser's work had not been in vain. He had played a major role in pioneering a strategy that would be central to one of the great mass movements in American history.

Hooked by Africa, 1949–54

IN 1949, WITH THEIR OLDEST CHILD APPROACHING SCHOOL AGE, the Housers began to look for another place to live. The public schools in their Bronx neighborhood were of poor quality, and George's busy schedule made it difficult for Jean to contemplate raising her children in such an area. After rejecting several other places within his family's meager budget, Houser learned from a fellow FOR member about some people who were seeking to buy land in the New York metropolitan area to establish an interracial cooperative community. Houser jumped at the chance to join the project. Ever since his prison days, Houser had always wanted to live simply and cooperatively. Looking for a piece of land they could afford, the group had discovered a heavily wooded 150-acre property in rural Rockland County, about two hours from the city. Rockland County at the time was largely an insular, white, politically conservative farming area. Thus, the decision to start an interracial cooperative community in that setting and at that time was a daring undertaking. Because the initiating group had insisted that the community they were building was to be interracial, none of the local banks would give them mortgages, thus they were forced to turn to city banks.

With $5,000 borrowed from Houser's parents, another $5,000 loan from a wealthy FOR board member, and a $2,000 bank mortgage, the Housers were able to purchase over an acre and a half of the total land parcel. They also had plans for a modest bungalow built according to a formula by a contractor hired to build the first ten homes in the community, soon to be known as Skyview Acres. On September 1, 1949, the Housers, with the help of George's brother, Henry, packed up their belongings in an old truck and drove through the pouring rain to their new home in Rockland County.

The Housers' new home was set in the middle of a stand of sugar maple and pine. George would later delight in tapping the sugar maples to make his own maple syrup. The decision to join the cooperative would prove to be judicious. History is rife with the stories of men who devoted their lives to great causes at the expense of their families—one thinks, in particular, of Gandhi and Tolstoy. With George away over the next decades on frequent trips and with his long commute by carpool into the city (neither the Palisades Parkway nor the New York Thruway had been built yet), it would be important for Jean to have a community of mutual support. Eventually growing to forty-five households, Skyview Acres was to be an ideal community for the growing Houser household. There were cooperative babysitting arrangements, children's play groups, a buying club, and summer activities run by members of the community—most of whom were professionals with a variety of skills and talents. A small stream that ran through the acreage was dammed to create a swimming hole for the summer months and an ice-skating pond in winter. An open area was left for baseball and soccer games and an annual "Skyview Day" picnic. Activities for children were available, ranging from music lessons and dramatics to arts and crafts; and the surrounding woods made an ideal playground for games of cops and robbers or for teenagers to escape parental supervision.

The cooperative babysitting arrangements allowed Jean to return to school and eventually to develop her own career. By 1955, a second son, Steven, was born. Not quite three years later, in 1958, came a third son, Thomas (Tom). In 1965 Jean would earn an MS degree in special education from Yeshiva University and begin working with special needs children. Observing that there was no school program in the area for developmentally challenged children, she developed one such program and eventually became the assistant director and educational director of a child development center, working closely with the outstanding African American child psychiatrist and psychoanalyst Dr. Margaret Morgan Lawrence, who developed some of the first child therapy programs in schools, daycare centers, and hospital clinics.[1]

At first, the cooperators debated about whether they were becoming too insular. Residents of the area looked on them with suspicion, and the colony had to endure accusations of Communism and "free love." But as they became involved in the wider community, such accusations began to dissipate. As PTA president of her local elementary school, Jean ran for and was elected to the district-wide school board and sat on the board of a music conservatory that had been started by two other Skyview residents.[2]

CORE HITS AN IMPASSE

By the early 1950s Houser was becoming increasingly frustrated with having to run CORE on a tiny budget with limited time. He thought it was time CORE sought funds for a full-time executive director. The proposal, however, met with little response from the dispersed and variable CORE chapters. The reality was that by the early 1950s, the momentum that had propelled the organization was waning. CORE had largely won its fights against northern discrimination in public accommodations. The struggle against employment discrimination was beyond the means of this small volunteer organization, and its members were becoming dispirited by exhaustion and internal disputes between the liberal factions of the movement led by Jimmy Robinson and the more radical factions that had coalesced around Wally Nelson. Nelson held to a more confrontational approach to the police. While under arrest, he preferred to go limp, whereas the more "respectable" factions sought to avoid arrests altogether. Nelson was also not averse to working with Communist-affiliated groups, whereas the liberals were staunchly anti-Communist.[3] Houser was ambivalent. Although he sympathized with Nelson's more radical approach, he tried in vain to mediate the two sides. The fact was that CORE had never been a coherent organization. It was always torn between two poles: the liberal, integrationist pole that viewed civil disobedience as a last resort after other attempts at reconciliation had failed and a more radical Black Nationalist pole that saw civil disobedience as the strategic means to the end, not necessarily concerned with reconciliation but rather with justice for African Americans. As long as the white, integrationist element dominated, the organization was unable to attract masses of African Americans. At the 1952 CORE convention, most delegates reported a decline in chapter membership. Houser admitted that the organization was "stronger as a principle than as an organization."[4]

During the next two years the deterioration continued, and Houser was forced to conclude that CORE was in a weaker position than ever before. CORE's decline during this time may be attributable both to the growing recognition of black rights in the northern states and to the threat posed by McCarthyism.[5] Although the organization had eschewed Communist affiliation, it had not solved the problem. Conservatives and racists continued to smear the organization with the "red" label, seriously impeding its growth.[6] Moreover, to continue to be successful it needed a more substantial funding and organizational base, as well as the ability to move into the Deep South.

Along with the troubles in CORE, Houser was also experiencing his own waning support within the FOR, which was beginning to move away from racial and industrial activism. A. J. Muste retired in 1953 and was replaced by John Swomley, who had long bridled at CORE's insistence on being independent from the FOR. These factors compounded with the FOR's financial difficulties meant that the handwriting was on the wall. The FOR Program Committee had recommended that staff time on CORE should be eliminated as rapidly as possible. Houser was offered a position as Midwest secretary of the FOR, which would have required him to move back to Chicago; but working with liberal pacifists on an agenda that did not include race relations had never excited him. At its executive committee meeting in early April 1954, Houser announced that he was resigning from both the FOR and CORE to become effective in 1955.[7] For a brief period Houser flirted with the idea of looking for a job as a cominister in an inner-city black church where he could concentrate on community organizing.[8] But in the meantime, a new interest had begun to capture his always restless imagination.

AFRICA BECKONS

In early 1952, Bill Sutherland, a New York CORE activist and friend of both Houser and Rustin, returned from a speaking tour in England. Sutherland was a fellow pacifist who had served four years in Lewisburg Prison as a CO where he took part in efforts to desegregate the prison. With fellow war resisters Dave Dellinger, Ralph DiGia, and Arthur Emory, he had just finished a bicycle trip from Paris to Moscow in what was billed as a "World Citizens' Peace Project," and he was in England to talk about it. The journey was conceived in the context of the hot war in Korea and the intensification of the Cold War.[9] While in Europe, Sutherland had met many African students, picking up from them a sense of enthusiasm about the possibilities of freedom from colonial rule. It was an exciting time for African intellectuals. India's achievement of freedom in 1947 was stirring dreams of freedom throughout the colonial world. In London, Sutherland had met South African journalist Jacob Nhlapo, editor of *Bantu World*, who had told him about African National Congress (ANC) plans then developing for a massive nonviolent Defiance Campaign in South Africa to defy unjust apartheid laws enacted by the government.[10] Founded in 1912, the ANC had up until this time been a somewhat cautious organization. But in 1944, with the rise of extreme Afrikaner nationalism, a new group of young turks had formed the ANC Youth League. It would be these leaders—Nelson Mandela, Walter Sisulu, and Oliver Tambo—who would lead the movement in a more militant direction for the next half century.

When he returned from his trip, Sutherland, an African American, felt that "the possibilities of progressive social change [in the US] looked rarer and more remote, but in Africa it seemed that there was a real possibility to put the values we were talking about into action."[11] By the next year he would move to the Gold Coast (now Ghana), and throw in his lot with the anticolonialist movement. But in 1952, upon his return to New York, he would urge CORE leaders to actively support the South African cause.

On learning about the Defiance Campaign, Houser and Rustin were immediately struck with the parallels to the work they had been doing in the United States. The Defiance Campaign, however, was on a much grander scale. Houser's first reaction to Sutherland's urgings, however, was hesitation. His knowledge of Africa was rudimentary, and he felt overwhelmed with existing commitments. In the meantime, Sutherland had sent the CORE literature to the South Africans, who wrote to Houser and Rustin asking for help. They needed to raise a million shillings (about $150,000) for "propaganda" as well as to assist some of the families whose members were being arrested and imprisoned.[12] A direct plea for help from a national movement on the rise, like the ANC, was enough to trigger the instinct Houser always had to respond to the next pivot of history. But he was also struck by the similarities between the Defiance Campaign and the civil disobedience campaigns he had been waging against Jim Crow laws in the United States.[13]

As executive secretary of CORE, Houser then began a long correspondence with African independence leaders. Among his first correspondents were Albert J. Luthuli, then president of the ANC; Walter M. Sisulu, secretary general of the ANC; Yusuf A. Cachalia, secretary general of the South African Indian Congress (SAIC); Manilal Gandhi, Gandhi's second son; and Z. K. Matthews, president of the Cape Province branch of the ANC and head of African studies at University College of Fort Hare, the only university-level school for Africans in South Africa.[14] Matthews would come to Union Theological Seminary the following year as a visiting professor of world Christianity, and he and Houser would become good friends.

Houser, along with Rustin and Sutherland, decided to form a new ad hoc organization: Americans for South African Resistance (AFSAR). They were excited by the internal ANC documents they were reading, the nonviolent approach the Defiance Campaign seemed to be taking, the prospect of helping an anti-imperialist national movement for liberation, and the knowledge that their offer of help was an inspiration to the African leaders.[15] Donald S. Harrington, Unitarian minister of the progressive Community Church of New York and Charles Y. Trigg, minister of the Salem Methodist Church of

Harlem, were chosen as cochairmen. Houser was designated as secretary, and their executive committee included Roger Baldwin, Norman Thomas, Bayard Rustin, A. Philip Randolph, and Conrad Lynn, who was now Houser's neighbor in Skyview Acres.

Manilal Gandhi had written to Houser that he was a "bit doubtful to what extent our struggle is going to remain nonviolent, as those who hold the reins are far from believers in the principles of nonviolence. . . . What I feel therefore, is that you should certainly give your sympathy and moral support to the cause and watch how things go. There is too much of Communistic influence working and very little of the spirit of non-violence as preached and practiced by Mahatma Gandhi." For these reasons Gandhi had decided not to align himself with the movement.[16] A different note of caution was supplied by Reverend E. E. Mahabane, who wrote, "I regret to say, . . . the proposed campaign by the African National Congress on the 6th April will bring more harm than good. My personal opinion is that the masses are totally ignorant of what is happening, to say nothing of being organized."[17] The African National Congress, he averred, did not represent the majority of the people. Despite these negative responses to his offers of help, Houser and his comrades decided to lend their support to the cause. The official policy of nonviolence would have an effect, and Houser felt they "should support the civil disobedience tactic as a practical measure that would at least minimize violence."[18] Fortunately they did not heed Manilal's warning. Had they done so, Houser and his AFSAR colleagues would have lacked credibility with those at the center of the resistance. Manilal's distrust of Communists had, according to his granddaughter, "obscured" his vision and kept him out of the mainstream of the resistance: moreover, his "penchant for individual activity and moralizing brought him little appreciation."[19]

Malcolm X came to some of the early organizing meetings. He mostly kept to himself and didn't say much. Houser once tried to set up a meeting with Malcolm, but he was apparently not interested.[20] As the group was discussing what actions they could take, the question of Communism within the ANC came up. At the time, the only other organization in the United States that was focused on Africa was the Council on African Affairs (CAA), several of whose leading members were members of the Communist Party.[21] Since 1934, the African American–led CAA, headquartered in Harlem, had been advocating solidarity with Africa and linking European colonialism in Africa, Asia, and the Caribbean to US Jim Crow policies through protest rallies, publications, speeches, sponsorship of African liberation movement speakers, and lobbying at the United Nations. It represented a long tradition

of transnational contact between African Americans and their African breth-
ren. Several scholars have argued that this transnational contact was the basis
for launching US support for South African liberation.[22] It was India and the
CAA that launched the earliest call for international sanctions against South
Africa at the first meeting of the UN General Assembly in London in 1946.[23]
The CAA thus laid the groundwork for the kinds of work the ACOA would
later engage in. Among its leaders it counted such luminaries as W. E. B. Du
Bois and Paul Robeson.

The CAA reached the height of its influence in 1945–46, a short period
before the onset of the Red Scare and McCarthyism.[24] Ironically, the Cold
War had motivated the Truman administration to move on civil rights for
blacks due to the propaganda that the Soviet Union could use against a country that prided itself on being a beacon of freedom and democracy while a
significant segment of its population was denied such freedoms. Such pressure, combined with rising agitation for civil rights among returning African
American war veterans, forced the US government to soften its international
image as a racist nation. In June 1947, President Harry Truman became the
first president to address the NAACP. Truman pledged his support for the
civil rights of all Americans. He followed that in 1948 with an executive order
desegregating the military and banning discriminatory hiring practices in the
federal government.

According to some prominent scholars, even though the Cold War had
provided an opening for remedying some Jim Crow policies, it also narrowed
the scope of African American aspirations and split the African American
community. Gerald Horne felt that "the price of the ticket for anti-Jim Crow
concessions for U.S. Negroes was obeisance to the new Red Scare consensus."[25] Manning Marable argued that by shunning Marxists, the NAACP and
middle-class African Americans "lost the most principled anti-racist organizers and activists" and "liquidated the moderately progressive impulse of
the New Deal years and 1945–1946," making African Americans "unwitting
accomplices of a Cold War domestic policy that was, directly, both racist
and politically reactionary."[26] Scholars like Gerald Horne, Penny Von Eschen,
Brenda Gayle Plummer, and Francis Njubi Nesbitt have argued that the Cold
War also resulted in distancing the NAACP from its previous attempts to
link the struggle for black rights in the United States with the anti-imperialist
struggle abroad.[27] Carole Anderson, however, refutes this thesis, finding in
the archives of the NAACP a continuing effort to link the rights of African
Americans at home to the anti-imperialist struggles abroad through its alliances with other organizations like the ACOA.[28]

Cold War pressure, however, split the CAA, with several of its prominent members leaving the group for fear of being labeled Communist sympathizers. CAA founder, Max Yergan, subsequently became a staunch anti-Communist, turning against his former comrades.[29] Those remaining in the CAA experienced a period of intense harassment by the Federal Bureau of Investigation (FBI) and Justice Department, which resulted in dwindling support for the CAA. In 1953 the CAA was ordered to register under the McCarran Internal Security Act as a subversive organization, and by 1955 it had ceased most activities. The US government's Subversive Activities Control Board finally shut the CAA down for good in 1956.[30]

It was in this atmosphere of liberal anti-Communism that ASFAR was born and sought to distance itself from the CAA. Some scholars have been critical of Houser and his colleagues' perceived anti-Communism, claiming that this limited their ability to attract more radical Africans and African Americans.[31] Houser himself was not a visceral anti-Communist, although he shared in the era's wariness of the Communist Party due to its ties to the Soviet Union. He might also have been burned by his run-ins with another ideologically oriented party, the Socialist Workers Party, during his days with CORE. Later, however, Houser would come to work with several people who were in the Communist Party (or sympathetic to its cause) as well as travel to Communist Cuba; but in the early Cold War atmosphere he and his recruits must have felt it would be difficult to gain financial support for AFSAR's mission if they were associated with an organization under siege by the US government. A contributing factor may have been the mistrust between certain CAA members and the founders of ASFAR dating back to World War II, when Max Yergan had worked with the Communist Party to wrest control of the National Negro Congress from A. Philip Randolph. Some of ASFAR's founders, including Houser, had been allies of Randolph, so it was no surprise that they might hesitate to work with the CAA.[32]

Unlike Manilal Gandhi, other South African leaders Houser had been in touch with encouraged more than just moral support for their cause. In response, Houser had proposed holding a demonstration in support of the Defiance Campaign on April 6, 1952, a day on which organizations in South Africa and the United Kingdom were also planning to demonstrate. This was also a date celebrated by the Afrikaners as the tercentenary of the first European settlement in South Africa, a settlement established by the Dutch East India Company in 1652.[33]

Learning of ASFAR's plans, the CAA, which at the time was also supporting the Defiance Campaign, had contacted ASFAR's cochair, Donald

Harrington, suggesting that the two organizations cooperate in supporting the South African resisters. Houser was assigned the task of writing
to Alphaeus Hunton, the CAA's executive director, to explain why AFSAR
would not work with the council: "Although I am sure you have people representing many points of view in your organization, there are many who
are not by any means unsympathetic to the basic policies of the Communist Party. Our feeling is that the Communists will tend to make the most
of the South African conflict not because of a basic concern for the South
African people, but because they may be able to use the situation to bolster
their own partisan interests in the international power struggle."[34] Hunton
responded immediately by chastising Houser and his group, pointing out
that their attitude was hypocritical, since the South African civil disobedience campaign was supported by all sectors of progressive South Africans,
including Communists. "They have learned a lesson of unity in struggle;
it is to be hoped that we in America will learn it too before it is too late,"
Hunton wrote.[35]

Although they had turned down cooperation with the CAA, Houser
and his comrades knew from their own experience that the "red" label was
often used to smear people who were working for social justice. Some of
their South African correspondents had acknowledged the strong influence
of Communist leadership in the ANC but denied that it was the dominant
strain. Although not well acquainted with the details of ANC-Communist affiliation, they did not easily accept the charge of Communist control made by
those they knew were opposed to racial justice, despite a warning from one
of the FOR's top leaders that the FOR would not support the demonstration
they were planning on behalf of the Defiance Campaign.[36] If opposition to
apartheid were synonymous with Communism, then by that definition "we
were all Communists," wrote Houser.[37]

One of the many tragedies spawned by Cold War hysteria was that
Houser and his colleagues were willing to overlook Communist influence
in South Africa, yet they were unwilling to apply this same principle to organizations like the CAA and people like Robeson and Du Bois who were
severely persecuted by the government for their alleged Communist ties. Yet
the decision probably saved Houser and the ACOA from being hauled before
the HUAC, enabling them to take up the African liberation cause that the
CAA had been forced to abandon. Years later, however, Houser confessed
to feeling a sense of shame for his part in the correspondence with Hunton,
averring that he had always had great respect for people associated with the
CAA such as Hunton and Robeson.[38]

On April 6, 1952, an estimated eight hundred people filled the Abyssinian Baptist Church in Harlem, then pastored by Adam Clayton Powell Jr.,
the outspoken activist preacher who would later serve twelve terms in the
US House of Representatives. It was the first major event organized by the
newly created AFSAR, and it was held on the same day as a rally and picketing sponsored by the CAA, which attracted five thousand people.[39] Canada
Lee, who had starred in the 1951 film *Cry, the Beloved Country* (based on Alan
Paton's novel of the same title), had recently arrived from South Africa and
was one of the speakers at the ASFAR event, while Paul Robeson spoke at
the CAA-sponsored rally. A resolution of support for the South African Campaign was passed by acclamation at the ASFAR meeting and sent to the Joint
Action Committee in South Africa, Prime Minister Nehru in India, Manilal
Gandhi, President Truman, and Secretary of State Dean Acheson.[40]

The rally at Abyssinian was followed by a fifty-block-long motorcade
from Harlem to the South African consulate in Midtown Manhattan where
a picket line was set up around the consulate, the first of many to follow.[41]
Through mass mailings and leaflets, AFSAR leaders called on their contacts
to join them in supporting the drive against Jim Crow in South Africa. The
meeting raised $300, which Houser sent to Sisulu. A few days before the De-
fiance Campaign began, Sisulu again asked for help, this time in the form
of publicizing ANC statements, bulletins, photographs, and other material,
since within South Africa it was becoming difficult to rely on normal channels of communication.[42]

Supplied with continuing bulletins from South Africa, correspondence,
press reports in American papers, and a stream of insider information from
Z. K. Matthews (who had arrived in late June to serve for a year as a visiting
professor at Union Theological Seminary), Houser began to issue monthly
bulletins about the campaign that went to a small list of supporters in
church, civil rights, trade union, and pacifist circles eventually growing to
some three thousand recipients.[43] Some of this material contained graphic
firsthand accounts of imprisonment and police violence. He also authored
a thirty-two-page booklet, *Nonviolent Revolution in South Africa,* published
under the joint auspices of the FOR, CORE, and AFSAR.[44] Although American interest in South Africa was limited at the time, some local and national
church bodies put the issue on their agendas, and a Boston-based group formally affiliated with AFSAR distributed their literature and helped to raise
funds. Though still a small, volunteer, ad hoc effort, AFSAR raised about
$5,000 to send to South Africa, much of it through Matthews. Contributions
came from around the United States, Canada, and even India. A woman in

Arizona sent her diamond ring, saying she could not conscientiously wear it knowing that it represented slave labor. A family in Ohio contributed $100 at Christmas, saying it represented funds they had saved for family gifts. Some seminarians sent funds saved by eating sacrificial meals, and a person who withheld the military portion of his federal tax sent $100.[45]

AFSAR also initiated a letter-writing campaign to the UN and the US mission to the UN seeking approval for Z. K. Matthews to give expert testimony to the UN General Assembly about conditions in South Africa. India, supported by a cross section of other Asian countries, had taken the lead in calling on the UN General Assembly to put this on the agenda. Testimony at the UN from such nongovernmental representatives was unheard of in 1952, but the UN, still dominated by the United States, rebuffed the request.[46] By this time, AFSAR's work had begun to receive some notice in South African government circles as indicated by a press clipping that one of Houser's correspondents, Arthur Blaxall, sent in which Minister of Economic Affairs Eric Louw called attention to AFSAR's support for the Defiance Campaign.[47]

By spring 1953, however, a series of increasingly repressive laws passed in South Africa had made it impossible for the Defiance Campaign to continue. Over eight thousand people had been arrested. Meetings of ten or more people in African locations or reserves were forbidden. The receipt of funds for any organized resistance was punishable by five years' imprisonment, a £500 fine (equivalent to $6,000 today), and fifteen lashes with the cane. Correspondence was subject to scrutiny, and a new registration by race was required of all citizens.

THE AMERICAN COMMITTEE ON AFRICA (ACOA) IS BORN

Since the ANC had decided to lay low, it was time for those who had begun AFSAR to consider whether to disband or shift focus. Writing years later, Houser confessed that although he didn't realize it at the time, he was "hooked by Africa."[48] After several meetings through spring and fall 1953, the group, primarily at Houser's urging, decided to form a new nonprofit organization: the American Committee on Africa.[49] The ACOA would have the potential to not only address the problem of colonialism throughout the continent but also apartheid in South Africa.

By this time the planning group, which was transformed into a provisional executive committee, consisted (in addition to Houser) of Norman Thomas; Roger Baldwin; A. J. Muste; James Farmer; Catharine Raymond, Houser's secretary; George Carpenter, Africa secretary for the National Council of Churches; Rayford Logan, a professor of history at Howard University;

Conrad Lynn, the civil rights lawyer who had accompanied Houser on the
Journey of Reconciliation; Reverend Donald Harrington and Reverend Maurice Dawkins of the Community Church; Dr. Martin Dworkis, a New York
University professor; Peter Weiss, a patent lawyer and director of the Inter-
national Development Placement Association who had experience in Africa;
Harold Isaacs, a freelance writer and expert on Africa; Dr. Homer A. Jack,
pastor of a Unitarian Church in Evanston, Illinois; Dwight Lawrence, City
College NAACP, New York; Reverend Walter Offutt, NAACP; Gladys Walser
of the Women's International League for Peace and Freedom; and Judge J.
Waties Waring.[50]

Except for Egypt, Liberia, Ethiopia, and Libya, most of the continent in
1953 was still under the colonial dominance of Britain, France, Belgium, Portugal, Spain, and to a lesser extent, Italy. (South Africa was also independent
but was ruled by a white settler minority.) An Afro-Asian effort to change the
direction of the United Nations on colonial issues was just beginning. Still
dominated by the colonial powers, the UN did little to challenge the status
quo. Then in thrall to Cold War ideology, the US State Department had no
Bureau of African Affairs, viewing African politics through the lens of their
colonial allies and fearing that independence movements might turn to the
Soviet Union for help. Aside from the CAA reports that reached a limited audience of leftist activists and the black press (which had always been interested in
Africa), there was little publicly available knowledge in the United States about
Africa at that time. Some major publications like *Life* magazine and the *Saturday Review* had run special issues on Africa, and there was sporadic coverage
in the national newspapers of the day, such as the *New York Times*. John Gunther's seminal book, *Inside Africa*, one of a series of sociopolitical portraits the
journalist had painted of each of the continents, and British diplomat Vernon
Bartlett's *Struggle for Africa* wouldn't appear until fall 1953.[51] Until this time the
only American groups with any long-standing experience in Africa were missionaries who, as Houser would later discover, had a very limited understanding of Africa or Africans even though they lived and worked among them.

Moreover, African studies within academia was just getting started.[52]
Houser recalled hearing former Kennedy administration undersecretary of
state Chester Bowles speak about his own attempt to find relevant material
about Africa in a Connecticut town library. To find books on the Congo he had
to search under "B" for "Belgium." In searching for material on Ghana (then
the Gold Coast) or Nigeria, he had to look under "Great Britain," and so on.[53]

World War II, however, had weakened the power of colonialism. The
Atlantic Charter, a joint declaration of postwar aims signed by President

Franklin D. Roosevelt and British Prime Minister Winston Churchill in 1941, had articulated support for the self-determination of formerly colonized peoples. The Atlantic Charter and India's achievement of independence in 1947 had given hope to colonized peoples across the world. This stirring was represented at the Bandung Conference, a gathering of twenty-nine newly independent Afro-Asian nations that met in Bandung, Indonesia, in 1955. The Bandung Declaration declared, among other things, "that colonialism in all its manifestations is an evil which should speedily be brought to an end" and that "the subjection of peoples to alien subjugation, domination and exploitation constitutes a denial of fundamental human rights, is contrary to the Charter of the United Nations and is an impediment to the promotion of world peace and co-operation."[54] The Bandung meeting marked the emergence of the so-called Third World, a new geopolitical order that would increasingly be characterized by the polarity between North and South as opposed to East and West; but this new order was not yet widely visible in the United States.[55] Groups similarly concerned with justice and self-determination for Africa were forming in some of the other colonial powers. Soon they would all be working together. But a New York–based organization with access to the United Nations, where debates over the colonial status of African territories and demands for subjugated peoples' human rights were beginning to be raised, would have a unique role to play.

The question remained, however, of who could pull such an organization together. The decision to form the ACOA was both quixotic and prescient. To take on an entire continent with virtually no money or staff must have seemed like a fool's errand. It would take determination, imagination, and plenty of faith for such a small handful of people to think they could have any effect on a continent thousands of miles away. Houser was still on the staff of the FOR while also running CORE. Already overextended and with a family to support, Houser found it difficult to even consider taking on another pro bono project.

It was around this time that George Shepherd, who would become ACOA's first part-time volunteer director, returned from a two-year mission in Uganda, where he had been providing technical assistance to a nationwide farmers' cooperative movement. Shepherd's intention was to return for a short tour to raise funds for the farmers' federation. However, upon arriving in the United States he learned that the US State Department would not renew his passport, claiming (falsely) they had received some information from the British colonial powers that he had supported the Mau Mau Uprising in Kenya by encouraging Jomo Kenyatta. The Mau Mau Uprising was a revolt against colonial and white settler rule in Kenya, which lasted from 1952 through 1960 and helped to hasten Kenya's independence. Kenyatta, then leader of the Kenya African Union (KAU), was accused by the British of directing the revolt, although Kenyatta would always deny the charge. Shepherd had met Kenyatta only once, in the home of a friend in Nairobi.[56]

When Peter Weiss, who had helped Shepherd with a US speaking tour, learned that he was at loose ends, Weiss invited Shepherd to apply for the part-time, nonsalaried position of ACOA director. The committee was at first hesitant, knowing that although he was well acquainted with Africa, Shepherd had no connections in the United States. But given the circumstances, they could hardly look this gift horse in the mouth. Besides, he had come with good recommendations from well-known Britons active in the antiapartheid cause.[57] Shepherd would have to raise his own funds and establish a program. Welcoming the chance to keep up his commitment to African work, Shepherd became ACOA's interim director for the next two years. With office space in the basement of the John Haynes Holmes Building donated by Harrington's Community Church next door; contacts supplied by Houser, Weiss, and Roger Baldwin; and a corps of volunteers who, according to Shepherd, "all had shabby jobs during the day and gave up many evenings and weekends to make the world a better place," he began his work.[58]

Shepherd continued the occasional news bulletins that provided information about Africa and criticized American policy for supplying the colonial powers with the means of repression through its support for NATO's ostensible protection of Europe from Soviet aggression. Occasional conferences on the decolonization question and seminars around a visiting African personality were also provided. *Africa Today*, now the longest continuously published journal of news and analysis of African affairs, began as a mimeographed sheet in the ACOA offices.[59]

Shepherd also began to provide a political defense of the liberation position at the UN.[60] At the time of its founding in 1945, almost a third of the world's population lived in non-self-governing territories. While most of these territories were still ruled by colonial powers, some were territories that had been placed under mandates by the League of Nations following World War I.[61] Articles 73 and 74 of the UN Charter, however, had set forth the principle of self-determination for all peoples and the requirement that those countries governing or administering territorial dependencies had an obligation to help them move toward self-government. Chapter XII of the UN Charter set up the Trusteeship Council to administer and supervise the governing of these former mandate territories to make sure they complied

with UN principles. The colonial powers, however, were to varying degrees
reluctant to grant independence to their former colonies. Thus, the United
Nations, which had enshrined the concept of universal human rights and
self-determination in its Charter as well as in the Universal Declaration of
Human Rights, became the forum through which liberation movements
and their leaders sought to gain recognition and legitimacy for their right to
self-governance.

The relationship between self-determination, a collective concept, and
universal human rights, generally seen as pertaining to individuals, has been
contested in the literature.[62] The history of these two concepts is a confus-
ing one, and anticolonialists were themselves conflicted about the relationship. One way to look at the transition from ASFAR to ACOA in the 1950s
may be as the transition from a single commitment to an individual human
rights perspective (ASFAR had begun as a way of supporting South African
blacks in their struggle for freedom from racially oppressive laws) to a double
commitment as ACOA took up support for collective self-determination as
expressed in the many anticolonial movements that were beginning to explode across the continent. Both concerns—individual rights and collective
rights—would thereafter at varying moments define the work of Houser and
the ACOA.

The human rights framework was of course most salient in the ACOA's
campaigns against the apartheid regime in South Africa. William Korey as-
serts that it was NGOs like the ACOA that transformed the words of the
Universal Declaration from a mere standard into "a critical element of foreign policy discussions in and out of governmental or intergovernmental
circles."[63] In response to Houser's letter offering support for the Defiance
Campaign in 1952, Walter Sisulu had written, "I am very delighted that your
organization has taken such a great interest in the struggle for fundamental
human rights by my organization."[64]

Much of the work the ACOA undertook over the following decades
would be focused on supporting—against the opposition of Western
powers—petitioners from liberation movements at the UN who were ar-
ticulating their right to self-determination. By doing so Houser was also
supporting the framework of collective rights as a necessary prerequisite to
the development of universal human rights. As he was later to write, "In the
euphoria of the upsurge of nationalism and the struggle for freedom in this
period, not much attention was given to the concepts of human rights [i.e.,
'universal rights'] or democracy. The cause of freedom and independence
was itself a basic human right of course, and the concentration was placed

on this struggle."[65] But Houser would always hold these two forms of rights, as he put it, in "creative tension": "The dynamic of the liberation movement is needed to point the direction, to gain the momentum for change. The human rights initiative must appreciate this initiative, but maintain some objectivity and stand in judgement on excesses."[66]

In supporting petitioners before the UN, Houser was even supporting their right to petition the world body, a right that was finally recognized in the late 1960s. He was also providing information to the public about the debates over Africa at the UN and testimony to help move the UN in the direction of its principles.[67] To facilitate its work at the UN, the ACOA initiated the Coordinating Council on Africa, inviting various organizations that had an interest in African affairs to name a representative to sit on the council. The council would meet during sessions of the UN General Assembly to coordinate work on issues that came before that body.

5

An African Odyssey, 1954

Z. K. MATTHEWS HAD OFTEN TALKED WITH HOUSER ABOUT THE NECESSITY of visiting Africa. Houser's knowledge of Africa was rudimentary, and from his time in Asia he knew that firsthand experience was the only way to really understand another continent and its people. Thus, in spring 1954 he took a leave of absence from the FOR and CORE. With funds raised through his various FOR and CORE connections, letters of introduction from well-connected friends, and press cards from NBC radio and the Associated Negro Press, he boarded the *Queen Elizabeth* for London for the first leg of a six-month tour of Africa.

On board the ship Houser typed a letter to Jimmy Robinson, then serving as CORE's finance secretary, announcing that he was resigning from his executive secretary position as of the June 1954 convention. "Remind our supporters," he wrote, "that consequent reorganization will necessitate additional expense for CORE in that I have been able to contribute my time and office facilities and it is unlikely that another person may readily be found who will be in a position to do the same thing."[1] This was an indirect acknowledgment that Houser's willingness to put in long hours for little pay had helped keep the organization afloat all those years.

Despite misgivings about leaving his young family for such an extended period, Houser confessed to feeling heady "about the romance of sailing into adventure in the unknown."[2] And indeed, he was literally sailing into the unknown. At the time of his departure he wasn't sure, given his antiapartheid work, whether he could get a visa from the South African government. He had received a Portuguese visa to visit Angola, a British visa for the Gold Coast (now Ghana), a French visa for colonies in West and Equatorial Africa, and a Belgian visa for the Belgian Congo (now the Democratic Republic of the Congo), but the rest of the itinerary was still up in the air.

Houser had planned to spend a week in London, contacting antiapartheid groups, members of the British Parliament, journalists, missionary leaders, and anyone else who could provide him with background and contacts in various African countries. Because of Britain's increasingly troubled relationship with its African colonies, London had become a center of thought and activity related to Africa, including concepts of anti-imperialism and Pan-Africanism, with a number of organizations emerging to challenge British imperial policy.[3] A small cadre of Labour MPs had begun to raise colonial issues in parliamentary debate, with Fenner Brockway emerging as the leading figure.[4] John Hatch, secretary of the Commonwealth Department for the Labour Party, began writing about Africa for the *New Statesman* as well as publishing longer pieces.[5] In 1952 the Africa Bureau was established, largely at the behest of Michael Scott, a British Anglican priest who had been radicalized in South Africa. The bureau was founded to provide the British public with accurate information on issues related to Africa.[6] The bureau also provided support for representatives of African organizations visiting the United Kingdom, and in 1954 the Movement for Colonial Freedom emerged with the backing of seventy Labour MPs in defiance of their party's refusal to endorse independence for Britain's colonies. By the end of the decade, the Africa Bureau would become the leading extraparliamentary Labour pressure group devoted to colonial affairs.[7]

Houser armed himself with a letter from liberal New York State Republican Senator Jacob Javits to the American ambassador in London asking for help in requesting visas from the British government for their East and Central African colonies—Kenya, Nyasaland (now Malawi), Northern Rhodesia (now Zambia), Southern Rhodesia (now Zimbabwe), Uganda, and Tanganyika (now Tanzania). Houser, however, waited futilely for the visas to come through and turned to Fenner Brockway for strategic advice about how to deal with the situation. Brockway was not on the best of terms with the Conservatives or the conservative wing of the Labour Party and advised Houser that his request for a visa should be handled by someone with more moderate credentials.[8] Houser learned from these intermediaries that the Colonial Office had written to the territories to find out what the trouble was. Eventually, word came back that his reputation as an agitator for racial justice had made him suspect to British authorities, who were then being confronted by the Mau Mau Uprising in Kenya. He had been declared a "prohibited immigrant" and would not be able to visit Britain's East and Central African colonies. If this was the case, he figured that any attempt to get a visa for South Africa would also be futile.

Houser did, however, make good use of his long layover. He met the
leaders of several organizations—both solidarity organizations and emerging African liberation movements—with whom he would work for years to
come. Brockway gave him letters of introduction to several people in Africa,
and John Hatch provided good advice and the names of people who could
be helpful. One evening he went to the home of Seretse Khama, a chief in
waiting of the Bangwato people from what was then the British protector-
ate of Bechuanaland (now Botswana). Khama's marriage to a white British
woman had stirred up an international crisis in the relations between Britain
and South Africa and had sent him into exile in Britain. Khama would later
become the first president of Botswana.[9]

Houser also met with the Trinidad-born Pan-Africanist theorist George
Padmore. Padmore provided Houser with a framework for understanding
the struggle against colonialism in several parts of Africa, as well as a letter of introduction to Kwame Nkrumah, then Ghana's prime minister and
a leading Pan-Africanist whom Padmore was quite close to and who would
become Nkrumah's adviser on African affairs.

When Houser first encountered Africa, he found a continent whose
once-storied past had been all but decimated by a century of Western imperialist aggression, conquest, and colonization. The "scramble for Africa" had
begun in the latter half of the nineteenth century when the slave trade was
no longer profitable, capitalist industrialization demanded assured sources
of raw materials that were abundant in many African countries, and the
inter-European power struggles dictated the carving up of the continent into
multiple spheres of influence. Europe's social problems also led to the export
of "surplus labor" to settler colonies in Algeria, Tunisia, South Africa, South
West Africa (now Namibia), Angola, Mozambique, Southern Rhodesia (now
Zimbabwe), and Northern Rhodesia (now Zambia). Such conquest was not
without retaliation. African rulers had organized militarily to resist the sei-
zure of their lands and the domination of European powers through guerrilla warfare and direct military engagement. But changing configurations
in the political geography of Africa, combined with the superior military
technology of the Europeans, led to Africa's conquest and domination. By
1900 much of the continent had been colonized by seven countries: Britain,
France, Germany, Belgium, Spain, Portugal, and Italy.

Houser was starting from scratch. Over the course of the thirty-five
visits he would make to Africa from the 1950s through the late 1990s, he
would gradually give himself what amounted to a graduate-level education
on colonial and postcolonial Africa. This was not an easy task. Africa was a

complex geopolitical reality. Each colonial power managed its colonies dif-
ferently, depending on the administrative traditions in the home country, the
specific imperialist ideologies of the colonizers, and the political conditions
in the territories they had conquered.[10] Moreover, the decolonization process
as it got underway was a multilayered and multifaceted one.[11] Added to this
complexity would be the impact of the Cold War, as the United States, the
Soviet Union, and China each sought to influence the outcome of the liberation struggles in their own terms. In addition, there was the rivalry between
and among the various and shifting liberation forces. It was enough to daunt
even the most diligent scholar.

Houser's modus operandi was that of a participant observer. The detailed journals he kept on his travels to Africa, along with tape recordings,
films, and reports, would capture both the excitement and tragedy as well
as the hope and disappointment of Africa's anticolonial and postcolonial
development struggles. They would provide numerous insights into how
the colonial powers sought to thwart indigenous development and stymie
self-governance and also exposed the ways in which the Cold War deranged
intra-African relations and catalyzed internecine warfare within certain liberation movements. Over the course of his travels, Houser would make it a
point to meet with as many people as possible who could give him varied insights into what he was witnessing. His list of contacts would grow into the
thousands and would include liberation fighters at all levels of their movements, heads of state and other government leaders, American government
officials, parliamentarians, journalists, economists, medical personnel, NGO
workers, lawyers, missionaries, peasants, refugees, and political prisoners.

As a white man, Houser had a somewhat unique perspective at the time.
He was a Westerner who traveled to Africa not to convert (like the missionaries) or cure (doctors and other humanitarians) anyone and certainly not to
exploit the African people and their lands (like most Western policymakers,
diplomats, and so-called development experts). Houser just wanted to try to
understand the continent.[12] Because he brought to this journey the perspective of someone who had been involved in a leadership position in a liberation movement in his own country, he saw things in a way that few other
white Americans did at the time and looked for signs of rebellion where
others saw only stagnation.

Houser's itinerary took him first to Dakar, Senegal, then the capital of
French West Africa, a federation of eight territories under French colonial
rule.[13] He spoke no French and because of this confessed that his ability to
understand the society was limited. But he was nevertheless quick to observe

the hollowness of the French policy of "direct rule" through which Africans were supposedly being "assimilated" as "Frenchmen" as they became educated and acculturated.

From Dakar, Houser flew to Monrovia, the capital of Liberia. This country on Africa's Atlantic coast had been founded by freed blacks and ex-slaves from the United States who had been transported to Africa by the American Colonization Society starting in 1820. The country was run by Americo-Liberians, the descendants of those who had emigrated. They occupied the capital, followed American culture and customs, and had established a republic in 1847 with a constitution and flag modeled on the American Stars and Stripes. Although a minority of the population, the Americo-Liberians ran the country, relegating a host of native peoples to second-class status.

William Tubman headed the True Whig Party, which ruled with absolute authority. Since government jobs were the only way of escaping abject poverty, there was a tendency, Houser observed, for those with the best educations and the most leadership potential to gravitate to the civil service and to toe the government line. The small population, the one-party system, and the lack of economic resources to support a viable political opposition resulted in an atmosphere of self-censorship and intimidation.

Liberia's economy at the time was dominated by two US companies, Firestone Rubber and Republic Steel, whose presence did little to benefit the native population. The government had little money for capital improvements. Thus, there were no taxis or buses even in the capital. Many of the capital's streets were still unpaved, the roads were pitted and rutted, and there was no easy way into the hinterlands. Houser found the poverty staggering. However fleetingly obtained, the observations Houser recorded in his journal identified several problems that would lead to the bloody 1980 coup that overthrew Americo-Liberian rule, resulting in a long period of repressive government and civil war.

Houser's next destination was the Gold Coast (now Ghana), a British colony whose frontiers were the result of bargains among the colonial powers of Britain, France, and Germany that did not correspond to the historical boundaries of the kingdoms that preceded colonization. In contrast to the French, British colonies were administered by a system of "indirect rule." A governor or governor-general reporting to the Home Office in London generally governed along with an appointed executive council and a legislative council of appointed and selected local and foreign members. At the provincial and district levels, however, the British established a system of local administration in alliance with preexisting political leadership and institutions.[14]

Growing national pressure for self-determination had increased in the Gold Coast after World War II, and Britain, exhausted by the war, had begun to concede more and more power to its African subjects. By 1946 the British were moving toward self-rule for Africa.

Houser was welcomed to Accra, Ghana's capital, by his old friend Bill Sutherland, who had settled there, marrying a Ghanaian poet and teacher named Efua Teodora.[15] For Houser the atmosphere in Accra was "utterly dynamic" as he had serendipitously arrived when the country was in the midst of electing its first all-African National Assembly, a prelude to independence that would come three years later.[16]

The Convention Peoples Party (CPP) was the most powerful of the three parties vying for power. The CPP had been founded by Kwame Nkrumah, who would determine the future of Ghana and much of Africa for the next several years. Three hours after arriving in Accra, Houser was whisked off by his British Quaker hosts to observe the long lines of jubilant, largely illiterate voters waiting to cast their ballots at two polling stations (some had walked five miles to cast their vote) and later that evening witnessed ecstatic young dancers as they wove through a crowd of some twenty thousand at the polo grounds shouting, "Nkrumah, Nkrumah!" The CPP had won 71 out of 104 seats in the National Assembly. Later, Houser would ride through the streets of the capital in a victory procession in one of the CPP's campaign sound trucks. Preceded by CPP youth on bicycles, the caravan wove through streets crowded with thousands of people shouting "Freedom!" while beating on drums and raising their hands in salute as Nkrumah followed in a jeep.[17] It must have been a poignant moment for Houser as he thought about the lack of voting rights for blacks in the American South.

With introductions from Padmore and Brockway, Houser met twice with Nkrumah in his home. He was impressed by his plans not only for Ghana's independence but also by his commitment to making Pan-Africanism a reality.[18] At the time of his meeting with Houser, Nkrumah was clearly not only a leader of his country but also an emerging leader of the Pan-African movement. Years later Houser would write, "I, as a young man, was enthralled by Nkrumah's charisma, his common touch, . . . his utter devotion to African liberation throughout the continent, and his espousal of nonviolent tactics which he called 'positive action.'"[19]

Houser was surprised by the friendly attitude Ghanaians showed toward Americans, so different from their attitude toward the British, their colonial overseers. They knew that Americans had fought for independence from Britain, and their experience with American soldiers in West Africa during

World War II (more than one million Africans had served in the war on the Allied side) had been positive, though they knew little about racial segregation in the United States.[20] Their attitude may also have been colored by the fact that the United States had no colonies in Africa, although this positive perception of the United States would soon change. Whether Americans deserved to be treated as friends, Houser noted in his journal, was debatable.

The northern part of the country was different than the area around the capital. Here, ethnic governance and traditions were much more in evidence and disease and poverty abundant. Traveling with Bill Sutherland near the border of Togoland, Houser commented on the patchwork that European colonialism had made of Africa. Togoland, originally a German colony, had been divided up by France and Britain when Germany was stripped of its colonies following World War I. The Western half bordering the Gold Coast went to Britain, and the eastern half, bordering Dahomey, went to France. This meant that the Ewe people were split between the two colonial powers. Single farms were divided, requiring farmers to sell part of their produce in a French market in francs and the other in a British market in pounds sterling.[21]

While the Gold Coast appeared to be on its way to a relatively peaceful transition to self-rule, Houser noticed problems that would manifest later: the 90 percent illiteracy rate and the lack of a diversified economy. Despite having resources of bauxite, industrial diamonds, manganese, gold, and timber, the country had an overdependence on one export crop: cocoa. While accompanying Nkrumah to a concert in his Cadillac, Houser speculated that despite his reputation as a man of simple tastes, Nkrumah might be prone to exploiting the growing privilege that many of those who acquire power inevitably succumb to, and he was unsettled by Nkrumah's unofficial remarks about wanting to ban the Moslem Association Party. Houser thought it might not be healthy for the CPP to have too much control.[22] These observations, small in themselves, were a foretaste of things to come. Nkrumah would later turn the country into a one-party state and indulge in a cult of personality, calling himself "Osagyefo," or "the Redeemer." He would be overthrown by a military coup in 1966.

When Houser visited Nigeria for the first time (it had not yet developed its oil reserves), it was still a largely agricultural country. He found, again, a friendly atmosphere toward Americans and a strong desire for independence from the British, who governed the country with a British governor-general and a cabinet of Nigerians and Britons. In meetings with many Westerners as well as leaders of various political groups in Lagos and Ibadan in the west and Enugu in the east, Houser learned that the country was divided geographically, ethnically, and religiously. The Yoruba dominated the west, an area that contained more large cities and large villages than the poorer and more scattered eastern region dominated by the Ibo. The Hausa and Fulani dominated the far more populous northern region. All three regions had their own political organizations, each vying to be the channel through which independence would play out. Houser met with many of the leaders of these groups, learning from them that unlike the Gold Coast's fight to self-govern, Nigeria's movement for independence was being conducted through constitutional channels without being preceded by a period of militancy and with no dominant political party. He also picked up on the dislike between the Yoruba and the Ibo as well as their mutual disdain for the less developed northern region. Houser did not travel in the northern part of the country and therefore was unable to gain an understanding of its dynamics. But he reflected in his journal on whether Nigeria, with its strong regionalist sentiments, would be able to form one national government.[23] Regional hostilities would plague independent Nigeria into the twenty-first century.

As the son of missionaries, Houser was interested in assessing the impact of Western missions in Africa. In the Gold Coast he had been told by Africans that missionaries generally kept themselves apart from the people and had tended to destroy traditional African cultural traditions such as drumming and dancing in their schools and churches. Though not especially conversant with the political situation, Houser concluded that at least they were not inhibiting independence but rather coincidently helping it by means of the education they provided. "The churches are leading the way in bringing African leadership to the fore," he observed, "this is especially true in the Anglican and Methodist churches."[24] The northern part of Nigeria, however, lacked Western-style educational facilities because missionaries had a difficult time gaining entry into this largely Muslim region. Although Houser felt that Western education was a prerequisite to independent governance, he considered it a mistake to throw the baby out with the bath.[25]

Houser confided to his journal that he was disturbed by what he observed as the superior attitude of Europeans to their African servants and wondered if he would become a part of such a system if he lived there. "The Africans," he wrote, "are taken for granted. They are treated as children. The Europeans tend to rely on them for simple things such as getting a chair. . . . There has definitely been a dulling effect on even the enlightened Europeans. A wide gap is opened up between them and the mass of people. This doesn't necessarily spread to the educated African."[26]

On July 22 Houser flew to Duoala, the largest city in French Cameroon. Prior to World War I, Cameroon had been a German colony. With Germany's defeat, 80 percent of the land had been placed under French mandate by the League of Nations while 20 percent went to the British. After World War II, the entire area was put under UN Trusteeship. Limited in French Cameroon by his inability to speak the language, Houser did manage to meet with the anticolonialist, nationalist Union of the Peoples of the Cameroons (UPC), which he found more politically sophisticated than the movements in either the Gold Coast or Nigeria that had assumed the imminence of self-government and were cooperating with the British colonial administration. The UPC was antagonistic toward the French government, suspicious of the United States, and not as friendly toward Americans or missionaries as those in the Gold Coast and Nigeria. The missionaries, he was told, generally took their cues from the government. This was an attitude that he would find common throughout most of the rest of Africa. Houser sympathized with the anticolonialists' antagonism toward the French. He had witnessed the brutal beating of an African boy by a Frenchman over a minor traffic accident. "I don't know what it was about but no man should be able to treat another that way. The African made no response," he wrote.[27] He had learned that the French government refused to light the streets on which Africans lived and that they had been trying to thwart Africans' desire for independence, which was "their right as a Trust Territory." "I was glad to leave Douala," Houser confided to his journal, "I didn't like it very much."[28]

VISIT TO ALBERT SCHWEITZER'S HOSPITAL

Before leaving for Africa, Houser had decided to take a side trip to visit Albert Schweitzer's hospital in Lambaréné, Gabon, part of French Equatorial Africa that also included French Chad, Ubangi-Shari, and French Congo. He was curious about this great humanitarian physician, scholar, theologian, and musician he had read so much about. Schweitzer's dedication to selfless service was just the kind of role model Houser found appealing.

Houser arrived at Lambaréné's primitive airport on July 29 at nightfall and was taken to Schweitzer's jungle compound in a canoe paddled by four rhythmically chanting and singing Africans. He was disappointed to find that the great man was in Europe at the time, but he was interested to see the institution he had read so much about.

While impressed with the medical care, Houser had conversations with the European staff that left him feeling critical of "le grand docteur," who at the time had been the recipient of several humanitarian awards including the

1952 Nobel Peace Prize and whom much of the Western world considered to be a model of altruistic heroism. Houser's observations of Schweitzer's setup differed from the general consensus of the time. John Gunther's mildly critical but mostly laudatory assessment of the doctor had appeared in 1953,[29] but it was not until a decade later that criticism of Schweitzer's racism, paternalism, and stubborn resistance to change began to appear in print.[30]

"In spite of the fact that Schweitzer was not there, his personality dominated everything," Houser wrote in his journal.[31] A paternalistic attitude seemed to be the modus operandi. Africans were called "natives" and "are looked upon as irresponsible children and treated that way."[32] "I understand the *Grand Docteur* really bawls them out on occasion," Houser wrote, "the philosophy of Mademoiselle Emma Haussknecht [in charge of the hospital during Schweitzer's absence] is that you can't be too friendly with them or they will take advantage of you. . . . There is a separation of white and black in everything." "I realize this is not a simple issue," confessed Houser, "but the attitude of always treating the African as if he was someone to be commanded is not good. . . . There seems to be no concept of preparing these people for eventual freedom." Houser was also critical of Schweitzer's apparent management style: "There is no doubt . . . that this is a one-man show. . . . He is a firmly fixed man in his opinions. He does not seem to respect the opinions of others. . . . There is no concept of partnership. . . . Anyone on the staff with independent ideas would have a very tough time. There is no such thing as a staff meeting. Schweitzer plays the cards very close to his chest." Nevertheless, Houser had to admit that "the creative genius was there. It took something to come out to this wilderness about fifty years ago with only the idea of service and build this project!"[33]

Houser's indictment of Schweitzer's management style is an implicit statement about his own preferred style of management. Houser's style was collegial where Schweitzer's was authoritarian. Houser was respectful of others' dignity, while Schweitzer was paternalistic. Houser was open to new ideas, while Schweitzer was set in the past. However, there was a larger vision within his critique of not only Schweitzer but of so many missionaries he met. Because of his experience in fighting racism at home he was equipped to sense a coming age of liberation even if those on the ground couldn't see it. He called a shot early on that Schweitzer's work was irrelevant (or beside the point) to this coming age.

From his brief stays in Libreville, Port-Gentil, and Lambaréné, Gabon, Houser concluded that there was scant nationalist organization among Africans in French Equatorial Africa, and not much was being done to bring them

along. Revealing the rather naïve paternalism of the young man newly encountering Africa, Houser wrote in his journal, "These people are too primitive to organize a country and as long as the Europeans are here, Africans will
serve them. The only thing that will change this picture will be a strong educational movement to give the African ideas and independent judgment and
then organization and struggle. . . . The African cannot be the master of his
own destiny unless he adopts enough of the Western culture to struggle effectively against it and build institutions that can challenge it. . . . The conviction
is growing on me that struggling for independence is best preparation for it. A
people are not worthy of independence until they have struggled."[34] Houser
was right about the necessity of struggle, and this comment may help to explain why this committed pacifist would come to devote the remainder of his
life to the support of self-determination movements—even if said movements
were armed ones. But reflections such as these also reveal the ethnocentrism
and liberal paternalism still latent in this young man's first encounter with Africa. His appreciation of indigenous African culture and agency would grow
as he became more acquainted with the continent.

Houser's next stop was the Belgian Congo (now Democratic Republic of
the Congo). In the 1950s this was one of the richest countries in Africa, pos-
sessing vast stores of copper, industrial diamonds, tin, cobalt, and uranium
as well as agricultural products like rubber, cotton, palm, cocoa, and coffee.
The Congo had been brutally plundered and its people viciously exploited
by its colonial overseer, King Leopold II of Belgium. When he couldn't get
the Belgian state to finance his lust for African territory during the great
nineteenth-century scramble for Africa, Leopold engineered the land grab
as his personal fiefdom. Accurately portrayed in Joseph Conrad's *Heart of
Darkness*, the entire country was run like a slave plantation with the most
horrific punishments meted out if the Africans did not meet their rubber
quota. An estimated two million to fifteen million people had been killed,
putting Leopold among history's top ten mass murderers.[35] Although the
horror ended in 1908 when the Belgian state, compelled by international outrage, took control of the colony, it was left a devastated and traumatized land
where many of the evils of imperialism continued to live on. Belgium still
looked upon the Congo as an overseas province whose resources (including
indigenous labor) were ripe for exploitation. The Belgians had no policy of
preparing the Congolese for self-government until just before they decided
to leave suddenly in the early 1960s.

Houser arrived in Léopoldville, capital of the Belgian Congo (now
Kinshasa, the capital and largest city) on August 2. In Léopoldville he found

his way to the Union Mission House where he would be staying. His impression of the missionaries in the Congo was decidedly critical. The people were "stuffy," they appeared to have no interest in the development of the country from an African point of view, and treated Africans as servants, calling them "natives" and "boys."

Governance in the Belgian Congo came directly from the government in Brussels, which appointed the governor-general and the governors of the six Congo provinces. A show of giving Africans more power was made by establishing a handpicked advisory council composed of thirty whites and five blacks with no power. "There is no sign of a protest movement here," wrote Houser. "I don't know who will provide leadership for the struggle. My theory is that the missionaries don't know what they are doing but by providing some education they help prepare for the inevitable revolution."[36]

The Belgian government's press attaché had told him that the government's approach was to assimilate Africans into European society on a high level. Eager to contrast the Belgian approach from that in South Africa where segregation was legalized, the attaché asserted that whatever segregation existed was on an educational, cultural, and economic level and that as Africans became educated and achieved a European level of economic and cultural status, the differences would be wiped out. Such "assimilated" Africans, however, would have to carry a card identifying themselves as *evolué* or "evolved." The Belgian government did provide some social services and was beginning to institute education. An employer was required to pay a minimum wage (which was increased for each dependent) and was also obligated to subsidize housing, some health services, and minimum food rations.

Despite the cultural attaché's attempt to paint a positive picture of Belgian rule, it was clear to Houser that racial segregation and suppression was the rule. Out of some three hundred thousand Africans in the city, only forty-two families, he learned, were "assimilated," meaning they had become "Belgian" and had more rights than ordinary Africans. He observed that blacks and whites lived in separate sections of the city and went to separate coffee shops. And whites could go to the head of the line in the post office. Unlike bustling, colorful Accra and Lagos, Léopoldville at night was eerily quiet. A curfew kept Africans indoors, and they were not allowed downtown without a pass. African policemen had guns (but no bullets) and were prohibited from arresting whites. Africans who were arrested were denied the right to bail and could be held indefinitely. Even religious gatherings had to be headed by a Belgian, the Catholic missionaries serving as a tool of the government.[37] Houser concluded that the social legislation was part of a two-pronged effort to keep the African subservient by satisfying them with social welfare services but suppressing any move toward organization. The same kind of segregation existed in the other Congolese cities Houser visited, such as Luluabourg and Elizabethville. "So far," wrote Houser, "I don't see how the Belgian policy of assimilation will work in the long run. At some point the dynamics of a racial conflict growing out of a cultural and civilizational conflict, as well as an economic conflict, will come to a head. The Belgians will try to put it down vigorously."[38]

On the morning of August 7, Houser conveyed in his journal that he had just written nine pages on the Gold Coast for a newsletter to be sent back home: "I feel as if I have something to say about Africa now."[39] It was a recognition that in order to understand the complex history and present reality of this fascinating continent, one had to spend sufficient time there and to weigh insights from one's own observations as well as from those on different societal levels.

At supper in Léopoldville the night before he was due to fly to the Angolan capital, Luanda, Houser received three visitors. Before he had left New York, his friend, Homer Jack, had given him the post office box number of Manuel Barros Necaca, an Angolan, and Houser had written telling him when he would be in Léopoldville and expressing the hope that they could meet. Another visitor was Necaca's nephew, Holden Roberto, who would later feature prominently in Angola's history. The third was a man who worked at the Portuguese consulate. The three were concerned about whether to let Houser board the plane for Luanda the next day. From incoming cables from Lisbon, the consulate worker had learned that the Portuguese had been monitoring Houser's movements. They knew that he had left Lisbon on June 7 and thought he would be flying straight to Angola. When he didn't arrive as expected, they had alerted their consulate in Léopoldville not to issue him a visa, only to discover the day before his departure that he had already obtained a visa in New York. Apparently, the Portuguese decided to let him go but would watch him carefully.

On this part of his Belgian Congo odyssey Houser traveled by car with one of the missionaries into the bush, covering about 150 to 200 miles and visiting twenty villages. Here he observed and recorded local customs. Interactions between the American missionaries and the villagers were teaching him just how deeply white supremacy had infected this group of do-gooders. For example, the missionaries would let the Africans do most of the work, and when they talked with villagers, his missionary host would draw a line in the sand indicating that the Africans should stand behind that line. One of

his hosts drew analogies between African Americans and Africans: this, to
Houser, revealed the man's ignorance of American blacks.[40]

Feeling unnerved by the revelation that the Portuguese were tailing him
but nevertheless determined to see Angola, Houser boarded the plane on
August 9 for the two-hour trip to Luanda.[41] He was met at the airport by
Methodist missionaries who took him to their headquarters. Houser felt
much more at home with these missionaries, not only because they were
Methodists but also because of their more liberal attitudes toward Africa and
Africans. They referred to Africans as "Africans" and "Angolans," not "natives" and were in the process of turning over leadership of the church to
Angolans. Houser felt that the Protestant missionaries were doing a revolutionary job in training Africans for leadership and independence through
their private schools. In contrast, the state-supported Catholic schools appeared not to be doing so well, as the illiteracy rate in the country was 95 percent, while a study of the Protestant missionary schools in Lobito indicated a
75 percent literacy rate.[42]

The Portuguese, he was soon to learn, looked on Angola not as a colony
but as a part of Portugal.[43] They encouraged white immigration and their
policy of *assimilado* meant that some Africans could allegedly rise within the
system through their own efforts and be assimilated as Portuguese. But assimilation was a smokescreen designed to hide a harsh reality. There was no
help for Africans who wanted to rise. As a result, only a small percentage of
the African population was "assimilated."

Behind the façade of apparent racial tranquility lay another reality. This
African "province" of Portugal was ruled, like Portugal itself, by the dictator António de Oliveira Salazar, its governor-general appointed by Lisbon. It
was, in effect, a police state. Advocacy for greater group inclusion and criticism of Portuguese rule was forbidden. Houser could detect no sign of organized resistance among the Africans. He learned that his missionary hosts
had to be very careful about what they said, as the Portuguese feared negative publicity.[44] Even if they withheld their criticism until they returned to the
United States, their missions in Africa could be jeopardized. A perk of being a
NATO member was that Portuguese intelligence sources reached all the way
to the United States. "The difficulty with a police state," wrote Houser, "is
that it makes one eternally suspicious. Who do you trust and who don't you
trust."[45] The missionaries, he realized, had adjusted to life under such conditions. They were careful not to do or say anything that could be construed
as critical of the state, but they appeared grateful to have their consciences
stirred by Houser's probing questions. "I feel rather humble about this,"

Houser confessed, "because who knows what kind of adjustment I would make were I here longer. One's insight can so easily be dulled by time."[46]

It turned out that the authorities had been calling the missionaries for weeks to ask when he would arrive, as he would be required to go to police headquarters to get a permit to travel in Angola. The permit gave him permission to travel to Malange on the high plateau that runs down the center of the country and to Lobito, further south along the coast. In both places he had Protestant mission contacts; but his passport was retained, which meant he would have to travel without it. For the remainder of his journey he would be required to check in with the local police as soon as he arrived at his destination. Such checking, he learned, was essential for each "assimilated" African and foreigner. An African could not even change jobs in a city like Luanda without getting police permission.[47]

One of Houser's main interests in visiting Angola was to learn about the "contract" or forced labor system in which the state acted as labor recruiter, ensuring private enterprise of a supply of cheap labor. It was in Malange that he got his most detailed understanding of this system, which was a form of slavery. The district administrator told him that Africans were lazy, so the contract labor system was a way of forcing them to work. While the administrator claimed that only unemployed people were subject to contract labor, as Houser soon learned, even some of those who were already employed—and those who couldn't prove they had paid the head tax required of every African—were subject to detention by a *chefe do posto*, or district administrator.[48] Night raids were often made, the authorities going from dwelling to dwelling looking at identification papers and then dragging the men off to the local jail for the night to be shipped to their employers the next morning.[49] They would be sent to do work on government projects or for private companies or landowners who had contacted the authorities saying they needed a certain number of workers. Bribes often passed hands between the employer and the *chefe*. The worker was supposed to be paid a salary and provided with food, housing, and medical care by the employer. But the pay was minimal at best, the state having first taken out a tax that was owed. Workers were at the mercy of their employers and were required to work anywhere from three months to several years. Some missionaries told him they had seen men picked up and roped together as they were sent off.[50] At a village near the Quessua mission outside of Malange, Houser witnessed another aspect of the labor system. Twenty Africans—men, women, and boys—were filling potholes in the road with dirt from large anthills carried in pots on the women's heads. Villagers were responsible for road maintenance, devoting one day a week or more to the task, even though they didn't own vehicles and weren't paid for their labor.

"It seems obvious to me," wrote Houser toward the end of his stay, "that a potentially revolutionary situation exists here in Angola." Although the missionaries to whom he was making this point disliked the contract system, they had made their peace with it in order to continue their work. They disagreed, however, on Houser's assessment that a potentially revolutionary situation existed. Houser recorded their pitiful rationales for the lack of revolutionary sentiment in his journal: "Africans weren't interested; it would be dishonest to work underhandedly against the Portuguese to see their rule overthrown; Africans would be worse off under their own rule; some things in the present situation aren't so bad; look how Africans treat each other so much more cruelly than Europeans do."[51] Houser tried to point out that Africans had been made ambitionless because the structures of their society had been destroyed by white men, plundered through invasions, decimated by the slave trade, and were now suffering under this forced labor system. This apparent lack of ambition might be a general form of futility and hopelessness. "What is the aim of mission work?" he asked them.

> Is it to prepare these people for freedom? For independence? To
> be men? If the people are not capable of it then the work here is
> just like hospital work. It is like Schweitzer's philosophy. Patch the
> people up but don't try to disturb their society, or their thinking, or
> get them excited. Put them back in what you find them, just a little
> more whole because of the treatment but not essentially changed.
> But if more is possible. If these can be men, if they can be free, then
> admit your policy is one of accelerating this trend. If you have to
> compromise, admit it is a compromise and don't fool yourself into
> thinking it is the principal of loving the Portuguese.[52]

On a visit to the beautiful port city of Lobito and its environs, Houser met with the Reverend Jesse Chipenda and attended a meeting at his church. Inevitably the discussion came around to the prospects for independence. Houser suggested the need to struggle for independence. Chipenda, however, was pessimistic, claiming that Africans were like the grasshopper that has had its wings pulled off and doesn't know how to fly anymore. Ironically, Houser would later come to know Chipenda's son Daniel as an important political figure in the Popular Movement for the Liberation of Angola (MPLA). The day after his visit with Chipenda, while walking around the residential area of Lobito, a young African boy suddenly dashed from behind a bush thrusting some papers into Houser's hands and then disappearing as quickly as he had appeared. Since the three sheets were in Portuguese, Houser stuffed them in his pockets. After returning home he had them translated. The writer had been at the meeting the night before and his message was the following: "We cannot win the struggle by ourselves. Help us."[53] It was a poignant cry for help to which Houser would spend the next quarter century trying to respond.

On his last day in Angola, Houser discovered that he was being tailed. He confessed to feeling tremendously uneasy and dragged out by the Angola experience—caught between the missionaries on the one hand and the government on the other. He had wanted to find some sign of an incipient movement for liberation, but he lamented that the leadership structure was not there. The police surveillance continued right up until and after Houser boarded the plane in Luanda when his passport was finally returned to him. "It was a relief to get on that plane," he confessed. "I didn't realize how tired I had gotten from this whole process until I got out of there."[54] He had been in Angola almost two weeks.

During his trip down the west coast of Africa, Houser had been trying to think of a way to get into South Africa without being noticed, as it was clear that his support of the ANC was known by authorities. By the time he reached the Belgian Congo he had figured out a plan. He already had a round-trip air ticket from New York to Johannesburg. At a travel agency in Léopoldville he had exchanged his one-way air ticket for a boat ticket from Cape Town to Southampton, England. Then he went nervously to the South African consulate to ask for a transit visa from Johannesburg to Cape Town so he could catch his ship. The young vice consul thought it could be arranged and told him to return in a couple of days. Nervous, again, that the ruse might not work, Houser returned and was given his passport with the transit visa stamped inside. The consul told him that in a case like this he did not have to contact Pretoria. Houser emerged from the meeting relieved and exultant. His subterfuge had worked.

It was late in the day in early September when Houser left Elisabethville (now Lubumbashi) in the southern part of the Belgian Congo for a five-hour flight to Johannesburg, South Africa, nervous that his visit to Africa might be at an end. As he flew over Rhodesia, he was haunted by the fact that he was prohibited from visiting the country. His anxiety deepened when he looked at the question on the immigration form distributed on the plane: "Have you ever been convicted of a crime in any country? If so, give details." Should he be honest? Should he lie? He decided to mark the space for the question with a dash. Much to his surprise, nothing was said, and the immigration officer placed a "no" on the sheet. They did not even ask him to open his bag. He emerged exhilarated and relieved from the customs area to greet Arthur Blaxall, the only person he had written to about coming to South Africa. Blaxall, secretary of the South African Christian Council, was a British Anglican priest and pacifist who had come to South Africa in 1923 to work with the deaf and blind and, as the Defiance Campaign emerged, had aligned himself with the liberation struggle. Houser had earlier corresponded with him in his capacity as a member of AFSAR.

Blaxall and his wife drove Houser through Johannesburg to their home in Roodeport, some twenty miles from the city. It was here that the Boers had settled on their trek in the early part of the previous century. "It is amazing," Houser wrote in his journal, "how things have come to life that were just names to me before."[55] He did not sleep well the first night, as his mind was racing. Here was the culmination of his trip to the country he feared he would never see. All the distant associations of the last two years were now becoming flesh and blood. Houser's original visa had given him only a few days in South Africa to be in transit from Johannesburg to Cape Town where he was to catch his ship, but he decided to take a chance and to apply for an extension until September 24, which would give him three weeks in South Africa. Again, much to his surprise, the extension was granted.[56]

Just a year before Houser's visit to South Africa, journalist John Gunther had described the South African government as "in some respects the ugliest government I have ever encountered in the free world."[57] But he didn't think the country was likely to explode into civil war. The apartheid situation was in the long run untenable, but it was likely to last a long time.[58] Houser, however, his antennae alive to signs of incipient social struggle, found a situation "clearly building to revolution." Most whites, he observed, could not possibly see this underground ferment because they had kept the Africans so effectively in their place that they could not possibly know an African without tremendous effort.[59]

By the time he reached South Africa, Houser had become so inured to the wretched living conditions he had witnessed in Dakar, Luanda, and Léopoldville that the slums of Johannesburg, Pretoria, Durban, and Cape Town did not surprise him. He was, however, pleasantly surprised by the amount of public criticism of the government in the press. In contrast to Angola and the Congo, "there was ferment in South Africa; it was by no means politically dead."[60] Evidence for this conviction came not only from the press but also from small observations. He noticed an African National Congress pin on the lapel of a young African he met at a nonpolitical gathering; the youth mentioned that he had been arrested twice during the Defiance Campaign. Houser was also affected by the sight of an African shaking his finger vigorously at a white driver who had narrowly missed hitting him, telling the driver to watch where he was going. "When I saw this—a black man telling a white man off—I knew I was in a different situation," Houser wrote.[61]

Houser's awareness of the potentially revolutionary ferment was deepened by his meeting with several of the leaders who would be key players in the coming struggle against apartheid. One of these was Chief Albert Luthuli, whom Houser had corresponded with earlier. Luthuli was serving his second banning order at the time. Banning was an important government tool in the suppression of antiapartheid activism. People could be placed in a kind of house arrest or have their travel limited to their home area. Publications could also be banned—that is, kept from being published if found "undesirable" for any number of reasons. The two pen pals met in the town of Stanger in Natal Province where the government had confined Luthuli to his immediate geographical area. Houser was impressed with Luthuli's unshakable convictions, his avowal of nonviolence in the struggle, his sense of humor, and his deep, resonant voice.

In Orlando, an African location near Johannesburg, Houser visited Walter Sisulu, another of his pen pals. Sisulu was Nelson Mandela's mentor and lifelong friend and would later be a fellow prisoner with him on Robben Island. Houser had to meet with Sisulu surreptitiously as he was in defiance of a government law requiring official permits for whites intending to travel to an African location. Since he was not likely to be given a permit if the government knew that he was in the country, Houser decided that defying this law was the only feasible way to meet the man who had been his correspondent for the past two years. Sisulu shared with Houser the history of the ANC and his assessment of the Defiance Campaign as having raised the political consciousness of the masses. He told him of the plans for the Congress of the People to be held in 1955: at this Congress, demands that had been solicited from the people would be incorporated into a Freedom Charter.[62] This meeting was the start of a lifelong friendship that would result many years later in Houser coediting a book of Sisulu's memories.

Houser also met with Oliver Tambo, who struck him as a warm and gentle person. Tambo was a young attorney who shared an office with Nelson Mandela. He had been a leader in the Defiance Campaign and was a close associate of Walter Sisulu. He would later head the ANC in exile. Houser had learned of a tourist attraction featuring traditional dancing and singing that was to occur one afternoon at the Crown Mines. Eager to record some African music, he asked Tambo about this, and the young lawyer agreed to take Houser to the event. Throughout this trip, and on his subsequent travels in Africa, Houser was intent not only on recording Africa's political turmoil but in bringing back artifacts of its rich cultural heritage to Americans unfamiliar with the continent. While sitting in the stands, suddenly, near the beginning of the program, Tambo remembered that he was under a banning order and sprang to leave, as this was a "gathering" he was prohibited from. Houser ran out after him. On the way to the car, Tambo insisted on carrying Houser's briefcase. When Houser demurred, Tambo replied, "In my country we will do it my way." It was a gesture of kindness Houser would remember almost a half-century later.[63] Little did Houser then suspect that decades later—in 2010—he would travel to South Africa, from which he would be banned for thirty-seven years, to receive the Order of the Grand Companions of Oliver Tambo Award from the South African government.

Manilal Gandhi also became flesh for Houser when he met him at the Phoenix Settlement near Durban. This had been the site of the first civil disobedience campaign his father had organized against racial restrictions on Indians. Houser spent a day and a night with Gandhi, imbibing the spirit of the man for whom he carried an unusual reverence and after whom he had modeled his approach to political activism and social justice. He also met with two more radical Indian leaders: Yusuf Cachalia, a leading figure in the South African Indian Congress who was instrumental in bringing Indians into the Defiance Campaign, and Yusuf Dadoo, who worked to persuade the Indian community and democratically minded whites to link their destiny with the African majority. Dadoo would also become an important figure in developing the international outlook of the antiapartheid movement.

Z. K. Matthews, the elder statesman of the ANC had by this time returned from his year of teaching at Union Theological Seminary and was living at his home in Alice in Cape Province. Houser renewed his friendship with Matthews, who told him that since the end of the Defiance Campaign, Africans were taking a deep breath before the next wave of protest that the ANC would spearhead.

Through meetings with these leaders who were under banning orders and had to watch their every movement, Houser gained a much better sense of what the South African people were up against. He also got a taste of it when he attended a court hearing near Cape Town and heard the stories of people who were brought before the Commissioner of Native Affairs for violations of the so-called pass laws. But it hit home with greater force when

Houser discovered that he himself was under police surveillance. As he was putting Houser on the night train to Port Elizabeth, Matthews mentioned that the police kept him under constant surveillance. Houser had thought that the only person who knew his whereabouts in the country was Matthews. But as soon as he entered his room in the hotel in Port Elizabeth, the telephone rang. On picking it up he heard a click on the other end. Later that day he called Joe Matthews, Z. K.'s son, agreeing to meet him later that night on the street outside the hotel. After dark, the two men, along with Dr. J. L. Njongwe, treasurer of the Cape ANC, met in the street and decided that the safest place to talk would be in the car while driving. As they were driving along an unlit road bordering the Indian Ocean, two cars, one in front and one in back, suddenly stopped them in their tracks. Although his companions seemed remarkably calm, Houser was frightened and nervous. A plain-clothes policeman whom his friends knew thrust his head inside the window and said, "I strongly suspect you are guilty of violating the ban by being in a gathering."[64] Both Matthews and Njongwe had been under a banning order.

The three were taken to police headquarters where they were interrogated for about an hour and a half. It was now about eleven o'clock at night. Houser was told that he was not under arrest but was interrogated as if he were. Houser gave no names except that of Matthews, whom he had known in New York.

Houser returned to his hotel, and after a short night's sleep he left the next day for Cape Town. He had three days before his ship was to sail. Almost immediately he spotted the plainclothes policemen, whom he now expected to see. They were hiding behind open newspapers, comically, Houser thought, like in a film based on a Raymond Chandler story. They continued to follow him everywhere he went. Houser's main concern was for his tape recordings and notes. At first, he thought of hiding these items in his hotel room in case it was searched, but on second thought he took them to the South African Institute of Race Relations where he thought the items would be safer. The constant surveillance unnerved him. He managed to give the officers the slip on his second day in Cape Town. Because he was walking and they were in a car, he was able to cut through parks, and for one day they had no idea where he was. On that day he was able to contact I. B. Tabata, the leader and socialist theoretician of the Unity Movement, a Trotskyist movement that had been critical of the Defiance Campaign and the ANC. Houser had previously corresponded with Tabata in connection with the Defiance Campaign. Tabata introduced him to others in the Unity Movement and took him to the African section and the colored areas of the city. While Tabata was driving him, Houser spied the unmarked police car that had been following him and ducked under the dashboard. Later that day the woman at the South African Institute of Race Relations called to tell him that she had received a strange call from someone who said they were a friend of Houser's. This "friend" said Houser had not shown up for a lunch date and wondered how he could reach him. She answered that she didn't know anyone named Houser. The police had obviously tracked him to the institute. That evening, back at the hotel, the police were there again.

For the rest of his time in Cape Town, Houser decided to act like a tourist. On September 23, 1954, Houser wrote to Catherine Raymond, his assistant at the FOR, that "this little piece of the Earth's surface is in for some stormy days. . . . The situation is revolutionary. . . . This place will have a whole series of blow-ups for years to come."[65] He was right on the mark.

On his last day in Cape Town, Houser picked up his tapes and notes from the institute and stuffed them in the pockets of his raincoat. It was September 24, 1954, six months after he had left home. With some trepidation he boarded the boat, fearing again that his tapes and journals would be confiscated. Much to his surprise, however, his bags were not even opened, even though only a few yards away the same police were watching. As the boat sailed away, he rather impishly waved to his pursuers. The wave was not returned.[66]

Reflecting on his trip through Africa the following month, Houser wrote, "I never realized before how really bad United States foreign policy vis-à-vis Africa looks from an African point of view. The so-called world democratic forces haven't a chance of influencing the people of Africa as long as their influence is on the side of the status quo. White Communists in South Africa, by their active participation in the movement, help to keep the movement of the non-Europeans from being just anti-white."[67] It was an admission that one could not really understand the complexity of the world through the imperialist lens of the US government and the anti-Communist obsession of so much of its culture.

A Mission the Size of a Continent, 1954–59

HOUSER'S TRIP TO AFRICA HAD BEEN THE BEGINNING OF A LOVE AFFAIR with the continent. Eventually he realized that he could continue his involvement with Africa by agreeing to take on the leadership of the ACOA.[1] The organization was in a stalemate. Since it began with virtually no funds, the only way George Shepherd had been able to volunteer his time to the fledgling organization was through a small grant from a local church in Queens and a three-month grant from an Indianapolis-based foundation. By spring 1955 it was becoming clear that this part-time setup was not going to be viable for the long term. A memo to the executive committee, presumably drafted by Shepherd, had urged a more politically active role for the committee but one that could not be implemented under current staffing and financial arrangements.[2]

Consequently, in May 1955 Houser began raising funds to hire a full-time executive director.[3] Shepherd was ready to move into academia and had received an offer to begin a teaching career. Houser himself had had three job offers that would have required relocation, but he was reluctant to move his family from Skyview Acres. After discussing the pros and cons of taking on leadership of the ACOA with Shepherd and board members, Houser decided to give it a try. He knew that taking this new position meant that he would have to raise his own salary.[4] But he also saw that there was a niche in the struggle for freedom that no one else at the time was filling. Thus, there were lots of program and project possibilities if they had the imagination and drive and were able to raise enough money.[5]

It was a difficult decision, knowing that he had a family to support. With two young children at home and a third on the way (Steven Houser would be born in October of that year), Jean was in no position to help. "I'll give it six months or a year," Houser thought, "to see if it works and if it doesn't, I'll have to look for another job."[6] Knowing that the family would once again be thrust into financial insecurity must have been hard on Jean, but there is no evidence that she complained about it. She had known from the beginning what she was getting into by marrying George. Yet Houser's instincts were right. His fierce commitment to human rights, extensive background and connections in the civil rights and religious communities, years of organizing and fundraising experience, dogged commitment to detail, and growing understanding of Africa meant that the ACOA board would now have a leader who could enable the organization to turn a corner. From a struggling volunteer organization without a funding base, the ACOA would eventually become one of the most important (if relatively small) African solidarity organizations in the United States and a key external player in the long struggle to topple South African apartheid. The ACOA's role was particularly critical in the early years when there was little American interest in Africa.[7]

HOUSER BEGINS WORK

Throughout spring and summer 1955, while traveling the country giving talks about his Africa trip, Houser was simultaneously trying to raise funds for the ACOA and engage in programmatic planning. His contacts included labor unions, civil rights organizations, church and peace groups, and any others he thought he could interest in the project. A prospectus for the revamped organization included educating the American public about Africa through *Africa Today*, as well as literature on specific topics, a speaker's bureau, and public conferences. The prospectus also conveyed the intention to influence US foreign policy through supporting African petitioners at the UN and other activities and raising funds to support "specific projects in Africa either of an educational/welfare nature or in support of democratic moves toward freedom by the people of a particular country in Africa."[8]

Houser officially began his work as ACOA director on September 1, 1955, with a planned budget of $30,000, which had yet to be raised. Over the summer he had gone through what he described as a "terrific struggle" over what to do. There was everything to do at once: raising funds for salaries and program work, reorganizing the ACOA board, and initiating a vital program based on his plan.[9] The ACOA was still occupying space at the Community Church, which provided free rent. But money for everything else needed to run a viable program had yet to be procured.

Over the spring and summer Houser had been able to raise $4,000 for a project fund, half of which was sent to support the educational work of antiapartheid activist Father Trevor Huddleston in South Africa.[10] The other half went to an educational project in the Gold Coast that Bill Sutherland had initiated. Until enough money could be raised for his salary, Houser and his family limped along on whatever he could earn through speaking engagements as well as a loan from his father.

The year in which Houser began as executive director of ACOA was a momentous one in the history of the African American struggle for freedom and dignity. It was the year of the Montgomery Bus Boycott, marking the start of the most active phase of the modern civil rights movement. If Houser had any regrets that he was no longer part of that movement, he could take satisfaction in knowing that he and his comrades had pioneered the way with their courageous actions in the 1940s. Now, however, he was involved in a freedom movement on a much larger stage.

The first decade of ACOA's existence saw long-subjugated peoples asserting their independence and agency throughout the dying colonial world. When the decade began only four of the continent's countries had achieved independence. By the end of the decade, twenty-two more states would be led by Africans. In addition to the Bandung Conference, the Algerian War that began in 1954 was also a symbol of this ferment. Amidst a world increasingly divided between the capitalist West and the Communist East, Bandung represented an independent perspective, a challenge not only to colonialism but to the neocolonialism of the two superpowers. It was a perspective that Houser found himself agreeing with, and for the next thirty-five years he would devote his life to supporting those principles through direct action campaigns, lobbying, and written analysis. It would not be easy steering one's way between the Scylla and Charybdis of the two Cold War superpowers while holding fast to the principles of political self-determination and equality between peoples. Houser would often find himself suspected of either Communist sympathies or capitalist loyalties. Moreover, as the struggles for independence in Africa grew more intractable, his commitment to nonviolence would be tested as never before.

At the beginning of the decade the United States was taking its cues on African policy from its European colonial allies. But the winds of change were blowing in the direction of decolonization, and a new approach to Africa would be needed. But the approach would be a cautious one. Caught between its NATO obligations to Europe, Cold War fears of Soviet influence on newly emerging African nations, the growing civil rights unrest at home, and congressional pressure, the Eisenhower administration gave lip service to the ideal of self-determination while either supporting its European allies on colonial issues at the UN or abstaining.[11] The overall effect was to identify the United States with the dwindling pockets of white rule.[12]

The year 1958 saw movement toward African liberation increase in many parts of the continent. One indication was the attention Africa was then getting at the United Nations, so much so that the session of the UN General Assembly that year became known as the "Africa Session." By the end of the year, the UN had established the Economic Commission for Africa. The US government responded by establishing the Bureau of African Affairs within the State Department, headed by an assistant secretary of state for African affairs.[13] In addition, new consulates and offices of the United States Information Agency were opened in various parts of the continent. By 1959 it was clear that African independence was exploding. In a two-part spread in its January and February issues, *Life* magazine noted that "Africa suddenly is in the forefront of the news. Almost every week it produces something new and startling: the birth of a new nation, the dedication of a great dam or steel mill, a bloody riot in Nyasaland or the Belgian Congo."[14]

While for the most part the United States stuck to its policy of viewing Africa as an extension of Europe, there were some signs that this was beginning to change. For example, the US representative directly criticized South African apartheid for the first time, although it would not be until 1986 that the United States, in passing the Comprehensive Anti-Apartheid Act, would do more than just verbally condemn it.[15]

THE MAKE OR BREAK YEAR

The first year of Houser's tenure was make or break for the young organization. For the first half of the year the only other staffer was Lydia Zemba, a volunteer who left in February 1956 to pursue graduate studies. At that point, Houser persuaded Catherine Raymond, his assistant throughout his CORE/ FOR days, to join the staff as his current assistant. During its first year, the ACOA continued to build its project fund, but basic operating expenses were dire, causing Donald Harrington to report that "we are down to bedrock [financially] and a real state of emergency exists." Committing himself to a monthly pledge of $10, Harrington sent out an appeal asking for a hundred such pledges so that basic expenses could be paid "without our personnel having to worry all the time about where their next meal is coming from."[16] This would be the first of many such appeals to keep the small operation afloat.

Despite financial difficulties, Houser, his lone staff, and volunteers pulled off a one-day conference, "Africa, the United Nations, and U.S. Policy," that coincided with the opening of the UN General Assembly in fall 1955. They also sponsored public presentations by Father Huddleston and South African authors Peter Abrahams and Alan Paton; held four public programs on "Africa and the Arts" and five programs on "Forces for Making Social Change in Africa"; hosted receptions for Nnamdi Azikiwe, premier of the eastern region of Nigeria, Reverend Michael Scott, and students from the Gold Coast; organized meetings with petitioners from Italian Somaliland; and continued to publish *Africa Today*, now with a formal editorial board.

In July 1955 the ACOA obtained accredited NGO status with the UN. Much of Houser's time, when he wasn't writing fundraising letters, was spent in the halls of the UN, where he began to meet many of Africa's emerging leaders. Among the earliest petitioners was Julius Nyerere, a teacher and at the time president of the newly formed Tanganyika African National Union (TANU). This meeting was the beginning of a long friendship between Houser and Nyerere, who would later assume the presidency of newly independent Tanzania.[17] Houser organized a public meeting in New York at which Nyerere spoke, as well as several invitations to speak to small groups of people in their homes during his stay in the city.[18]

The other memorable petitioner was Sylvanus Olympio, who was from the Trust Territory of French Togoland.[19] Olympio, a polyglot who had been educated at the London School of Economics, was later elected president of the Republic of Togo. He would be tragically assassinated in the compound of the American Embassy in the capital city of Lomé in 1963, just two years after he had taken office, the first of several African leaders befriended by Houser who would meet a similar fate.[20] Olympio was also introduced to the American friends of Africa, whom Houser had been cultivating.

The importance of ACOA's work in hosting UN petitioners might not be fully appreciated today. Too often in those early days petitioners from Africa to the UN remained unseen and unheard by those outside the UN Trusteeship Council. They would arrive without any welcome and with no hotel reservations or provisions for office space or secretarial assistance. There was no advice given to them on arranging press interviews and no opportunity to meet Americans who were sympathetic to their cause. The result was that they had virtually no opportunity to inform Americans about themselves or their country and learned very little about the United States.[21] The ACOA's work with African petitioners would change all that by arranging meetings for them with UN and American government officials; providing housing, often in the homes of ACOA supporters; organizing press conferences and speaking engagements with American audiences; and providing office space and secretarial services so that they could put their petitions into the proper format and language. But most of all, the ACOA offered them the gift of friendship. The role played by this small organization was critical to these African leaders' ability to gain international attention and legitimacy for the cause of independence.

As the pace of international events grew, so did the work of the tiny band of people occupying the ACOA office. Letters and visitors were now flooding in. Of most immediate attention were the dire letters Houser was getting from South Africa. On December 5, 1955, the South African government carried out a military-style early-morning raid on the homes of 156 leaders of the Congress Alliance, a coalition of all the major antiapartheid organizations, spiriting them off to prison under heavy guard. Those arrested included almost the entire executive boards of the ANC, the Congress of Democrats (COD), the South African Indian Congress (SAIC), the Coloured People's Congress (CPC), and the South African Congress of Trade Unions (SACTU).[22] Among the prisoners were Chief Albert Luthuli, Walter Sisulu, Oliver Tambo, Nelson Mandela, Z. K. Matthews, and Matthews's son, Joe. On December 10, 1955, Z. K.'s wife, Frieda, wrote to Houser: "You have heard the news. My husband and son are both in gaol and likely to be there for some time. . . . The charge is of course a fantastic one I think—high treason. Just because they have tried to fight for our rights."[23]

The cause of the arrests was the Freedom Charter that had been adopted at a Congress of the People attended by three thousand delegates in a field outside Johannesburg in June 1955. The congress had been spearheaded by the ANC and organized by the Congress Alliance. Earlier that fall the government had raided over a thousand homes and offices searching for documents related to the charter. From the government's perspective, the Freedom Charter amounted to an act of high treason, since it declared the abolition of all racial discrimination and the granting of equal rights to all.[24] During his visit with Sisulu the year before, Houser had learned about plans for the Freedom Charter.

Faced with desperate letters requesting support for those arrested (and knowing some of them personally), Houser moved into action, setting up a South Africa Defense Fund. This fund was cochaired by the Reverend James Pike, dean of the Episcopal Cathedral of St. John the Divine in New York City, and John Gunther, along with a host of distinguished college presidents and figures from the worlds of literature, labor, and theology as sponsors. One of the first appeals for the fund was signed by Martin Luther King Jr. Donations began to come in from forty-nine states and from over a dozen foreign countries.[25] Over the course of two years, a total of $75,000 would be raised by the ACOA.[26]

In 1956, Sudan, Morocco, and Tunisia won their independence and became members of the UN. Elated by this news, Houser organized a public reception in honor of their independence. But his initial optimism about this event would prove to be naïve. Almost immediately after independence Sudan fell into a series of civil wars that continues unabated to the present day, and independent Morocco would itself become a colonial power in the Western Sahara.[27] Houser would soon learn to temper his enthusiasm with a dose of realism about postindependence problems.

Kenya was still under British colonial administration, but aspirations of independence were rising. The most visible expression of these aspirations—because it was covered in the news—centered on the Mau Mau Uprising. In the Western press the Mau Mau were branded "criminals or gangsters, certainly not freedom fighters."[28] Britain fought back with a counterinsurgency program that was portrayed as a "war between savagery and civilization," creating even more death and destruction than the Mau Mau had.[29]

Tom Mboya, the twenty-six-year-old general secretary of the Kenya Federation of Labor, was also emblematic of this stirring for independence. Houser had learned of Mboya from Michael Scott of the Africa Bureau in London. On leave from his duties in Kenya, Mboya had been attending Oxford's Ruskin College. He was interested in visiting the United States to meet with labor unions. Houser invited him to come for a two-month speaking engagement under ACOA auspices. Although Mboya was virtually unknown in the United States, Houser was the first to pick up on his importance to the African liberation struggle. According to his biographer, David Goldsworthy, Mboya was "a major and indeed brilliant political figure, a man of extraordinary intelligence and dynamism, a prolific and protean achiever" and would become for a time "the most visible of politicians" second only to Nkrumah.[30]

Despite the ACOA's lack of funds to underwrite such an itinerary, Houser banked on getting support from trade unions. The relations he established with President George Meany of the AFL-CIO, President Walter Reuther of the United Auto Workers (UAW), David Dubinsky of the International Ladies Garment Workers' Union (ILGWU), Philip Murray of the United Steelworkers, Sidney Hillman of the Amalgamated Clothing Workers, Ralph Helstein of the United Packinghouse Workers, and A. Philip Randolph (with whom Houser already had a connection) would prove to be invaluable in the ACOA's work for the next three decades.

This was a pivotal time for American labor. After the Communist purge of the 1940s, white labor leaders had concentrated their efforts on winning workplace goals for their members; but the resurgence of the civil rights movement during the late 1950s had begun to nudge the newly merged AFL-CIO back in the direction of a concern for wider social justice. Through his connections with the civil rights community, Houser was positioned to introduce Mboya to almost all of the important African American civil rights leaders. And through his connection with this African labor organizer, Houser was also pivotal in winning US labor's support for the cause of African self-determination.

From August 14 to October 6, 1956, Houser and Mboya traveled to nine cities. Radio and television appearances were also arranged, and Houser's admiration for the articulate and charismatic young man grew as he watched the audiences' reactions. The tour was so successful that it was extended from eight weeks to eleven, including ten days in Canada. The tour netted Mboya $35,000 toward the establishment of a trade union center in Kenya—something he had been unable to get from the Brussels-based International Confederation of Free Trade Unions (ICFTU)—and the start of a scholarship program to help train African union leaders as well as scholarships to bring Kenyan students to study in US universities.[31] This was to be an important contribution to Africa's development, as there were few trained and educated Africans who could take over the reins of government after independence.[32] Upon his return to Kenya, Mboya wrote to Houser saying that he would never have obtained the $35,000 had it not been for Houser's initiative. A direction to help solve a problem for the future of Kenya and indeed of Africa had been identified, even if the resources were at first inadequate to do more than establish a program and an idea. Mboya's visit was the start of a relationship that would continue until his tragic assassination in 1969.

ACOA BECOMES THE "GO-TO ORGANIZATION" ON AFRICAN AFFAIRS

By the end of the first year it looked as though the fledgling ACOA might survive. Houser had met his budget of $30,000. More than a third of that went to the project fund, while the remainder was used for salaries, travel, publications, and office expenses.[33] Because of the ACOA's work in supporting African independence movements—which violated the policy of noninterference in the domestic affairs of the United States' allies—as well as its willingness to criticize US foreign policy, the ACOA could not count on getting government or corporate money; and major foundations were not a reliable source of funds. Thus, Houser would have to count on developing a list of individuals who were committed to the liberation cause and willing to support it financially. This meant that the organization was in a nearly constant struggle for funds. That it was able to survive for almost half a century is due in no small part to Houser's indefatigable energy and the sacrificial efforts of his small but dedicated staff. But it was also a function of the remarkable board that Houser had brought together. This interracial group was firmly committed to the values represented by this quixotic experiment in international solidarity. Although they were at different levels of understanding with regard to Africa, the group's members were willing to devote many hours of their own time to attend meetings, consider policy, contribute money from their own pockets, host African visitors in their homes, sign fundraising letters and letters on behalf of the ACOA to the UN and members of Congress, testify before Congress or the UN on behalf of the organization's priorities, and travel to Africa on the ACOA's behalf—sometimes risking their lives.

By the beginning of Houser's second year, the ACOA had established itself as the go-to organization on African affairs in the United States with an expanded eighteen-member executive committee, a professional fundraiser in Harold Oram,[34] and a new "national committee" that read like a who's who of liberal sentiment during the Cold War. Represented among the fifty-five people were the following luminaries: former first lady Eleanor Roosevelt, fifteen members of the House of Representatives; four senators; one governor; one former assistant secretary of state; one former attorney general; ten intellectuals from the fields of journalism and literature; two from the entertainment field; three university and seminary presidents; four educators (including Houser's old seminary professor, Reinhold Niebuhr); six members of the clergy, including Dr. Martin Luther King Jr.; one labor leader; and baseball hero Jackie Robinson.

The list of distinguished names on the organization's letterhead, however, masked the reality of the work faced by the still minuscule staff. In addition to continuing appeals from South Africa, there were journalists needing information on Africa, college students seeking projects to work on with African petitioners, students asking for information on Africa for academic papers, and people planning trips to Africa requesting names of contact people. There were also hundreds of letters each year from African students studying in the United States—or those wishing to come to the United States—requesting loans, travel grants, scholarship funds, and help in obtaining part-time employment. Houser felt obliged to answer every one of these letters and always did his best to provide the kind of help requested.

At midnight on March 6, 1957, a new Ghanaian flag was hoisted over the first sub-Saharan country to achieve independence. It was a milestone for Africa, setting into motion a rush for independence throughout the rest of the continent. Houser was thrilled. In preparation for the event, the ACOA had formed a Gold Coast Celebration Committee cochaired by Eleanor Roosevelt and civil rights leader Channing Tobias. More than five hundred people (including well-known leaders in public life) signed a letter of greeting to the Kwame Nkrumah, the new president. Homer Jack, representing the ACOA, presented the letter to Nkrumah at the independence celebration in Accra. On the same day as the celebration in Ghana, Houser and his staff organized a large independence celebration at New York's Town Hall. Eighteen hundred enthusiastic people, half of them black, filled the hall to overflowing, while hundreds had to be turned away. A taped message sent by Nkrumah was played, and the new Ghanaian flag was presented by the official representative of Ghana.[35]

BACK TO AFRICA

That June, Houser was back in Africa, this time for a five-week visit. The Council on Student Travel had hired him to provide an orientation for a dozen American students who had gone to Nigeria to learn about its history and customs under the auspices of the Experiment in International Living. His arrival in the country occurred just as a constitutional conference to decide the country's future was occurring in London. Houser's earlier observation that Nigeria's tribal and regional differences would become more pronounced was now more apparent with all of the parties ready to conclude that the country would have to be a federation. This would be no easy task, but "one thing is certain," Houser wrote, "a free Nigeria will be a very powerful influence on the continent. . . . This is the most populous country in Africa. . . . Nigeria's independence will spark rapid developments elsewhere on the continent."[36]

After completing his paid assignment, Houser traveled to Accra, Ghana, where he stayed with his friend Bill Sutherland, then working for A. K. Gbedemah, Nkrumah's finance minister. It had been just four months since the country had achieved its independence. Houser noticed a great deal of new construction and detected a change in the people's attitude. Now that they were no longer united in a common struggle, groups opposing the new government were already arising over what appeared to be ethnic rivalries and economic issues. "He [Nkrumah] will have to concentrate his efforts on some fence mending at home if he wishes to be in a position to proceed with his announced objective of aiding other African countries in their struggles for independence," Houser observed.[37] In discussions with Gbedemah, Houser picked up undercurrents of differences between Nkrumah and this man who had engineered Nkrumah's election, a prescient observation that would play out later in Ghanaian politics when, in 1961, Nkrumah would force Gbedemah into exile over worsening relations between the two.[38]

The contrast between independent Ghana, where Africans were in charge, and the Belgian Congo (his next destination) was striking. Houser again picked up no sign of emerging nationalism except for the existence of a newspaper called *Congo*, edited by Africans and critical of the government. Nevertheless, he continued to believe, beyond any outward sign of rebellion, that the road to independence would be inevitable.[39]

Houser had hoped to visit the Central African Federation as well as Tanganyika but was turned back from Northern Rhodesia and sent back to the Belgian Congo.[40] He then took a plane from Elizabethville to Entebbe-Kampala in Uganda but was ordered by Ugandan immigration authorities to leave on the next available flight for London five days hence, an indication that he was still a "prohibited immigrant" barred from entering Britain's East and Central African colonies. Houser lost no time in writing a letter of protest and clarification of his intentions to the governors and prime ministers of the countries he had been barred from. The *Christian Science Monitor* carried the story in its August 12, 1957 issue, quoting the *Central African Examiner* as saying that "they had very little sympathy for the American Committee on Africa.... Had Mr. Houser been allowed to tour the federation he might well have closed his eyes to anything good and seen only the evil he wanted to see. He might also have stirred the wilder elements of the African National Congress to new agitation."[41] When he read this, Houser must have chuckled over the preposterous idea that his efforts could stir up the ANC, which had plenty of its own reasons for being stirred up.

By late fall 1957, the ACOA Executive Committee had decided not to renew the fundraising contract with Harold Oram, as the cost of his services no longer fit within the organization's still meager budget.[42] Several committee members pledged and others agreed to try to raise enough money for their own fundraiser. By the end of the year, the ACOA was in debt.[43] Still, despite dwindling funds and inadequate staff, the frantic pace of ACOA's work continued. The ACOA commissioned and prepared two documents on Portuguese Africa, one on Portugal's violation of the UN Charter and the second on its continuing oppression of labor. The documents were sent to all of the delegations to the United Nations, providing them with a unique perspective on the problems in this area of Africa.

On December 10, 1957, Human Rights Day, ACOA sponsored a large gathering in New York as part of an "International Day of Protest" against

South Africa's apartheid policy to coincide with events in other countries. In preparation, the ACOA had issued a Declaration of Conscience, with Eleanor Roosevelt serving as chair of the International Endorsement Committee, Episcopal Bishop James Pike as US chair, and Martin Luther King Jr. as national vice chair. One hundred twenty-three world leaders from thirty-nine countries signed the declaration, which condemned the actions of the apartheid regime and called on the South African government "to honor its moral and legal obligations . . . to the United Nations Charter." The declaration also urged people to petition their organizations and governments "to bring about a peaceful, just and democratic solution in South Africa" and "to mobilize the spiritual and moral forces of mankind . . . to demonstrate to the Government of the Union of South Africa that free men abhor its policies and will not tolerate the continued suppression of human freedom."[44] The highlight of the International Day of Protest was an address by Dr. King.

The Declaration of Conscience generated a great deal of publicity, with at least fifty countries reporting some kind of action—a considerable feat considering this was long before the internet made such international solidarity actions feasible.[45] Francis Njubi Nesbitt has argued that such appeals were, by this time, becoming outdated in South Africa and the United States, "where petitions and declarations had been replaced by strikes, economic boycotts and talk of armed struggle."[46] But the importance of such international opprobrium should not be so easily dismissed. South Africa had always been very protective of its international image and sensitive to criticism. Its ability to attract investment and continue trade with other countries depended on it. Thus, it was not surprising that the South African government reacted with characteristic outrage. In a radio address on September 12, Minister of External Affairs Eric Louw deplored "in the strongest terms this concerted effort to undermine our international position," calling George Houser "a known leftist," painting the ACOA "with a decidedly pinkish tinge," and characterizing Mrs. Roosevelt as "not a stranger in American left-wing circles."[47] Despite the South African government's concern that the Declaration of Conscience had tarnished its international image, Louw maintained that the policy of the South African government would not change. However, on December 17, the South African government announced that it was dropping the case against 61 of the 156 who were arrested for treason the previous year. The ACOA surmised that the international attention brought to South Africa's behavior by the Declaration of Conscience may have played a role.[48] Certainly, the timing would suggest this.

Beyond raising funds for the defense of those on trial for treason in South Africa, the ACOA arranged an itinerary for two speakers from South Africa at venues around the United States and sent a letter to Avery Brundage, president of the International Olympic Committee, urging him to place the question of apartheid in sports in South Africa on the agenda of the semi-annual meeting of the International Olympic Committee in Tokyo on May 14–17, 1958. In the late 1950s South African poet and teacher Dennis Brutus had been instrumental in initiating the idea of an international sports boycott as secretary of the nonracial South African Sports Association (SASA). In 1962 Brutus helped found the South African Non-racial Olympic Committee (SANROC), becoming its president. SANROC would become the main vehicle of the international sports boycott. Houser had learned of Brutus's efforts in the late 1950s and would meet him for the first time in London in 1965 after Brutus's release from prison. The two would work closely together on these issues over the next two decades.[49]

HARD CHOICES FOR A PACIFIST

Until 1958, Houser had not paid much attention to the liberation struggle in North Africa, having focused most attention on events south of the Sahara; but the Algerian revolution had been in full swing since 1954, the Battle of Algiers had taken place in 1957, and the quest for independence had become the focus of UN debates. Moreover, American and NATO support for the French was becoming an important foreign policy issue. Since France considered Algeria an integral part of France, the US State Department—then headed by John Foster Dulles—refused to get involved in what they considered an internal French issue. Except for John F. Kennedy, then chairman of the Senate Foreign Relations Subcommittee on Africa, few prominent Americans criticized French policy.[50]

Prior to the debates about Algeria at the UN, the limited extent of Houser's involvement in the Algerian struggle was including news about North Africa in ACOA's publications, meeting with the National Liberation Front (Front de Libération Nationale; FLN) representative M'Hammed Yazid when he was in New York lobbying for the Algerian cause at the UN in 1956, and sending a letter to President Eisenhower to protest the arrest and imprisonment of five Algerian leaders by the French, also in 1956. Aside from his preoccupation with swiftly moving events elsewhere in Africa, one reason for Houser's neglect of Algeria was that this revolution was of a different order from the largely nonviolent transitions to independence he had witnessed thus far. Here, an armed guerrilla movement faced a French army sixteen times its size. What was a pacifist to do when faced with such a situation? Houser wrestled with himself over whether he could support such an independence movement.

As he began to study the history of Algerian occupation and realized that French policy was unpopular among a significant segment of the French public, he became more sympathetic to its cause. In the end, he decided that he could not remain uninvolved if he believed in the principle of self-determination. "Thus, somewhat uneasily," he wrote later, "I found it possible to rationalize my support for the Algerian revolution."[51] Since there was no nonviolent alternative, he decided that the ACOA's function would be to interpret the justice of the FLN's cause to the American people and attempt to influence US policy against giving military aid to France. The ACOA published a thirty-two-page pamphlet by an academic well versed in the field. This pamphlet analyzed the conflict in Algeria in some detail, as well as including articles in *Africa Today*. Influencing US policy on Algeria, however, was to prove difficult for the ACOA. Several attempts to issue public statements or to formulate a policy on the Algerian situation remained elusive.

In fall 1958, board member Gilbert Jonas wrote a memo to the steering committee giving an ultimatum that the board must come to an agreement on whether they would support Algerian independence and publicly endorse the Provisional Government of the Algerian Republic (Gouvernement Provisoire de la République Algerienne; GPRA), a successor to the FLN, so the GPRA could have its case heard in the United States and at the UN. Jonas argued that the ACOA should make Algeria its priority, since this was the only place in Africa where a shooting war existed and where hundreds if not thousands of Africans were being killed each week.[52] Replying to Jonas's memo, Houser wrote that there was no doubt about the immediacy and urgency of the Algerian problem, but it was not so clear what they could do about it. "From a narrowly organizational point of view," he wrote, "we could not sustain ourselves financially with this emphasis. Furthermore, a program concentrated on Algeria would lose us members rather than lead to expansion."[53]

Despite the failure of the board to agree on a policy statement, Houser had been quietly providing some support for the Algerian cause. In addition to publishing articles about Algeria, Houser had facilitated contacts for two FLN representatives who traveled around the United States speaking before student, church, and labor audiences, while participating in radio and TV programs and meeting with members of Congress. In December 1958 Houser organized a public meeting at the Carnegie Endowment International Center at which speakers from the *New York Times*, the FLN, and City College spoke.

AN ACOA LEGAL OBSERVER AT THE SOUTH AFRICA TREASON TRIAL

The South African Treason Trial, which had begun in 1956 was, by summer 1958, still in progress, fraught with delays and procedural complexities.[54] It was at this time that the ACOA arranged for Erwin Griswold, then dean of Harvard Law School, to attend the trial as an expert legal observer. This had to be done discreetly. Had it been known that Griswold was traveling under the auspices of the ACOA, he might have been barred from entering the country. After leaving South Africa, Griswold wrote to Houser that he had found considerable hostility to the ACOA in South Africa, and considering the doors that had been opened for him, it was fortunate the government had not known about the connection.[55] On Griswold's return, the ACOA organized a two-day program for him consisting of a press conference, radio interviews, and a luncheon at which Griswold neglected to acknowledge the role Houser and the ACOA had played in his going to South Africa. Houser was hurt by this omission but figured that Griswold was "trying to keep his skirts clean."[56] He could take some comfort, however, in the fact that in giving widespread publicity to the absurdity of the indictments and their ultimate legal failure, the trial enormously enhanced the prestige of the ANC and that he and the ACOA had played a small but important role in helping to publicize the white regime's embarrassment.[57]

While the Algerian war was raging and the treason trials were continuing in South Africa, in Ghana, newly elected president Nkrumah was positioning himself as leader of the Pan-African movement. During summer 1958, he made his first trip to the United States in ten years. Nkrumah met with President Eisenhower and other officials, spoke to the press and led a parade through Harlem. In honor of his visit, the ACOA, in coordination with the NAACP and Urban League, sponsored a dinner in the Grand Ballroom of the Waldorf Astoria. Organized by ACOA volunteer Cora Weiss, the dinner was attended by eleven hundred people. They would hear Nkrumah speak of the role the ACOA was now playing in facilitating intercontinental friendship and understanding.[58]

ACOA AT THE FIRST ALL-AFRICAN PEOPLE'S CONFERENCE

Eight months later, from December 8–13, 1958, Nkrumah convened the All-African People's Conference (AAPC) in Accra, Ghana, the first Pan-African meeting to be held on African soil and the first of three to be held on the continent.[59] This was an event Houser did not want to miss. Through his contacts with Nkrumah and George Padmore, Houser had secured fraternal delegate status for the ACOA at the conference.[60] This was an exciting and hopeful moment in African history and a recognition that the African peoples, despite their differing cultures, shared a common history of colonial oppression. The conference was also a forceful declaration that African peoples could create their own destiny: it was Nkrumah's vision of a "united states" of Africa that animated the proceedings. Only by unifying politically and economically could they hope to harness the economic potential and resources of the continent for the betterment of its people.[61] In attendance were three hundred people from both independent and nonindependent states representing the continent's emerging leadership; there were others from the African diaspora and individuals and organizations like the ACOA that had supported African liberation. Except for the top leadership of the ANC (who were not allowed to travel), it was the most representative gathering of African leaders ever assembled and included movements and organizations representing many political tendencies.[62]

At the conference Houser renewed his friendship with Tom Mboya, with whom he had been corresponding throughout the previous spring. And he met Patrice Lumumba for the first time. Lumumba represented the newly formed National Congolese Movement (Mouvement Nationale Congolais; MNC) and would later become the first prime minister of the Congo (later Zaire and today known as the Democratic Republic of the Congo). Houser would forge ongoing relationships with other leaders at the conference such as Kenneth Kaunda from Northern Rhodesia (who would become the first president of independent Zambia); Joshua Nkomo from Southern Rhodesia (a leader with Robert Mugabe in the independence struggle that resulted in Zimbabwe's independence);[63] Hastings K. Banda from Nyasaland (who would lead the country to independence as Malawi and become its first president); and Kanyama Chiume (who would be the first foreign minister of Malawi). Leaders of the FLN were also in attendance.

It was at this first AAPC that the other African leaders were introduced to an emerging liberation movement in Angola. Houser had been the go-between. Ever since meeting Manuel Barros Necaca and his nephew, Holden Roberto, in Léopoldville in 1954, Houser had maintained a correspondence with the older man as his political movement transformed from an ethnocentric movement to a more nationalist-oriented liberation movement, which became the Union of the Peoples of Angola (União das Populações de Angola; UPA). On learning of the conference from Houser, Necaca, referencing Houser, wrote to conference organizer George Padmore to ask about sending a representative. Padmore replied: "I am delighted to know that you are

associated with Mr. George Houser of the ACOA. Mr. Houser is well known
to us and is being a helpful colleague. We in this part of Africa get very little information about what is happening in either the Belgian Congo or the
Portuguese territories."[64] It took an outsider like Houser, who had kept in
touch with leaders of emerging movements—both in his travels throughout
the continent and in New York, London, and other major cities—to connect
leaders in one part of the continent with those in another.

For Houser, the conference's significance lay in its focus on anti-imperialism
and anticolonialism. Also important was its reinterpretation of Pan-Africanism,
which was now not just seen as a racial identity but also as a residential identity that could include whites as long as they respected the basic principles
of democracy and independence. This approach provided an alternative to
the Communist-inspired attempt in Cairo the year before to harness Pan-
Africanism. In his conference report, Houser noted that although greetings
from Nikita Khrushchev and Chou en-Lai were cheered by the delegates, Soviet influence was not yet highly visible. There was no official greeting from
any US official until at the end of the conference when Congressman Charles
Diggs (D-Michigan) and Claude Barnett of the Associated Negro Press, who
were there as observers, reportedly went over the head of the American ambassador to Ghana to force a lukewarm statement out of the Eisenhower
administration.[65] "It is fortunate that no mention of it was made at the Conference, for it would have hurt American prestige further," Houser wrote.[66]
Soviet influence, while currently only a potential, would certainly grow, he
averred, "unless the problem of racism in the multi-racial areas of Africa
moves toward solution and unless the Algerian war is brought to an end."
Houser continued: "Unless the United States takes a much more forthright
position on crucial issues in Africa, American influence will decline steadily.
. . . The United States can and should be much more vocal in its support of
responsible independence movements for independence in Africa, including
Algeria."[67]

The fact that the United States continued to drag its feet, however, made
the role of a nongovernmental organization like the ACOA more important,
especially as it could demonstrate to nationalists in Africa that at least they
had some US support. Having witnessed the ferment over independence at
the conference, Houser and his fellow observers could, in turn, more effectively convey to US authorities the need for a change in United States policy
toward Africa, which they did in a visit to members of Congress and State
Department officials on their return.

THE ACOA MEETS A TEST

Attendance at the AAPC was an uplift for Houser. It had been only two months since he had been criticized rather harshly in a memo sent to the steering committee by board member Gilbert Jonas for the scattershot nature of the ACOA's approach to issues: resulting in the organization's lack of productivity, Jonas argued. Scattershot, possibly, but lack of productivity was certainly not a fair description of Houser's efforts. In reply to Jonas, Houser acknowledged that no one was more conscious of staff failure than he was, but he went on to try to explain the kinds of pressure his staff was under.[68]

Looking at Jonas's behavior from the perspective of history might raise some questions about his motivations.[69] Jonas was one of two people (the other being fundraiser Harold Oram) who had attempted to oust A. J. Muste from the executive board, claiming that he was too radical. Jonas's attempt was shot down by the rest of the board but had left a bad taste in some of their mouths about this effort to get rid of one of the most respected pacifists in the country. Eliott Newcomb, another board member who had been associated with Harold Oram, argued that the ACOA should adopt a more conservative strategy, one focused on the hiring of public relations consultants and one on lobbying Congress and the State Department rather than a strategy that supported the liberation movements. The issue came to a head at a March 1959 board meeting at which Newcomb ran for chair against incumbent Donald Harrington. Newcomb was narrowly defeated. Thereafter, he and Gilbert Jonas, along with three others associated with the Oram faction, were dropped from the board as members.

If Muste was too radical for the ACOA board, why then had Jonas pushed to make the armed rebellion in Algeria the major focus of ACOA's work, when Algeria was obviously a difficult subject for Houser's board? Perhaps Newcomb's attempt to steer the organization in a more conservative direction was simply the decision of a man with a more conservative public relations mentality. Oram, however, was disturbed by the board's decision not to dismiss Muste and sent a letter to the board saying that if they persisted, he would inform the National Committee members that they were on a board with a known socialist. Oram said, "I would anticipate not only 50–75 percent resignations within this group, but also a public scandal." Houser looked on this letter not only as a threat but also as blackmail.[70] Luckily, whatever the motivations behind these actions were, the attempts to undermine Houser's work were not successful. Houser believed that if Newcomb had won the chairmanship of the organization, the ACOA would have distanced itself from the liberation movements, and he would have been out of a job.[71] The majority of the executive board remained firm in their commitment to the values that had brought them to the work, and Houser had had the good sense not to allow the organization to be dragged into a vulnerable position where it could easily be destroyed. Although this was the only major internal struggle for control of the organization, it would not be the last time he would face controversy over his work.

1959: A YEAR OF NEW INITIATIVES

Houser began 1959 with another trip to Africa from January 20 through February 25. His main purpose was to attend the second All-African People's Conference that was convened this time in Tunis from January 25 through February 1. The principal policy issue at the conference was the question of whether an all-African trade union federation should be established. At the time, the Western-dominated International Confederation of Free Trade Unions (ICFTU) was in contention with the Soviet interest in destroying the ICFTU in Africa and of many African leaders to achieve real neutrality in their international outlook and a federation they could control. This would pose a serious problem for Mboya, as Houser pointed out: "Will he be able to maintain his generally neutralist outlook on the international power struggle while remaining affiliated with an international trade union organization that is tied in with the Western European countries?"[72] Following the AAPC, Houser took the opportunity to make brief visits to the United Arab Republic (a short-lived political union of Egypt and Syria), the Sudan, Ethiopia, Tanganyika, Belgian Congo, Nigeria, and Ghana.

It was fortunate that the ACOA had not been destroyed, because by 1959, its fifth year of operation, the organization was beginning to hit its stride. On April 15, 1959, in New York's Carnegie Hall, the ACOA hosted a gala "African Freedom Day," the first of three such events to be held in support of the AAPC's call for the founding of an African Freedom Day "to mark each year the onward progress of the liberation movement."[73] The program's roster was filled with prominent progressives. Eleanor Roosevelt and Marian Anderson served as honorary cochairs. Theodore W. Kheel, New York's preeminent labor mediator and then president of the Urban League, was chair. And George Meany and Jackie Robinson were cochairs. Keynoting the event, which was attended by some three thousand people, was Tom Mboya, whom Houser had brought back for a second tour of the United States. Mboya cut a dramatic figure, striding onto the stage in his African garb waving a rhinoceros tail, a symbol of authority to the Masai in his native Kenya.

Also on the program were Governor G. Mennen Williams of Michigan (an early supporter of African freedom), ambassadors from most of the newly independent states, A. Philip Randolph, Harry Belafonte, Langston Hughes, and William Warfield. Messages from many African leaders were read at the event.[74] Typical was a message from Sylvanus Olympio of French Togoland: "May I express the hope that your organization will continue to be a source of inspiration and hope for millions of African freedom fighters, for there can be no lasting world peace when so many African territories are subjected to foreign rule."[75]

As the decolonization process proceeded, the ACOA stepped up its attempts to influence United States policy on Africa. The executive board finally approved a statement on Algeria calling on the United States to support a UN-conducted plebiscite on self-determination. It was signed by eighty-eight prominent Americans as well as several members of Congress. The statement received wide publicity, especially abroad.[76] "The importance of issuing public statements of this kind to offset the absence of a clear American policy," Houser wrote, "cannot be overestimated in our attempt to build good American relations with a future independent Algeria."[77]

After French Guinea gained its independence in September 1958 as Guinea, Houser had immediately sent congratulatory messages to President Sékou Touré as well as telegrams and letters to President Eisenhower, Secretary of State Dulles, and the assistant secretary of state for African affairs, urging recognition of Guinea and the sending of US aid to the country. Houser believed that the ACOA's efforts had helped to facilitate official US recognition of Guinea, which occurred a month later. The following year, the ACOA would host a dinner, which would be attended by over three hundred people, for President Touré when he visited New York.

Between February and March 1959, a crisis developed in the Central African Federation. The crisis came to a head when the white settler–dominated governing body declared a state of emergency, banning the three African nationalist congresses whose members had been protesting nonviolently and arresting thousands and imprisoning their leaders over a false "plot" to massacre whites in Nyasaland. Houser was particularly attuned to this crisis as he saw parallels between the way Africans were treated in the federation and Jim Crow practices in the American South. He had also come to know four of the Africans who were leading the movements for independence and majority rule in this part of Africa: Kenneth Kaunda, Hastings K. Banda, Joshua Nkomo, and Kanyama Chiume. On learning of the state of emergency, the ACOA called on the US government to support African desires for independence, an end to racial discrimination, and participation of African leaders and banned organizations in the constitutional discussion that was to take place in 1960.[78] When the emergency was over, Houser arranged for all four leaders to tour the United States during fall 1959. Had the ACOA's case been heeded, Africa might have been spared some of the agonies of its subsequent history.

At its June 1959 meeting the ACOA executive board approved the transformation of the South Africa Defense Fund, through which money had been raised to support the Treason Trial defendants, into the Africa Defense and Aid Fund of the American Committee on Africa. This decision grew out of numerous requests the committee was now getting from all over Africa for help in supporting people who had been arrested and imprisoned, as well as requests for educational and other kinds of welfare aid. The fund would continue to be subject to ACOA control in both policy decisions and fundraising.[79] Raising funds for cases that could arise anywhere in Africa, however, meant a new kind of work for Houser and his staff. Each of the requests for funds would have to be carefully vetted in order to appeal to the public, but it would also be a way of raising the visibility of the ACOA as an organization that had its hand on the pulse of an awakening Africa. The first public announcement of the fund was made at the dinner for Guinea's President Sékou Touré that fall.[80]

AN AIRLIFT THAT HELPED CHANGE A NATION AND A CONTINENT

Mboya's second tour of the United States, from April 8 to May 15, 1959, was another roaring success for both the ACOA and Mboya himself. It was also an important moment for the African American community: their struggle for freedom had been recognized as part of a worldwide movement for freedom and equality. At the time, Mboya was at the height of his prestige, having been elected chair of the first AAPC and chairman of the ICFTU for the eastern, central, and southern African regions. *Life* magazine called him "not only the outstanding personality in Kenya, but among the most important in all Africa."[81] His nearly one hundred speaking engagements were packed to overflowing, according to Houser, who had accompanied him on much of the tour. He spoke not only to college and university groups but also to conventions of labor and political groups, to the Senate Foreign Relations Subcommittee on Africa, and various city councils on foreign relations. He met with the editors of *Time*, *Life*, and the *New York Times*, and appeared on over two dozen radio and TV shows, including NBC's *Meet the Press*.[82] He also had private meetings with then senators John F. Kennedy and Hubert Humphrey, two-time presidential candidate Adlai Stevenson, Vice President Richard Nixon, and civil rights activists like Martin Luther King Jr., Roy Wilkins, Harry Belafonte, and Jackie Robinson, among others. He presented the commencement address at Howard University and was awarded an honorary LLD. David Rockefeller held a dinner in his honor, Ralph Bunche arranged a luncheon for him at the United Nations, and the Liberian ambassador held a reception for him in Washington, DC. Houser was "greatly impressed with his responsibility and integrity," his unusual effectiveness in breaking stereotypes, and his willingness to meet all his commitments despite being tired.[83] Houser could have been speaking about himself, as the sheer number and variety of the engagements he and his staff had arranged for Mboya were a testament to his own inexhaustible energy and responsibility.

During his first visit to the United States in 1956, Mboya had met William X. Scheinman, a member of the ACOA executive board and a small plane parts manufacturer who had underwritten some of the tour expenses.[84] The two men, who were nearly the same age, hit it off after a long night together at a Harlem jazz club, and they continued their friendship through subsequent correspondence. The result was that Scheinman agreed to underwrite the transportation expenses for the first seventeen African students to take up the scholarships that Mboya raised the money for on that first trip.[85]

Since his initial meeting with Mboya, Scheinman, with the help of Houser and ACOA board members Frank Montero and Peter Weiss (as well as Weiss's wife, Cora), had set up the African American Students Foundation (AASF) to raise additional money for the transportation of the African scholarship students Mboya was recruiting. Although the foundation was set up as a separate nonprofit entity, it had clearly been spawned by the connections Houser had made through his work with the ACOA.

During Mboya's second US visit, the "Airlift to America" got off the ground. With small donations from all over the country as the result of a fundraising letter signed by Harry Belafonte, Jackie Robinson, and Sidney Poitier, eighty-one students were able to travel to the United States and take their places in American universities that first year.[86]

Over the next four years the airlift would bring nearly eight hundred students from Kenya, Tanganyika, Nyasaland, Uganda, Zanzibar, and Northern and Southern Rhodesia to study in the United States. One of the first students to arrive in the United States was Barack Obama Sr., whose story would only become known when his son was elected to the US presidency in 2008. The importance of this effort needs to be considered in light of the paucity of educated Africans who were ready to take their place in government and in the economy when independence was finally achieved. There was one technical school in Uganda, but in all of East Africa, for example, there were no schools of higher learning.[87] Despite being pilloried by the traditional international education organizations, this small group of people was thus remarkable for its vision and commitment to the cause of African-directed development, as well as for the ability to make big things happen.[88]

According to Tom Shachtman, who wrote the story of this dramatic airlift, the African American Students Foundation was doing several "radical" things: "They were circumventing the British colonial education system, which rewarded only a handful of Kenyans each year with a scholarship to study in Great Britain; they were finessing the U.S. foreign-student establishment, which only accepted Africans from already-independent nations; and they were attempting to bring over large groups rather than a few 'elite' students."[89]

They were also providing a liberal Western-oriented education as an alternative to that presented by the Soviet Union, which with the advent of the decolonization movement had begun actively recruiting African students with full scholarships to study in the Soviet Union as a means of enhancing its standing and popularity in the Third World.[90] For Houser, the airlift was the fulfillment of the conviction he had come to during his second visit to Africa. He had hoped that the ACOA might play a role in helping such students return to their countries committed to the development of their people rather than to their own aggrandizement; and to a large extent that vision, which was shared by Mboya, Scheinman, Montero, and the Weisses, was fulfilled. Over 90 percent of the eight hundred students returned to their homes, which was unheard of in foreign education in this country.[91] Shachtman wrote the following: "The 'airlift generation' would achieve a remarkable record of accomplishment. Upon returning home, they would become the founding brothers and sisters of their countries. For the next quarter century they would make up half of Kenya's parliaments and account for many of its cabinet ministers and even more of its high-level civil servants, in addition to staffing the professorships and deanships of its nascent universities, starting medical clinics and schools, growing multimillion-dollar businesses, and leading international environmental programs."[92]

The airlift would last only a few brief years. In 1963 it became a regularized activity funded by the US government and carried out by its grantor organizations. But this private, idealistic effort by a handful of committed individuals would have far reaching implications for the United States. Not only would it play an indirect role in the election of the first black president, but it also played an important but underrecognized role in boosting the African American turnout that was key to John F. Kennedy's narrow electoral victory in 1960.[93]

The airlift would also benefit civil rights in the United States. Some of the African students with higher degrees who chose not to go home went on to become leading African scholars at US universities, helping to integrate their respective faculties and steer them toward becoming more inclusive of students of color, as well as inspiring language and area studies programs on campuses across the United States. By dint of the Africans' principled behavior and hard work, the airlift also opened doors for African American students, breaking down stereotypes about people of African descent. African students frequently encountered racial prejudice in the communities they were studying in. But in dealing with these incidents of bias, colleges and universities were pushed to intervene on the students' behalf and became better prepared to work with and help integrate the students of color who came after them. According to Shachtman, African students often served as guest speakers for American communities and as interviewees on local radio and TV stations: "Their nonthreatening demeanor, intelligence and thirst for learning helped to dispel generations of distrust of people of darker skin,"[94] especially in small towns that had never encountered a person of color.

A final contribution of the East African students was to change how foreign exchange programs were administered. Prior to the existence of the AASF, US government authorities had controlled the selection process. Now it was being handled by Africans themselves, enabling many more than just the tiny elite who had been filtered through the government-run programs to obtain a higher education. It thus pioneered a large rise in the number of foreign students admitted to the United States.[95]

The story of Mboya's meteoric rise had a footnote. At some point in his relations with the United States, Mboya began to accept money from the CIA, and in Africa he affiliated his Kenyan Federation of Labor with the US-backed International Confederation of Free Trade Unions, which had grown out of a Cold War split of the international trade union movement. Neither Houser nor the ACOA staff or board members knew of this CIA connection at the time, although Cora Weiss later remembered driving him to an appointment with Jay Lovestone, remaining in the car while Mboya went upstairs to pick up a check.[96] Lovestone, a founder of the American Communist Party, had turned anti-Communist and was on the payroll of the CIA while working with the AFL-CIO. Houser's introduction of Mboya to US officials may unwittingly have begun the process through which Mboya came to be touted by the West as the anti-Communist spokesman for Africa.[97]

UNDER GEORGE HOUSER'S energetic leadership, the ACOA had grown in the space of just five years from an organization with a nonexistent budget to an organization with an estimated budget for 1959 of $93,000. They had blossomed from a miniscule staff to a staff of eight full-time people and several volunteers. The ACOA was once a lone voice crying out in the wilderness, but now it was the leading American voice on African affairs. Houser himself had developed contacts all over the African continent, and the ACOA had a growing network of American supporters who, by the start of the 1960s, loosely numbered some twelve thousand people.[98] Houser weathered a board threat to his own leadership, worked through the difficult decision as a pacifist to support movements that eschewed nonviolence, and was beginning to make his way through the thorny thickets of Cold War politics.

The Houser family in Buffalo, New York, one year after their return from the Philippines, 1925. L to R: Ethel Houser, Otto Houser, Martha Houser holding Henry Houser, Margaret Houser, George Houser in front. *George M. Houser Private Collection.*

Houser and Bayard Rustin at sit-in, Toledo, Ohio, 1945. *George M. Houser Private Collection.*

Participants in the CORE/FOR Summer Workshop, Washington, DC, 1947. Houser is in front holding the sign. *Swarthmore College Peace Collection, used with permission.*

Some of the participants in the Journey of Reconciliation, in front of Spottswood W. Robinson's law office, Richmond, Virginia, 1947. L to R: Worth Randle, Wally Nelson, Ernest Bromley, James Peck, Igal Roodenko, Bayard Rustin, Joe Felmet, George Houser, Andrew Johnson. *Used with permission from Fellowship of Reconciliation.*

Houser and Rustin receiving the Thomas Jefferson Award for the Advancement of Democracy by the Council against Intolerance in America, 1948. *George M. Houser Private Collection.*

ACOA delegation at the first All-African People's Conference, Accra, Ghana, December 1958. L to R: John Marcum, Homer Jack, George Houser, Kwame Nkrumah, Frank Montero, William X. Scheinman. *George M. Houser Private Collection.*

Houser and Tom Mboya meeting with Adlai Stevenson, 1959. Back row, L to R: Homer Jack, George Houser, William X. Scheinman. Front row: Adlai Stevenson, Tom Mboya. *George M. Houser Private Collection.*

Houser with UPA guerillas in the Angolan jungle, 1962. *George M. Houser Private Collection.*

Houser leading a picket of the *South African Pioneer* on the docks in Brooklyn, New York, 1963. *Amistad Research Center, used with permission.*

ACOA-sponsored picketing of Chase Manhattan Bank, New York City, 1966. Photo by Collin Gonze. *American Committee on Africa Collection, Amistad Research Center, Tulane University.*

Houser at UN meeting on divestment from South Africa, 1981. *George M. Houser Private Collection.*

Houser, 1989. *George M. Houser Private Collection.*

Houser with Nelson Mandela outside Mandela's office at the South African
Parliament building, 1997. *George M. Houser Private Collection.*

Houser presenting his coedited book, *I Will Go Singing*, to Walter and Albertina Sisulu, 1999. *George M. Houser Private Collection.*

Houser holding the staff presented to him by the government of
South Africa on the occasion of his being given the Order of the
Grand Companions of Oliver Tambo Award, 2014. Suzun Lucia
Lamaina, copyright 2014. *Used with permission.*

7
The End of Euphoria, 1960–68

ON THE CUSP OF THE 1960S, AFRICA HAD SEEMED A PLACE OF GREAT expectations for Houser. He was enthralled to see nationalist movements being born and new leaders arising on a continent that had been left deliberately underdeveloped by colonialism.[1] It represented something new on the world stage. Even Britain's conservative prime minister, Harold Macmillan, acknowledged the change: "The wind of change is blowing through this continent, and whether we like it or not, this growth of national consciousness is a political fact."[2]

In 1960 alone, seventeen sub-Saharan states became self-governing, most without widespread violence. This new African bloc led the effort to pass UN General Assembly Resolution 1514, which for the first time declared colonial subjugation a "denial of fundamental human rights, . . . contrary to the Charter of the United Nations and an impediment to the promotion of world peace and co-operation."[3] By the end of the decade another fifteen countries would achieve independence. African countries had become the largest single group of nations in the UN. On May 25, 1963, the long-sought dream of Pan-African unity was institutionalized when the thirty-two independent countries founded the Organization of African Unity (OAU) in Addis Ababa, Ethiopia. The OAU's principles included promotion of solidarity and cooperation among African states, defense of the sovereignty, territorial integrity and independence of African states, and the eradication of all forms of colonialism. On Houser's many subsequent travels to Africa, one of his primary points of contact would be the secretary of the OAU, who was headquartered in Dar es Salaam, Tanzania.

The existence of two dozen independent countries by the end of 1960 inspired the formation of new nationalist movements in the southern African countries still under colonial rule. Seeing this, white settler minorities sought to resist independence through cooperative military action and increased police repression, forcing the movements to move toward armed struggle. The independent states would provide legitimation and support for these movements in the form of asylum for their exiled revolutionaries, field offices for movements that were outlawed in their own country, facilities for military training, efforts to unify movements from the same country, and other necessities.[4]

Achieving independence, however, did not guarantee a conflict-free future, and continental solidarity was easier said than done. If anything, independence made the political situation more complicated. Internal dissention arose when economies that had been devastated by colonialism failed to produce full employment and prosperity. Struggles for power between political groups and personalities led to coups (and attempted coups) and sometimes to prolonged civil war. When in February 1966 Ghana's Kwame Nkrumah, architect of Pan-African socialism, was deposed in a violent coup, Houser was led to lament that an era seemed to have ended.[5]

Further complicating the picture, Africa would now become the new Cold War arena. With European powers abandoning the continent, the United States could no longer count on its allies to thwart Soviet influence in the region. Both superpowers had their eye on securing access to the vast mineral deposits on the African continent. They also sought strategic positions in extending their spheres of influence and were choosing sides among liberation movement factions. Seeking help from wherever they could get it, African leaders were often caught in this Cold War proxy fight, sometimes succeeding in playing one rival off against another. Nevertheless, the relations among liberation movements were often affected by international alignments.[6] The disillusionment with the continent that often set in among Westerners, Houser realized, was based on ignorance of what African countries were actually doing or of progress being made.[7] Nevertheless, these new realities made the work of external solidarity organizations like the ACOA infinitely harder and would require a reevaluation of the ACOA's approach to events on the continent.

SOUTHERN AFRICA: A DECADE OF TURMOIL

The Belgian Congo

In January 1959, rioting shook Léopoldville, indicating to Belgium that its colony might be the next domino to fall. Less than thirteen months later, unwilling to deal with the political crisis caused by surging nationalism, Belgian officials agreed on an independence date of June 30, 1960, moving up a date they originally thought would take fifteen years to reach.[8] The independence of what was now called the Democratic Republic of the Congo had taken even African nationalist leaders by surprise. Democratic in name only, the country was almost immediately engulfed in internal chaos. This was the result of regional and tribal power grabs, vengeance against the hated Belgian settlers and troops, and the deplorable conditions bequeathed by the Belgians.[9]

Two months after independence, secession (aided by Belgium) was declared by Moïse Tshombe, a leader in the Katanga province, which was the center of the Congo's mineral wealth.[10] The ACOA immediately initiated a full-page ad in the *New York Times* opposing this effort and backing the UN force, whose purpose was to forestall a big power clash and to try to preserve Congo unity.[11] Lumumba traveled to the United States in July 1960 seeking US and UN help in restoring order and unity to his country. Houser welcomed him with an "open letter" and along with two board members met with Lumumba declaring the ACOA's support and their intention of pressing Eisenhower's help in resolving the Congo crisis. During their discussion, Lumumba agreed to be an international adviser of the Africa Defense and Aid Fund.[12] But Washington was rattled by Lumumba's fiery speeches calling for economic and political independence and for control of the country's resources to benefit his own people. When Lumumba threatened to turn to the Soviets for help if others refused aid to Congo, Eisenhower took this as a sign that Lumumba was a "Castro or worse."[13] After being rebuffed by Eisenhower, Lumumba turned to the UN Security Council for help in stopping the secessionists, but this also failed. In desperation he requested and received Soviet military aid and advisers.

Less than two months after being named prime minister, Lumumba was targeted by the CIA for assassination.[14] Belgium had also wanted him dead, and the deed was carried out in January 1961 by Belgians still working in the Congo's army and anti-Lumumba factions in the government with close ties to the CIA.[15] The assassination was a devastating blow to Africans throughout the continent who were striving for independence, setting off a wave of anti-Western passion throughout the Third World and among the African diaspora. It stunned the rest of the world as well, signaling that a neocolonialist counteroffensive was underway. Houser was disheartened by the news of Lumumba's assassination and the Congolese turmoil. In contrast to the Eisenhower administration's portrayal of Lumumba as a dangerous Communist-inspired radical, Houser saw him as a committed freedom fighter whose death was that of a martyr in the struggle for freedom and self-determination.

The key figure in the assassination plot was Joseph Désiré Mobutu, a sergeant in the old colonial Force Publique whom Lumumba had asked to head his army but who, unbeknownst to Lumumba, had been tapped by the CIA as useful to the West. Mobutu set up a new government. But in 1965 he staged another coup, setting himself up as dictator and changing his name to Mobutu Sese Seko and the name of the country to Zaire.[16] Despite Houser's earlier plea that the United States should remain neutral in the Congo crisis, Mobutu would remain a client of the West for the next three decades, ruling as a kleptocrat.[17] He would make a name for himself as perhaps the most corrupt leader in the world during the thirty years he ruled Zaire.

Revolution in Portuguese Africa

If the Congo's unexpected independence had left it with corrupt governance, elsewhere in southern Africa the fight for independence would be prolonged and bloody. The Portuguese were the last colonial power to relinquish control, ruthlessly suppressing any movement toward political or even cultural organization among Africans.[18] Portuguese repression of any rebellious movement meant that the organizing had to be done outside the country, thus fragmenting nationalist networks. Differing exile environments also affected the prospects for unity.[19] To make matters worse, just as the revolutions broke out in Portuguese Africa, the area became the nexus of a struggle for power between Cold War adversaries. Such outside interference guaranteed that the struggle for self-determination would be fraught with unimaginable tragedy.

Mozambique

Between 1959 and 1960, three nationalist organizations composed of Mozambican refugees were founded in neighboring countries. In June 1962, representatives of the three formed a new organization: the Front for the Liberation of Mozambique (Frente de Libertação de Moçambique; FRELIMO). The organization's president, Eduardo Chivambo Mondlane, had studied at Oberlin College and had met Houser as early as 1951 at a conference site near there.[20] That meeting led to a long and close friendship between the two. After earning a doctorate and marrying an American woman, Mondlane worked for the UN Trusteeship Council, held a professorship at Syracuse University, and then returned to Africa to lead his people's struggle for liberation. It was through frequent correspondence and meetings with Mondlane in New York and Africa that Houser would view the unfolding liberation struggle in Mozambique.[21]

Mondlane succeeded in establishing a bureaucratic structure, a program of political action within Mozambique, and a military wing. After its founding, FRELIMO gained the recognition of the OAU as the legitimate representative of the Mozambican people and the active support of the Tanzanian government. "No struggle for freedom from colonial domination," wrote Houser, "had more idealism, optimism, and hope for a radical change in the way of life than that of Mozambique. . . . I was one of many in Africa and around the world who looked to Mozambique with particular hope and faith."[22] FRELIMO's armed guerrilla struggle against the Portuguese began in 1963, but it, too, would not be without internal dissention.

Angola

During Houser's 1954 visit, Angola had appeared incapable of mounting a movement for independence, but by 1960, it had two operating underground liberation movements. The Popular Movement for the Liberation of Angola (Movimento Popular de Libertação de Angola; MPLA) had been organized secretly in Luanda in 1956 by members of the urban intelligentsia. Its principal figures were Mario de Andrade, Viriato da Cruz, and Agostinho Neto. Upon independence in 1975, Neto would become Angola's first president. Unable to operate openly inside the country, the MPLA made its headquarters in Conakry in newly independent Guinea. The other movement was the Union of the Peoples of Angola (União dos Povos de Angola; UPA), headed by Barros Necaca and Holden Roberto. It was based in Léopoldville in the newly independent Congo and was more heavily peasant based. In 1962 the UPA joined with the Democratic Party of Angola to form the Revolutionary Government of Angola in Exile (Govêrno Revolucionário de Angola no Exílio; GRAE) whose guerrilla wing, the National Front for the Liberation of Angola (Frente Nacional de a Libertação de Angola; FNLA), was headed by Roberto.

Early efforts by the MPLA to form a united front with the UPA proved futile, each portraying its competitor as a tool of foreign interests and Cold War politics. Underlying the rivalry, however, were class, ethnic/racial, religious, and regional differences.[23] Marxist-oriented students formed the base of the MPLA, although Neto hailed the virtues of nonalignment and sought support from "progressive" forces in the United States as well as from the Eastern bloc.[24] The UPA combined populist rhetoric with promises of security for free enterprise.[25] After 1966, a third force entered the scene: the National Unity for the Total Independence of Angola (União Nacional para a Independência Total de Angola, UNITA). UNITA was headed by Jonas

Savimbi, who had been foreign minister of the GRAE but left the post in 1964. Ambitious, charismatic, and unscrupulous, Savimbi would eventually become a willing tool of the Portuguese secret police, the United States, and South Africa in an effort to prevent the MPLA from controlling this resource-wealthy and strategic African country.

When the Angolan rebellion broke out in 1961, it was swift and unexpected, catching the colonial authorities and nationalist leaders unprepared.[26] The armed struggle would extend beyond independence, devolving into a bitterly fought civil war that pitted the triumphant Cuban- and Soviet-supported MPLA against UNITA, which was supported by the United States and South Africa. It was a devastating civil war that lasted until 2002 and was to leave large swaths of the country in ruins.

Portuguese Guinea

In Portuguese Guinea, the African Party for the Independence of Guinea and Cape Verde (Partido Africano de Independência de Guiné e Cabo Verde; PAIGC) emerged to wage the struggle for independence. Headed by agricultural engineer, intellectual, poet, and revolutionary theoretician Amílcar Cabral, the PAIGC was, in Houser's estimation, "probably the most successful and advanced of all the freedom organizations in the 1960s and early 1970s."[27] Houser had first met Cabral in 1960 at the second AAPC in Tunis and again at the third AAPC in Cairo. Through increased contact over the years his admiration for the man grew. "His great organizing ability, clarity of purpose, clear analysis, superb tactical sense and innovative ideas made him a leader almost without peer in the African liberation struggle," wrote Houser.[28] The armed struggle began between 1962 and 1963, but it would take ten years before Portuguese Guinea won its freedom as Guinea-Bissau. Tragically, Cabral would not live to see the fruits of the movement he had built. Just six months before Guinea-Bissau was recognized as an independent nation by seventy other countries, Cabral was assassinated by two disgruntled former PAIGC members who were directed by the Portuguese secret police and supported by dozens of other PAIGC members.[29]

Central African Federation

After years of nonviolent protest and the imprisonment of nationalist leaders, African politicians in two of the three territories making up the Central African Federation—Northern Rhodesia and Nyasaland—won increasing power in their legislative councils and were working toward a breakup of the federation. In March 1963, the British government conceded, and the federation was formally dissolved on December 31 of that year. The following year Northern Rhodesia was granted independence as Zambia, with Kenneth Kaunda becoming president. Nyasaland became Malawi, with Hastings K. Banda serving as prime minister.

Self-determination for blacks in Southern Rhodesia, the third member of the Central African Federation, would not be so easy. Its white settler government was more deeply entrenched. A mass movement, the National Democratic Party (NDP), was formed in 1960 to seek majority rule. Through strikes and mass protests they had hoped to compel Britain to intervene and force a handover of power to black majority rule. What they got instead was a compromise that fell far short of the one-person, one-vote result they had hoped for. The NDP rejected the white minority government's constitutional proposal: it was banned in late 1961 but replaced in 1962 with the Zimbabwe African People's Union (ZAPU) led by Joshua Nkomo. Under continuing repression, ZAPU leaders decided to go underground. In 1963, internal conflict within the party led to a split and the formation of the Zimbabwe African National Union (ZANU) under the leadership of Ndabaningi Sithole and Robert Mugabe.

The split dismayed Houser. He had known Nkomo best but also knew and respected many of the ZANU leaders. Since the split could affect which of the two groups the ACOA would support, he sought to ascertain the reasons for it—as they didn't seem to be ideological ones. Houser admitted that as an outsider it was hard to disentangle the conflict and decided that the ACOA would have to support both parties.[30] There would be still later splits that would enable the white settlers to exploit the differences and stymie the formation of a cohesive national identity.[31]

Determined to maintain their dominance, the white settler Rhodesian Front thrust Ian Smith into the office of prime minister. In 1965 he issued a Unilateral Declaration of Independence (UDI), essentially ignoring Britain's pleas for concessions to the black majority and stripping blacks of all rights. The response was an embarrassment for Britain. International outrage resulted in economic sanctions supported by the UN. The struggle for independence would drag on until the end of the next decade.

South Africa

After decades of protest and nonviolent civil disobedience, the antiapartheid movement in South Africa turned from nonviolent protest to armed struggle. The catalyst was the Sharpeville Massacre of 1960. On March 21, 1960, the Pan-Africanist Congress (PAC) organized between five thousand and seven thousand people in a peaceful demonstration, marching to the municipal office and central police station in a Johannesburg township in protest of the pass law that required black Africans to carry identification papers. The PAC had split from the ANC the year before over the latter's policy of multiracialism.[32] The police suddenly opened fire on the crowd, killing 69 and wounding some 180 others.[33]

The event immediately provoked international outrage and spawned the birth of antiapartheid organizations across Western Europe. A UN Security Council resolution, signed by the United States, deplored the actions of the South African government. Calls for a boycott of South African goods and refusal to unload ships from South Africa came from trade unions in eight countries. President of the AFL-CIO, George Meany, called for a halt to the purchase of South African gold. Beleaguered and ever more defensive, the South African government issued a state of emergency, banning all groups, arresting two thousand demonstrators, and outlawing the ANC and PAC. The two groups decided that to carry on the struggle they would have to go underground and wage a protracted guerrilla war. Some three hundred to four hundred leaders from both movements then left the country to set up headquarters in Ghana, Algeria, Egypt, Britain, and independent Tanzania to raise international support and develop training camps for a new armed unit of the ANC, Umkhonto we Sizwe, that would engage in acts of sabotage.

Responding to the Sharpeville Massacre, Houser went into emergency mode with several programs designed to protest the massacre and provide help for its victims. An emergency "Call to Action" was circulated, listing actions Americans could take to respond to the crisis. The idea of a boycott of South Africa had been growing internationally as the result of a call by ANC leaders, and Houser decided that the idea needed to be accelerated in the United States.[34] Even before Sharpeville, he had recommended to his board that the ACOA explore the boycott as a means of pressuring the apartheid regime.[35]

In March, Houser called a meeting of representatives from labor, student, and religious groups to discuss the idea. The group decided that a consumer boycott would not work in the United States, as there were too few Americans consuming South African goods. They thought a wider kind of boycott, such as boycotting tourism, artists' tours, and investments, might be more effective. Houser was authorized to work on the outlines for a broad campaign with the ACOA acting as the domestic branch of the international boycott effort.[36]

The ACOA's second Africa Freedom Day rally, held in April at New York City's Town Hall, was called to protest Sharpeville and to announce the start of a nationwide boycott of South Africa later that month. Attended by hundreds of people who erupted frequently with shouts of "Tell 'em. . . . Give it to 'em!" the event was keynoted by Hastings K. Banda of Nyasaland (later, president of Malawi) and Kenneth Kaunda of Northern Rhodesia (later, president of Zambia). NAACP attorney, Thurgood Marshall, was among the other speakers. A drive to raise funds for the victims and their families resulted in $19,000 sent to South Africa.

Later that spring, Houser convened the Emergency Action Conference on South Africa. Chaired by Jackie Robinson and cosponsored by thirty-eight national organizations, the conference was attended by over two hundred people. The featured speaker was to have been Oliver Tambo, Deputy President of the ANC, who had recently escaped from South Africa and was now organizing the international work of the ANC from exile. Following the conference Tambo was scheduled to embark on a month-long lecture tour arranged by the ACOA. Shortly before the event, however, Houser received word that the State Department had denied Tambo a visa. Houser immediately telegrammed the State Department and organized protests among church, labor, and community groups.[37] His intervention succeeded in June when Tambo was issued a visa. Although it had come too late for the conference, the ACOA managed to arrange some speaking engagements for him around the country.

The conference produced two dozen recommendations for ending apartheid, as well as a commitment to raise $100,000 for the defense of detainees and their families.[38] The ACOA published the actions and recommendations as a pamphlet. Circulated widely, *Action against Apartheid* amounted to a blueprint for the broad antiapartheid movement that would blossom in the following decades.[39]

The growth in antiapartheid NGOs, coupled with pressure from the new African members of the UN, led to the establishment in 1962 of the UN Special Committee against Apartheid. From its beginnings in 1963 until the end of apartheid, the UN Special Committee served as a focal point around which NGOs like the ACOA and African leaders could focus international attention on the festering wound of the apartheid state. The UN Special Committee's mission was to press for effective international sanctions against South Africa, arrange assistance to apartheid's victims and liberation movements, ensure constant publicity to South Africa's transgressions, and assist antiapartheid organizations like the ACOA in organizing public campaigns.[40]

Houser would work closely with E. S. Reddy, head of the UN Special Committee, and later when he was director of the Centre against Apartheid. He felt a special bond with Reddy, an Indian who had Gandhi "under his skin" so to speak.[41] "I know that I felt I had an ally in this huge international edifice [the UN]," Houser later recalled.[42]

US AFRICA POLICY DURING THE 1960S

Until John F. Kennedy's election as president in 1960, US policy toward southern Africa had been "not to unduly disturb the status quo."[43] Kennedy's election inaugurated a shift in US rhetoric and policy. This change resulted from the explosion of the civil rights movement, the fact that Kennedy owed his election in part to the black vote, the negative international publicity the United States was getting while promoting itself as a beacon of democracy, and the independence of most of sub-Saharan Africa—whose new status on the international stage could no longer be ignored.[44] With Africa now being linked by both African leaders and the Soviet Union to civil rights unrest at home, US government policies toward one would have to be calculated for the possible impact on the other.[45]

Unlike Eisenhower, Kennedy openly expressed tolerance for African neutralism, invited African leaders to the White House, and encouraged his advisers to work up programs for US economic assistance. After a Portuguese slaughter of fifty thousand Angolans in March 1961, the United States voted to condemn Portuguese policy in the Security Council, terminated commercial arms sales to Portugal, and reduced its military aid from $25 million to $3 million. The administration also inaugurated a scholarship program for students from southern Africa—partly to counter the Soviet Union's more expansive scholarship program—and began the Peace Corps.

Kennedy's appointment of former Michigan governor G. Mennen ("Soapy") Williams as assistant secretary of state for African affairs, a man whom Houser had tapped to be one of the speakers at his first Africa Freedom Day event in 1959, as well as Kennedy's brief appointment of civil rights activist Chester Bowles as undersecretary of state, gave Houser some reason for hope. With such men in the State Department, the ACOA would now have greater access to Washington policymakers.[46] This became more explicit when Houser was named one of twenty people to serve on a State Department Advisory Council on African Affairs.[47] Over the next four years, the council would meet six times. Williams and his deputy used the council to push the Africanist position with the government and press and urged

Kennedy to back up verbal disapproval of apartheid with a full arms embargo against South Africa. The administration responded with a unilateral declaration that the United States would sell no additional arms to South Africa as long as apartheid remained in place. Subsequently, the United States voted for a UN resolution calling on all states to voluntarily cease the sale and shipment of military hardware to South Africa.[48]

The positive policy changes initiated in the early days of the Kennedy administration, however, soon began to unravel. The United States was still beholden to its European allies and to NATO, and its foreign policy remained colored by Cold War ideology.[49] African Americans were still politically weak, with only a handful of representatives in the US House, none in the Senate, and few in state governments. And for most whites, African policy was not on their radar screen. The result was a mixed message that gave verbal assent to African nationalism while refusing to take actions that would undermine its European allies or the needs of American corporations doing business with South Africa.[50]

The United States' continuing racial problems at home left African diplomats suspicious of Kennedy's intentions, especially when they met with incidents of racist behavior on their visits to the United States, or when fragments marked "Made in America" from bombs dropped by the Portuguese were found in a war-torn Angolan village.[51] Eventually, the Kennedy administration's reversal of past support for Portugal in UN resolutions regarding its African colonies was eroded by its commitments to Portugal under NATO and a new Berlin crisis that dramatized the strategic value of American refueling facilities at its military base in the Azores.[52] Fearing the rupture of its security and economic ties to South Africa, the administration opposed UN resolutions calling for economic measures against the regime as well as calls for the regime's expulsion from the UN. All of this led Houser to believe that the president did not give much weight to the advice given by the Advisory Council on African Affairs.[53]

Southern Africa would also prove a dilemma for the Johnson administration. The economic problems on the continent seemed intractable and continued internal conflict in so many of the countries "soured the Johnson administration on deeper involvement in what seemed potentially an African quagmire."[54] No doubt his own quagmire in Vietnam weighed heavily on him. A reluctant Congress also prevented Johnson's attempts in 1966 to recover the momentum behind US policy toward Africa with an economic development program.

HARD QUESTIONS FOR HOUSER AND THE ACOA

The militarization of the struggle for liberation in southern Africa, the rivalry between contending liberation groups, and the impact of Cold War politics raised new and difficult questions for Houser and the ACOA. How could a committed pacifist support movements that were now engaged in armed struggle? Furthermore, if Houser wished to continue supporting self-determination, which among the contending groups should the ACOA support, and what criteria should be applied to differentiate among rival groups and claims? Cold War rivalries and South African intrigue made such decisions even more complicated. How could the organization avoid being used by one side or the other, especially when the people they were working with were sometimes getting money from either the United States or the Soviet Union?

Except for Algeria, which began its armed struggle in 1954, Houser's faith in nonviolence had not faced a major test. Although there had been acts of violence against African nationalists by colonial authorities, the countries that had achieved independence thus far had done so through relatively peaceful means. But at the second AAPC in Tunis in 1960, Houser had noticed that anti-American sentiment was growing, nonviolence was eroding, and Africans were beginning to fear that the end of political colonialism would result in economic neocolonialism.[55] If the ACOA hoped to counter this anti-American feeling, it would have to champion the viable liberation movements even if they turned to armed struggle. In moving from an absolutist position on nonviolence to one conceding that nonviolence was sometimes not a viable option, Houser was distancing himself from the nonviolent beliefs of his mentor, A. J. Muste, as a universal blueprint for social transformation and its implied ethnocentrism.[56]

Yet which among the competing organizations should he support? Until now, Houser had based his support on the personal contacts he had made, his assessment of the strength of the support they had within their own countries, opinions of trusted colleagues, and those organizations supported by the UN. After the OAU's formation in 1963, he would back those movements it considered legitimate. But what to do when the OAU recognized more than one competing liberation movement as in Southern Rhodesia (Zimbabwe)? Houser was dismayed by the split in ZAPU that had created ZANU, but both were recognized by the OAU. He knew the leaders of both groups, and there was no clear ideological or tactical distinction to be made between the two. "We foreign supporters of the struggle," he reluctantly concluded, "had to adjust to the fact that there were two viable movements after the split in 1963."[57]

However, his policy of not taking sides when there were internal struggles for leadership within and among liberation movements would sometimes get him into trouble. Houser had never sought to apply a Cold War
test to his loyalties. But in the ensuing years, Cold War realities would occasionally come back to bite him. In mid-1961, the CIA secretly placed Holden
Roberto on its payroll in an effort to prevent the MPLA from taking power.[58]
For the better part of the 1960s, a rumor circulated in papers in Africa, Europe, Cuba, and the Soviet Union that the ACOA had passed CIA money to
Roberto and the UPA to forestall the MPLA from taking power. One rumor
even suggested that the ACOA had created the GRAE. The existence of this
rumor caused the leadership of the MPLA to treat Houser with suspicion.[59]
At the time he was supporting Roberto, Houser was unaware that he was
receiving CIA funds, although there was an incident that might have made
him suspicious. During one meeting in Léopoldville, Roberto handed him an
envelope to take back to the United States asking that it be spent correctly. Inside were four crisp $100 bills. Houser later recalled that he wondered where
Roberto was getting these newly minted bills.[60] Nor could Houser have anticipated that his enthusiastic support of Mboya would lead to Mboya's being
touted by the West as the anti-Communist spokesman for Africa or that his
early support of UNITA would prove to have been a mistake.

Houser was not concerned about being labeled a Communist, Communist sympathizer, or supporter of "terrorists" by the right-wing Portuguese-
American Committee on Foreign Affairs, the government of South Africa,
or by right-wing members of Congress.[61] He knew where such smears were
coming from; besides, he had been used to this "Communist" label since his
days with CORE. But what hurt his ability to be trusted by some he considered allies were the accusations that he and his organization were fronts for
the CIA. Consequently, Houser found himself trying to explain to his friends
and the numerous sources of such disinformation that the rumors were simply untrue. "There can be a McCarthyism (guilt by association) of the left as
wrong as that of the right," he wrote.[62] But in the murky waters of Cold War
intrigue and covert operations it was easy for the forces opposed to African
liberation to sow distrust among those working for self-determination.

Yet if he doubted his ability to be effective, Houser had only to cite a series of articles written by a major Afrikaans journalist who called the ACOA
the principal enemy of the white supremacist government, or a speech by Sir
Roy Welensky, prime minister of the Central African Federation, in which
he complained to his Federal Assembly that the visits of members of his
legislature to the United States did not get the same attention as the visits of

African liberation leaders sponsored by the ACOA. "I can only describe the assistance given to these people by the American Committee as monumental," Welensky stated. "I am amazed at the power and influence that they have and the ability to get the viewpoints of these people across."[63]

Houser returned to Africa in November 1960 to attend the swearing-in ceremony of Nnamdi Azikwe as first African governor general of Nigeria,[64] using the occasion to meet with liberation leaders and to make another visit to the Congo in the midst of its turmoil. His discussions in Léopoldville convinced him that there was little hope for a resolution to the Congo crisis short of stronger UN intervention. The ACOA could not do much except to urge the United States to keep its hands off the region.[65] The organization was still needed in other areas, however. Appeals to the Africa before Defense and Aid Fund were now coming from South Africa, South West Africa, Portuguese Africa, and South African refugees. The Algerians still saw the ACOA as one of their chief supporters in the United States (Houser had kept in almost constant contact with their UN representatives). The ACOA's voice was still needed in UN policy deliberations in resisting the introduction of the Cold War into Africa and in pressing for a change in US policy. Moreover, they remained a critical source of information needed by delegations to the UN, and their office was functioning as an overseas "office" for numerous African petitioners as well as the ANC.[66]

THE CHALLENGE TO WHITE LEADERSHIP

Another set of difficulties for Houser during the 1960s arose because of the entry of new organizations into the field of African solidarity work.[67] The wave of independence activity in Africa had coincided with a resurgence of the civil rights movement in the United States. And increasing exposure to African leaders and independence movements had catalyzed a resurgent interest in Africa among the African American diaspora, resulting in calls for African Americans to be in the forefront of African solidarity work.

Furthermore, radical expressions of Black Nationalism were emerging on both sides of the Atlantic. In South Africa these developments were represented by the formation of the Pan-Africanist Congress (PAC) in April 1959, and by the Black Consciousness Movement (BCM) associated with Steven Biko toward the end of the 1960s, and in the United States by Malcolm X and Elijah Mohammed of the Nation of Islam. Later in the decade the Black Panther Party, challenging the nonviolent approach of the civil rights leaders with whom Houser was most closely associated, espoused armed black self-defense.[68] In 1966 Student Nonviolent Coordinating Committee (SNCC) chairman, Stokely Carmichael, ignited a firestorm with his slogan of "Black Power" and his demand that whites leave SNCC and work on racism among their own people.[69]

Within the ACOA, a nucleus of black staff and board members, feeling ties to the Black Nationalist movement, began to exert pressure for a black executive.[70] There had been expressions within the radical African American community that the ACOA was a "white" organization and therefore not to be trusted with the liberation of blacks.[71] E. S. Reddy told an interviewer later that such remarks were "unfair to George Houser,"[72] pointing out that Houser had been a founder of CORE, had started working with the African liberation movements from the very beginning, and was friendly with many African American leaders whom he brought to be active with the ACOA during the McCarthy era when most black organizations toed the State Department line on Africa. He also pointed out that although the African American Leadership Conference on Africa was headed by African Americans, it was George Houser who had organized and promoted it.[73]

Nevertheless, with African Americans now questioning white leadership of their movements, Houser would have to rethink his role as a white man heading an organization devoted to the support of black Africans. Should he give up his Africa work and concentrate on working against racism at home among whites? Was his decision to devote himself to Africa a result of CORE's deteriorating membership and finances and waning support from the FOR, or was it a way of sidestepping the unease with his own white privilege and the increasingly fraught relationship between the liberal civil rights movement and Black Nationalist politics that made increasing demands on white activists? It may have been a bit of both, although he never admitted to being burned by Black Nationalist politics. Houser's son, Steven, reported that he had seemed to make his peace with it and never heard him say a negative word about Malcolm X, Stokely Carmichael, or the Black Panthers. "I know he believed that it was right that African Americans should be the leaders of the Black Liberation Movement."[74] In fact, he had sought opportunities where possible to work with Black Nationalists. For example, early on he had sought to work with Malcolm X, only to be rebuffed. Later, he would invite Elombe Brath to serve on his board. Brath, the New York–based head of the Patrice Lumumba Coalition, had been recognized by Stokely Carmichael as the "Dean of Harlem Nationalists." In a 1969 letter to E. S. Reddy proposing a UN seminar on the US and South African apartheid, Houser had suggested, among those to be invited, representatives of SNCC, particularly James Forman.[75]

Houser had always seen his Africa work and the struggle for civil rights in the United States as the same struggle; and it may have been his belief that his unique experience in the civil rights movement had given him a perspective on the relationship between the two that few other white people had. Yet to his executive board he suggested that he might step down if the board felt a different leadership was necessary.[76]

Between 1960 and 1961, the ACOA executive board engaged in an intensive period of soul searching over whether the organization should continue, and if so, under what kind of leadership. Much would depend on what specific contribution the new leadership could make to the process of African liberation. Responding to criticism that the ACOA was a "white" organization, Houser hired Chuck Stone as Associate Director in 1960, but the appointment was to be short lived. Stone left after four months to take a more lucrative position as managing editor of the Washington edition of the *Afro-American*, perhaps indicating the difficulty in forging genuinely biracial managements in organizations like the ACOA where the hours were long and the pay low. The ACOA was not the only organization going through such soul searching. The liberal mainstream churches were feeling the pressure of wider black participation in funding and programs that affected them.[77] And the African Studies Association faced several tense annual meetings over black accusations of white paternalism, resulting in the secession of most African Americans (though not most Africans) from the association and the formation of their own association.[78]

In January 1961, feeling that his attempts to influence US Africa policy might be more effective if the black community took the lead, Houser proposed the idea of holding a conference of African American leadership organizations on Africa. Since the demise of the Council on African Affairs, there had been no black-led organization willing or able to assume such leadership. In 1959, Michigan congressman Charles Diggs had failed to convince the NAACP to establish a special office on African issues.[79]

After consulting with civil rights leaders, plans for a conference entitled "The Role of the American Negro Community in U.S. Policy toward Africa" were begun.[80] The conference took place the following year.[81] The call to more than seventy-five of the nation's top African American organizations had been issued by the entire roster of civil rights leadership, thus indicating the evolution of liberal African American thought on Africa after its earlier attempts to distance itself from events in Africa.[82] Although Houser had initiated the idea for the conference, the ACOA's steering committee decided that the ACOA should stay in the background. Consequently, it was listed as one of some two dozen sponsoring organizations.

During the next six years, the American Negro Leadership Conference on Africa (ANLCA), led by Ted Brown of the Brotherhood of Sleeping Car Porters, endorsed armed struggle in South Africa and political and material assistance for its national liberation organizations. It also secured a historic meeting with President Kennedy—the first time a large group of African American leaders had been given a chance to discuss the nation's relations with Africa. The group urged Kennedy to adopt a "Marshall Plan" for Africa, impose sanctions on South Africa, and support a UN proposal for an arms embargo against Portugal. Three successive conferences were held, and the ANLCA succeeded in stopping United States naval vessels from visiting South African ports. The organization, however, failed to establish a firm institutional base. Houser had hoped that King's association with ANLCA would bring the African American community to a new level of involvement in the antiapartheid struggle, but King's preoccupation with domestic racism dictated that his involvement would be largely symbolic.[83] Internal conflict caused partially by rising militancy among a younger cohort of African Americans, financial problems, and the inability to focus on a distant struggle when there was a more pressing one at home caused the ANLCA's demise in 1968.[84] The end of the ANLCA meant that until the formation of TransAfrica in 1977, the ACOA would continue to be the major US organization lobbying for policy sympathetic to anticolonialism and black majority rule.

In the end, the ACOA board did not take Houser up on his offer to step down. They were probably aware that few people had the breadth of his experience or the willingness to put in long hours on a modest salary. The short life of the ANLCA indicated the difficulty for African Americans of carrying on two major struggles at once. The result was that the ACOA, during a time of intense interracial conflict and mistrust, remained one of the few interracial organizations to survive the black revolt. Yet the lack of African American leadership on the organization's staff would continue to nag.

A TREK THROUGH REBEL ANGOLA

When Holden Roberto visited the United Nations in 1961, Houser had spoken with him about the possibility of going into northern Angola with the UPA guerrillas. He had learned of medical needs in the areas controlled by the guerrillas that he wanted to help meet. He also felt that by going into the rebel areas he would be able to better interpret what was happening inside Angola.[85] There was also a measure of curiosity and excitement about the prospect of seeing a guerrilla operation from the inside. Houser had always been drawn to risk and adventure. He knew that the Portuguese would likely find out that he was going to be with the UPA and could use this information against him and the ACOA. "Are the risks worth the gains?" he asked himself.[86]

Having answered that question in the affirmative, Houser found himself on a heavily overcast night in early January 1962, traveling by car from Léopoldville in the Congo toward the Angolan border, a five-hour journey.[87] He was accompanied by his friend, Professor John Marcum of Lincoln University, who would later write a seminal history of the Angolan revolution. While in Léopoldville the suspicion that they were being followed by the Portuguese added to the tension of going into a war zone, so they decided to slip across the border under cover of night so that reports of their movements could not get back to the Portuguese or Congolese authorities. Given the anti-Western feeling among so many Africans that Houser had picked up on at the third AAPC the year before, it is a testament to the trust that Houser had won among African freedom fighters that he was welcomed by the UPA guerrillas.[88]

Driving through a heavy tropical rainstorm with faulty windshield wipers, the car moved at a snail's pace. As the rain let up, they turned onto a pitted dirt road that led to the border, meeting up, as planned, with a UPA truck filled with eight heavily armed combatants. When both the car and the truck broke down and had to be abandoned, the party was forced to travel by foot for the next five kilometers, crossing the border near dawn.

Houser had been awake all night but described himself as "amazingly keyed up."[89] The rainy season had brought out the landscape's lushness. Houser took in its beauty—the fresh, moist air, the rolling hills and valleys, grass higher than Iowa corn, and thick forests with small streams meandering through them. He could hardly believe that a war was going on. Only a few hundred yards from the border, however, that pacific reverie was dispelled when they encountered a cache of weapons being distributed to a group of young nationalists. For the next five hours, Marcum and committed pacifist Houser accompanied the guerrilla band with their load of rifles, grenades, machine guns, ammunition, and land mines on a trek to the place where they would spend the night—an abandoned village that was now a guerrilla training center. There they were besieged by requests for medical help. They had brought 250 pounds of medical supplies to be distributed throughout rebel-held territory, but that was hardly enough to satisfy the dire medical needs that existed in the territory. Houser recorded that he and Marcum treated about fifty people who had open sores that looked like raw meat. The following day the two men distributed the medicines to representatives from communities scattered around the northern part of the country.

For the next eleven days Houser and his companions trekked through rebel territory. The UPA forces were organized into small, mobile units suited to guerrilla warfare. They operated out of forest villages that were linked by an intricate system of paths through an area that appeared to have the beginnings of a political state. UPA authorities had issued "passports" that had to be checked at guard posts along the paths and at makeshift gates at village entrances. Customs posts, a communications and information system, village councils—as well as party, trade union, and youth organizations—all appeared to be operating.

Hiking for six or more hours a day, Houser and his companions followed narrow, rooted paths up and down through deep forests, crossing streams bridged by narrow logs sometimes high over the water. As the party threaded its way through elephant grass fifteen or more feet high, Houser stubbed his toe on a hidden rock. By the time they stopped for the night the toe was discolored and painfully swollen; Houser thought he must have broken it. The following day it was no better, but they had to move on. For a while he hobbled slowly, but it wasn't enough. Despite Houser's objections, one of the guerrillas, hardly larger than Houser himself, picked him up and carried him piggyback until Houser felt guilty and asked to be put down. Houser continued to hobble on, feeling strengthened by this act of kindness. It was a gesture he would never forget.[90]

The group subsisted on one meal a day, usually of manioc and tropical fruit, occasionally chicken with hot palm oil sauce, wild buffalo, peanuts, and palm wine. On one occasion they had wild pig, fish, and eel. Passing through each of twelve villages they were greeted warmly by the villagers who lined up for whatever medical treatment these two nonmedically trained men could offer. Mostly this consisted of dressing open sores and distributing what pills they had on hand.

The routine in each village usually began with a flag-raising ceremony, a lecture on civic duties or national goals by the village president or military chief, and a presentation of arms. Older people tended the fields guarded by soldiers. The large numbers of teenagers spent their time drilling, learning patriotic songs and, in the larger centers, studying from a tattered school syllabus or Bible. Houser was somewhat surprised by the religious orientation of the guerrillas, evidence of the influence of Western missionaries.

Because of the peril of air raids, in some villages women and children spent the day under protective boulders secluded in the forest. When planes were heard approaching, warning whistles would sound, and people would flee into the forest with whatever supplies they could carry, while military personnel ran to lookout posts prepared to fire at approaching aircraft.

Along the way, Houser heard stories of recent fighting between the Portuguese and the UPA, listened to firsthand accounts of Portuguese atrocities, and came across the effects of war: bomb fragments from a Portuguese air attack with "Property of the U.S. Airforce" printed on it and villages left burned out and abandoned by indiscriminate bombing. On one occasion they felt the concussion of rockets and incendiary bombs and saw fires engulfing two villages they had just left.

By the end of twelve days of walking, Houser and Marcum had covered two hundred miles. As they neared the border to return to the Congo they learned that Congolese authorities were waiting for them at the place where they had originally crossed and thus decided to cross at a different spot to avoid being detained. They arrived in Léopoldville in the early morning hours tired and dirty but exhilarated by what they had experienced. "We had seen the great courage and self-sacrifice of a whole people," Houser would write. "We had seen the birth of a nation from the ruins of a colony; and we had confirmed that we, as Americans, could contribute to the struggle for dignity and freedom."[91]

During their stayover in Léopoldville, Houser met with Dr. José Liahuca, director of the FNLA's medical and refugee program, about the possibility of providing some medical aid to the UPA rebels and to the estimated 150,000 Angolan refugees who had fled to the Congo. But in a meeting with the MPLA executive committee he found its members guarded with him. Having failed to find the kind of support in the United States they had obtained in Europe, the MPLA were still suspicious of Americans; or perhaps they had seen the disinformation about his alleged connections to the CIA that were circulating in the Marxist press at the time.

In a report on his findings, Houser concluded that there was no hope for a common front among the liberation organizations.[92] Given the uncertainty of the leadership struggle in Angola, Houser decided that for the time being he would put most of his effort into supporting the UPA/FNLA-GRAE (the organization he was most acquainted with), but he would not close off aid to the MPLA if it were needed.[93] When in 1963 the OAU recognized the FNLA/GRAE as the legitimate representatives of the Angolan liberation struggle, Houser's decision found more legitimation. The assumption behind that recognition, however, began to unravel the following year when Roberto rebuffed all efforts to align with the MPLA, and it became clear that disorganization and authoritarian leadership were hobbling the FNLA/GRAE's effectiveness as a revolutionary force. Throughout the rest of the decade, a complex pattern of constantly changing fortunes and interrelationships among the FNLA/GRAE, MPLA, and UNITA—which had formed in 1966 when Savimbi broke with the FNLA/GRAE—would make relationships with outside groups like the ACOA difficult.[94]

On returning to New York, Houser decided that the best way he could help the UPA rebels was to raise funds for medical aid. He also wanted to find a doctor who could help with the swelling number of war refugees in the northern areas of Angola, which was controlled by the UPA and the Congo. At the fourth annual Africa Freedom Day rally at New York's Town Hall that April, the ACOA announced the launching of an emergency relief fund for Angola. By May, the US labor movement had sent $5,000 worth of medical supplies.[95]

A young Canadian doctor, Ian Gilchrist, who had been raised by missionary parents in Angola and who spoke some Portuguese, Umbundu, and French, learned of the ACOA's effort and wrote to offer his services. Gilchrist began his work in early January 1963, assisting Angolan physician Dr. José Liahuca, who was struggling to get a relief service going under the auspices of the UPA.[96] Gilchrist had no salary, but the ACOA had taken out an insurance policy, opened a small savings account for him in the United States, sent him a small stipend to support his family, and purchased a Volkswagen van that was converted into an ambulance.[97]

A NEW URGENCY IN SOUTH AFRICA

After the South African government's passage of the Sabotage Act in June 1962, which reinforced the state's power to curb antiapartheid activity (including the possibility of the death penalty for violators of the act), Houser saw a new urgency to respond to the crisis with an appeal to the international community. In addition to printing a pamphlet entitled *South African Crisis and U.S. Policy*, the ACOA issued "An Appeal for Action against Apartheid" on December 10, 1962, Human Rights Day. Sponsored by Martin Luther King Jr. and Albert Luthuli, the appeal called on people of conscience across the world to demonstrate their opposition to apartheid. In preparation, the ACOA had contacted groups in Britain, Holland, France, Germany, India, various parts of Africa, and organizations across the United States. Over two hundred thousand copies of the appeal, which had been signed by some two thousand people, were sent to individuals and organizations. In response, the ACOA received reports of actions across the United States as well as Canada. This was one of the first big efforts to enlist student organizations in the antiapartheid movement. The US National Student Association included the "Appeal for Action against Apartheid" in a mailing to its thirteen thousand members and sent a telegram to the First National City Bank in New York urging it to withdraw its investments and other forms of financial support from South Africa.[98] The student movement would come to be one of the most important constituencies for antiapartheid activity in the years ahead.

WITNESS TO THE FOUNDING OF THE ORGANIZATION OF AFRICAN UNITY

From May to June 1963, Houser again traveled to Africa accompanied by his friend Irving Wolfe to attend the founding meeting of the OAU on May 25, in Addis Ababa, Ethiopia. This historic event brought together the heads of state of all but two of the independent countries. Having been represented at the earliest gathering of heads of independent states in 1958, Houser was able to assess what that five-year difference had made in the situation in Africa. "The focus still is on anti-colonialism and freedom, but just as urgent are solutions relating to economic, educational, and political unification problems," he wrote.[99] Cities in the independent areas of Africa—Algiers, Cairo, Dar es Salaam, Léopoldville, Accra, Dakar, Conakry—were now serving as headquarters for the offices and training of freedom fighters in the unliberated regions. "Emphasis in the struggle for freedom in southern Africa has very definitely shifted from the non-violence of the All African Peoples Conference in 1958, to violence," he reported.[100] From his talks with leaders of the ANC and the PAC, Houser learned that both groups were planning sabotage.

After the conference Houser traveled to Nairobi, arriving on the day Jomo Kenyatta was sworn in as prime minister. He and Wolfe lunched with Tom Mboya, who by this time had been made minister of constitutional affairs. Afterward, Mboya drove them to Kenyatta's home. In Dar es Salaam, Houser had a long discussion with Eduardo Mondlane, who informed him that the insurrection in Mozambique was about to begin. From Dar es Salaam, Houser and Wolfe traveled to Léopoldville and several villages along the Congo-Angola border to study the refugee problem. In Léopoldville, Houser had dinner with Zimbabwean nationalist Ndabaningi Sithole and Sam Nujoma, who would later become Namibia's first president. From Nujoma he learned that there were some fifteen hundred to three thousand South West Africans (Namibians) training in camps in the Congo who were eager to go into South West Africa to begin the insurrection against South Africa.[101]

Houser also met with Dr. Gilchrist who was now providing medical aid to about fifty refugees a day of some thirty thousand Angolan refugees who were in Léopoldville, as well as making periodic trips of 150 to 200 miles south to the Angolan border to do what he could to meet the medical needs of people who could not get to Léopoldville or other urban centers. Houser was impressed with Dr. Gilchrist's effectiveness and deep commitment and felt gratified that in his efforts to supply the area with this doctor he had helped to mitigate the terrible suffering he saw among the refugees.

However, from the start of Gilchrist's work it was clear that in a revolutionary setting there would be multiple challenges: differing political agendas, personality and ethnic tensions, Portuguese sabotage, and the ever-stressful problem of limited resources. One of those challenges arose over Gilchrist's commitment to meeting the needs of those most affected by war, and Holden Roberto's commitment to his supporters, who expected to be looked after first. By 1964 it would become apparent to Gilchrist that disorganization within the FNLA/GRAE, political intrigue, and Roberto's commandeering of the medical operation to serve his own interests was interfering with his work. Through letters from Dr. Gilchrist, Houser learned of how Roberto's problematic behavior was affecting the relief work. Gilchrist wrote that he suspected a plot was being hatched to get rid of him and that his days there might be numbered. Roberto and some of the others in the UPA/GRAE suspected Gilchrist of being implicated in an unsuccessful coup against him by his own minister of defense.[102]

Not being on the scene, it was hard for Houser to discern what was going on in the chaotic and bewildering atmosphere of the plots and counterplots, assassinations, and coup attempts that Dr. Gilchrist confronted. After talking with John Marcum, Houser told Gilchrist that he could see no alternative except to continue supporting Roberto, since there was no alternative to him. He could understand how difficult this was for Gilchrist and reassured him that he would support whatever decision he needed to make. If Gilchrist felt he had to leave, Houser pledged to try to find another position for him. Gilchrist thanked Houser for his support, agreeing that Houser didn't have much of an alternative to supporting Roberto at the moment but cautioned him that "for the time being there should be a great emphasis on support of the people with a softened support for the man."[103]

Houser managed to have some talks with Roberto on his trip to Africa later that fall but continued to hope that Roberto, despite Gilchrist's warning, would correct the situation so that Gilchrist could continue. Gilchrist did, in fact, continue to soldier on. But by July 1965, realizing he was the object of a hunt by UPA security agents, Gilchrist left the country with the assistance of a consortium of aid and development agencies.[104] Arriving in New York, he had long talks with Houser about the series of events. Despite Houser's deep respect for Gilchrist's dedication to the cause of relieving human suffering, he continued to relate to Roberto and Necaca, giving them the benefit of the doubt that these difficulties arose as a result of misunderstandings that occur in the midst of a revolution. He admitted later that his relationship with Roberto never quite recovered from this development.[105] It would take a few more years, however, for Houser to fully realize that he had backed the wrong horse, although Gilchrist averred that at the time "there were no right horses, and there was a constant evolution of conditions."[106]

Although Houser rarely talked about defeat or failure, he must have been bitterly disappointed that his humanitarian instincts had led to Dr. Gilchrist being placed in harm's way by the very movement and man— Holden Roberto—his organization had been supporting; but such was the nature of trying to work in solidarity with people caught up in the labyrinthine and uncertain world of an armed struggle for independence.

A BITTERSWEET ANNIVERSARY

In November 1963, just a month after the Rivonia Trial that would put apartheid in the dock and send Nelson Mandela, Walter Sisulu, and eight other antiapartheid activists to life sentences on Robben Island, the ACOA celebrated its tenth year.[107] From a small voluntary organization with no funds, it had expanded its support base to sixteen thousand and was operating on a budget of $151,000, which, as usual, was in the red.[108] It now had a staff of eight to ten people. It had enlisted in its various events and campaigns a veritable who's who of figures from the worlds of civil and human rights, politics, literature, religion, entertainment, and sports. Its Africa Defense and Aid Fund had sent thousands of dollars to assist political prisoners and their families, refugees from the fighting, and liberation movements with nonmilitary aid. In the United States it had serviced the need for information and expert analysis of countless students, journalists, activists, and UN and US government officials. For African liberation leaders who came to New York, the ACOA had provided introductions to people and officials who could be helpful. They also provided these leaders with office space and secretarial services, assistance with housing and transportation, and exposure to US audiences.

If not a household name in the United States, the ACOA had achieved a reputation across Africa as one of the liberation struggle's best friends in the United States. A special anniversary issue of *Africa Today* contained messages from several of Africa's emerging leaders. Among them was Oliver Tambo, who wrote the following: "The untiring work of the American Committee on Africa has been one of the influences that have compelled world recognition of the rights of Africans and all oppressed peoples to freedom and independence."[109] Amílcar Cabral wrote that "no one can doubt the important role played by your Committee. By your firm anti-colonial stand you are effectively contributing to the isolation of the Portuguese colonialists," but perhaps Eduardo Mondlane best summed it all up: "The American Committee on Africa is to me the conscience of the American people in relation to the problems and needs of the African peoples."[110]

But almost halfway into the 1960s it was clear that the euphoria that had swept supporters of Africa's independence was encountering hard new realities. Houser reluctantly reported these harsh developments to his board: assassinations, growing evidence of authoritarian leadership, coups and attempted coups, border disputes, and apparent infiltration of Chinese and Russians into the continent.[111] Moreover, the Congo crisis had led to a rift in relations between Africans and Americans.[112] Compelled to acknowledge the disillusionment that had set in among some of his supporters, Houser sought to rally his executive board for the work that still needed to be done.

> We have never taken the view . . . that with the coming of independence
> utopia would be ushered in. . . . Our position has been based on
> the justified assumption that the way people are prepared for
> independence is by struggling to achieve it, and then by accepting
> the responsibilities that go along with it. The kinds of problems
> which attract our attention in newly-independent Africa today are an
> essential beginning to accepting responsibility.[113]

In July 1964, Houser took another extended trip to Africa, this time to attend the celebration of Malawi's independence. Invited by future Malawi president Hastings K. Banda, Houser witnessed the autocratic tendencies that would become more pronounced after Banda's installation as president in 1966, when he called himself "Ngwazi" (meaning "conqueror") and after a few years declared himself "President for Life." Traveling to other capitals to speak with numerous people, Houser concluded that turmoil in the region would lessen the pressure on the United States and Europe to challenge the racist regimes. If this scenario came to pass, Houser insisted that "the task of the American Committee on Africa is to point out again and again . . . that this present stage is purely momentary. . . . The contradictions between apartheid and equality are too great to permit an accommodation to be made for an indefinite period."[114]

For the next two years Houser remained in the United States, sending others on various ACOA-sponsored tours to Africa so that he could attend to the business of running the organization. As always, the ACOA struggled for operating funds. Since its founding, there had been unsuccessful attempts to obtain tax-exempt status so the organization could attract foundation and large donor funding, but by late 1964 it had become obvious that their political activity was the source of the government's inaction. Houser's solution was to spin off a separate "nonpolitical" entity that could apply for tax-exempt status. The original fund would continue to support political work, while the new fund, the African Aid and Legal Defense Fund, would support UN work, educational and medical projects, and the families of political prisoners. The ACOA would appoint the new fund's trustees and staff both funds, and Houser would oversee both. Given the confusion about the names of the two funds, the ACOA decided in 1968 to change its name to the Africa Fund.

A FOCUS ON SOUTH AFRICAN ECONOMICS

In the mid-1960s, Houser sought to increase American attention to the crisis in southern Africa. It was not easy to pry Americans' attention away from the dramas happening at home. Civil rights protests and the deepening war in Vietnam were absorbing the attention not only of government leaders and Congress but also of civil society. Yet he was encouraged by the fact that local groups were springing up in a number of cities and that organizations like the National Student Christian Federation, the National Student Association, Students for a Democratic Society (SDS), and some major religious denominations were now giving some staff and program time to African issues.[115]

Despite Houser's momentary pessimism, the vehicle that would be the most important tool yet available to draw activists to the cause was already on the horizon. Prodded by board member Peter Weiss, the ACOA decided to begin work on African economics. It had become clear to Houser and his colleagues that US investments in South Africa were helping to keep the apartheid regime afloat. Consequently, in 1964, the opening salvo in what would become a sophisticated, multifaceted campaign to expose and cripple the structure of US economic support for apartheid was launched with an article in *Africa Today*. Using some preliminary statistics the ACOA had gathered, the unnamed author—possibly Houser—made the case that US investments had saved the apartheid regime from economic collapse in 1961 by contributing almost the entire amount of foreign exchange needed to reverse the precipitous decline of the South African economy. Increasing US investment in South Africa embarrassed the United States on the world stage. These investments were also dangerous and inconsistent, since the United States had banned arms sales to South Africa but continued supplying oil and other strategic commodities that were equivalent to weapons. Moreover, such investments violated America's democratic ideals, flouted UN resolutions, and encouraged the exploitation of South African labor.[116]

To launch its attack on American investments, the ACOA organized the South African Crisis and American Action Conference at which papers on the extent of American private involvement in the South African economy were presented, and options for legal action were explored. The conference was sponsored by the Consultative Council on South Africa, a coalition of about thirty organizations the ACOA had been instrumental in initiating in early 1964. Held March 18–20, 1965, and attended by four hundred to five hundred people, the conference resulted in a list of action recommendations that a delegation subsequently presented to Secretary of State Dean Rusk, National Security Advisor McGeorge Bundy, and members of the US Congress.[117] Realizing they were on to something, Houser hired four graduate students during summer 1965 to undertake more advanced research on South Africa's economy and American corporate involvement. The results were subsequently published in the January 1966 issue of *Africa Today*.[118]

That same year Jennifer Davis, a South African woman who had studied economics at the University of Witwatersrand, arrived at the ACOA office. As the daughter of liberal Jewish parents, she had been a fierce opponent of apartheid since high school and was determined that every Jew should resist religious and racial oppression wherever it occurred. After university she worked with the labor movement and organized with the Unity Movement, an antiapartheid movement with Trotskyist tendencies. As an outspoken activist, it was natural that her days in South Africa would be numbered. Getting word that she and her husband, a lawyer who had defended apartheid's political victims, were about to be placed under house arrest, she made her way to New York with her two children. Her husband, who was visiting his brother at the time, had preceded her.[119]

Jennifer Davis turned out to be just the person Houser needed to carry on the economic research begun by the summer interns. Appointed under the title of research director, Davis got to work, organizing the chaotic files in the ACOA office into a usable system. Over the ensuing decades the sophisticated economic research produced by Davis would become the major source of information used by journalists, African liberation leaders, legislators, and antiapartheid activists like Randall Robinson, who in 1977 would found TransAfrica, the black-led organization credited with bringing US support for the apartheid regime to its final end.[120] Analyses of neocolonial exploitation of commodities such as oil and diamonds, the extent of US corporate investments in South Africa, and the effects of economic sanctions on

Southern Rhodesia and South Africa would find their way into congressional and UN testimony, newspaper articles, pamphlets, and flyers. Such research would prove to be one of the most effective ACOA contributions to the effort to topple apartheid.

Recognizing that the economic information the ACOA was now uncovering could form the basis for local actions by Americans, and disappointed by the American Negro Leadership Conference's organizational difficulties, Houser once again tried to broaden the racial composition of his senior staff with someone who could take the ACOA program to the African American community. In September 1965, Wendell Foster began work as associate director. An ordained minister, he had served a predominantly black church for nine years and had been active in civil rights work. He had also served as tour leader on two ACOA summer tours to Africa.[121] Foster remained on the ACOA staff for the next two years, resigning in mid-1967.

During 1965, Houser sought to get Congress to hold hearings on the South African crisis and the following year succeeded in securing the first major review of US policy. He also spearheaded a statement condemning Rhodesia's Unilateral Declaration of Independence and the US government's weak response to that action. With Wendell Foster's help, the ACOA coordinated the organization of two vigils to mourn the plight of political prisoners in South Africa at the South African consulate and the South African Tourist Corporation in New York City and held a Human Rights Day rally at Hunter College in New York City on December 10, 1965. At the latter rally, Martin Luther King Jr. gave his first major address on South Africa to an audience of some eighteen hundred.[122] The rally raised $9,500, which was sent to the South African victims.

The September 1966 assassination of South Africa's prime minister and the architect of apartheid, Hendrik Verwoerd, and his succession by the brutal minister of justice, John Vorster, convinced Houser and his associates of the urgency of stepping up their campaign of economic pressure on South Africa. A few countries had announced their own unilateral trade restrictions against South Africa, but for the most part, the economic price to each nation was too high. The United States was dragging its feet, preferring to shift responsibility to the business community, while American businessmen argued it was a foreign policy decision best left to the White House.[123]

An indication of the real reason behind the United States' abdication— and proof of the powerful forces Houser was attempting to challenge—can be found in a story the ACOA had a hand in exposing when it made its offices available in the late 1970s to British freelance journalist Bernard Rivers. While in Africa with a British documentary film crew, Rivers had become intrigued with how Rhodesia, which had been slapped with comprehensive UN Security Council sanctions in December 1966, managed to continue to get its oil.[124] A landlocked country, Rhodesia would have been brought down within a matter of weeks had a massive international oil conspiracy not been put in place. An elaborate chain of bogus companies that secretly transported oil through South Africa into Rhodesia was contrived by major oil giants like Shell, British Petroleum, Mobil, and Texaco and protected by the major powers, including Britain and the United States. The story that Rivers and his partner, Martin Bailey, uncovered reads like a cloak-and-dagger thriller and has been compared to Watergate, including the existence of a "Deep Throat" from within the Mobil Oil Corporation.[125] But it is mostly a story about the deep character of the military industrial complex and the relationship between governments and multinational corporations that allowed the racist Rhodesian regime to survive unhampered by international sanctions. Although just a footnote in the saga of the ACOA's years of effort challenging white supremacy in southern Africa, this story illustrates just how important it was that the ACOA existed when it did.[126]

DISENGAGING FROM SOUTH AFRICA

If the US government would not impose limits on US investment in South Africa, Houser and his colleagues reasoned that perhaps pressure could be applied on the companies themselves. That opportunity arose when two Union Theological students, who were also enrolled in a one-year intensive program at Columbia's School of International Affairs, decided to focus their study on US bank lending to the apartheid regime. Their research revealed that Chase Manhattan and First National City Bank (later Citibank) were the lead players in extending financial assistance to the regime. Armed with this information, the two recruited students from nearby schools to remove their accounts from the two banks. They were quickly supported by the ACOA and the National Student Christian Federation.

Soon afterward, ACOA staff, in consultation with the students, developed a plan for a fall city-wide campaign against the two banks.[127] In preparation, Houser drafted "Rationale for the Protest against Banks Doing Business with South Africa," a document that Robert Kinloch Massie, author of a monumental work on the United States and South Africa in the apartheid years, called "one of the most succinct arguments for economic disengagement from South Africa."[128]

To launch the wider campaign, Houser and the National Student Christian Federation formed the Committee of Conscience against Apartheid.

With more than 120 prominent sponsors, this committee urged individuals and organizations to withdraw funds from the two banks by Human Rights Day, December 10, 1966, and to direct pressure on a consortium of ten banks involved in a $40 million revolving loan fund to South Africa.[129] A. Philip Randolph led demonstrations against these banks and began negotiations. By December 1966, he reported that $23 million had been withdrawn from the targeted banks.[130] Though the banks made no immediate change in their policies, the growing movement began to create public relations problems for them. In 1969, Houser and his colleagues were surprised when the Associated Press announced that the South African government was pulling out of the $40 million revolving loan fund presumably because of the country's "strong gold and foreign exchange position."[131] Houser surmised that the real reason for the withdrawal must have been that the highly visible loan was more bother than it was worth.[132]

RETURN TO AFRICA

After two years of working in the trenches at home, Houser was itching to get back to Africa. Thus, from May 11 to June 1967 he was on the road again. His purpose was to get a feel for the current atmosphere from the liberation movements and to look into possible ACOA projects. After a two-year absence, Houser detected the realization among southern African leaders that they could not expect much help from independent Africa—which was struggling with internal dissension and its own developmental problems— the United Nations, or a weak OAU.[133] Considering this, he concluded, the ACOA "cannot realistically call for an overall program of economic sanctions with any hope of success. But we can try to move in the direction of economic disengagement unilaterally. We can urge an American policy against new investments. . . . We must be satisfied to work on small but specific projects, where there is a chance for some degree of success."[134] His friends in the nationalist movements agreed on the soundness of this approach.

A DARING CONFRONTATION IN THE SKY

Earlier that year Houser had begun to turn his attention to the long-simmering events in South West Africa (later Namibia). At the end of World War I, the League of Nations had given the Union of South Africa a mandate to administer this former German colony for the "well-being and social progress" of its inhabitants, but with the birth of the UN that mandate was to be transferred to its Trusteeship Council. South Africa, however, refused to abide by the decision and sought to annex the territory, extending its apartheid system and building military installations in obvious violation of the terms of the mandate. For years, petitioners on behalf of the Herero people of South West Africa had been attempting to get the UN to act against South Africa, but the regime had remained obdurate.

In July 1958, Houser had received a copy of a petition addressed to the UN secretary of the Committee on South West Africa from three leaders of the Ovamboland People's Congress, a forerunner of the South West African People's Organization (SWAPO), requesting that the territory be placed under the UN Trusteeship system.[135] Houser sent the petition to the secretary of the UN Committee on South West Africa. On September 24 of that same year a package postmarked "Cape Town, South Africa," arrived at the ACOA office. Inside Houser discovered a copy of *Treasure Island*, and in a hollow that had been cut out was a tape from one of those leaders, Herman Andimba Toivo ja Toivo, containing music. In the middle of the tape was a message requesting that it be played at the UN, since he had been denied permission by the South African government to appear as a petitioner. Houser duly sent the tape to the UN, arguing that it was against its charter for petitioners to be prohibited from leaving their countries in order to appear at the UN.[136] The playing of that tape at the UN helped pave the way for direct testimony by liberation movement representatives from South West Africa. This appeal for help illustrates the trust that came to be invested in Houser by those on the front lines of the struggle and the name recognition he had developed among liberation movements that were little known in the United States at the time.

When Houser got word in December 1959 that the South Africans were forcibly removing Africans from their homes to a new location to set up an apartheid system, Houser had again taken the issue to the UN and made several unsuccessful attempts to get the International Court of Justice (ICJ) to rule on the dispute.[137] Sam Nujoma, Chief Hosea Kutako, and Chief Samuel Witbooi wrote to thank the ACOA for placing its legal experts at their disposal and for assisting in other ways, including the attempt to get the territory referred to the ICJ.[138] But in the meantime, an indigenous movement—the South West People's Organization (SWAPO)—had arisen to challenge South African rule. Its guerrilla campaign began in August 1966.

The unsettled status of the territory had made it difficult for Houser to figure out an action plan in relation to South West Africa. However, the passage of Resolution 2145 by the UN General Assembly in October 1966, and a subsequent resolution (2248) to implement UN authority through the establishment of a UN Council for South West Africa, presented an opportunity.[139]

The resolution declared that South Africa's mandate was now terminated and that from then on the territory would be placed under the direct responsibility of the UN, which began referring to the country as "Namibia," its local name. Still, South Africa continued its intransigence, and the international community, dominated by the big powers, gave no indication of its willingness to effectively challenge South Africa's refusal to comply with the UN resolutions. For Houser, this meant that the apartheid regime had won both a political and psychological victory.[140]

South Africa's recalcitrance reminded Houser of the American South's refusal to abide by the Supreme Court's *Irene Morgan* decision and the Journey of Reconciliation he had helped organize to challenge the South's defiance. While lunching with his old friend Lyle Tatum in February 1967, the two began to speculate on what could be done to implement the UN resolution. Over several months of brainstorming, during which they were joined by two other men with broad experience in Africa, they hatched a plan.

Calling themselves the "Ad Hoc Committee for the Development of an Independent South West Africa," they raised funds and recruited an interracial group of volunteer specialists to attempt to fly into the country to search for projects that could be developed in farming, nutrition, health, and cooperatives. Given the inability of the UN to enforce its resolution, the plan represented what was then a rare case of civil society actors trying to enforce a UN decision using nonviolent direct action. It was a risky venture. The South African government would surely get wind of it, and there could be a confrontation. Houser and his colleagues, however, thought the confrontation would occur inside South West Africa. The UN Council and SWAPO gave the plan its imprimatur, and President Kenneth Kaunda of Zambia promised help on the African end.

In the predawn hours of December 6, 1967, ten men boarded two small chartered planes at the airport in Lusaka, Zambia, with the intention of flying into South West Africa without South African visas and therefore in defiance of that country's continuing control of the territory. In addition to two pilots, Houser, and Tatum, on the plane were Dr. John L. S. Holloman, former president of the National Medical Association and the Medical Committee for Human Rights; Professor Flemmie P. Kittrell, a nutrition specialist at Howard University; Samuel F. Ashelman, economic consultant with the International Cooperative Association; and three journalists, one from the *London Times* and two from Zambian papers.

Houser confessed to being intensely nervous. He had not been able to sleep for the three nights they were en route to the Lusaka airport, constantly mulling over the details and possible repercussions of the trip.[141] Neither pilot—one an American and the other a white Rhodesian—had been apprised of the flight's purpose, nor had any advanced public notice been given of the planned flight. It was only the night before their departure that they had informed the newspapers and the American ambassador to Zambia about the reasons for their journey.

From Livingstone, Zambia, where the plane refueled, the route took them across a corner of Rhodesia before entering Botswana. Soon after, Rhodesian police radioed the planes that they had received word from South African police that the passengers did not have visas and would not be allowed to enter South West Africa. This was the first indication the pilots had that anything out of the ordinary was happening, but they assumed that the visa problem could be straightened out once they reached Windhoek. Halfway across the Botswanan desert the radio crackled, and a voice with a heavy Afrikaans accent came over the airwaves. "We know what your mission is," the voice said. "You will not be allowed to land in Windhoek. What is your intention?" The puzzled pilot turned to Houser. "What is this all about?" he asked. The men had prepared a brief written statement explaining that they had no visas, did not recognize South African jurisdiction in South West Africa, and planned to land to identify development projects. The grim-faced pilot then replied, "This is a gritty position."[142] But he told the South African police that they would fly on.

When the pilot announced that they had crossed over into South West Africa territory, the radio crackled again. A voice asked for the names of all passengers, to which the pilot complied. Then the voice continued: "Listen carefully. . . . You will not be allowed to land at Strijdom Airport (Windhoek) or any other airport in South West Africa unless all documents of crew and passengers meet all local legal requirements. We know the reason for your mission, and should you land against this instruction, you shall have to bear the consequences."[143] They were to learn later that the South African government had received advance warning of their flight.

The pilot was not about to get arrested nor have his plane confiscated. Ten minutes from Windhoek he turned the plane around, radioing the other pilot to do the same. Houser's heart sank. It seemed as if their months of planning had come to naught. But by this time there was a more onerous danger. The plane's fuel gauge was registering near empty, but the pilot's request to land for refueling was denied. They would have to find a place to land in the desert. The pilots knew of an airstrip at Maun, Botswana, but there was only a beeper tower to indicate how to find it. Then the plane

jerked, and the right engine went dead. Houser, sweating profusely and unaware that the plane had an emergency tank, peered frantically for a place to
land. The pilot turned on the emergency tank, which meant they could go a
little farther. Then the left engine went out.[144] Just then, the other plane radioed that they had got a line on Maun. To everyone's great relief, the airstrip
appeared just in time. They landed and were able to refuel.

The men then went through an agonizing discussion. Should they pursue their backup plan, which was to be dropped at a town near the Caprivi
Strip—a panhandle running east of Namibia between Botswana on the south
and Angola in the north—and try to enter South West Africa by Land Rover?
They would return to Lusaka and decide from there. Three hours later, hun-
gry (Houser had been too nervous to eat that day) and tired, they faced a raft
of reporters who were waiting at the Lusaka airport. It had been a harrowing
fourteen-hour journey.

Knowing that the world was now aware of their plan, the men decided
not to try to enter South West Africa by land. "I had never felt more let
down," Houser recorded later. "We had worked so hard and then it was all
over in a day."[145] From Lusaka they cabled a protest to Prime Minister Vorster
of South Africa as well as the UN Council on South West Africa, informing
them of what had happened and stating their willingness to give a report to
the council.[146]

In a press conference the following morning the men explained why
they had undertaken the mission. There was brief coverage on radio and
TV. Stories appeared in the southern African press as well as in the *London
Times*, *New York Times*, and *Washington Post*. A *Times of Zambia* editorial
commented: "The gallant band of Americans who set the record straight
on just who controls the voiceless people of South West Africa deserve the
praise and thanks of every Pan-Africanist."[147] Prime Minister John Vorster, in
a statement that was widely carried in the South African press, was quoted
as saying, "Mr. George Houser . . . was well known for his interference in
South African affairs, and his action was arrogant and provocative. . . . The
whole move was merely an attempt to revive the South West Africa debate
in the UN. . . . Nobody will be allowed in South Africa or South West Africa
without proper documents and Houser will definitely, with or without documents, not be permitted."[148]

Though disappointed in the failure of their mission, Houser could take
some satisfaction in dramatizing South Africa's refusal to abide by UN resolutions and in demonstrating to the people of South West Africa that there
were those elsewhere in the world who believed in South West Africa's right

to independence and were prepared to take some risks to implement their beliefs.[149] Later, testifying before the UN Council on South West Africa, Houser admonished the rather sclerotic agency that "the government of South Africa must be continually reminded, not just by vocal protestation, but also by action, that the world challenges its continued control over South West Africa."[150]

A David against Goliath, 1968–73

BETWEEN 1968 AND 1973 EVENTS IN BOTH SOUTHERN AFRICA and the United States reached a critical peak. The repression in South Africa was now complete, with the banning of all antiapartheid organizations and the imprisonment, banning, or departure of nearly all their former leaders. Faced with increasing rebellion on its borders, the Vorster government stepped up attempts to shore up its position by sending troops into Rhodesia, Angola, Mozambique, and South West Africa (Namibia) to support faltering minority regimes while simultaneously offering access to South African resources, technology, and markets to surrounding black states like Zambia and Botswana. It also engaged in a propaganda campaign intended to soften its international image by extending invitations to everyone from critics to entertainers and sports figures to visit the country.[1] Continuing to flout UN directives, the regime hardened its defiance by establishing the first "apartheid homeland" in South West Africa in 1970. South Africa was now a powerful military and economic power, supported by American corporations like General Motors, IBM, Union Carbide, and the Polaroid Corporation, with arms supplied by the Conservative British government elected in 1970. American support for the apartheid regime gave the ACOA an opening to challenge it, but clearly the organization had its work cut out for itself.

Nineteen sixty-eight was a pivotal year in American politics with a hotly contested presidential election, turmoil in the streets over the seemingly never-ending war in Vietnam, increasing militancy among segments of the black community frustrated by the intransigence of their economic plight, and the assassinations of Dr. King and Robert Kennedy within two months of each other. To Houser, it must have seemed as if the causes he had committed his life to were more distant than ever. Yet the harder the challenge, the more determined he was to persevere.

The troubles at home were hardly a propitious time for the ACOA's attempts to call attention to southern Africa. But for Houser, the upcoming presidential electoral campaign was an opportunity to link a pro-imperialist American policy in Southeast Asia to American support for Portugal in southern Africa and the white minority regimes of Namibia, Rhodesia, and South Africa. Thus, he plunged into the fray with an unsuccessful attempt to get all the presidential candidates to take a stand on the southern Africa issue with a position paper endorsed by 130 prominent Americans. It was a radical proposal that was unlikely to go over well with a government whose main foreign policy imperative was fighting not only the Cold War but a "hot" war as well. However, the connections this statement made between America's foreign policy and its treatment of racial minorities at home was as prescient in 1968 as it would be today.

> White Americans are racially myopic. Few, regardless of their
> views about the war in Vietnam, think of it in racial terms. Many
> Vietnamese and other Asians, many Africans, and many black
> Americans see it as the latest episode in a continuing race war. Men
> who are not white remember that it was yellow men on whom the
> first atomic bomb was dropped. It is yellow men and their country
> that now suffer napalm, defoliation, and other forms of ever more
> savage warfare. The presence of 540,000 Americans in Vietnam is
> seen as a continuation of the old imperialism—the white world
> ruling the non-white.[2]

The maverick Democrat, Senator Eugene J. McCarthy, was the only presidential candidate to take a position on southern Africa. With so much at stake on other fronts, neither the Democratic nor Republican parties even mentioned the crisis in southern Africa in their platforms. Moreover, the Democratic Party platform, repudiating the ACOA's position on southern Africa, castigated the "self-serving revolutionaries who employ illegal and violent means" to exploit the aspirations and frustrations of the people in Asia, Africa, and Latin America.[3] While disappointed in the outcome, Houser reasoned that the value of the committee's political activity was in the contacts that were made.

Racial polarization and Black Nationalist militancy were not just engulfing the United States. They had now become issues of contention within global Protestantism. In 1968, pressured by militant African and American blacks, the World Council of Churches (WCC), a federation of mostly Protestant mainline denominations, had decided to establish the Programme to

Combat Racism. In the next few years it would funnel nonmilitary support to the armed liberation movements in southern Africa.[4] The question of whether Christians, who adhered to a gospel of love, should be supporting those involved in armed struggle was not a dilemma for Houser alone. The ethics of support for liberation movements that practiced violence had become a subject of extensive debate within religious circles. Both the WCC and the ACOA would come under a firestorm of criticism from right-wing and even some liberal circles for supporting "terrorists" and "Communists." Houser would be obliged again and again to justify his apparent abandonment of pacifist values.

When an interviewer questioned him about the apparent contradiction between his "religious duty" and his "patriotic duty," Houser replied, "To believe in freedom and justice and to try to realize it to the greatest extent possible. That's a good foundation both for a patriotic view and a religious view of the world. . . . And from that point of view, I don't see any contradiction between the two."[5]

Houser gave a more nuanced justification in the July 10, 1972 issue of *Christianity and Crisis*, the publication of record for progressive Christians, which was devoted to a discussion of Christianity and violence. The turn to violence in southern Africa, Houser explained, was fairly recent, a response to the increasingly violent repression of the remaining colonial powers, but the fact that violence was being used did not mean that nonviolence was theoretically irrelevant. The problem was that in the southern Africa struggle no one was ready to lead a nonviolent movement. "I find it impossible," Houser wrote, "not to support the liberation struggle because it is so patently just. . . . [Nonmilitary aid] does not violate my conscience, although I realize this also involves me implicitly in support for the violent nature of the struggle." "Considering the fact that the demand of the Christian Gospel is one of love," he continued, "my rationale is not entirely satisfactory. I am sure that the World Council of Churches has used something of this same rationale in justifying its support for the African liberation movements."[6] In their willingness to countenance support for armed movements, Houser and the ACOA were outliers in the white liberal religious community in the United States.[7]

A REACTIONARY TURN IN US AFRICA POLICY

Richard Nixon's election to the presidency in 1968 signaled a new setback in the government's Africa policy. Under Nixon's new national security adviser, Henry Kissinger, the administration had secretly moved to relax South Africa's political isolation and economic restrictions while publicly mouthing opposition to racial repression. The policy was outlined in secret National Security Study Memorandum 39 (NSSM 39).[8] Over the next five years, the White House would effectively abandon any opposition to white rule (however weak and disingenuous) and provide John Vorster with unequivocal evidence of American confidence.[9] The Nixon administration also renewed support for Portugal, even supplying the country with arms and herbicides, which they began to use in Angola. In 1971, an amendment attached to a successful military procurement bill by Senator Harry Byrd of Virginia further eroded the gains that had been made by the antiapartheid movement in moving US policy away from its support for racist regimes. The amendment effectively broke the first mandatory and comprehensive sanctions program against Rhodesia ever approved by the UN by allowing Rhodesia to sell large amounts of strategic minerals such as chrome.[10]

AN ACOA PRESENCE IN WASHINGTON

Houser had long felt the need to have a presence in Washington, DC, to monitor Africa policy and exert pressure at its source; however, he was under no illusion that simply lobbying Congress or the State Department would change American policy without persistent grassroots pressure. By 1968, this long-standing dream had come to fruition with financial help from several Protestant denominations. The Washington Office of the ACOA would mobilize support for legislative efforts by providing background material to members of Congress, as well as arranging for African leaders and others with specific knowledge of African affairs to confer with legislators and other government officials. It would also relate these government activities to a wider public by organizing public events concerning US Africa policy, publishing memoranda on African issues, and coordinating activities with other groups in the Washington area.[11]

In 1972, the ACOA's Washington Office was spun off as an independent entity with a separate staff, changing its name to the Washington Office on Africa (WOA) and broadening its support base to include unions in addition to faith-based organizations. Edgar (Ted) Lockwood, an Episcopal priest and lawyer who had been a civil rights activist, was hired to head the WOA. Though operating independently, the WOA would continue to work closely with the ACOA. The office the ACOA had started would become the model for the Washington Office on Latin America, established after the 1973 coup in Chile to provide a counternarrative to US policy in the region.[12] This was yet another example of how Houser's initiatives set precedents for future action by others.

One example of the ways in which the Washington office worked in
tandem with grassroots mobilization was in ACOA's efforts to defeat the
Byrd Amendment. While Lockwood worked the hill, ACOA organizers were
tracking ships suspected of carrying cargo from Rhodesia to ascertain their
port of destination. They would then alert local groups that were prepared
to protest. Major demonstrations were held at ports in New York, Philadelphia, Maryland, and Louisiana. Although the demonstrations were unsuccessful in preventing the cargo from being offloaded, they managed to delay
some shipments. The actions, however, continued to call attention to Rhodesia, eventually pressuring Congress to restore the embargo in 1977.

The 1965 Civil Rights Act had begun to diversify the racial composition of Congress. Over the next decades, the ACOA would find a more
receptive audience for its initiatives in the Congressional Black Caucus and
particularly its founder, Charles Diggs, Democrat from Michigan, who had
a long-standing interest in African independence. He and Houser would develop a close relationship, sharing information and ideas for action. Diggs
would provide an amplified voice for Houser and the ACOA within Congress
and in the media.[13]

DEEPENING THE DISENGAGEMENT STRATEGY

With the consolidation of the South African police state by the late 1960s
and the stifling of resistance, the United States began to tacitly accept a con-
tinuation of apartheid by engaging in practices such as increased foreign investment, calls for dialogue with the regime, and approving entertainers or
sports figures' visits to South Africa. For Houser, engaging with the regime
in these ways was a tragic error. What was needed was increased pressure on
the regime. Testifying before the House Sub-Committee on Africa in March
1966, he had pointed out the hypocrisy of the US government's policy: on
the one hand making eloquent statements about apartheid while claiming
that South African ports were "highly useful" to the US Navy, that tracking
station facilities were "important," that American business was providing a
"useful channel of communication with influential South African private
and official circles," and that disinvestment "might harden South African
policies." Houser also called out the US government's dubious claim that
American disinvestment would have no effect on the South African economy.
He then offered a set of specific proposals that Congress could take to disengage from complicity with the apartheid regime.[14]

Knowing that he could not count on an unwilling Congress to take up his
recommendations, Houser devised a strategy of pressuring Congress, while

concurrently increasing grassroots mobilization around disengagement. The goal was to isolate South Africa in the international community, turning it into a pariah and thus weakening its external support. This strategy would take both economic and cultural forms.

With the approach of the 1968 Summer Olympics in Mexico, Houser saw a promising opportunity to put South Africa on the front burner. Since the 1950s there had been international calls to ban the regime from international sports competitions. As early as 1958 the ACOA had supported the idea of a sports boycott and had participated in the unsuccessful international effort to ban South Africa from the 1960 Olympics in Rome. But by 1964, thanks to the efforts of Jackie Robinson and Eleanor Roosevelt, they were successful in banning the regime from the Tokyo Olympics. In the interim, however, Prime Minister Vorster had announced some cosmetic changes to their rigid policies of racial segregation in sports. An interracial team would be allowed to compete but would be chosen in separate tryouts. Succumbing to this ruse, the International Olympic Committee (IOC) reinstated South Africa. The announcement was met with declarations by African nations that they would boycott the Olympics. Houser immediately moved into action to prevent the country's readmission.

Houser had met Dennis Brutus, the South African poet and leader of the South Africa Non-racial Olympic Committee (SANROC) the year before in London, and the two had agreed to work together on a sports boycott of South Africa.[15] In furtherance of that goal, the ACOA issued the statement "South Africa and the Olympics," sending this call to action to several hundred athletes.[16] Sports, the statement argued, could be South Africa's Achilles' heel. The country bristled with sports fever, and a second ban could deliver a real blow to the white supremacist population and the country's international image.

In February and April the ACOA held press conferences to publicize a statement supporting a boycott signed by sixty-four outstanding athletes. Subsequently, Major League Baseball player Jim Bouton and South African footballer Steve Mokone, representing the ACOA, traveled to Mexico City to assist Brutus and Chris DeBroglio, a member of SANROC, in lobbying the IOC for the exclusion of South Africa from the games. Faced with the prospect of a massive international boycott, the Olympic Committee retracted its reinstatement of South Africa. The ACOA's efforts no doubt contributed to the pressure on the IOC, but Houser was under no illusion that they alone had accomplished this important victory, attributing it to the unrelenting pressure of the African-based Supreme Council for Sport in Africa (SCSA), an arm of the OAU. Nevertheless, Jim Bouton reflected that "probably our most significant impact was simply our presence which had the effect of making every delegate aware that their days of operating in secrecy are over."[17]

The pressure on South African sports would continue, led by the unrelenting efforts of Dennis Brutus and the dynamic leadership of Richard Lapchick, founder of the American Coordinating Committee for Equality in Sport and Society (ACCESS). As a young doctoral student, Lapchick had been inspired by Houser to write his dissertation on how South Africa used sport as part of its foreign policy.[18] Working closely with the ACOA and Brutus, ACCESS successfully garnered support from even those who had at first refused to heed the boycott. In the coming decades, the sports boycott would emerge as one of the more successful weapons against apartheid.

A variant of the sports boycott that the ACOA played an instrumental role in initiating in the United States was the cultural boycott.[19] In 1965 the ACOA had issued "We Say 'No' to Apartheid: A Declaration of American Artists." The sixty-five signers of this declaration—all luminaries in the arts—pledged to "refuse any encouragement of, or indeed any personal or professional association with, the present Republic of South Africa: this until the day when all its people—black and white—shall equally enjoy the educational and cultural advantages of this rich and lovely land."[20] The cultural boycott would blossom over the coming decades, adding many more names to those unwilling to have their talents exploited by an apartheid regime.

Houser's effort to undermine the South African regime economically was to take yet another turn in 1968: targeting shareholders in corporations that did business in South Africa and urging them to purge their portfolios of South African equities.[21] Accordingly, plans were made to send ACOA representatives armed with proxy votes to stockholders' meetings where they would raise questions about their investments and urge shareholders to withdraw their stocks from the business. As Jennifer Davis explained, "If we could knock out the corporations we could change the relationships of power much more easily rather than dealing with governments."[22] Houser acknowledged that they were fighting an uphill battle, but he believed that over time the efforts would bear fruit.

The campaign began in April 1968 when Houser, using a proxy, attended the shareholders' meeting of First National City Bank. Other delegations followed at meetings of the Gillette Company and IBM in Boston, Chase in New York, and Texaco in St. Louis. ACOA also helped organize protest demonstrations at the Engelhard Chemicals and Minerals meeting in Newark, New Jersey, and at the General Motors meeting in Detroit. The pressure on stockholders would soon be adopted by others. Church pension funds and religious orders had large investments in companies doing business in South Africa and, after initial reluctance, were more amenable than other organizations to applying a social justice test to their portfolios.

Facilitating the stockholder campaign was the Interfaith Center for Corporate Responsibility (ICCR) established by member denominations of the National Council of Churches in 1973. The ICCR's mission was to engage in research on corporate performance and employment practices and to organize resolutions challenging shareholders to withdraw their investments from socially reprehensible companies. The ICCR was headed by Tim Smith, who as a young man had spent a summer in Kenya. Like Houser he had attended Union Theological Seminary, and over the years the two would work closely together on these campaigns, Smith serving on ACOA's executive board.

Throughout the 1970s the shareholder resolution campaign would spread, drawing in scores of institutional investors: religious bodies, universities, trade unions, philanthropic organizations, and state and county pension funds. At first reluctant to countenance such challenges, the corporations, under mounting pressure, began to adopt incremental policies to head off disinvestment like hiring black workers and putting blacks on their corporate boards. Under such pressure, General Motors, one of the most visible targets of the shareholder campaign and the largest employer of blacks in South Africa, recruited its first black board member, Baptist minister Reverend Leon Sullivan. In 1977 Sullivan would articulate what became known as the Sullivan Principles, consisting of seven requirements for corporations doing business in South Africa.[23]

Requirements such as equal pay for equal or comparable work would widely influence the practices of corporations in the years to come, but in Houser's eye they were merely a sop to the regime. They would give the impression that South Africa was changing but "would have virtually no effect on apartheid in the larger community," he argued. Moreover, American-dominated companies employed only 1 percent of South African workers.[24] Any accommodation to the apartheid regime—especially in the case of foreign investment—only strengthened it: "The small reforms which might be made are outweighed by the assurance this aid gives to the South African government. Further, it gives those investing a stake in the status quo," said Houser.[25]

In 1973 the ACOA and churches put together another campaign aimed at bank loans after they discovered that forty banks, including eleven from the

United States, had made $210 million in loans to the South African government since 1970 through the European-American Banking Corporation (EABC). After protests in the United States and Europe, the EABC was forced to end further credit to South Africa, except for the financing of current trade.[26]

In another effort to isolate South Africa, the ACOA initiated a campaign during the early months of 1969 to protest the granting of an air carrier permit to South African Airways (SAA) to fly into Kennedy International Airport. Largely because of ACOA's urging and Congressman Diggs's shepherding of it, hearings on the issue were held by the Subcommittee on Africa of the House of Representatives Foreign Affairs Committee, and Congress introduced a bill to ban foreign airlines whose countries practiced racial or religious discrimination. The ACOA next placed an ad in support of the campaign in the *New York Times* that was signed by over 150 black leaders. Both the *Evening Star* (Washington) and the *New York Post* reported that the statement "was particularly notable for the wide scope of organizational affiliations" among sectors of the African American community who didn't usually manifest such unity.[27]

Despite these efforts, SAA continued to land. The ACOA then mounted continuous protests at Kennedy International Airport, the offices of South African Airways, and the British Overseas Airline Corporation, which was providing facilities for the South African company. The initial SAA flight was met at the airport by more than two hundred shivering demonstrators in a heavy snowstorm. It was followed by five more demonstrations. In 1969, organizing several hundred people to attend protests at Kennedy, an airport that must be approached through miles of heavy city traffic, was not as easy in the days before the airport air train made transportation easier and social media made instant mobilization possible. The ACOA's efforts resulted in a minor victory when Congressman Diggs announced that he had obtained a Civil Aeronautics Board ruling prohibiting SAA from advertising any segregated facilities in the United States.

The ACOA won another victory when New York City's Commission on Human Rights, in a case brought by the ACOA, enjoined the *New York Times* from printing advertisements for employment in South Africa because of their racially discriminatory practices, illegal under New York City law. Additional tactics to bring attention to the rogue regime were ones Houser had adapted from his days in CORE such as a "stand-in" at SAA reminiscent of the stand-ins pioneered by Houser in the 1940s at movie theaters and roller-skating rinks. Some small victories were won through the ACOA's efforts to stigmatize traffic with South Africa. The United States cancelled port calls by its ships in South Africa rather than accept the racial conditions imposed by the apartheid regime. Reacting to the negative publicity they might get, some media outlets refused to accept SAA advertising; and publicity about Holiday Inn's decision to open facilities in South Africa resulted in its decision not to publicize these facilities in the United States.

To support its grassroots work on exposing US economic support for South Africa, the ACOA had published in 1966 a special issue of *Africa Today* on "American Involvement in the South African Economy." This was followed in 1970 with "Apartheid and Imperialism: A Study of U.S. Corporate Involvement in Africa."[28] Without the benefit of either computers or the internet, Research Director Jennifer Davis of the ACOA and a host of volunteers had by now developed a sophisticated research operation. Data from a wide range of sources was used: US government and UN documents, internal documents from the governments and movements in question, articles from a variety of foreign presses, and specialized studies. These data were combined with an astute understanding of how institutional racism and colonialism operated to demonstrate the yawning gap between the euphemistic rhetoric of governments and corporations and the reality on the ground. The value of such research to the anticolonial support movement has not been widely enough recognized.

That same year, ACOA became the most important ally of a small group of Polaroid employees who called themselves the Polaroid Revolutionary Workers' Movement. These workers had discovered that Polaroid had been furnishing the technology used to make the hated identification passes black South Africans were required to carry. With its ability to disseminate information about what Polaroid was doing to its national network of activists, the ACOA was able to amplify the voices of the Polaroid Revolutionary Workers' Movement beyond their base in Boston, thus exerting pressure on the corporation. Publicly embarrassed, Polaroid directors sought to maintain their liberal image but were reluctant to give up their South African market. They responded with a promise to ban all sales to the government, military, and police and would train black employees for important positions, commit a portion of their profits to black education, raise black wages, and make a grant to bring some blacks to the United States in an exchange program. In a carefully reasoned article in the *Christian Century* and in a *New York Times* op-ed, Houser pointed out that the "Polaroid approach" would provide the rationale for many American companies that wanted to stay and even expand their businesses under the false assumption that they could help end apartheid while making a profit.[29]

The attack on Polaroid made headlines in the South African papers, some of which blamed the demonic influence of the ACOA.[30] ACOA and its allies would continue the pressure until 1977, when it learned from a South African Polaroid employee that its South African distributor had been secretly selling Polaroid film and cameras to a South African government agency in violation of a 1971 agreement.[31] With the ACOA's exposure of this information, Polaroid announced on November 21, 1977, that it was pulling out of South Africa completely, the first company to do so. Polaroid credited the ACOA for its decision.

AN ASSESSMENT OF THE LIBERATION MOVEMENTS IN SOUTHERN AFRICA

Toward the end of 1968 Houser made another trip to Africa for the purpose of getting a firsthand look at projects that the Africa Fund was helping to support but also to renew old contacts with African leadership and to check on developments that were impossible to follow closely enough from New York. In a confidential assessment of the liberation movements in southern Africa made to his board, Houser revealed the delicacy with which he approached discussions with liberation movement leaders:

> In spite of the fact that I have known many of the leaders of the
> various movements for many years, a person who is trying to
> look too closely into what is being done in the struggle or in the
> preparation for it can be looked upon with great suspicion. . . .
> Knowing this, I am fairly careful how I talk even with old friends. I
> don't press for inside information on the military situation. I don't
> ask to visit military training camps. I don't seek information on the
> minutiae of tactics involved in the struggle. If any facts regarding
> these security matters emerge, I don't talk about them and I certainly
> do not put them in writing. If something is told me in confidence,
> I keep it in confidence. Nevertheless, certain impressions emerge
> which I can pass on for whatever they are worth.[32]

One of the most important findings from his trip was that the plight of political refugees from southern Africa was becoming increasingly difficult. Refugees who were members of liberation movements recognized by the OAU found support in liberated countries as "freedom fighters," but unaffiliated or dissident individuals were having a much harder time. Prior to 1963, such nonaffiliated refugees were welcomed everywhere. In those years, aid from outside Africa was available. But with the realization that change would be a long time coming, such aid had been cut back, and the resources in most African countries were inadequate even for their own people.[33] From Tanzania, Houser wrote to his board president, Peter Weiss: "We must not only help political refugees, but also must tell the story of why there are refugees."[34] This is a sentiment that could be applied to today's US refugee crisis.

As to ACOA's capacity to affect change in southern Africa, Houser was characteristically modest: "American private groups cannot hope to run competition with the kind of overwhelming support coming through governments. Therefore, we should act in accordance with what we are. . . . Our commitment is to the struggle for freedom and not to any particular leader or particular faction. . . . We cannot act as if we were supplying overwhelming support either financially or materially. Therefore, we cannot really be a decisive factor in the internal struggles of the various movements."[35]

A FOCUS ON PORTUGUESE AFRICA

That the struggle for freedom in southern Africa would be long and hard was brought home to Houser once again in early 1969. He received a phone call with the shattering news that Eduardo Mondlane, president of FRELIMO, had been assassinated by a Portuguese parcel bomb sent to FRELIMO's office by the Portuguese secret police, who had managed to infiltrate FRELIMO.

Houser organized memorial services for Mondlane in New York and Washington, DC. He also provided the opening remarks at the New York service in February 1969: "Eduardo had it made, we might say. . . . He could have lived a comfortable life in the U.S. and talked about revolution. He could have been a successful professor in innumerable universities in the U.S., Britain. . . . But Eduardo shunned these easy solutions to his life work. It was not of any simple necessity that Eduardo returned to Africa to engage in the struggle. He chose to do it. This led to his tragic death, but much more important is the fact that this gave ultimate meaning to his life."[36] These remarks about shunning a comfortable life for one of uncertainty in the struggle for freedom could have been said about Houser himself.

Perhaps jolted by Mondlane's death into recognizing that by being focused on South Africa he had been neglecting the continuing struggle in Portuguese Africa, Houser decided that for the next year they should place a major emphasis on ending the US military alliance with Portugal and supporting the liberation movements in Portuguese territories, while continuing work on the South African initiatives they had begun. In support of this emphasis, the executive board approved a budget of $188,861, the largest it had ever tried to raise since its inception. In December 1971, the Nixon administration announced that it was giving $435 million to Portugal in exchange for use of the Azores as a military base. An essential part of the ACOA campaign, then, would be to end American military support for Portuguese colonial domination as well as to discourage growing US economic involvement.

The ACOA staff's focus on Portuguese territories produced a series of spot radio announcements beamed primarily to the black community in New York, Chicago, and Washington, DC, aimed at educating listeners on the issues of the freedom struggle and stimulating action. The FRELIMO representative in the United States, Sharfudine Khan, was also given financial and logistical support for office space, travel, a speaking schedule, and contacts in Washington, DC. As the principal American company involved in the Portuguese colonies, the Gulf Oil Corporation became a major focus of ACOA's divestment work. In April 1970 the ACOA sent three dozen protesters inside the Gulf shareholders meeting in Pittsburgh while four hundred protesters picketed and leafletted outside. "Amid loud shouting and occasional ejections of demonstrators Gulf Oil struggled through a two-hour annual meeting," the *Wall Street Journal* reported.[37] Inside, protesters armed with proxies, submitted for symbolic nomination to the Gulf board, MPLA President Dr. Agostinho Neto and the PAIGC's Amílcar Cabral.[38]

While Gulf's security detail kept the demonstrators short of their goals, the ACOA's efforts were but the opening wedge in a decades-long campaign to expose the role of these giant corporations in contributing to oppression in Africa.[39] Universities that invested in Gulf stock and allowed recruiting by Gulf Oil on their campuses became another target of the campaign. The ACOA and its allies issued a call to boycott Gulf products and to return Gulf credit cards. By 1973, the Gulf Oil boycott had expanded nationally. Gulf responded by attempting to intimidate people not to give the movement their proxies and by sending spies into various meetings of the antiapartheid groups.[40]

A fourth area of work on the Portuguese territories was exposure of the military and economic ties between Portugal and the United States. A special issue of *Africa Today* provided evidence of the falsity of the US claim that its military and economic ties to Portugal related solely to NATO defense purposes and had nothing to do with its wars in Africa.[41]

RETURN TO AFRICA

From May through August of 1970, Houser found himself again back in Africa. Houser's trip included stops in nine countries as well as a stop in Rome, where he and Prexy Nesbitt, a member of the ACOA staff with strong ties to the black liberation struggle in both the United States and Africa, attended the International Conference in Support of the Peoples of Portuguese Colonies. Among the leaders he met with were Oliver Tambo; President Kenneth Kaunda of Zambia; newly elected MPLA president, Samora Machel; and Diallo Telli, first president of the OAU, as well as his old friends Bill Sutherland; Mondlane's widow, Janet; and Mboya's widow, Pamela.[42] As always in his African travels, Houser was besieged by requests for help. He delivered a $25,000 check from the Africa Fund for a PAIGC hospital and $1,000 to ZAPU for the Zimbabwe African People's Welfare Trust, but upon learning that ZANU had a similar fund, he told himself he would have to send a check to them as well; and he was obliged to give out small amounts of money to refugees he ran into who were stranded without funds.

By now, the grand vision of revolutionary Pan-Africanism was losing its luster. Africa's first two presidents, Kwame Nkrumah and Sékou Touré of Guinea, had both become increasingly autocratic. Touré had "set aside his youthful dreams of creating a utopian socialist state and become a vengeful tyrant who tortured his real or perceived opponents,"[43] while Nkrumah, the father of Pan-Africanism, had made some disastrous economic decisions and was developing some autocratic tendencies of his own. Ousted by a military coup in 1966, he was now living in exile in Conakry as Touré's honorary vice president.

From several sources Houser gathered the impression that Holden Roberto was in trouble. Not only was there animosity toward his increasing authoritarianism within the FNLA/GRAE, but his troops had killed about forty MPLA militants. "This is shocking, to me," Houser lamented, "but I suppose I shouldn't be surprised. I suspected it all along. This kind of enmity spells tragic difficulties ahead for Angola."[44] Earlier suspicions about Roberto had not deterred him from supporting the FNLA/GRAE since the OAU had recognized the movement as legitimate, and it was not yet clear which of the three movements in Angola would emerge the winner.[45] Houser's support for Roberto could also have been conditioned by the kindness he experienced from the UPA guerrillas on his trek through rebel territory and by his effort to work with the AFL-CIO which supported Roberto.[46] Now, however, his belief in Roberto as a legitimate leader of the liberation movement in Angola was shaken.

MULTIRACIAL LIBERALISM MEETS A TEST

While Houser was away from the office for four months, a controversy had arisen over the focus of the ACOA, reflecting differences between the old guard, who had come of age within the liberal pacifist-oriented multiracialism of the civil rights movement and a younger cohort who had been nurtured in the turbulent era of Black Nationalism and anti-imperialist protest. One of these was Rozelle (Prexy) Nesbitt. As a college student he had spent a year studying at University College in Dar es Salaam, Tanzania. Nesbitt had once flirted with joining FRELIMO as a militant. Instead he went to work for about a year between 1968 and early 1970 at the FRELIMO-sponsored Mozambique Institute. Here he would meet many of the leading figures in the liberation struggle in southern Africa.[47]

Between 1970 and 1971 Nesbitt was brought on to the ACOA staff to do Midwest fieldwork in his hometown of Chicago through a one-year grant from a group of African activists who felt the ACOA was too limited to the East Coast. His focus was to work with young African Americans and progressive whites, whose communities he described as a "media wasteland." In outlining his approach to this work, Nesbitt argued that the ACOA needed to develop more popular modes of communicating with the younger generation.[48] Nesbitt's work in Chicago began to take on a more radical coloration than the more measured rhetoric emanating from ACOA's home office in New York.

At an ACOA executive board meeting in September 1970, Nesbitt surfaced some difficulties he was having with the way the ACOA was operating. He complained about a letter the ACOA steering committee had sent to its Washington director, Charles Hightower, asking Hightower to withdraw a statement he had made criticizing some other African Americans who had signed a full-page *New York Times* advertisement in June in support of Israel. Hightower's statement had hit a raw nerve in Washington. The *Washington Star* reported that "the fragile alliance of anti-apartheid forces in Washington has been blown apart by an intemperate attack on six Negro congressmen for their support of Israel which was published at the week-end by the Washington office of the anti-apartheid American Committee on Africa. White liberals and Jews on Capitol Hill, especially those who have been active supporters of ACOA, were stunned and angered by the attack."[49]

It was clear that for the ACOA criticism of Israel was a delicate subject for some of its Jewish board members. The ad had been sponsored by the A. Philip Randolph Institute and signed by several people Houser had worked closely with over the years. In addition to Randolph, they included Congressman Charles Diggs, Bayard Rustin, Frank Montero, and Jackie Robinson.[50] A counter ad was subsequently drafted by several radical black Americans who objected to American military support for Israel. Appearing in the *New York Times* in November, the ad stated that the signers were not anti-Jewish but anti-Zionist. Charles Hightower was among the signers as was Bob Van

Lierop, a member of the ACOA board, and Conrad Lynn, Houser's neighbor and one of the riders on the Journey of Reconciliation. A division that had developed within the black community over Israel was now erupting within the ACOA itself.[51] The controversy forced the board to issue a policy statement that ACOA policy positions from then on were to be confined to the liberation struggle in Africa and American responsibilities vis-à-vis Africa generally and southern Africa in particular. ACOA representatives who wished to speak on issues not within this purview were to do so only in their personal capacity.[52]

A larger bone of contention was Houser's policy of maintaining neutrality among the contending liberation movements, especially in Angola. According to Nesbitt, most of the staff felt that Houser should take a more ideological approach to choosing which groups to support.[53] In the circles Nesbitt moved in, the MPLA was the favored movement. Why, for instance, was Houser supporting Holden Roberto when the MPLA was the legitimate Angolan liberation movement? The ACOA's lack of clear policy and politics was making Nesbitt's fieldwork difficult as was the perception among militant blacks that the ACOA was a white racist organization and perhaps even had CIA ties. Nesbitt argued that a special meeting of the board was needed to iron out these issues.[54] Such issues were to occupy several months of intense discussion within the organization.

Suspicion of the ACOA among radical Black Nationalists had probably arisen because of ACOA's perceived anti-Communism and Houser's tendency to work with anyone he deemed devoted to the cause of African liberation. This included known anti-Communists both in the United States and South Africa, some of whom, like Roberto, were suspected of having CIA ties. A book that had been published in Cuba and that circulated in leftist circles identified Houser as linked to the CIA because of his support for UNITA and the FNLA. Houser may perhaps be forgiven for his naiveté in supporting those who turned out to be untrustworthy. In the treacherous environment of Cold War politics it was the business of the CIA and powers like Portugal and South Africa to sow suspicion and discord among and between liberation movements, but it was not always easy to discern who could be trusted. African Americans as well as Africans themselves could fall victim to such manipulation. Even SWAPO, according to Houser, spoke "well" of UNITA in 1972.[55]

In a subsequent memo to the board, Houser responded to Nesbitt's critique in his characteristically forthright but nonaccusatory manner.[56] Nevertheless, Nesbitt's memo had raised troubling questions for Houser and the ACOA's direction in an era of increasing contestation between black and white radicalism and white liberalism. The following month, a special board meeting was held to discuss the ACOA's overall direction and policy. The discussion that ensued was the most intense of any of the board meetings. Peter Weiss, then president of the ACOA, stated that some of the questions raised in Nesbitt's report (presumably those about Israel) had been raised before and that the ACOA had compromised in the past over these issues because of related financial considerations. On the issue of the racial composition and orientation of ACOA, he noted that in the past it had been a white liberal organization that behaved paternalistically toward the black community before realizing that black people had to work things out for themselves. Perhaps, he argued, it was time for a black executive director. One board member suggested that there had been some fear of a "black takeover" of the ACOA. Others argued that the issue wasn't having an African American director but rather the relationship between a liberal executive board that sets policy and a more radical staff who had little input into policy. Houser, on the other hand, argued that most of the program initiatives came from the staff and then were taken to the board for action. Another argued that ACOA policy must come to terms with the strong growth of knowledge and awareness in the black community about African issues such as the odd role of Israel in Africa—most especially as an ally of South Africa.

As to the ACOA's neutrality regarding liberation movements, some argued that there had to be some firm criteria upon which decisions could be made as to which groups merited the ACOA's support. Houser admitted that there was a need for in-depth discussions about the groups, nevertheless asserting that a position of neutrality did have viability. It is not always easy, he argued, to determine which group has the most political support, as situations change over time. The arguments were not settled, and by the end of the meeting a decision was made to set up a subcommittee composed of representatives of both the board and staff to come up with some clear policy proposals around both decision making and political posture vis-à-vis the liberation movements.[57]

In a subsequent board meeting Houser responded to the sub-rosa subject behind this series of contentious meetings: the issue of continuing white liberal leadership of a movement devoted to the support of radical African self-determination. He pointed out that in the last several years there had been an emphasis on having black staff. He had not seen this in terms of a "black take-over," but if there were a time when that should happen, it would. Despite talk about disagreements among the staff, he averred that there had been agreement and unity on the policies and programs. If that changed, he would be ready to step down.[58]

But there had not been agreement and unity. By the end of 1970, the criteria for choosing "sides" among liberation movements had not been settled, and a special meeting of the board with program staff attending was set for the following February 1972. Houser opened this meeting with a discussion of some of the considerations that had guided his relationships with African independence movements over the years. The situation in Angola, he pointed out, lent itself most readily to making choices. He admitted that circumstances in Angola had changed and that the UPA-GRAE had weakened: as a result, the MPLA was now the most viable movement with popular support. "But in each case," he argued, "the historical situation must be taken into account." Still, Houser argued that he had to deal with people from the different groups as individuals; he did not want to be in a position of having to shut the door on them purely on the grounds that ACOA had made policy decisions to support only certain groups. Houser had, for example, been supporting a school run by the FNLA/GRAE. Was he to stop supporting children now that the GRAE had been demoted in favor of the MPLA? Here was the Christian liberal, always seeking to meet humanitarian need regardless of ideological clarity. By the end of the meeting, the board had voted to make the MPLA the primary recipient of support, leaving it up to further discussions about what "primary" meant.[59] In fact, Houser had begun to communicate with Neto and had already sent $1,000 from the Africa Fund for the MPLA's medical needs. In the following month, Houser would send another $3,000 and invite Neto to come to the United States for a speaking tour. From then on Houser would continue to be in contact with both Roberto and the UPA/GRAE and Neto and the MPLA, sending funds to each and writing that he hoped they could find a path to unity.

In July of 1971 Houser announced to his board that Prexy Nesbitt would be leaving the ACOA staff to continue his academic studies.[60] Nesbitt's memory of why he left the staff after only a year is at odds with the ostensible reason given by Houser. Nesbitt's recollection was that Houser was to have matched the money that had been raised by the group of African activists so that he could continue after the one-year grant ran out. That money was apparently not raised, which upset those initial funders who had hoped Nesbitt could continue.[61] Perhaps this was because Houser had been uncomfortable with Nesbitt's rather freewheeling work in Chicago, or the fact that, as Nesbitt recalled, the two had had intense arguments over Houser's support for Holden Roberto and Jonas Savimbi (UNITA).[62] Or perhaps Houser's four-month leave of absence had not left him time to raise the requisite amount. In fact, the budget for 1970 was again in the red, and the payroll due on December 2 could not be met.[63]

Houser told his board that Nesbitt's work in Chicago had been valuable in bringing southern Africa news to the Chicago community and campuses, and the two men parted on friendly terms. It was hard to get mad at Houser. One could disagree with him over political issues, but he always deserved credit for his total dedication to the cause over so many years. "While I disagreed with George on these questions I also had an immense respect for George," Nesbitt told this author many years later.[64] Houser also apparently had respect for Nesbitt, as he brought him back later in that decade to run the ACOA's bank campaign.

Nesbitt's work in Chicago had raised an issue that had been kicking around within the ACOA for a few years but had been left unresolved. That was the question of whether the organization could or should support fieldworkers. Some short-term fieldwork projects had been carried out in New Jersey and Brooklyn, but there was never enough money to fund a full-fledged fieldwork operation. A special executive board meeting in March 1972 decided that while fieldwork programs were needed and could have positive results, the ACOA could not handle the task of funding local fieldworkers; however, it could try to work with local groups to raise money and provide a portion of the fieldworker funding.[65] Following Nesbitt's departure, the ACOA would provide a token amount for the maintenance of a storefront literature library on Africa in Chicago, run by volunteer Eileen Hanson who took over the work Nesbitt had been doing there.

In June 1971 the ACOA issued a brief report on the status of the liberation movements. The report gave assessments of each of the movements in the six countries still waging wars for independence. The report characterized the MPLA as "the most successful" resistance movement, with a reported eleven thousand troops in 1970 and control of one third of the country.[66] The journals Houser had kept containing records of his conversations in Africa with dozens of people reflect far more drama and intrigue than the rather dry statistics marshalled for the public report. He had been privy to the infighting and splits that were then occurring among the various liberation movements and personalities. Houser's penchant for talking with all sides to a controversy, seen by some as politically incorrect, had actually enabled him to gain a deeper understanding than many of his contemporaries of the trials Africa was undergoing as it sought to overcome its colonial past and chart a different future. However, he was reluctant to air these internal conflicts in the midst of southern Africa's ongoing struggles against a more pernicious enemy. Instead, Houser saved them for the more detailed account he was to give almost two decades later in his book, *Nothing Can Stop the Rain*.

In May 1972 Houser left for another trip abroad. He attended a conference in Brussels on the Namibian situation (organized by SWAPO), had meetings in London with a number of groups and individuals, and then attended the OAU meeting in Rabat, Morocco, followed by visits to Lusaka, Dar es Salaam, and Nairobi. He again visited with Zambian president Kenneth Kaunda and Tanzanian president Julius Nyerere. Nyerere expressed deep interest in the disengagement issue and asked Houser for background materials on activities of US corporations in southern Africa. From discussions with these leaders he was now more convinced than ever that the ACOA's decision to back the MPLA, a decision he had long balked at, was the correct one.[67]

A SECOND ATTEMPT TO ENTER NAMIBIA

From Kinshasa, Houser attempted for a second time to fly to Namibia, which had once again claimed his attention after twelve thousand contract laborers had begun a sustained strike in December 1971, bringing the mining industry to a near standstill with little notice from the outside world. On June 21, 1971, the International Court of Justice had handed down its advisory opinion on Namibia, ruling that the illegality of South Africa's continued presence in Namibia after the termination of its mandate in 1966 obliged other states to recognize South Africa's illegality there and to refrain from dealings with South Africa that would imply recognition of or support for South Africa's administration of Namibia. Testifying to the UN Council on Namibia in January 1972, Houser gave the information he had obtained about the strike from his sources inside the tightly sealed country, urging the council to widen its immediate and long-term action to support Namibia's people.

Without waiting for UN action, the ACOA had engaged in its own support efforts, circulating a fact sheet on Namibia, calling on the US government through a visit to George H. W. Bush, then UN ambassador, to support the World Court decision. ACOA also issued a public call to two American mining companies, the Newmont Mining Corporation and American Metal Climax, to stop their exploitation of African workers. Together the two companies owned Tsumeb, the largest base mineral mine and other properties in Namibia. The ACOA also threatened to support a congressional inquiry into the companies' mining practices. In February, the committee convened a press conference outside the corporate headquarters of Newmont Mining. Five members of the Congressional Black Caucus, along with Theo-Ben

Gurirab of SWAPO, South African attorney Joel Carlson, a member of the International Committee of Jurists, and representatives of other organizations called on the mining company to recognize the United Nations as the lawful authority in Namibia. In a meeting afterward with company representatives, these members requested an end to cooperation with the illegal administration of South Africa.[68]

In March, Judge William H. Booth, head of New York City's Commission on Human Rights and newly elected ACOA board president, was commissioned by the International Commission of Jurists to observe the trial in Windhoek of ten striking workers who had been arrested by the South African government. Upon his return he testified to the UN on what he had learned as well as appearing on radio and TV and at a public meeting arranged by the ACOA. That same month the ACOA's Africa Fund, in conjunction with the World Council of Churches Programme to Combat Racism, published a thirty-three-page pamphlet detailing US corporate involvement in the Namibian economy, especially in mining, which was experiencing a boom in Namibia.[69]

As before, Houser sought to test South Africa's compliance with UN resolutions and the opinion of the World Court, knowing full well that his announced visit would likely set the South African security apparatus into operation. For his second effort to enter Namibia, Houser decided he would not attempt another risky flight. This time he would try to travel on a commercial Pan-American flight to South Africa, where he would have to switch to South African Airways since SAA was the only airline that flew into Namibia. He would travel on a visa that had been issued by the UN, the first such visa issued to anyone for entry into Namibia but one that the US State Department refused to recognize.

He had not tried to get a South African visa, which would have been impossible. But he had been told that transit visitors at Jan Smuts airport did not need a visa. While prepared for being refused entry to Namibia, he was a bit surprised by a certain newspaper article on the front page of the *Zambia Times* the day before his scheduled departure. The article stated that the South African government would not allow him beyond the airport at Johannesburg and that it was unlikely that a recognized airline would allow him to board in Kinshasa without a South African visa.[70] He was to discover later that the story had appeared in the press all over Africa.

On the morning of June 14, 1972, Houser arrived at the airport in Kinshasa and was met by the airport manager who informed him that the South African government had told Pan-Am in South Africa that he should not be permitted to board the plane without a South African visa. The manager said that South Africa was exercising the right of "no transit without visa." This was unusual, he said, but Pan-Am had to abide by it or risk being fined by the South African government. The following day Houser met with the Pan-Am airport services manager and gave him a fuller explanation of his position, handing him a letter protesting Pan-Am's action. During his conversation he learned that the airline's New York headquarters had given their office in Kinshasa instructions on how to handle the situation and considerable background about him and the ACOA.[71]

Once again, Houser's attempt to enter Namibia had been thwarted. But the real purpose of his gambit—to expose South Africa's defiance—had not failed. Although the US press ignored Houser's exploit, press accounts of his aborted trip appeared all over Africa and in the British press.[72] While persona non grata in South Africa, Houser was given surprisingly positive coverage by the *Johannesburg Star*, given the fact that newspapers during that time were embedded in the apartheid system and closely monitored by the government. Detailing his entire biography, the paper portrayed him as a David going up against Goliath, in a struggle "that indicates a strength of conviction deeper than any desire for self-aggrandizement":

> For all the radicalism and liberal bigotry that conservative South
> Africans may see in his actions, Mr. Houser is no wild-eyed fanatic.
> Certainly his manner does not give this impression. His speech
> is quiet, even when appealing to a United Nations committee for
> impossibly tough action against South Africa. His movements are
> deliberate and his short frame is always conservatively clothed.
> Whatever passions might burn beneath his stolid exterior to drive
> him to seemingly desperate ventures like the South West Africa
> "fly-in," Mr. Houser at least gives an outward impression of calm
> sincerity.[73]

The South African writer seems to have gotten it just right.

BEHIND THE LINES IN GUINEA-BISSAU

In summer 1973 Houser made another trip to Africa, this time for six weeks. His itinerary included Guinea, Tanzania, Zambia, Zaire, and Liberia and had meetings scheduled with almost every liberation movement leader, including those of Guinea-Bissau, Mozambique, Zimbabwe, Namibia, Angola, and South Africa, as well as with government officials in Zambia and Tanzania. A highlight was a visit to the liberated areas of Guinea-Bissau. This visit was particularly poignant as Amílcar Cabral, the continent's most visionary leader, had been assassinated at the beginning of the year by PAIGC liberation fighters to whom Portuguese officials had promised high positions in a new Portuguese-friendly regime.[74] In Conakry, Guinea Houser met with Cabral's widow, Ana Maria Cabral, and learned of the hair-raising circumstances of Cabral's assassination from Aristides Pereira, one of the six founding members of the PAIGC, who had been with Cabral and had himself narrowly escaped being delivered to the Portuguese. Pereira would succeed Cabral as Secretary General of the PAIGC. Other PAIGC officials told him of the esteem in which they held their fallen leader: "I was told that one of his greatest contributions to the movement was the spirit in which he dealt with people. One of the leaders told me that he never recalls Amilcar losing his head in anger. This person said that whenever others of them occasionally were in bitter argument, Amilcar would say, 'if we who are working here together cannot love one another how can we expect to love the people whom we are trying to serve in Guinea Bissau whom we can't even see now.'"[75]

Three years earlier, Houser had arranged a US speaking tour for Cabral, and just two months before Cabral's assassination, Houser had hosted a small gathering in a Manhattan apartment for him when he came to the United States. There, Cabral had spoken eloquently of the deep chord of friendship that had been struck with these intrepid American supporters of liberation. "For me," said Cabral, "it is a pleasure to be here with you, friends of our people in the struggle, people that we view as our brothers and sisters. This meeting helps us better to know what constitutes our dream of America—all kinds of people, simply seated on the floor with the heart and the head, dedicated to the marvelous adventure of man in this controversial planet, very simply man and woman. Our hearts, maybe more than our heads, have the same rhythms of pulsation."[76]

After Cabral's death, Houser wrote that the African continent had lost a man of "almost unparalleled ability" and that "no leader of a liberation movement in Africa has spelled out the essential theory of political organization more clearly than has Cabral."[77] "Cabral combined a pragmatism with an unusual humanitarianism," Houser continued, "he opposed terrorist methods that might endanger the lives of innocent people. He believed optimistically in the possibility of rehabilitating the defectors from the party, even those who later killed him. He was always open to a political rather than a violent solution to their liberation struggle."[78] It had been just four years earlier that another visionary leader, Eduardo Mondlane, had been assassinated. For Houser, the tragedies were beginning to pile up.

Before dawn on June 19, 1973, Houser and several PAIGC leaders took off from Conakry for a trip inside PAIGC territory in Guinea-Bissau in an armored Land Rover and jeep to a base camp on the border at a place called Kandiafara. The ten-hour trip took them over rough roads: the last three hours of the journey Houser described as the stony bottom of a not quite dry mountain streambed. Since it was the rainy season, the vehicles were sometimes under water. Remembering his earlier foray into UPA guerrilla territory on foot, Houser considered that the road, however bumpy, was a lot better than a long hike. Just two days before, the camp had been bombed by the Portuguese. Houser saw several wounded civilians being operated on in a nearby PAIGC "hospital" beneath a canopy of trees that protected them from Portuguese planes. From there his party traveled further inland to a Portuguese military camp on a road that was littered with burned-out jeeps and trucks, which was a testament to the strength of the PAIGC. They had captured the twenty-two-acre military base in order to prevent the Portuguese from returning. The PAIGC had destroyed everything but the airstrip, a generator, and a six-month food supply that was now being put to use. Barely ten miles away Houser could hear the guns of another battle in progress. This trip, he wrote, "was a grim reminder that a war was going on."[79]

In the wake of Cabral's death, Houser was pleased to find that Cabral had his people well prepared for independence. Inside PAIGC-controlled areas he witnessed nation-building projects such as a network of schools, hospitals, and trading centers called "People's Shops" through which the people were able to trade what they themselves produced and other needed items that were supplied by friendly countries, such as Holland, Sweden, Norway, Cuba, East Germany, and a number of Eastern European nations. Houser was deeply impressed by the communal living arrangements that PAIGC leaders and workers had developed in which everything was shared, and everyone took some responsibility for the welfare of the group. In a jungle setting in Africa perhaps he had discovered the fulfillment of the youthful dream he once had for his own life while in prison in Danbury.

On September 24, 1973, the Republic of Guinea-Bissau was proclaimed by its leaders. By the end of the year the new nation was recognized by seventy-five countries. The United States, however, was not one of them. Accordingly, the ACOA formed an ad hoc committee to support the Republic of Guinea-Bissau with the names of seventy-seven prominent Americans as sponsors. The committee would work to organize citizen support for the new republic and for US support for its membership in the UN.

DESPITE THE ACOA'S HEROIC EFFORTS to support the liberation movements and challenge apartheid, the number of Americans across the country
who paid ample attention to what was happening in Africa was still relatively
small. Civil rights activists were preoccupied with the fight for their own
liberation, and the war in Southeast Asia was commanding the attention of
many others. The ACOA and its dedicated band of Africanists was hardly a
match for the well-funded white racist groups that mobilized to influence US
Africa policy, but for Houser, the ACOA's work was still needed. This David
would continue to catapult his stones at Goliath, making a few dents in its
armor but never quite felling the giant.

Some of the Toughest Battles Still Lie Ahead, 1974–80

ON APRIL 25, 1974, A RADICAL FACTION WITHIN THE PORTUGUESE Armed Forces, demoralized by the futility of the African wars that had drained the financial and human resources of the most underdeveloped country in Europe, revolted against the authoritarian regime of Prime Minister Marcelo Caetano. This revolt established a new socialist and democratic government committed to civil liberties for its citizens and independence for its colonies.[1] For Portugal's African colonies, as for the populace at home, the lifting of over four hundred years of authoritarian rule unleashed a space for democratic forces that had long been suppressed. The event would have far-ranging consequences for the geopolitics of southern Africa.

The Portuguese coup had taken everyone by surprise, particularly Houser. A month after the event he wrote a lengthy memo to his board speculating on what the coup might mean for Portugal's African colonies and for the work of the ACOA.

> The liberation movements have been geared to a protracted conflict
> in which their nation-building activities were part and parcel of their
> armed struggle. They will continue to need all the help they can
> get both in support of their demand for independence and in their
> national reconstruction work. . . . We hope that the time for ACOA
> to decide whether to close up shop will come in the future, but it
> is not here yet. The issues we have related to have not been solved.
> Some of the toughest battles still lie ahead.[2]

Five months before the coup, Guinea-Bissau had proclaimed its status as an independent state and was recognized by seventy countries. Now Guinea-Bissau could take its seat in the United Nations unless blocked by the United States, which was still refusing to recognize the new reality. The

ACOA quickly formed the ad hoc Committee to Support the Republic of Guinea-Bissau, which declared a kind of people's recognition of a sovereign nation and called on its supporters to pressure the US government not to use its Security Council veto to block Guinea-Bissau's membership. The call was supported by seventy-five prominent people and organizations.[3] Recognizing a fait accompli when Portugal recognized the new republic, the Ford administration followed suit, officially recognizing it on September 10, 1974. The ACOA celebrated Guinea-Bissau's new international status with a public celebration on September 24, 1974.

In fall 1965, six months after the Portuguese coup, Houser embarked on his eighteenth trip to Africa, invited by President Kenneth Kaunda to attend the tenth anniversary celebration of Zambia's independence, all expenses paid. He characterized the mood of most of the existing liberation movement leaders he met with as one of "great expectations," but unlike the mood that prevailed in 1960, it was "not based on the false premise that independence and freedom will be handed to the people from some force outside of themselves."[4]

In Dar es Salaam, Houser sat down with Janet Mondlane and Samora Moisés Machel. After Mondlane's death, Machel had been elected president of FRELIMO following a leadership crisis.[5] From them Houser learned of the uphill battle Mozambique would face once independence was declared. The economy and the land itself had been devastated not only by colonial rule but also by war, massive floods, and locust infestations. Moreover, a mass exodus of Portuguese professionals was causing a shortage of trained people in schools and hospitals. In addition, Mozambique's leaders had inherited an import-dependent economy, one that was geared to trade with its sworn enemies, South Africa and Rhodesia. Its desperate economy also depended on the remittances Mozambican migrant labor sent home from South Africa as one of its few sources of foreign exchange. Mozambique would need a great deal of help, far more than Houser's small organization could possibly provide. Nevertheless, at Machel's invitation, he was determined to visit Mozambique the following year to see what the needs were and how the ACOA could assist. Houser was impressed with Machel: "Everything about him seemed dynamic—his ideas, his easy laughter and many gestures, his erect and rapid walking pace. He did not like to talk about himself. When I asked about his personal background, he responded, 'That is not important. What is important is the movement! . . . We don't believe in personality cults.'"[6] Houser also wrote that Machel was "a forceful, engaging, unpretentious person who gives strong leadership to FRELIMO and no doubt will to the government of Mozambique."[7]

All of the Zimbabweans Houser talked with felt that the Smith regime's days were numbered, as it was taking ever more desperate measures against its perceived enemies. The two independence movements, ZANU and ZAPU, were still operating independently. It remained to be seen if a viable movement for independence could thwart Ian Smith's determination to cling to power. As for South Africa, no one Houser talked with felt optimistic about changes in the country itself.

On June 25, 1975, Mozambique declared its independence. Paul Irish, an ACOA staff member, attended the independence celebrations, the ACOA being one of the few American organizations invited. In New York, the ACOA sponsored a reception in honor of the Mozambique delegation to the United Nations and a meeting in celebration of Mozambican independence. The ACOA also issued a seventy-one-page booklet entitled *Mozambique: Dream the Size of Freedom*. Authored by Houser and Herb Shore, the publication detailed the history of Portuguese colonialism and FRELIMO's struggle for independence.[8]

On November 11, 1975, Agostinho Neto, in the name of the MPLA, declared Angola's independence. But the prospects for a peaceful transition did not look hopeful. In departing, Portugal had failed to designate any party as its legitimate government. Moreover, Portugal's retreat had left a resource-rich country with an 85–90 percent illiteracy rate.[9] Mozambique's rate was, if anything, even higher. But FRELIMO had made a concerted effort to reduce it, and within five years the adult rate would drop from 97 percent to almost 72 percent.[10] Mondlane's leadership and the relative political unity established in Mozambique as compared with Angola explain the difference. Even after the Portuguese coup, the three Angolan movements—the FNLA, MPLA, and UNITA—continued to fight each other. Their competitiveness was complicated not only because Portugal had prohibited political relationships among Africans during their colonial domination but also because of the influence of outside forces that were pulling each movement in different directions.

Prior to the coup, Prime Minister Vorster had thought that the decolonization process in southern Africa could be managed, repeatedly emphasizing Pretoria's desire to work with whatever regimes came to power in Angola and Mozambique. However, the coup had raised fears of Communist influence and possibly even military bases on South Africa's border as well as terrorist incursions into South Africa, especially among hardliners. Vorster, however, thought South Africa could be given breathing space to resolve its internal problems. In a policy that came to be known as "détente," he volunteered to sign nonaggression pacts with any African state, signaled that he wanted to help resolve the Rhodesian civil war, and dangled economic aid and trade concessions in front of black-led states. This would help soften South Africa's image in the UN and elsewhere and hopefully stave off greater sanctions that could cripple its economy.[11] But to Houser and his discussants, the contradictions between South Africa's attempt to appear conciliatory toward black Africa belied the escalating repression inside the country.[12]

Houser's skepticism about South Africa's appearance of change was soon validated when the Vorster and Smith regimes began a counterinsurgency campaign in Mozambique and Angola, exploiting differences within the countries. Barely free of Portuguese oppression, Mozambique was plunged into war again, this time fomented by Rhodesia in retaliation for Mozambique's harboring of Zimbabwean guerrillas fighting for majority rule in Rhodesia. The vehicle was a counterinsurgency force sponsored by the Rhodesian Central Intelligence Organization known as the Mozambican National Resistance (MNR), later known as Renamo. The Ford administration, which had succeeded Nixon's, could have helped with economic aid for the struggling country. But instead, President Ford turned a blind eye, spurred on by propaganda against the Mozambican government from right-wing sources and corporations anxious about investments in southern Africa.[13]

In October 1975, just four months after Mozambique's declaration of independence, Houser made good on his determination to visit the country. "To me," he wrote, "Mozambique was the most exciting independent country in Africa just then, not simply because the liberation struggle had been won, but also because of the integrity of the FRELIMO leadership."[14] Even though it was still early in the process of transition from colonialism, Houser was impressed with the steps FRELIMO was taking. Whites were invited to stay and identify with the revolution, partly because their skilled manpower was needed. But in his inaugural speech, Machel mentioned another reason: "Because our struggle never took on a racial character and because our people were always able to distinguish between the colonial-fascist regime and the Portuguese people, today we can extend a friendly hand to the Portuguese people, without any complexes of any kind, so that we can build a future of friendship together, without hatred or feelings of revenge."[15] In an effort to stop the exploitation of people, the legal profession, education and health systems, and funeral proceedings had been nationalized. Unused land and rental apartment buildings were also nationalized but not private homes, private industries, or stores. The government's budget prioritized education and culture, agriculture, health, and armed services in that order. Drugs, alcoholism, and prostitution were outlawed in neighborhoods, schools, and businesses. Houser saw evidence of self-organized Dynamizing Groups that engaged in neighborhood clean-up, organized safety patrols to discourage petty thieving, and sent delegations to FRELIMO headquarters to seek help for such problems as unemployment, violations of women's rights, and isolated acts of racial discrimination. At places of work these groups served as a kind of trade union through which grievances could be presented to management. Janet Mondlane was in charge of the division of the Ministry of Health that provided services for the elderly, children under five, and those dealing with issues of mental illness, drug addiction, homelessness, and prostitution. A shelter for homeless children and a rehabilitation center for prostitutes were also in operation.[16]

Traveling into rural Tete Province, hundreds of miles from the country's capital, Lourenço Marques (now Maputo), Houser saw the beginnings of the construction of communal villages where, except for small subsistence plots, the land would be worked communally. These were considerable accomplishments for a country that had been left underdeveloped by colonialism and was still being ravaged by war. Houser's assessment, however, was not a starry-eyed one, as there were tendencies that merited criticism: "One hopes that an elitism will not grow up and that the common touch which has been an important part of Frelimo success during the liberation struggle, will be maintained and strengthened in the years ahead."[17] Houser would travel to Mozambique several more times in the ensuing years. He would witness progress but would also see severe problems due to droughts and floods, shortages of machinery and consumer goods, and constant attacks by Renamo, which would be given new life by South Africa after Zimbabwe declared its independence in 1980, thus ensuring that Mozambique's development would not go smoothly.

In Angola, the postcoup Portuguese government had announced that it would recognize a government only if the three warring parties agreed to unify. In January 1975, in a tenuous agreement known as the Alvor Accord, the parties agreed to form a transitional government with representation from the three movements and the Portuguese. It was to operate for about ten months prior to the election, which was set for late October, followed by independence in November. It was during this period that Houser made his third visit to Angola. He had entered the country on his own after a nine-day visit to Guinea-Bissau and a week in the Cape Verde Islands. While he had made a brief visit to the southern liberated part of Guinea-Bissau in 1973, he had never been to Cape Verde. "To be able to go into these former Portuguese areas of Africa through the 'front door,'" he wrote, "was an exciting

experience."[18] Houser was anxious to learn whether the new government
of Guinea-Bissau would stick to the principles that its late leader, Amílcar
Cabral, had articulated. He was pleased to find that "the way in which the
PAIGC leadership is facing its overwhelming task gives one hope that in spite
of its small size, Republic of Guinea-Bissau will serve as something of a
model of what can be done in other parts of Africa as well."[19]

Houser's visit to Angola, however, left him with a less positive outlook
on the future. He reported that the general atmosphere was tense. Political graffiti abounded. There were, at the time, five military organizations in
operation, all of which the provisional government was supposed to be in-
tegrating: those of the three contending movements, the Portuguese forces,
and a so-called integrated force. Soldiers representing one or another of
these forces were everywhere. Each party's headquarters was guarded by
armed soldiers, and many of the political leaders carried revolvers. Though
political competition appeared to be fierce, the real danger lay in the fact
that each party was backed by an independent military force. In every conversation the real possibility of civil war came up. "It is sobering to realize,"
Houser lamented, "that there is no country in Africa in which a coalition of
parties has been able to form a government and maintain a coalition over a
period of time."[20] On his last day in Luanda, Houser could hear gunfire: one
of the many signals that a full-fledged civil war was about to begin.

Barely back in New York, Houser received word that the FNLA had attacked an MPLA training camp north of Luanda, killing fifty recruits. During
April and May the intensity of the conflict increased. In June, Kenyatta,
backed by the OAU, made one last attempt to bring the three sides together
to forestall civil war. But by then it was too late.

With each side scrambling for outside support to increase its internal
leverage, the region became the site of a proxy war by the Cold War powers
with the Soviet Union coming to the aid of the MPLA, China training FNLA
troops, and covert aid from the United States via Zaire flowing to the FNLA.
The country was a special target of outside interests because of its rich resources—oil, iron, uranium, phosphates and manganese, diamonds, coffee—
and its strategic location in the geography of southern Africa.[21] By the late
summer, South African troops, encouraged by the United States, began fighting in Angola in support of the FNLA and UNITA against the MPLA, which
by then controlled twelve of Angola's fifteen provinces.[22] By the second half
of 1975, UNITA was receiving aid from the United States and South Africa. In
what was described as "the largest covert operation ever undertaken outside
Southeast Asia," the US secretary of state, Henry Kissinger, had instructed

the CIA to funnel $14 million in military aid to Jonas Savimbi to "prevent an easy victory" by the MPLA.[23] In response to the US and South African interventions, Cuban military personnel and Yugoslavian and Soviet weaponry began arriving to support the MPLA.[24] With this help the MPLA succeeded in destroying the FNLA and repelling South African forces, emerging in early 1976 as the dominant military power and winning recognition by the OAU, as well as the nine European Community member-states, as the de facto government of independent Angola.[25] Not so the United States, which was the only country on the fifteen-member Security Council to veto Angola's application for UN membership.[26]

In the United States many liberals in Congress, stung by the Vietnam experience, were wary of another US involvement in a war thousands of miles away. In late December 1975, they passed the Tunney Amendment to the Defense Appropriation Act of 1976 (named after its sponsor, Democrat senator John Tunney of California).[27] Subsequently, the Clark Amendment, sponsored by Democrat senator Dick Clark of Iowa, was also passed. This amended the US Arms Export Control Act of 1976 to prohibit the United States for the foreseeable future from conducting military or paramilitary operations in Angola unless authorized by Congress.[28] However, just nine days after the Clark Amendment became law, in defiance of Congress, Secretary of State Kissinger cabled the US Charge d'Affaires in Kinshasa, instructing him to tell UNITA leaders that the United States would "continue to support UNITA as long as it demonstrated the capacity for effective resistance to the MPLA."[29] It is likely that covert aid continued through the end of the Ford administration.[30]

Alarmed by this flouting of Congress's will, Houser sought to rally public support for enforcement of the Tunney and Clark amendments. To that end he raised funds for an ad in the *New York Times* headlined "Angola . . . a New Vietnam?," which appeared on January 18, 1976. The following day a coalition of forty organizations organized by the ACOA met in Washington, DC, for a congressional briefing and rally against US intervention in Angola. The ACOA held a press conference to announce a statement supporting recognition of the People's Republic of Angola. The statement, which had been signed by a number of peace organizations, called for action in response to the threatened veto of Angola's membership in the United Nations, arranged a meeting of an MPLA delegation with congressional leaders, and set up public meetings for the delegation in New York. ACOA staff and board members gave radio and TV interviews; spoke about Angola at rallies, churches, university and community forums; and distributed literature on what was happening.

Among this literature was an op-ed authored by Houser that appeared in the *New York Times* on December 14, 1975. Figuring that parallels to Vietnam might arouse the public's interest, Houser wrote that the "conflict of opposing political movements for control of an independent Angola is rapidly escalating into an international confrontation reminiscent of Vietnam." Houser went on to characterize the United States' portrayal of the civil war as one of "Communism vs. anti-Communism," which was a gross distortion of the reality, pointing out that all three movements were socialist in orientation: "In a continent where there is little private accumulation of capital, socialism of one sort or another is an accepted norm. Capitalism is a reality in most of Africa only through the interests of foreign corporations and enterprises."[31] From his own contacts with the MPLA he could state that during the war with Portugal they would have been glad to get help from wherever they could, including the United States. "Where was the United States during the years of struggle?" he asked rhetorically. "It was firmly welded into an alliance with Portugal and had a policy of avoiding contacts with the liberation movements in Portuguese colonies."[32] For the United States to now claim that Soviet help for the MPLA equaled Soviet control was hypocritical, Houser argued, given the United States' own covert support for the other two movements and its refusal to mention South Africa's intervention. "It would be a tragedy for the United States to repeat the errors of Vietnam because it looks upon the Angolan conflict as an occasion for another anti-Communist crusade,"[33] said Houser. If the United States had heeded Houser's insight, years of unnecessary suffering and destruction might have been averted—or at least mitigated.

In testimony before the Subcommittee on African Affairs of the Senate Committee on Foreign Relations on February 4, 1976, Houser repeated the analysis he had given in his op-ed. He urged the United States not to give overt or covert financial or military assistance to Angola and to stop recruiting mercenaries to fight in that country's conflicts. He also recommended that the United States stop pressuring the Gulf Oil Corporation to cease its operations in Cabinda.[34] The MPLA, Houser told the Senate, was practical. It had been working cooperatively with Gulf Oil, but American pressure on the company to cease its operations deprived the new government of needed revenue.[35]

The ACOA admitted that the quantity of its response to the Angolan crisis did not match the hoped-for outcomes. The ferocity of the administration's response and the divisions within the black community over support for the three warring factions in Angola were among other factors limiting the ACOA's ability to rally traditional allies on this issue.[36] The scope of the ACOA's influence, however, could be seen in the number of local solidarity organizations around the country that immediately sprang up to take up the Angolan cause. Some of them were formed specifically around the Angolan issue while others were existent organizations that joined the "out of Angola" bandwagon.

A VISIT TO CUBA

From February 25–29, 1976, Houser was one of twenty-six leaders of American solidarity groups and members of the black press invited to Cuba for a seminar on the MPLA. From this invitation it was apparent that the MPLA, which had once suspected Houser of being a front for the CIA, now considered him an ally. It was to be the first of several visits he would make to this small island nation that the United States still considered an enemy.

In meetings with MPLA representatives Houser gathered a deeper understanding of the MPLA's worldview, their relations with their rivals and with other countries, the problems they faced, and their hopes for the kind of society they were seeking to build. Participants were told that the MPLA had a policy of nonalignment and that it wanted to establish relations with all countries under the principle of noninterference and reciprocity, including the United States if they would recognize the movement. But the MPLA would not beg for such recognition. They were not interested in exporting their revolution. They spoke of building a nonracial society where there would be absolute equality between men and women. The solidarity participants were impressed with the MPLA and left with a list of coordinated support actions they planned to take upon their return.[37] Houser was one of five people tasked with coordinating the stateside work of the coalition. Houser subsequently provided members of the US delegation with a packet of materials on Angola. With the ACOA's excellent research capacity and on-the-ground knowledge of events in southern Africa, it was perhaps the only organization capable of pulling together such informative pieces.

Undeterred by the limited response to his initial frenzy of activity around the Angolan crisis, Houser proposed to his board three courses of action for the ACOA on Angola: a public campaign to win US recognition of Angola's government, a national tour of a delegation from the MPLA, and a national conference to be held in late May in Chicago to acquaint a broad section of people with the MPLA and the problem of Angola in the southern Africa context.[38] That conference, cosponsored by representatives of twenty-two organizations, was held May 28–30, 1976.

A month and a half after his first trip to Cuba, Houser was back in Cuba to participate in a seminar sponsored by the UN Special Committee against

Apartheid. Houser's role was that of a critical interpreter of US policy in southern Africa.[39] Though Houser was frustrated by the formalities of the conference, he managed to make two suggestions that were favorably received. First, he invited national antiapartheid movements in different countries to expand the "We Say No To Apartheid" campaign where people in the arts and sports announce their refusal to perform or appear in South Africa; secondly, he proposed holding national antiapartheid poster competitions for professional artists and students. Around the edges of the conference, Houser spent about an hour with Black Panther founder, Huey Newton, who had been in Cuba for about six months and engaged in a long talk with Aida Montalvo of the Organization of Solidarity with the People of Asia, Africa and Latin America (OSPAAAL), which was a Cuban anti-imperialist organization. From her he learned that OSPAAAL wanted to try to make up for the mention in their literature of the ACOA as a CIA conduit. They now believed that the ACOA was a serious group that distributed valuable material, and Montalvo invited Houser to write an article for their internationally circulated magazine, *Tricontinental*.[40]

After returning from Cuba, Houser testified before the Democratic Party Platform Committee on May 19, 1976. It was another presidential election year, and this time, given Congress's passage of the Tunney and Clark amendments, there was a chance that his perspective on southern Africa might be heard. Houser warned the committee that despite Congress cutting off funds for UNITA, a big power confrontation could still happen in southern Africa given the volatile conditions in the region. Pointing out that US investment in South Africa had increased by more than a billion dollars, he laid out a number of steps that a Democratic administration should take.[41] Unlike the Democratic Party of 1968, which had ignored the ACOA's entreaties, this one was more receptive. Twenty-seven lines in the platform were devoted to Africa, and although still couched in aspirational terms, the platform supported almost every one of Houser's recommended policy actions.[42] It is not known if Houser's testimony before the committee was responsible for this change. Certainly, the Tunney and Clark amendments and the aroused public attention to southern Africa were at play, but the striking resemblance between Houser's recommendations and the platform's planks suggest that his testimony may have had an effect.

RETURN TO GUINEA-BISSAU

In the fall of 1976, Houser was again back in Guinea-Bissau. He was the only American attending what was the first major event since independence, a celebration of the twentieth year of the PAIGC's founding. The PAIGC had made it clear that they were only inviting governments and a few nongovernmental representatives who had been their special friends during the long years of the liberation struggle. One of the first things Houser noticed was that many of the streets had been renamed for fallen heroes of the southern Africa revolution. While in the country Houser took the opportunity to meet with officials and to visit some of the schools and hospitals that the Africa Fund had supported during the long independence struggle. Although his time in the country was limited to a week, he was pleased to see that slow progress was being made since his last visit in the field of education. However, in other areas the progress was less evident. Still, Houser was impressed with what he saw of the careful planning and practical thinking of the PAIGC leadership.[43]

A DISAPPOINTING POLICY SHIFT

Jimmy Carter, who ran for the presidency in 1976, had campaigned on a pro-majority rule platform calling for many improvements in southern Africa policy. Shortly after Carter's accession to the presidency in 1977, Congress, at the president's urging, repealed the Byrd Amendment, which since 1972 had permitted the importation of strategic materials from Rhodesia. That and Carter's appointment of Andrew Young as UN ambassador, as well as the administration's signing on to the 1977 mandatory arms sanctions against South Africa, suggested that there might be a real change in southern Africa policy. In Young, Houser felt he had an ally, someone he could talk with in the administration. Like Houser, Young was a clergyman and had worked closely with Dr. King in the southern civil rights movement.

But if Houser had entertained such hopes, by mid-1978 they had been dashed. Although the United States supported passage of the mandatory UN arms embargo against South Africa, the US government did little to enforce it, and later evidence suggests that some munitions got through.[44] Despite a campaign by the ACOA to get the United States to recognize the MPLA as Angola's government, opposition within the Carter administration (especially from his fiercely anti-Soviet national security adviser, Zbigniew Brzezinski)—and Congress prevented such recognition. Houser acknowledged that some improvements had been made in the administration's African policy, yet there were still three critical areas in which US policy had not fundamentally changed. First, the administration was still in thrall to Cold War ideology; second, US policy toward African regimes remained infected by the fear of Marxism and socialism as ways of organizing economic and

political life, preventing the United States from supporting genuine nationalist movements; and third, the Carter administration was still supporting US
investment in South Africa under the assumption that this would help bring
about change.[45] Houser argued that the Carter administration was still operating out of the reformist paradigm associated with the civil rights movement. A new paradigm, he insisted, was required to understand what was
happening in southern Africa:

> The trouble with Young's view, and that of the Carter administration,
> is that it does not come to grips with the revolutionary dynamics
> involved in the southern African struggle. The civil rights struggle in
> the US was not essentially revolutionary against discrimination and
> segregation. The ownership of property, control of industry, was not
> basically at stake. . . . If US policy is to be relevant to the liberation
> struggle in southern Africa, it cannot cling to the hope that changes
> will be brought about by remedial reforms in business practices which
> will bring the black population into the system. To still hold to this
> philosophy is to delude the American people, to attempt to delude the
> Africans, and to lead toward national strife with the US again backing
> up a white minority intent on preserving its position and power.[46]

Perhaps at one time in his history, Houser might have been where Andrew
Young was. But it is clear that his experiences in Africa had changed Houser's
own thinking about the conditions needed for real political change in that
part of the continent.

HOUSER RESPONDS TO A NEW ERA OF REPRESSION IN SOUTH AFRICA

Although challenging the apartheid regime in South Africa had been a constant part of the ACOA's work, Houser's major preoccupation throughout 1975
and the first half of 1976 had been Angola; however, his attention to the ongoing repression in South Africa was suddenly riveted by news of the police
killing of thirteen unarmed black students and the injuring of hundreds of
others in what has come to be known as the Soweto Uprising. On June 16, 1976,
the police opened fire on thousands of students in Soweto Township outside
Johannesburg. They had been protesting the compulsory use of the hated Afrikaans language in their schools. News of the killings spread quickly around the
world, and the rebellion soon spread across the country with thousands more
marching and boycotting work and school. It was the first great mass uprising
in South Africa after a lull of almost a decade. The apartheid regime responded
with more killings, beatings, arrests, torture, and imprisonment.

In response to Soweto, Houser went into immediate action, accelerating both his focus on the violation of human rights in South Africa and on the disengagement campaign. In the following weeks, the ACOA issued a call for demonstrations across the country to condemn the killings and to protest Secretary of State Kissinger's meeting on June 23 with South African Prime Minister John Vorster. Activities on college campuses increased dramatically. At Houser's urging an "Emergency Coalition for Human Rights in South Africa" was formed, drawing representatives from over one hundred organizations. Six hundred people gathered across from the UN, over one hundred set up a picket line outside the South African consulate, and thousands more marched in other cities in support of the black struggle in South Africa. Houser testified before the UN Special Committee against Apartheid, exposing ongoing US administration collaboration with the South African government and spoke on the *Today* show. The ACOA also initiated a nationwide antiapartheid poster competition with an exhibition of the art at the UN in June 1977 and in various venues across the country.

On learning of the death of black consciousness leader Steve Biko while in detention on September 12, 1977, Houser quickly called a press conference at which Judge Booth excoriated the Carter administration's hypocrisy in expressing shock at Biko's death while continuing to support the flow of hundreds of millions of dollars to South Africa. The ACOA also circulated the last and only surviving tape interview with Biko that had been recorded around March 1977 and delivered to the ACOA office by a supporter who had obtained it in South Africa.

The Soweto uprising and consequent crackdown by the apartheid regime had produced a new flood of refugees from South Africa. One of these was Tsietsi Mashinini, the escaped leader of the Soweto uprising whom Houser invited to come to the United States to speak to American audiences in December 1976.[47] That March a benefit concert to raise funds for the refugees was held at Carnegie Hall. Although essentially Houser's idea, the concert was a coalition effort. During spring 1978, the ACOA sponsored a nationwide campus speaking tour by Rhodes Gxoyiya, a South African exile with close ties to the black student movement. In support of its work on disengagement from South Africa, staff members appeared before legislative bodies and participated in scores of TV and radio programs, some of which were beamed as far away as Australia and Africa.

In late 1975, South Africa had initiated an advertising campaign to sell gold Krugerrands to Americans to help earn its critical foreign exchange. On learning of this, the ACOA encouraged its supporters across the country to engage in boycotts, demonstrations, and city council resolutions banning such sales. One of the principal targets was Merrill Lynch, Pierce, Fenner and Smith, the nation's largest brokerage firm whose offices in half a dozen cities were picketed by protesters. By March 1978, the ACOA was able to announce that in addition to Merrill Lynch, other prominent entities had stopped selling or advertising the coins as a result of the protests: four banks; seven city councils; the Massachusetts House of Representatives and eleven television stations in New York, Boston, Chicago, and Portland, Oregon; three major department stores in New York, Cleveland, and Chicago; one New Jersey newspaper; and nine coin and jewelry stores in Cleveland, Oakland, Boston, and Pittsburgh.[48]

New campaigns against corporate practices included a successful campaign to stop the Seagram Distillers Company from going through with a plan to invest in a South African Bantustan. When twelve major American corporations doing business in South Africa announced that they were signing the Sullivan Principles, the ACOA struck back with a press conference denouncing the move and an article by Jennifer Davis demonstrating the fig leaf these principles were throwing over a racist regime.[49]

In 1979, the ACOA opened a new front in drawing out connections between environmental groups in the United States focused on energy issues with the activities of the nuclear and fossil fuel industries in South Africa. A report describing how Fluor Corporation of California was constructing coal-to-oil facilities for the South African government and at the same time pushing this costly synthetic fuel process in the United States was circulated to the press and key contacts across the country. The ACOA also took the initiative in trying to promote an oil embargo against South Africa, sending letters to the governments of nearly twenty-five oil-exporting nations, seeking a clear statement of policy on oil supplies to South Africa and encouraging participation in an embargo against South Africa. In addition, the ACOA sent letters to Mobil, Texaco, and Standard Oil of California reminding them of OPEC policy banning the sale of OPEC oil to South Africa and asking whether they had supplied OPEC oil to South Africa.[50]

Perhaps the most important campaign undertaken during this period was a revival of the bank divestment movement. In the fall of 1976 the ACOA had learned that a consortium of ten banks, headed by Citibank, was planning to make a new set of loans estimated to total at least $2 billion to South Africa. In response, Houser recalled Prexy Nesbitt as the ACOA's associate director, tasked with heading up the newly established Committee to Oppose Bank Loans to South Africa along with Gene Jones of Clergy and Laity Concerned.[51]

By the end of the year the campaign had local organizations operating in fourteen or fifteen different cities. Over a thousand people across the country had distributed more than one hundred thousand fliers. The ACOA's research efforts had produced a list of nearly sixty banks known to have South African loan involvement with details on the extent of their commitments. In November of that year the governing board of the National Council of Churches, representing thirty denominations with constituencies estimated at thirty million people, unanimously approved a statement calling for support "to end all economic collaboration between South Africa and the U.S. government and its private institutions which have investments in South Africa." Trade unions, religious bodies, and civic groups responded with plans to withdraw in excess of the total withdrawn during the previous campaign of the 1960s.[52]

By the end of 1977, Prexy Nesbitt reported to the UN Centre against Apartheid that heightened awareness of South African issues in the United States had ignited a "bush fire" of antiapartheid activism across the country. With it came a tenfold call on the ACOA's small staff to provide specific information from the ACOA library and research files and to serve as speakers.[53] Some idea of the scope of the challenge faced by the ACOA was indicated by a lengthy article appearing in early 1978 in the *Wall Street Journal*, a publication that seldom paid attention to those challenging corporate rule. Fairly glowing with praise for the plucky little ACOA, the author stated the following:

> The immensity of the task that ACOA has set for itself is indicated
> by the fact that Mobil Corp. alone has annual South African sales
> of $500 million, and Ford and General Motors each do better than
> $200 million a year business there. Pitted against giants like these,
> ACOA has an annual budget of $264,000, raised largely through
> donations, speakers' fees and the sale of booklets and posters, which
> it shares with a tax-exempt affiliate called the Africa Fund. These
> funds are dwarfed by the reported $4 million that South Africa is
> spending on advertising and public relations in the U.S. just to sell its
> Krugerrand gold coins to U.S. investors. And they are only a fraction
> of the public-relations budgets of the U.S. corporations that are the
> principal targets of ACOA's stinging broadsides. Nevertheless, in the
> last year or so ACOA has scored some notable victories in its long-
> running battle with the South African regime.[54]

Later that year, the ACOA's efforts to keep up with the now multiplying demands on its energy would be complemented by those of another organization: TransAfrica. By fall 1975, Congressman Charles Diggs and other members of the network of blacks interested in foreign policy had decided that the time had come to form a black-led organization focused on Africa policy.[55] Crucial civil rights legislation had been passed, and there was now a strong nucleus of African Americans in Congress so that attention could be given to the international role of the African diaspora. Since the demise of the American Negro Leadership Conference on Africa there had been no such outlet for African American leadership. As an African American lobby on Africa and the Caribbean based in Washington, DC, TransAfrica began to operate in spring 1978 with civil rights attorney and activist Randall Robinson as its executive director. From then on, the ACOA and TransAfrica would serve parallel and sometimes overlapping roles in coordinating the increasingly large configuration of national and local groups challenging apartheid.

By 1979 there was so much activity on the nation's campuses that Houser saw the need for a coordinator who could network these disparate groups together. Josh Nessen was hired and began publishing the *Student Anti-Apartheid Newsletter* as a way of connecting students engaged in antiapartheid work on various campuses as well as providing useful information on companies and investments. In its inaugural issue the newsletter reported the following: "Though divestment has remained the cutting edge of the movement, many successful campus committees have developed material aid campaigns for the liberation movements, and have linked their work to anti-racist struggles. On several campuses strong ties have also been forged with the anti-nuclear movement, and divestment activists have recently taken an active role in combatting the reactionary hysteria over Iran."[56]

That same year the Committee to Oppose Bank Loans became the Campaign to Oppose Bank Loans to South Africa (COBLSA). It would continue after that as an independent entity although still headquartered in the ACOA office. When Prexy Nesbitt stepped down in 1979, Houser hired Dumisani Kumalo, who would later become free South Africa's first ambassador to the UN, as the second national coordinator. Kumalo's initiation into the American antiapartheid movement came in spring 1979 through an ACOA-sponsored ten-week cross-country tour of American high schools, colleges, universities, churches, and trade unions. Kumalo was met with larger-than-expected crowds of the well informed and those with burning questions about apartheid. On his return, Kumalo reported to the ACOA that "more and more people find that they have to contend with names and places they never heard of. . . . This explains why ACOA literature is much sought after as an authoritative source."[57] It was not only authoritative but was also made readily accessible to those who needed information. One NAACP member wrote to Houser that he had "the most efficient office in town. Two days before leaving for the NAACP convention, I requested information on the U.S. Arms Policy, or lack of it. I received very useful information on the morning of our departure."[58]

The Campaign to Oppose Bank Loans to South Africa would continue to grow, gaining support not only from religious denominations, universities, trade unions, and civil rights leaders but eventually cities, counties, and states. By the 1980s one could find local groups committed to the campaign in virtually every state and city in the country.[59] While in 1981 the bank campaign's office was moved to the Institute for Policy Studies in Washington, DC, the ACOA would continue to be the most prominent national point of contact and source of activist-oriented research on South Africa. By then, however, the proliferation of diverse groups and shifting patterns of coalitions was, according to William Minter, "beyond anyone's capacity to track."[60]

NAMIBIA AND ZIMBABWE: THE CONTINUING STRUGGLES

While Angola and South Africa had been Houser's major preoccupations during the second half of the 1970s, Namibia and Zimbabwe were not far behind. He had kept in close contact with SWAPO's representative at the UN as proposals for internationally supervised elections in Namibia were being negotiated. This was the beginning of a tortuous process of negotiations that would drag on for years, the South Africans drawing out negotiations with the UN and constantly undercutting every attempt at a breakthrough. South Africa's intransigence in Namibia would continue to fester throughout the rest of the decade and into the next.[61]

As the armed insurgency in Namibia increased, thousands of refugees poured into neighboring countries. It was another refugee crisis that Houser, through the Africa Fund, would attempt to address with a large shipment of donated high-priority medicines for the estimated sixty thousand Namibian refugees who had fled to neighboring Angola.

In Rhodesia, the two liberation movements, ZANU and ZAPU, were still operating independently. Houser had kept in constant touch with the leadership of both movements, arranging for their visits to the United States and supplying them with needed equipment such as photostat machines, typewriters, stationery, books and magazines, and funds for correspondence courses for political detainees. Starting as an exile movement, they had penetrated farther inside the country.

There had been an unsuccessful attempt in 1971 by Kenneth Kaunda and Julius Nyerere (presidents of Zambia and Tanzania, respectively) to get ZANU and ZAPU to come together under an umbrella organization to be known as the United African National Council (UANC) with Methodist Bishop Abel Muzorewa as president, but the failure of this attempt at unity meant a reescalation of guerrilla activity.

By 1976, the struggle had intensified, with Zimbabwean rebels using independent Mozambique as a base from which to infiltrate eastern Rhodesia. The white Rhodesian government was now under increasing diplomatic, military, and economic pressure for a settlement. Another attempt to forge a settlement was proffered by Henry Kissinger, but the terms—which left whites in control of the Ministries of Defense and Internal Security in an interim government—were unacceptable to the nationalists. Still a third effort pushed by the British and the Americans to convene a conference in Geneva in 1976 broke down when it was clear no progress was being made.

By 1978 the situation had become increasingly untenable, and Ian Smith was forced to accept the necessity of a settlement. Smith made a last desperate effort to achieve a semblance of majority rule. Called the "Internal Settlement," the scheme was to have a black prime minister and a black majority cabinet while whites controlled the police, army, civil service, and prison system. Whites would also have more than enough votes to block any constitutional change. ZANU and ZAPU opposed the plan. Elections were held in April 1979 and Muzorewa's United African National Council won, with Muzorewa, beholden to the Internal Settlement plan, becoming the prime minister of so-called Zimbabwe-Rhodesia.[62] Houser testified before the Senate Subcommittee on Africa and mobilized opposition to efforts in the US Congress to send election observers and lift sanctions against Rhodesia after the vote. Houser argued that any election based on an inherently racist constitution—one already denounced by the Patriotic Front (the alliance of ZAPU and ZANU), the frontline states, and the OAU—would do nothing to bring a fair settlement in the struggle for majority rule. Moreover, the United States would once again be aligned with South Africa. Houser failed to win over the Senate, but his effort succeeded in getting the House of Representatives to reject sending election observers and persuading President Carter to veto the Senate's bill to lift sanctions.[63] Rejected by the major guerrilla forces, the new government failed to win any international support.

The guerrilla war in Zimbabwe would continue with no settlement emerging. During this period, the ACOA was providing analyses of the complex day-to-day events through frequent radio interviews, articles—including a detailed fourteen-page chronological history of Rhodesia/Zimbabwe authored by Houser. The ACOA and Washington Office worked hard to prevent any of Smith's schemes for holding on to white power from gaining support in the Carter administration or Congress. While these efforts were in progress, the ACOA was also assisting the liberation movements and providing large quantities of medicine and equipment to centers for Zimbabwean refugees in Mozambique and Zambia through its Africa Fund.

Amid frenzied activity, both Houser and Nesbitt made trips to Africa to assess the refugee situation and needs of the liberation movements. From August 24, 1978, to October 1, 1978, Houser was in Tanzania, Zambia, Botswana, and Mozambique to connect with leaders of both independent and still struggling countries gathering information he would write about on his return. As he did so many times before, Houser took notes on material aid that was needed, especially in the refugee camps. In Gaborone, Botswana, Houser ran into Joe Matthews, the son of Z. K. Matthews, whom he had been arrested with on his first and only trip to South Africa in 1954. Matthews reported that he had recently had dealings with the South African police in relation to a case he was handling and found himself talking to the same officer who had arrested them some twenty-five years earlier. At the end of the conversation the policeman asked, "Whatever happened to that white American that was picked up with you many years ago?" To which Matthews replied, "He's still at it!"[64]

WITH THE POLISARIO IN WESTERN SAHARA, COLONIAL AFRICA'S LAST FRONTIER

Although his attention was riveted on the struggles for independence in South Africa, Namibia, and Zimbabwe, Houser could not help but be drawn to the last (and least known) bastion of European colonialism in Africa. On the rim of the Atlantic, bordering Morocco to the north, Algeria to the northeast, and Mauritania to the east and south sits a long strip of desert known as the Western Sahara. Its population, known as Sahrawis, are a nomadic collection of tribes, formed from a mixture of Arabic, Berber, and black African cultures—referred to by one journalist as "one of history's forgotten peoples."[65] Western Sahara had been a Spanish colony since 1884, but it wasn't until the early 1970s that a nationalist group, calling itself POLISARIO (the Popular Front for the Liberation of Saguia el Hamra and Rio de Oro; or Frente Popular de Liberación de Saguía el Hamra y Río de Oro), arose to challenge Spanish domination. Spain relinquished administrative control over the territory in 1975, dividing it between Morocco and Mauritania (both of which claimed

parts of the territory as their own) and subsequently occupied it. But when
Mauritania made peace with the POLISARIO and withdrew, Morocco (which
until 1956 had been a French colony) continued its annexation. King Hassan
II of Morocco claimed that ties existed between the sultans of Morocco and
certain Saharan tribes prior to Spanish colonization. But the rich phosphate
deposits (the fourth largest in the world) discovered in the north near Bu Craa,
the potential to mine vast stores of other minerals—titanium, vanadium,
zinc, uranium, copper, gold, natural gas, magnetite, iron, petroleum—and
the abundant fishing area off the coast were probable reasons for Morocco's
interest in the region.[66]

In 1975, the United Nations sent an investigative mission to Western Sahara that reported strong popular support for the POLISARIO and its policy
of independence; that same year the International Court of Justice issued an
advisory opinion that found no legal justification for Morocco's occupation.
The POLISARIO then announced the formation of the Sahrawi Arab Democratic Republic (La République Arabe Sahraouie Démocratique; SADR).
In 1979 the UN General Assembly affirmed Western Sahara's right to self-
determination, recognized POLISARIO as the legitimate representative of
the people, and urged Morocco to terminate its occupation of the country,
which it refused to do.[67]

Sometime in 1977, Houser learned about the POLISARIO's struggle for independence. The situation was not well known in the United States and on
learning about it Houser immediately proposed to his board that the ACOA
support the POLISARIO struggle. The following year he met POLISARIO's
representative in New York, Madjib Abdullah, and received an invitation to send
a representative to the third anniversary of the SADR on February 27, 1979.
Houser dispatched ACOA staff member Richard Knight to Algeria and Western
Sahara with a mission not only to attend the celebration as an ACOA representative but to study the military, political, and refugee situation of the Western
Sahara particularly with a view to developing possible projects that the Africa
Fund could support. Knight was the only American present at the celebration.

Knight returned with such a fascinating report that Houser was itching
to go himself. With only two weeks to spare from his constant work on Zimbabwe, Houser left for Western Sahara, arriving in Algeria on May 5. His intention was to spend about a week visiting the refugee camps near Tindouf
in Algeria, close to the border of Western Sahara, and then to have about
two days in POLISARIO-controlled areas of their country. He would return
home by way of Algeria and Geneva, where he would talk with officers in
the UN High Commissioner for Refugees.

Houser visited three sprawling refugee camps where perhaps as many as one hundred thousand Sahrawis had fled to escape the bombing and occupation by Morocco and Mauritania. Scattered widely apart, the camps were erected near a source of water that was drawn in buckets from wells. Although the large tents had no furniture, Houser was amazed at the homey atmosphere created by the colorful wall tapestries, rugs, mats, and pillows and found sitting on the floor to be surprisingly comfortable.

Houser could hardly think of these Sahrawis as refugees: "I have visited many refugee camps in Africa over many years but I have never seen a group of people who are as self-reliant and well organized as are these Sahrawi people." Indeed, the refugee camps appeared more like settled communities. Each was divided into *wilayas* (or provinces) corresponding to the divisions of the country and then into *dairas* (districts). The political structure consisted of cells with eleven members in each. Everyone he talked with was a member of a cell, which was the basic unit from which representatives were elected to the popular committees in each of the *dairas* and from there to the *wilaya* councils and from there to the General Congress, the top policymaking body of the POLISARIO.

With the men off fighting or away on other duties, the camps were mostly populated by women and children and some elderly people. In this Islamic culture, it seemed that women had taken on the responsibilities of running the society and were proud of their changing role—and they were eager to talk about it with Houser. They had organized the population into functional committees to provide health care, education (the literacy rate was between 85 and 95 percent), food distribution, justice, and handicrafts. "I had the feeling, . . . that in visiting these camps I was seeing something of what the nation of the Western Sahara would be like under the independent control of POLISARIO," Houser wrote.[68] Although the Sahrawi were well organized, this was still a refugee situation, and they were in need of critical supplies. There were ways the ACOA could help. In his journal Houser made notes of what was needed. Upon his return, the Africa Fund shipped $25,000 worth of donated antibiotics for use by the Saharan Red Crescent in the refugee camps. These shipments were but one part of three tons of medical goods the Africa Fund sent to Africa in 1979, some of which went to Namibian refugees in Angola and Zimbabwean refugees in Mozambique.[69]

After five days in the Algerian refugee camps, Houser's plans suddenly changed when a POLISARIO host came into his room around midnight and suggested that he spend a week riding with them across the expanse of the country through the heart of Moroccan-occupied areas. Houser had about a

half hour to make up his mind and began to marshal reasons for not going:
"We would go through areas where POLISARIO guerrillas and Moroccan
troops were fighting. Did I want to risk it? It was one thing to visit refugee
camps in Algeria and quite another to go into a war zone in the Western
Sahara."[70] But Spanish freelance journalist José Martin Artajo, who had
also been visiting the camps, urged him to go: "George, you can't miss this
opportunity. You may never have another chance to cross the desert. You
will always regret it if you don't go."[71] Houser's sense of adventure was
piqued, but a moment later his trepidation returned when he was asked
to sign a waiver indicating that he absolved the Algerian government of
any responsibility in case of "accident." Not one to turn down a new adventure, however, Houser decided to go, writing a letter to Jean explaining
the change in his plans. Houser would be the first American to cross the
Western Sahara Desert—one of the most inhospitable places on earth—
with the POLISARIO guerrillas.

After only about three hours' sleep, the men left while it was still dark in
two Santanas, each with six occupants: nine armed combatants and three foreigners. In addition to Houser, there was Artajo, whose father—from whom
he had severed ties politically—had been Franco's foreign minister, and there
was also Italian metallurgist Dominico Palumbo.[72]

The two-car caravan headed west over trackless desert in vehicles without roofs or windshields, which could have reflected the desert sun, thus
making them a target for Moroccan aircraft. It was a mystery to Houser how
the guerrillas knew where to go as they had neither compasses nor radios,
but they seemed to know the desert intimately.

It was general practice to rest during the worst heat of the day on blankets beneath whatever small thorn trees they could find. By three or four
o'clock in the afternoon a lunch would be served, with everyone eating
and drinking from a communal bowl after which they would resume their
journey. Water was carried in large barrels and used sparingly. Protecting
the fair skin on Houser's head and face from the scorching sun, wind, and
sand was a *shesh*, the traditional turban worn by the nomads. But when his
hands began to burn, Houser wished he had brought gloves as well. During
the trip Houser would bathe in a pocket of rainwater found in a mostly
dry streambed. He dined on rabbit, camel, goats, gazelle, and desert birds.
He would endure bread laced with sand and drink water that occasionally
tasted of gasoline—having been siphoned into a drum with a fuel hose—or
looked like dishwater and tasted of mud. Houser, at the age of sixty-three,
was grateful for the early camping experiences that had prepared him for

roughing it, but his formidable constitution no doubt helped. He didn't get sick once, except for when he contracted a cold on the last leg of the trip.

At about 10:30 that night they arrived at the abandoned town of Tifariti, the scene of a recent battle that had been won by the POLISARIO and that Richard Knight had witnessed a bit of on his previous trip to the territory.[73] After a night sleeping on the sand, Houser and his companions spent some time the next morning surveying the forlorn area: a burned-out school, empty shops, an abandoned airstrip, discarded helmets, weapons, bullet casings, and a large graveyard where the bodies of civilians, POLISARIO, and Moroccan combatants were all buried.

Pushing on, they came to the town of Amgala where similar signs of destruction signaled the aftermath of a battle that had taken place two weeks before. It was midnight before the group stopped for the first meal of the day over a fire under the stars, then slept on blankets spread over the sand. The remainder of the trip to the Atlantic coast was largely without incident. The POLISARIO appeared to be in command of the desert while the Moroccan troops kept to the towns they occupied.

The last part of the trip to the Atlantic coast was a bit more harrowing. They would be traveling close to Bu Craa, a Moroccan stronghold and site of some phosphate mines. The guerrillas decided to make a dash for the sea under the cover of darkness. "I shall never forget that ride," wrote Houser afterward. "The waning moon rose about 11:00 P.M. and by 12 was high enough to give needed light. Four Santanas were in our party now. We moved across the moonlit desert . . . headlights off, skimming over the flat, smooth sand at high speed. The beauty of it was overwhelming. We didn't stop for more than three hours."[74] Two hours before they reached the ocean, they were taken to the site of a downed American F-5 fighter jet. The Moroccan pilot had parachuted and was now a prisoner of the POLISARIO. Houser photographed the American markings in case evidence might be needed to demonstrate that the United States, in arming Morocco, was violating a 1960 US-Moroccan military agreement prohibiting the use of US weapons outside internationally recognized borders.[75] Before they even reached their destination on the Atlantic coast, Houser felt the cool sea breezes and could smell the salt. On arriving at the point where the sea met the sand he remarked later, "What a thrill! I felt like an explorer who had just made a great discovery."[76] After bathing and washing their clothes in the ocean, the party began their return journey.

Taking a more northerly route, the return trip would not be as pacific. As the caravan came within twenty miles of Semara, the second-largest town in the country, they saw a US-made 75mm cannon manned by the POLISARIO and were told that a bombardment of Moroccan defenses was about to begin. The three foreigners were given long Saharan gowns to wear so they could not be distinguished from the guerrillas if planes gave chase. Houser commented that he had not asked to experience combat, but there was no escape. In the early afternoon, the three foreigners clambered up a hill to watch the bombardment—Houser would film and tape record it—and were told to lie low. The rocks were scorching, and Houser found it difficult to hold the equipment yet stay below the brow of the hill. As he watched, six POLISARIO shells landed about four miles away. Houser and his friends could see the puff of smoke and then heard the explosion. The Moroccans then returned fire. Suddenly, his POLISARIO companions told them to run downhill to the cars immediately as Moroccan planes might come. The Santanas raced at high speeds for about two miles, stopping to hide beneath a grove of trees where Houser removed his gown. About half an hour later they drove onto a base where many guerrillas were gathered. Trenches and camouflaged nooks in the rocks provided shelter, but they decided to press on back to the reception center in Algeria. After eating at around midnight, they set out once again in darkness. Houser had not slept for two nights in a row and could feel a cold coming on. Dead tired and thirsty, he fantasized all night about drinking from a cool mountain stream, the kind he would find on his camping trips back home in the Adirondacks or the Tetons. Arriving the next morning at the reception center Houser fell into a delicious sleep.

Houser found the POLISARIO combatants to be "a remarkable people—hardy, friendly, companionable, hardworking, and efficient. . . . I heard no bickering, arguments, or angry voices. When meeting other POLISARIO guerrillas in the desert, they stopped, embraced, laughed, and said touchingly genuine farewells. I felt their sense of unity in a cause."[77]

Later in November that same year, Houser again made a trip into POLISARIO country, having been invited by the Algerians to attend the twenty-fifth anniversary of the beginning of their struggle against the French. Still entranced by his adventure in the desert, Houser went to POLISARIO headquarters to see about arranging a visit to Mahbes, the most eastern Moroccan stronghold, which just three weeks before had been the site of a ferocious battle the POLISARIO had won.

After having again signed a "waiver," Houser was off on another trip across the desert. At Mahbes he would find not only destroyed property but also the grisly human remains of the recent battle. The POLISARIO claimed that seven hundred Moroccans had been killed. Houser would later write:

> Who knows how many had died in the battle for Mahbes. . . . I
> counted perhaps 50 Moroccans lying as they had fallen three weeks
> before, in various stages of decomposition from sun, wind, and sand.
> . . . I had been on African battle sites before, but this was the first
> time I had actually seen the dead on the field. . . . It was a shock to
> me, who had never shot anything more powerful than a BB gun my
> father gave me when I was 10 and who had gone to prison in 1940
> protesting the peacetime conscription before U.S. involvement in
> World War II.[78]

Later that day Houser and his hosts went to a spot in the desert about the size of a football field where the POLISARIO had stored captured weapons. "Here was more military equipment than I had ever seen," he wrote.[79] Nearby were about fifty prisoners of war. He talked with one of them who spoke good English. The man had trained at Randolph Field in Texas and had piloted an American F-5 when it was shot down near Semara. It was likely this pilot was from the wrecked plane Houser had seen in the desert on his first trip. While talking to the pilot and another English-speaking prisoner, Houser learned about their families and their desire that this "foolish" war would end so they could go home. "I could not avoid a feeling of sympathy for them with the bleak future they faced," wrote Houser.[80]

Back at the reception center Houser talked with the SADR minister of the interior, who told him that the United States had been supplying Morocco with sophisticated weapons in violation of a neutrality agreement. The Carter administration's rationale was that this would help nudge the POLISARIO Front toward the negotiating table. Apparently there had been differences within the Carter administration. Back in Algiers, Houser made an appointment with US ambassador Ulrich Haynes. From Haynes he learned that the US mission had been instructed not to talk with POLISARIO. Haynes grilled Houser, the only American (except for Richard Knight) who had talked with the POLISARIO, about the chances for a political settlement. Houser informed Haynes that the POLISARIO saw the entire region as their own property and that by backing Morocco the United States was supporting an occupation just as imperialist as that of Spain. The United States was also sabotaging a possible peaceful solution to the controversy through a UN-sponsored referendum.

On his return, Houser, in addition to sending medical supplies, exposed the fact that South Africa was now sending weapons to Morocco for use in Western Sahara. He continued to do what he could to stop new US arms

shipments to Morocco, writing a letter to President Carter, testifying before congressional committees, writing letters to the *New York Times* and a
magazine article for *The Progressive*, and appearing with POLISARIO representative Madjib Abdullah on ABC's *Like It Is*—but to no avail. As in Angola,
US support for the aggressor, Morocco, was serving to prolong the war just
at the point where the POLISARIO was gaining significant victories.

Houser had not shaved the entire time he had been in the Western Sahara. He decided to keep the beard until independence was won, but the
struggle for independence in the Western Sahara would continue indefinitely. In 2016, UN Secretary General Ban Ki-Moon would call it "one of the
forgotten humanitarian tragedies of our times."[81] Houser continued to wear
a goatee for the remainder of his life, a reminder of the one African independence movement whose victory he would not live to see.

AN ELECTIONS OBSERVER IN ZIMBABWE

With the situation in Zimbabwe stalemated, international pressure, particularly by Britain hoping to forestall a radical government in Zimbabwe, finally
helped bring the war to an end in 1979 after almost fifteen years of armed
struggle. Andrew Young had worked with British foreign minister David
Owen to lay the foundation for a set of proposals that would be the basis
for negotiations. Subsequently, Britain convened a conference of the parties
at Lancaster House in London to negotiate the terms of independence. The
meeting lasted from September to December 1979. Robert Mugabe arrived
for the talks in a suit that Houser and his ACOA colleague Paul Irish had purchased for him.[82] "There were no optimists as the discussions began either in
the conference or among informed observers," wrote Houser. "Nevertheless,
the desire for a resolution on the part of all concerned was powerful enough
to move the discussions forward, and finally the effort was successful."[83]

The parties arrived at a constitution providing for majority rule, the conditions for a cease-fire, and a date for elections. Four parties would contend
for the election. Robert Mugabe's ZANU and Nkomo's ZAPU maintained a
fragile unity as the Patriotic Front (PF) but retained their own separate organizations, and rivalry between the two persisted. Muzorewa, heavily bank-
rolled by South Africa, headed the United African National Council; and a
group that had split off from ZANU was headed by Ndabaningi Sithole.

It was not clear that the elections in Zimbabwe would go smoothly, but
Houser felt there was no more important place to be than in Zimbabwe in
the run-up to the vote. Since provisions had been made for both official and
unofficial election observers, he decided to organize an unofficial delegation.

Their group would be a small part of a much larger set of outside observers. The group consisted of Houser and Dr. Tilden LeMelle, representing the ACOA; Cynthia Canady, a lawyer representing TransAfrica and the NAACP; Dr. Robert Edgar of Howard University's African Studies Center; and Ted Lockwood, representing the Washington Office on Africa. Mike Shuster, a journalist with National Public Radio (NPR), was also part of the group. He would be sending daily reports to NPR through a difficult communications channel.

Until this point Houser had been prohibited from entering Zimbabwe. To make sure he could get in, he requested and received an official letter from the British UN ambassador affirming that the interim governor's office in Salisbury (now Harare) had approved his entrance. Houser and his team arrived in mid-February 1980, just two weeks before the election.

The atmosphere in Salisbury when the group arrived was tense and intimidating. Police searches for weapons and explosives existed at the entrance to every public building, hotel, and bank, and body searches were carried out at the offices of each of the political parties. Having just emerged from a decade-long civil war, the truce between the four Rhodesian and Zimbabwean armies was obviously shaky. Outside Salisbury the situation was even more volatile. The British had decided to rely solely on the Rhodesian establishment to manage and control the cease-fire. While the forces of the Patriotic Front were required to remain at assembly points scattered around the country, the Rhodesian military, Muzorewa's Auxiliaries (the private army of Bishop Muzorewa), and the police were allowed to roam at will. This resulted in intimidation tactics—beatings, arrests, torture, and sometimes murder—against those working for the Patriotic Front. During their stay in the country several journalists would be killed, reportedly caught in the crossfire of the combatants. Police and troops had set up roadblocks, permitting whites to go through but searching blacks and requiring them to produce identification papers. On highways one came upon signs that read, "Warning to Motorists. It is dangerous to travel on this road after 3:00 PM." "The presence of guns/armed troops of the Security force and the Auxiliaries, the threat of bombs, the hundreds of arrests of political campaign organizers all added up to an unmistakable tension," wrote Houser.[84]

The white Rhodesian establishment that controlled the media was rabidly opposed to Mugabe, blaming most of the violence on his ZANU party. Houser and his group, however, observed that the principal blame appeared to lie with the security forces and Bishop Muzorewa's Auxiliaries.[85] So hated was Mugabe by the white Rhodesians that he had to cancel his appearances on the final two weekends of the campaign because of several near assassination attempts and continuing death threats.

Houser's presence in Zimbabwe did not go unnoticed in South Africa. A typical reaction to Houser was a South African newspaper headline, "Rabid Anti-White in a 'Warehouse of Radicals.'" Singling out Houser as part of a group of "radicals and terrorist supporters, many of whom have been banned for years from entering either Rhodesia or South Africa," the writer said that since Houser became executive director of the ACOA in 1955, "he has seldom strayed far from his pre-occupation with making things as hot as possible for the Whites of Southern Africa. . . . Mr. Houser denies that he himself is a Marxist, but there is no record of him ever supporting any moderate Black cause in Africa. His links lie particularly with the Moscow-orientated terrorist movements."[86]

The plan was to meet with all of the contending African candidates and their supporters on separate days and travel through different parts of the country to see whether the election campaigns and the actual balloting were being conducted in a free and fair manner. To accomplish this, the group would split up and meet in the evening at their lodging to discuss their findings. Mike Shuster would summarize the substance of their discussions as the basis for filing his live reports with NPR. To cover the entirety of the country, Houser's group rented two cars, dividing up so that they could visit all eight provinces. Part of the trip was also by plane and helicopter, courtesy of the Commonwealth countries. They also attended political rallies and visited the offices of each of the major political parties, meeting with all the major candidates with the exception of Muzorewa, who was unavailable. Everywhere they went they were met by men with guns.

Given the tense situation in the country, it was inevitable that Houser and his group would be caught up in it, given the fact that they would not be traveling with the government-orchestrated junkets as the official delegations were doing.[87] It happened on a sunny Sunday morning shortly after their arrival in the country as Houser and his companions, in two cars and accompanied by four ZANU campaigners, were on their way to the Chiota Tribal Trust Land about sixty miles south of Salisbury. A frightened, disheveled man suddenly came running up to their car. He told them that he had just been beaten by soldiers who were heading their way. Just then an armored truck came speeding along the dirt road throwing up a cloud of dust as it braked to an abrupt halt. A dozen shouting members of the regular Rhodesian security forces jumped from the truck with their nervous trigger fingers on machine guns and their automatic rifles pointed at the group. Ordering them to get out of the car, a sergeant shouted a warning that if anyone moved, they would be shot. The soldiers were searching for "terrorists," and ZANU supporters were considered "terrorists." "We didn't know what to expect," recalled Houser. "We were not only fearful for our own safety, but particularly for our Zimbabwe companions. . . . I was not alone in thinking that this might be the end of the road for us."[88] The group was then separated into the two cars and the truck, each with soldiers pointing their guns at the heads of the observers. Houser, who was driving one of the cars, was told not to go more than five miles an hour or he would be shot. With a gun pointed to the back of his neck, the soldier told Houser that the "gooks" (the name the Rhodesian soldiers used to describe ZANU and ZAPU members) loved to kill white people and that those accompanying Houser's group were likely bent on killing them. "I should point out," Houser recalled, "that I never felt safer than with our ZANU or ZAPU friends. The Security Forces and Auxiliaries made me nervous. They had guns.[89] Houser told one of the other members of the group who had arrived after the incident took place that if he were to be killed, he had led a good life.

The caravan proceeded to a military base where the group was interrogated. At a police headquarters in a nearby town they were again interrogated and then released. It had been a harrowing four-hour ordeal. With characteristic understatement Houser later recalled, "We profited from the experience at least knowing what intimidation was like. Our Zimbabwe friends credited us with probably having saved their lives. We were glad to escape with our own."[90] In his later public statements about the incident, Houser admitted to being scared. But to his friends, he apparently showed no fear. "None of that ever really fazed George in any way," Tilden Lemelle remembered. "I guess with George the cause was right, it was God's work and he had no fear. That was a dangerous time because when we went to report to the British guy in charge—we used to call him General Whiskey because he was constantly drunk—his response to our report was, 'You're lucky you didn't get killed.'"[91]

Before the voting started, Houser's group, along with two of Houser's old friends who represented the American Friends Service Committee, Lyle Tatum and Bill Sutherland, along with a group of observers from Canada, issued a joint statement and held a press conference calling on the British to correct their bias in favor of Muzorewa, suggesting steps the British might take to insure free and fair elections.[92] Their statement received front-page publicity in the press, several minutes of commentary on the BBC, and careful consideration from the spokesman for Lord Soames, the British governor.

While there is no way to tell whether the observer group's recommendations had an effect, the voting was remarkably peaceful in contrast to the violent atmosphere leading up to the election. Ninety-three percent of potential voters had gone to the polls. On March 3, the day before the results were known, Houser's group issued a detailed report about their findings on the freedom and fairness of the elections.[93] "Our experiences were representative enough to make us feel we could express opinions on what was happening with confidence," said Houser. "We had a good entree with the Zimbabwean political leadership because of our work with them covering more than 20 years."[94]

Much to the shock of the white Rhodesians and South Africa—and to the surprise of the British and Americans (but perhaps not to Houser, given what he had seen on his trip to Africa two years before)—ZANU-PF won an overwhelming fifty-seven seats out of eighty reserved for blacks or almost 64 percent of the vote, while ZAPU took another twenty seats and Muzorewa's group only three.[95] After the vote was announced, jubilant crowds took to the streets, singing and dancing and crowing like the rooster, the symbol of the ZANU-PF party. The British governor then asked Mugabe to form a government, and so the two frontrunners agreed to a coalition government.[96] Given the pervasive press bias in favor of Muzorewa (the favorite of Rhodesian whites) and the attempts by whites to prevent ZANU and ZAPU from coming to power, the result was, to Houser, nothing short of a "miracle." Now that the fighting was over, however, the hard part of development and reconstruction would begin, and Houser would again seek to monitor its trajectory and support it with material aid.[97]

Five months after his election as prime minister of Zimbabwe, Robert Mugabe came to the United States to participate in ceremonies surrounding Zimbabwe's acceptance into the UN. As Houser had done with so many heads of state with whom he had worked, he organized a reception for Mugabe at the Church Center for the United Nations, which was attended by three hundred people. Calling out George Houser and Judge William Booth by name, Mugabe thanked them and the countless others who had supported their struggle in the face of a media barrage from the Rhodesians and South Africans, who had painted those struggling for their freedom as "monsters," "terrorists," and "Communists."[98]

10

One Step Enough for Me, 1980–2015

"How is George Houser?" asked the [Botswana immigration] official. My experience, criss-crossing the U.S. on speaking tours, was that whenever a person asked about George Houser, it means they knew something good about us, even though they might disagree with it.

"George Houser is retired now," I said.

"Oh, man," said the official, waving his hand in a manner to express disbelief. "George will never retire, man."

—*Dumisani Kumalo, in a letter to Jennifer Davis written from Harare*[1]

IN JUNE 1980, GEORGE HOUSER INFORMED THE ACOA BOARD of his decision to retire in June 1981 when he reached the age of sixty-five. The complex, exciting, and often tragic travails of the African continent had been his life's work for over a quarter of a century. Though Houser would never get Africa out of his blood, he told his board that he thought a change would be good for the organization and for himself. He expressed the desire for more time to pursue other interests, to spend time with his family, and to write and reflect on his life.

The ACOA executive board had managed to scrape up a small pension for Houser enabled by a grant from a generous benefactor. With Jean's pension and Social Security, it would be enough for the Housers to maintain a modest lifestyle. On June 17, 1981, George Houser's nearly three decades of work for the cause of African freedom were celebrated at a gala retirement event at the Community Church of New York, the church that had donated space to the fledgling organization when it was just getting started in 1953. Doubling as both a tribute to Houser's work for peace and justice and as a fundraiser for the always-in-debt ACOA, the evening featured the reading of statements from a wide range of African political leaders; leaders of antiapartheid movements from as far away as New Zealand, Ireland, Britain, France, and South Africa; and performances by well-known artists.[2] Even though Houser was still barred from South Africa and Namibia, the UN Communications Network broadcast the entire program to those countries, a gesture that must have galled the South African authorities.

Minister of Local Government and Housing E. J. M. Zvobgo of Zimbabwe wrote, "It is difficult to pay a fitting tribute to George Houser, a man who has done so much for so many around the world. . . . No problem was ever too small or too big. He worked untiringly for the liberation of the whole of Africa and I am convinced that he will continue to do so."[3] Judge William H. Booth, the ACOA's president, characterizing Houser's work with the organization, said, "To pay tribute to George is to recall a seemingly endless number of involvements. . . . He is at the center of activity . . . hunting a new angle, meeting new people, trying a new strategy. Even his detractors testify to his commitment."[4] President Julius K. Nyerere of Tanzania perhaps best summed up the arc of Houser's life:

> The most important people in the world are often those who work quietly in the background of events, devoting their skill, their commitment, and their lives, to the causes they believe in. They receive no acclaim; but without them there would be no triumph. George Houser is such a man, and his service has been given wholeheartedly and without reserve to the cause of human freedom and human equality, with special reference to the struggle against colonialism and racialism in Africa. Many who are now, or have been political leaders in Africa during the last three decades have been helped to become effective on the international scene by the assistance and the friendship of George Houser. I am one of those who he helped in this way.[5]

Just a month before he was scheduled to retire, Houser had made his last trip to Africa in his role as executive director of ACOA. It was a five-week trip from March 15 to April 21 that took him to the front-line states of southern Africa: Angola, Mozambique, Namibia, Zimbabwe, Tanzania, and Zambia. Among the many dozens of people Houser met with were several he had known at one time simply as "freedom fighters" but who had since risen to become heads of state or foreign ministers.

At the time of Houser's 1981 visit, a new wave of unrest had broken out in South Africa when a nationwide boycott campaign was triggered by the regime's Republic Day celebrations. Coupled with a series of sabotage attacks by the ANC, this unrest had resulted in another round of repression by the government. The African leaders with whom Houser spoke were naturally anxious about the direction of US foreign policy under President Reagan, probing Houser for his insights into the new administration.

Houser's visit to Africa coincided with a tour of the southern African states by Chester Crocker, the man newly in charge of Reagan's Africa policy and the architect of the administration's policy of "constructive engagement," an approach that was supposed to encourage change in South Africa through dialogue with its white leaders. Houser's itinerary happened to cross with Crocker's in Maputo and Luanda. On the same day in Maputo both men had discussions with Mozambique's foreign minister, Joaquin Chissano, Crocker meeting with him in the morning and Houser in the afternoon. The discussions took place against the background of Mozambique's discovery of a CIA spy ring whose members were in the process of being expelled from the country. The two discussions could not have been more different. Crocker's attempts to ingratiate himself with Chissano backfired. When Crocker told Chissano that he had "come to negotiate" on the Namibian question, Chissano countered, "If you want to negotiate you will have to do so with SWAPO. We are only here to exchange views." The discussion ended abruptly. According to the press, Crocker was "grim-faced" when he left Mozambique.[6]

In his own discussions with Chissano, Houser was given a frank blow-by-blow account of the conversation between Chissano and Crocker as well as information about the evidence Mozambique had amassed on the CIA operation. Sharfudine Khan, FRELIMO's New York representative, told Houser afterward that Chissano had given him the most detailed report of the discussion with Crocker he could imagine. Crocker's attempt to broker a solution to southern Africa while leaving in place the apartheid regime in South Africa did not meet with any further success. The presidents of Angola and Mozambique—and even South Africa's then prime minister, P. W. Botha, had all rebuffed his overtures.[7]

Part of the purpose of Houser's trip was to follow up on Africa Fund medical assistance projects and to discuss the needs of refugees in Zimbabwe, Mozambique, Angola, Zambia, and Tanzania. On Houser's return to the United States, the Africa Fund Trustees approved a $10,000 grant to the Women's Council of the ANC of South Africa to help finance a daycare center for South African refugees in Zambia, prepared a special brochure on the refugee centers, and distributed nearly fifty thousand copies to alert the American public to the critical needs of these refugees. The fund also contributed $11,000 to the SWAPO Women's Council for a project designed to provide vocational training to equip women refugees with skills needed in building a new Namibia as well as eyeglasses and audio-visual equipment for classroom use in the camps. As 1981 ended the ACOA was preparing to ship over half a ton of penicillin to the refugee centers and $50,000 worth of medicines, equipment, and books.

The fears of the Africans with whom Houser met about the direction of US policy were justified. Ronald Reagan's election to the US presidency in 1980 and a Republican majority in the Senate came with a ratcheting up of anti-Communist rhetoric. Arguing that "constructive engagement" was necessary to reestablish Pretoria's trust in the United States, the Reagan administration vetoed a UN Security Council Resolution to impose sanctions on South Africa; cast the only vote against a Security Council condemnation of South Africa's invasion of Angola; loosened regulations on exports to South Africa; increased contacts between US and South African police, military, and intelligence personnel; and began a campaign to repeal the Clark Amendment, which had prohibited the United States from aiding groups engaged in military or paramilitary activity in Angola. The Reagan administration was also secretly financing UNITA through Saudi accounts in exchange for the sale of AWACS planes to the Saudis.[8] "There seems to be considerable evidence," Houser would write in 1984, "that this administration has proceeded further than any other in identifying its own interests with those of the South African state."[9]

"Constructive engagement" was to be anything but constructive, serving only to undergird the apartheid regime and increase its repressive behavior. As a result, the number of arrests, tortures, and deaths in detention in South Africa increased dramatically, while the regime, aided by US military, diplomatic, and political support, was emboldened to launch large-scale attacks into Angola.[10]

Following intense pressure from pro-UNITA lobbyists, Congress repealed the Clark Amendment in 1985, after which Reagan immediately authorized $15 million for Savimbi's UNITA forces. These decisions came as a reaction to an MPLA offensive, aided by Cuban troops, which the Reagan administration depicted as Communist aggression.[11] With the FNLA now defunct, American support for UNITA continued to increase, serving to prolong until 2002, with the death of Jonas Savimbi, a civil war and unrecorded holocaust that left by some estimates more than a million dead, untold wounded (including seventy-seven thousand amputees), and massive devastation of natural resources and the economy.[12]

Houser had done his best to forestall such a reactionary turn in southern Africa policy, yet he had always known that the struggle would be long and that he might not see its completion. Although his formal work with the ACOA was at an end, he was determined to continue the fight in other ways. Retirement, then, was more like recycling.

He was leaving the ACOA in capable hands. Two South Africans would carry on the ACOA's work for a free southern Africa until its conclusion. Under Jennifer Davis's leadership and Dumisani Kumalo's charismatic role as projects director, the organization would take the work Houser had begun into all fifty states. Reagan's election had convinced activists that hope for action at the federal level was probably foreclosed. In late 1980 the ACOA, along with the seven other organizations, created the Campaign against Investment in South Africa to focus efforts on getting public pension funds to vote their shares or sell their stocks in companies that did business with South Africa, which could represent an enormous source of economic leverage.

Throughout the 1980s the antiapartheid movement would expand exponentially to become the most important protest movement organized around a foreign policy issue.[13] Historians date 1984 as the year the tide against South Africa began to turn. By this time, in addition to the ACOA, three other national organizations—TransAfrica, American Friends Service Committee (AFSC), and the Washington Office on Africa—were playing complementary and overlapping roles in loosely coordinating the work of scores of local networks and specialized groups. These local organizations, which became more militant as the 1980s progressed, would carry the freight of the antiapartheid movement to its conclusion.

It was in 1984, after the arrest of over one hundred United Democratic Front (UDF) leaders in South Africa,[14] that Randall Robinson decided to turn to more disruptive tactics. Forming the Free South Africa Movement, TransAfrica staged sit-ins at the South African embassy in Washington, DC. By 1985 there had been more than twenty-nine hundred arrests of protesters—among them twenty-three members of Congress as well as the children of Martin Luther King Jr., Jimmy Carter, and the Kennedys.[15] Massive protests inside South Africa, which led the government to declare a state of emergency, combined with escalating international pressure to force substantial capital flight, caused the value of South Africa's currency to drop dramatically.[16]

As he had in the civil rights movement, Houser had been a pioneer when few others saw the possibilities of action, but it would be others who were credited with the final victory. It was the large, grassroots mobilization that finally convinced Congress to pass the Comprehensive Anti-Apartheid Act in 1986 over President Reagan's veto. Passage of this legislation catalyzed similar sanctions in Europe and Japan, signaling there would be no rescue from outside and dealing one of the penultimate blows to the faltering apartheid state.

Houser had technically retired from the ACOA, but his activism for peace and justice would continue for the next thirty-three years. Shortly after his retirement, with a grant from the Ford Foundation and office space provided by the Board for Homeland Ministries of the United Church of Christ, Houser began the work of preparing the ACOA and Africa Fund records for their eventual placement in a library archive.[17] He was also able to work on the book he had always wanted to write about his encounters with the African liberation movements. *Nothing Can Stop the Rain: Glimpses of Africa's Liberation Struggle* was published in 1989. Written when southern Africa was still in the midst of its struggle for liberation, the book provides fascinating insights into the tangled relationships between African leaders and movements and Houser's assessment of these personalities and events. He would also serve as interim executive director of the FOR and as coordinator for programs on southern Africa at the Stony Point Conference Center, a multifaith retreat center run by the Presbyterian Church in Nyack, New York. With the outbreak of wars in Afghanistan and Iraq he would participate with his neighbors in weekly street-corner antiwar vigils in Nanuet, New York.

Houser would continue to write and speak on Africa and to work with the Africa Fund as a trustee and executive board member, reporting on fund recipients and searching for new projects on the several visits he would make to Africa. Over the next eighteen years he would make thirteen more trips to Africa. These trips in his "retirement" were to be something of a victory tour, and they speak to the tremendous goodwill he had earned in his thirty years as head of the ACOA. On a trip in 1983, accompanied by his son, Steven, Tanzanian president Julius Nyerere shared his intimate assessments of the many African leaders with whom Houser had worked over the years, providing details of the clashes between them that had shaped the liberation struggles and postliberation history. In Zambia, he had another frank discussion with President Kenneth Kaunda. Houser was probably the only American who could be invited (and trusted enough) to partake in such private discussions with Nyerere and Kaunda. Both presidents shared impressions of President Reagan that they certainly would not have wanted publicized. And in Zimbabwe, in conversations with ZAPU and ZANU officials, ZAPU members of the Zimbabwean government told Houser things that they wouldn't have wanted Mugabe or ZANU officials to hear.[18]

In the fall of 1984 and again in the summer of 1987, Houser made two trips to Algeria, one of them accompanied by his wife, Jean, to attend anniversary celebrations of the war against the French. By this time, however, Houser was beginning to weary of the endless military parades that accompanied each celebration. While he had rejoiced at the victories won by successful liberation movements, commemorating militarism with displays of tanks and weaponry was distasteful to this man who was still, at heart, a pacifist.[19]

In fall 1989 Houser traveled to Namibia to observe preparations for the UN supervised election for a constituent assembly that would draft a national constitution, with independence to follow.[20] For the first time he could enter the country he had been banned from for thirty-four years. In the intervening years the South African regime had become increasingly isolated. Its military operations were eating into its budget, the number of white casualties on the battlefield was eroding support for the war even among Afrikaners, civil unrest at home was growing, and international sanctions were having an effect. The government realized that if it got out of Namibia it might be able to set the terms for its independence and protect its business interests.

Unlike his earlier attempt to enter Namibia by way of South Africa, this time Houser met with no problems at Jan Smuts International Airport. As usual, his visit to Namibia was spent meeting with various political leaders as well as UN officials, church leadership, teachers, and trade unionists.[21] His visit included a briefing by Sam Nujoma, who had been exiled from his country for twenty-nine years and was now back leading the liberation struggle. A huge crowd turned out at the homecoming rally for Nujoma, where he was hailed as something of a folk hero. While standing in the hot sun having had hardly any water for hours, the seventy-three-year-old Houser was suddenly called to the stage where he was introduced as an old friend of SWAPO who had greeted Nujoma when he came to New York in 1960. "I was a little embarrassed. No other non-SWAPO person was so introduced," Houser confessed to his colleague Jennifer Davis.[22]

On his way back through Jan Smuts International Airport, Houser had sought out a public phone and put through a call to Walter Sisulu, who had recently been released from twenty-six years of imprisonment on Robben Island. The two had not met since Houser's 1954 visit to South Africa. Houser reached the veteran ANC leader and was exhilarated to hear Sisulu inform him that he had spoken frequently to his fellow political prisoners on Robben Island, including Nelson Mandela, of the work of the organization that

Houser led for some three decades. With characteristic modesty, Houser would later recount that it was "gratifying that even after all the years in prison he [Sisulu] remembered me."[23]

In March 1990, Houser was back in Namibia to celebrate the country's independence under the new African constitution. The day before the celebration, foreign guests had been arriving from all over the world, among them was Nelson Mandela, who on February 11 had been released from twenty-seven years in prison. In the Windhoek Athletic Stadium the following day, Sam Nujoma was sworn in as the president of the independent Republic of Namibia and Hage Geingob as the first prime minister. Thus had ended seventy-five years of South African occupation and over a century of foreign rule. The mood in the stadium was euphoric, yet the challenges for the new country would be tremendous. South Africa had bequeathed its former colony a legacy of grinding poverty, 33 percent unemployment, a budget deficit, rampant illiteracy and malnutrition, as well as deep racial and ethnic divisions among the people.[24]

Arriving home after his visit to Namibia, Houser received a notice from the Mozambican government that he had been awarded the Bagamoyo Medal by the Fifth Congress of the FRELIMO Party so named for the Tanzanian coastal town of Bagamoyo, which hosted the FRELIMO Secondary School and vocational training center used by FRELIMO fighters. It was the first of several awards that would come to Houser in his later years for his work in supporting African liberation.

SOUTH AFRICA REDUX

Between February and March 1991, Houser made his first visit to South Africa, from which he had been banned for thirty-seven years. He had waited a long time to see this day. On the one hand it was exhilarating to be back and to see so many of the comrades in the ANC and PAC offices he had worked with (or for) over the years when they were either in exile or in prison. Among them were Walter Sisulu, Nelson Mandela, Yusuf Cachalia, Joe Slovo, and Helen Suzman.[25] Others who had been active in the struggle he would meet for the first time, such as George Bizos, a member of the legal team who had defended Mandela, Govan Mbeki, and Sisulu at the Rivonia Trial.

Although the apartheid state was crumbling, it was still extant.[26] No one knew whether the far-right would unleash more violence. It remained to be seen if a new constitution could be written, given the huge gap between the two sides. "This is a risky time in South African history," Houser wrote. "A moment of truth lies just ahead when the rewards of agreement between contending sides can be great and the tragedy of failure enormous."[27]

As Houser drove through the crowded townships of Soweto, Alexandra, Gugulethu, and Crossroads, past houses in the township of Mpophomeni in Natal that had been burned out by Inkatha forces (the private army of the autocratic Chief Mangosuthu Buthelezi), and as he visited prisoners in the notorious Robben Island prison it became clear to him why this trip was a sober one. "I am not a neophyte," he confessed. "I have too much awareness of the enormity of the problems in South Africa. The changes in apartheid are important but leave untouched the great problems of poverty, of land distribution, of crime and internal violence."[28] It was the statement of a man who had learned to temper his original idealistic enthusiasm for the vast potential of Africa with the sobering realities of the difficulties that lay ahead: "One thing is certain in my mind—if a new democratic South Africa can emerge from all the struggle and suffering and turmoil over the past decades, it will be a historic miracle."[29]

Houser's first trip to the new South Africa had whet his appetite for more.[30] As William Minter and Sylvia Hill pointed out, "Understanding the complex process under way in South Africa during the transition years was not easy inside South Africa, much less from an ocean away."[31] The following year Houser would get another opportunity to try to understand South Africa's trajectory. From April to May 1992 he led a study tour to South Africa where he found that internal violence had escalated, threatening the negotiations that were to lead to the end of apartheid and a democratic election.[32] "Change has not filtered down," Houser lamented.[33]

One of the highlights of Houser's trip was his visit to Oliver Tambo's home. The veteran freedom fighter who had led the ANC from exile was now seventy-five and was recovering from a serious stroke. Houser, who was a hearty seventy-six, found Tambo to be "a shadow of his former self," his speech slow and his uncertain gait steadied by a cane. It would be the last time Houser would see Tambo. The following year he would succumb to another stroke.

DEFYING THE CUBAN EMBARGO

Later that fall, Houser and Irving Wolfe embarked on another adventure that would once again pit Houser against the foreign policy of the United States. The two joined 103 other people in a forty-three-vehicle caravan carrying fifty tons of humanitarian aid to Cuba that had been collected at stops throughout the United States by dozens of churches and community groups.[34] It was an effort to circumvent the American blockade of the island nation and deliver needed supplies directly to the people of Cuba. Since 1962, all exports and imports to or from Cuba had been prohibited by various US presidential executive orders. But in 1992, the US Congress passed the Cuban Democracy Act, which made the economic embargo an official law, as well as not only prohibiting US citizens from traveling to Cuba but also banning family remittances to that country.[35] It was a measure the rabidly anti-Communist Cubans, who had gained significant political influence in Congress, had been pushing for years.

The caravan was dubbed "Pastors for Peace" (or "Friendshipment") and had been the brainchild of the Reverend Lucius Walker, a black Baptist preacher who had founded the Interreligious Foundation for Community Organization (IFCO) in 1967. The IFCO's stated mission was to support the disenfranchised through community organizations, both domestically and internationally, that were fighting human and civil rights injustices. Pastors for Peace was just the kind of project Houser was naturally attracted to. During his previous trips to Cuba he had seen for himself a different reality from that painted by the US government, which had long demonized the country and its colorful leader. Moreover, Pastors for Peace was the kind of direct nonviolent action that Houser himself had orchestrated during his days with CORE and the ACOA.

Houser's fellow "caravanistas" were, like him, political activists who were mostly from religious backgrounds. They came from twenty-five states and nine countries. Following nine different routes on the way to the rallying point in Laredo, Texas, the caravan stopped every evening in a different city or town where the participants loaded more supplies into the vehicles and took part in solidarity rallies, church services, press conferences, and educational gatherings in which they discussed how US foreign policy was affecting the lives of Central American residents. Apart from the fact that Houser and his caravanistas had to drive their own vehicles, the whole trip was reminiscent of the Journey of Reconciliation, although on that excursion Houser and his comrades were upholding US law—in this case they were flouting it. No longer a young man, now Houser was having to ride for long hours, load and unload cartons of material aid, and sleep each night on a different stranger's couch or church floor, often getting as little as four hours' sleep. At age seventy-six, this kind of travel was not easy.

When the caravan reached Laredo, the organizers received a letter from the State Department stating that if they wished to export humanitarian goods, they would have to apply for a government-approved license.

Violation of the requirement could mean conviction under the Trading with the Enemy Act, carrying penalties of up to ten years in prison for individuals and a $100,000 fine and a possible additional civil penalty of $50,000.[36] After intense discussion, the group decided that they would not try to block traffic but would challenge the embargo by walking their supplies across the bridge no matter how long it took. Ten people—all clergy—were chosen to be the first to court arrest. Houser felt honored to be among them.

Wearing clerical collars (it was the first time in his life Houser had ever donned one), they approached the bridge across the Rio Grande River, which demarcated the border, and found they were able to walk across without incident. But on the third try they were blocked by the police and pushed to a fenced enclosure where customs officers wrested the equipment from them. Several were roughed up. Houser and several others were briefly detained but not arrested. After discussions between the group's lawyers and Treasury and Commerce officials, the government officials decided that the caravan could go through without a license if they listed everything they were taking. Computers and some medicines would not be allowed. Houser and his comrades were elated: they had broken the embargo, at least temporarily!

Once in Mexico, the caravan participants found a very different reception. Cars honked as they passed the caravan with its colorful banners, and people in the street stopped to talk with them. The Mexican government had given the caravan complete backing, and the exploit received front-page coverage in the Mexican papers. When they reached Tampico, a five-hundred-mile journey from Laredo, a large and exuberant rally was held in the central plaza. From there they went to the port to unload the aid, which would be transported to Cuba by freighter.

An hour's flight took Houser and his fellow travelers to Havana, where they were greeted at the airport by a throng of Cubans, newspaper and TV journalists, and dignitaries. The Cuban press hailed them as "heroes." They held a press conference and were given the first of a series of receptions that would be repeated over the next several days. In one ceremony in Old Havana, Houser and nine others who had been the first to defy the embargo were presented with symbolic keys to the city. During the following days the group visited schools, hospitals, the Trade Union Confederation, a bicycle and cigar factory, and a Pioneer Camp that had been turned into a facility for children of the Chernobyl nuclear accident who were not only being educated but were also receiving medical treatment for their cancers and other diseases as well as psychological counseling by a medical staff of 504.[37] During one evening at a church service Fidel Castro appeared and spoke for over an hour. Houser confessed to having a "restrained enthusiasm" about seeing Fidel.[38] Having seen so many promising African leaders succumb to the enticements of power, Houser was wary of the cult of personality that can develop around a strong leader.

The effects of the blockade were everywhere. Although the material aid they had delivered was only a drop in the bucket, Houser and his cohorts felt they had made a significant contribution to friendship across borders. Despite the hardships caused by the blockade, they learned that no child went without shoes, no poor people could be found begging in the streets, education and health care from birth to death was available to all, and Cuba had the lowest infant mortality rate in Latin America. In 1959, the year before the revolution, there were six thousand doctors. In 1992, there were forty-seven thousand.

Yet Houser and his fellow travelers would soon hear about a different side of Cuba. They were told of the strained relations between the Catholic Church and the government, the extensive black market the blockade had given rise to, the economic mistakes the government had made, and the sometimes arbitrary arrest of government critics. Still, Houser was impressed. "One has to admire the determination of the Cuban people to survive," he wrote.[39] "Whatever the ultimate significance of the fact that the U.S. government 'blinked' at Laredo, I am entirely convinced of one thing by this project—the absolute importance of continuing, persistently, to open up friendly contacts between the U.S. and Cuba."[40] In subsequent years Houser would participate in two more Pastors for Peace caravans.

AN UNEXPECTED BRUSH WITH MORTALITY

Although Houser had dozens of near-death experiences in his life, he was unprepared for what happened in August of the following year. It was on a hot, humid day as he was playing golf with some friends near his home that he felt a tightening in his chest, weakness, and a pain radiating down his arms. Amazingly, he drove himself to the hospital (a twenty-minute ride) and was treated for a heart attack. Houser had always considered himself immune to the aging process. For a man who had prided himself on his physical stamina, this sudden realization of his vulnerability was a rude awakening. "How could this happen to me?" he asked in notes written from his hospital bed. "This whole episode makes me realize my mortality. Life doesn't go on forever. . . . I think I shall watch my priorities. I'll spend more time with Jean. I won't try to go on every project or make every meeting."[41]

VISITS TO A FREE SOUTH AFRICA

Starting on April 26, 1994, South Africa held its first truly democratic elections, and on May 10, Nelson Mandela became the first black president of a free South Africa. Houser was not present for the elections, but a delegation from the ACOA was part of the international observer team. Gail Hovey, who was part of that delegation, recalled that Kenneth Kaunda had asked where George Houser was.[42] Despite vowing to slow down, Houser could not stop his lifelong penchant for being where the action was. That July he led another study tour to the new republic. His wife, Jean, and granddaughter, Emily Leys, were among the participants. As usual, Houser packed the itinerary with visits to schools, hospitals, religious, and civic organizations; tours through the townships; and visits with government officials. His granddaughter, Emily, recalled that the trip was billed as a "study tour," but it really felt like "a star-studded post-revolutionary victory tour."[43]

In August of that same year, Houser received a letter from Walter Sisulu. "At 83," the letter said, "I have been persuaded that I should not depart this life without recording for history and the archives my reminiscences and experiences, not only of my personal life, but also of those events in the long struggle for this 'New South Africa' that we are now beginning to build." Sisulu requested Houser's help with that project. Thus, on September 18, 1995, Houser and his friend Herb Shore, then a professor of writing at the University of California and a longtime southern Africa activist, departed for yet another trip to South Africa. The project was not designed as a formal biography but as an oral history, an account of the struggle as he remembered it that would be placed in the archive at the Mayibuye Centre at the University of the Western Cape, in the ANC archives at Fort Hare University, and at the Africa Fund. That Houser was asked to shepherd such a project is evidence of the unique reputation he had earned with African leaders.

Between September and early October, Houser and Shore collected over fourteen hours of tape recordings they would transcribe, correct for factual errors, and organize topically and chronologically the following autumn in New York. In January and February 1997, the two men spent a few more weeks with Sisulu in Johannesburg and Cape Town, collecting fourteen additional hours of recordings. After months of writing and reorganizing taped material, the result was *I Will Go Singing*. The book's titular phrase was taken from Sisulu's thoughts as he was awaiting sentencing at the Rivonia Trial. If he had to go to the gallows, Sisulu thought, he would go singing "for the sake of the youth who follow us, so they will know that we fulfilled our task in life"[44]

During the hours he spent with Sisulu, Houser's love and admiration for the man grew. "In addition to his courage," Houser said, "he is a man of great goodwill. He amazingly carries no bitterness after the long years of struggle which involved long periods of banning and imprisonment not only for himself, but for his wife, Albertina, and his eight children, three of them adopted. . . . He sees good points even in those in opposition to him. . . . He is a peacemaker. He holds things together."[45] The schedule of taping and visits would have taxed a man half his age, and Houser, now eighty-one, confessed to feeling tired at the end of each day. He was sleeping only fitfully, another admission that his age was catching up with him. Nevertheless, he kept up a full schedule of meetings and visits to various historic sites such as Liliesleaf Farm, the secret meeting place for ANC activists in the 1960s and the site where many prominent ANC leaders were arrested, leading to the Rivonia Trial. The history Houser had watched from afar became a vivid reality for him after visits to Pollsmoor Prison and Robben Island and hearing the stories associated with the famous prisoners who had been incarcerated there.

Between January and February 1997, Houser and Shore returned to South Africa to finish taping Sisulu's story. On that occasion, the two of them attended a meeting of parliament at which Mandela spoke and were afterward ushered into Mandela's office. As Mandela came striding into the office where several people were waiting, he called out, "Where is George Houser?"[46] The two men then settled in for a long talk, at the end of which the great man embraced Houser warmly and on a copy of the speech he had just given inscribed the following: "To George, Best wishes to a remarkable freedom fighter." Afterward, they went outside for photos. Two elderly men, one towering over the other, joined by a common yearning for freedom and justice but kept apart by years of oppression, were now smiling brightly at the camera and uniting in a heartfelt handshake.

Despite being diagnosed with lymphoma that same year, Houser could not stop his activity. In addition to his trips to South Africa and Cuba, he would visit Costa Rica, where he had been invited to give a talk; travel to China accompanied by his wife, Jean; and go to Brazil to take part in the marriage ceremony of a grandson. At the age of ninety-three he would participate in a fact-finding trip to Israel and Palestine where, at a Palestinian protest, he was hit with tear gas from Israeli soldiers. Experiencing the many government checkpoints, the five-hundred-mile wall built to divide Palestinians from Jews, and an area where Palestinian homes had been taken over by Israeli families while the former owners camped in tents on the street outside, Houser was reminded of the apartheid he had seen in South Africa.[47] "I felt," Houser told this author, "that if I were younger I would probably have gotten involved."

During his later years Houser also became an advocate for the release of two controversial reformed political prisoners, Kathy Boudin and Judith Clark, members of the Weather Underground who had been convicted of murder for their role in the robbery of a Brinks armored car at the Nanuet Mall in Rockland County, New York, in October 1981. Houser visited both women dozens of times, writing letters to the editor and state officials on their behalf, as they had become model prisoners.[48] Boudin was released in 2003, but Clark would remain incarcerated until 2019. In a letter to the *Journal News* Houser expressed his reasons for supporting Judith Clark, whom law enforcement continued to paint as an unrepentant terrorist: "I would like to express the hope that the bereaved families of the victims of this tragic event two decades ago would find it in their hearts to believe that the punishment has been sufficient and that forgiveness might help relieve the pain."[49] It took real courage on Houser's part to have supported these women in a conservative climate in Rockland County, which had been dominated by long-simmering anger among the law enforcement community.

Houser's later years were filled with many well-earned tributes. Among them was an honorary LLD awarded to Houser and James Farmer in 1994 by Antioch College and a Distinguished Alumni/ae Award in 1996 from Union Theological Seminary, the school that had refused to allow him to graduate. In December 2007, the *New York Times* paid tribute to the then ninety-one-year-old peace and justice activist: "At a time when religion in American politics almost invariably means the religious right, he's a vibrant reminder that faith cuts through politics from more than one direction, with more than one message."[50]

Perhaps the most coveted award Houser received was from the government of South Africa. On April 9, 2010, Houser received a telephone call from the South African consulate in Los Angeles. "We have a very important message for you from the President of South Africa," the caller said. Some days later, a letter was sent by diplomatic pouch inviting him to participate in a ceremony in Pretoria, all expenses paid, at which he would be awarded the Order of the Grand Companions of O. R. Tambo. After a gap of eleven years, Houser and his wife, Jean, flew to South Africa for the last time. They were met at the airport and given a car at their disposal. "VIP treatment that we're not used to!" Houser quipped. In a ceremony at the Presidential Guest House attended by hundreds of people, South Africa's then president, Jacob Zuma, hung a medal around Houser's neck and presented him with a

handsomely carved wooden staff entwined with a copper snake to symbol-
ize the work of people who have labored for peace and justice.[51] "I felt good
about it, [the award] not ecstatic," he told a journalist later, "because there
are many people who struggled hard against apartheid. I felt humbled."[52]

For Houser, this trip was like an "old home week." Although many of the
friends he had wished to see had since died, he was able to visit with several
who were still alive. The day before they were to leave, the Housers visited
Soweto, and Houser was pleased to see that many of the ramshackle huts
were gone. There had been some improvements. But in his conversations
with these old friends Houser sensed a feeling of disillusionment about the
future of the country. There was already rampant corruption in the government, crime was a serious problem, gated communities were in abundance,
and the gap between rich and poor continued to be a stubborn problem.[53]

In 2009, the Skyview Acres community bid a fond farewell to the Housers, who were leaving their home of sixty years to take up residence at
Friends' House, an assisted-living facility in Santa Rosa, California, run by the
Quakers not far from the home of their daughter, Martie Leys. The Housers'
farewell party was written up in the regional newspaper, Houser having been
a longtime icon in the Rockland County community. "He's among those
incredible people who go where angels fear to tread," said civil rights activist
Stella Marrs.[54] In Santa Rosa, Houser continued his agitation for peace and
social justice, giving talks to local audiences, arranging speakers as head of
the Friends' House Program Committee, participating in peace vigils, and
writing op-eds and letters to the editor until his health no longer permitted
such activities. On June 2, 2015, he celebrated his ninety-ninth birthday in the
nursing unit of Friends' House surrounded by a chorus of family and friends
singing old campfire songs and treasured hymns.

George M. Houser died peacefully of congestive heart failure on August
19, 2015. The Fellowship of Reconciliation announced his passing with the
words that "one of the most important yet least-heralded activists of the 20th
century" had just died.[55] Lengthy obituaries appeared in the New York Times
and Washington Post.[56] Two memorial services were held, one in California
and the other in the chapel at Union Theological Seminary in New York
City where, seventy-five years before, the Union Eight had held their prayer
service before being sent to prison. Although Houser had outlived most of
those he had worked with, both services were attended by hundreds of people who either knew him or knew of his work. South Africa's consul general attended the New York City service. Recollections of family members
were combined with memories and tributes from several who had worked

with him through the ACOA. Richard Lapchick, who had worked with him on the sports boycott campaign, remarked that "George Houser was the American most responsible for awakening Americans to the injustices on the continent," while Prexy Nesbitt testified that "as an African American man . . . I have to say a particular note of thanks to George for working both sides of the pond. He never just worked on African issues. He always saw the relationship between working on Africa and working on the injustice in this country." Messages were read from Max and Elinor Sisulu, the son and daughter-in-law of Walter and Albertina, as well as from Dumisani Kumalo, who recalled that as South Africa's ambassador to the UN, "It was always a joy to invite George Houser to diplomatic receptions because he knew so many ambassadors and leaders of African countries long before they were members of the U.N."[57]

ONE STEP ENOUGH FOR ME

When he began his work for social justice, Houser could not have foreseen the florescence of his initial efforts to break the back of racial segregation, nor could he have predicted the ultimate results of his efforts to get companies, investors, sports figures, and artists to disengage from South Africa. In a time of restricted space for dissent, his cultivation of action and advocacy had helped lay the groundwork for the eventual end of de jure racial segregation in the United States and apartheid in South Africa.

Houser refused, however, to take credit for the subsequent developments that were the work of thousands of others in the United States, Europe, and most significantly those in Africa who were sacrificing their lives on a daily basis for freedom. "I have lived during exciting times and have managed to latch on to some of the historical developments that have made this period meaningful," he once said. "I have played a role, but I certainly do not exaggerate my contribution. I wouldn't want to make it more than it is."[58]

Perhaps Houser's signature gift to the movements he was associated with was his emphasis on reconciliation. This could sometimes be seen, perhaps mistakenly in Houser's case, as too facile an accommodation to the forces of oppression. In the American race relations context what was needed, according to more militant sectors of the black community, was reparations, not reconciliation. Yet in light of his support for the African liberation movements and his advocacy for Kathy Boudin and Judith Clark, we can surmise that his idea of reconciliation was not to be equated with gradualism or accommodation. Although he didn't articulate it as such, his idea was more in keeping with South Africa's Truth and Reconciliation Commission, where reconciliation was to be the end point of a process of restorative justice that included repentance by wrongdoers and reparations to those who had been harmed.

Although apartheid's defeat was the result of a multicausal process, Houser had helped to lay the foundations for a solidarity movement that by the 1980s would begin to shake the foundations of business as usual, contributing to a significant shift in geopolitics and in the domestic culture of the United States. During his years as executive director, Houser's hand was often hidden in the collective policy decisions made by the board and steering committee and in the materials produced by the ACOA, ranging from thousands of pages of print to large public events, conferences, speaking tours, public demonstrations, boycott campaigns, exhibitions of African art and quiet dinners for African guests. Yet behind it all was George Houser, acting as goad and catalyst with his indefatigable energy and vision. He was a man who believed that persisting against all odds was the only way forward.

The bank campaign Houser had helped to catalyze would prove to be one of the most successful weapons in the solidarity movement's arsenal of tactics used to help weaken the system of apartheid. "The boycotts that were put into effect against South Africa," according to Nelson Mandela, "hastened the day that I was released from prison and hastened the day when I became president."[59]

The shareholder divestment campaign Houser and the ICCR had begun in 1968 was to have wide-ranging effects on the way American corporations did business. Over the ensuing decades it would result in the movement for socially responsible investing and have wider consequences as well, helping to sustain a student movement after the Vietnam War ended. Students who staged sit-ins in their universities' administrative offices to compel them to divest from companies doing business in South Africa came to see that their education was more than attending classes: it was also about the goals, values, purpose, and principles of the institution of higher education itself. They would not only protest the investment portfolios of their universities but also challenge the ties of academics and trustees with South Africa. They would protest racism and corporate recruitment on their campuses and begin demands for a change in curricula, such as adding courses and majors in black studies.[60]

Yet for someone so devoted to improving the human condition, the long arc of history Houser lived through could sometimes be unforgiving. Throughout his life Houser had seen many hopes rise and triumph only to be dashed by betrayal or disillusionment. He began his activist career trying to bring about the end of war and was always a devout pacifist; but a world without war seemed to be even more distant with the terrorist attacks of September 11, 2011, in the United States and the US government's belligerent response in Afghanistan and Iraq. His characteristic response, however, was to denounce the use of retaliatory weapons. In a speech entitled "The Other 9/11," he told the story of Gandhi announcing his first campaign of nonviolent civil disobedience in South Africa on September 11, 1906. The point was to contrast the moral power of nonviolent direct action with the senseless (and immoral) violence and paranoia that has characterized US policy since September 11, 2001.[61]

If global peace was still elusive, so was the cause of racial justice in the United States. The African self-determination that Houser had worked so hard for failed to produce the peace and prosperity it had once promised. Looking back on such failures might have seemed a cause for cynicism, but Houser rejected such an attitude. "The struggle for a better person, a better life, a better country and a better world never ends," he once wrote. "Perhaps the moment of greatest freedom is found as we engage in the struggle to achieve it. And that moment is always with us."[62] He was always comforted in that struggle by a theme from one of his favorite hymns, "Lead Kindly Light," a refrain of which goes, "I do not ask to see the distant scene/One step enough for me."[63] "I believe that," said Houser. "I believe one step is enough and you take it, as long as you have faith you're doing the right thing to begin with."[64]

Notes

INTRODUCTION

1. George M. Houser, *No One Can Stop the Rain: Glimpses of Africa's Liberation Struggle* (New York: Pilgrim, 1989), 3; personal reflections as told to the author.

2. Houser, interview by the author, May 3, 2010; Houser in email to the author, March 20, 2009.

3. Aldon D. Morris, *The Origins of the Civil Rights Movement: Black Communities Organizing for Change* (New York: Free Press, 1984).

4. Dumisani Kumalo, message read at memorial service for George Houser, New York City, November 6, 2015.

1

1. Houser, interview by the author, March 19, 2009.

2. Houser, interview by Philip Greenspan, July 21, 2006, GMH PP.

3. Two of these books were particularly persuasive: H. C. Engelbrecht and F. C. Hanighen, *Merchants of Death: A Study of the International Armament Industry* (New York: Dodd Mead, 1934) and retired, decorated Marine Corps General Smedley D. Butler's *War Is a Racket* (New York: Roundtable, 1935).

4. John Howard Yoder, *Nevertheless: Varieties of Religious Pacifism*, 2nd ed. (Scottdale, PA: Herald, 1992).

5. For a biography of Muste's life, see Leilah Danielson, *American Gandhi: A. J. Muste and the History of Radicalism in the Twentieth Century* (Philadelphia: University of Pennsylvania Press, 2014).

6. A. J. Muste, "Evanston: After Three Months," *Fellowship* 20, no. 11 (December 1954): 13.

7. See Sheila D. Collins, "Public Attitudes toward Government," in *When Government Helped: Learning from the Successes and Failures of the New Deal*, ed. Sheila D. Collins and Gertrude Schaffner Goldberg (New York: Oxford University Press, 2014), 3–4.

8. The Social Creed called for the alleviation of Sunday working hours, the abolition of child labor, a living wage, the negotiation and arbitration of labor disputes, social security for workers in old age, disability insurance, poverty reduction, and a fairer distribution of wealth. However, it stopped short of advocating cooperative ownership and made no reference to racial justice. For a history and critique of the Social Gospel movement see Gary Dorrien, *Social Ethics in the Making: Interpreting an American Tradition* (Oxford: Wiley-Blackwell, 2011), 60–145.

9. See Gertrude Schaffner Goldberg, "A Decade of Dissent: The New Deal and Popular Movements," in Collins and Goldberg, *When Government Helped*, 86–119.

10. For histories of this movement see Robert Cohen, *When the Old Left Was Young: Student Radicals and America's First Mass Student Movement, 1929–1941* (New York: Oxford University Press, 1993); Hal Draper, "The Student Movement of the 1930s: A Political History," in *As We Saw the Thirties: Essays on Social and Political Movements of a Decade*, ed. Rita James Simon (Urbana: University of Illinois Press, 1969); Eileen Pagan, *Class, Culture and the Classroom: The Student Peace Movement of the 1930s* (Philadelphia: Temple University Press, 1982); and Patti McGill Peterson, "The Young Socialist Movement in America from 1905 to 1940: A Study of the Young People's Socialist League" (PhD diss., University of Wisconsin–Madison, 1974), ProQuest (7430124).

11. Cohen, *When the Old Left Was Young*, xiii.

12. Cohen, xiv.

13. Cohen, xvi.

14. The World Student Christian Federation was established in 1895 at Vadstena Castle, Sweden, by students and student leaders from ten North American and European countries.

15. Rick L. Nutt, *The Whole Gospel for the Whole World: Sherwood Eddy and the American Protestant Mission* (Macon, GA: Mercer University Press, 1997), 4.

16. Sherwood Eddy and Kirby Page, *The Abolition of War: The Case against War and Questions and Answers Concerning War, Christianity and World Problems*, Christianity and World Problems Series no. 7 (New York: George H. Doran, 1924), 43.

17. Sherwood Eddy quoted in Michael G. Thompson, *For God and Globe: Christian Internationalism in the United States between the Great War and the Cold War* (Ithaca, NY: Cornell University Press, 2015), 2. A. J. Muste was among the members of the committee.

18. Thompson, *For God and Globe*, 1.

19. Nutt, *The Whole Gospel*, 4.

20. Houser to parents, August 8, 1935, GMH PP.

21. Houser to parents, August 8, 1935.

22. Houser to parents, August 29, 1935, GMH PP.

23. Houser to parents, August 29, 1935.

24. Houser to parents, September 12, 1935, GMH PP.

25. Houser to parents, September 12, 1935.

26. Houser to parents, September 12, 1935.

27. China was then engaged in a civil war between the Nationalists and Communists, and Japan was occupying parts of the country.

28. Houser to parents, October 1, 1935, GMH PP.

29. Houser to parents, November 13, 1935, GMH PP.

30. Houser to Parents, n.d. 1935, GMH PP.

31. Richard L. Deats, "No Moratorium on the Sermon on the Mount," accessed February 24, 2013, http://deatspeace.tripod.com/muriel.html. For more on Muriel Lester, see Jill Wallis, *Mother of World Peace: The Life of Muriel Lester* (Enfield Lock, UK: Hisarlik, 1993).

32. Wallis, *Mother of World Peace*.

33. Houser to parents, November 7, 1935, GMH PP.

34. Houser to parents, December 12, 1935, GMH PP.

35. Houser to parents, December 12, 1935, GMH PP.

36. Dr. Hu Shih (1891–1962) was a leading liberal nationalist scholar and philosopher, leader in the New Culture movement, and author of "The Chinese Renaissance." His reputation fell into decline as revolutionary Communism spread in China. In *The Heritage of Asia*, published in 1932, Kenneth Saunders called him the greatest modern leader of China. "Writes of 3 Leaders of the 'New Asia,'" *New York Times*, June 30, 1932, https://timesmachine.nytimes.com/timesmachine /1932/06/30/100831531.html?pageNumber=21.

37. Houser to parents, December 12, 1935; Houser, "Impressions of an American Exchange Student at Lingnan" (unpublished manuscript), GMH PP.

38. Houser to parents, December 19, 1935, GMH PP.

39. Houser to parents, February 13, 1936, GMH PP.

40. Houser to parents, March 18, 1936, GMH PP.

41. Houser, "Impressions."

42. Houser to parents, May 28, 1936, GMH PP.

43. Harry Ward represented the far-left wing of the Social Gospel movement. His enthusiastic support of the Soviet Union and his inability to explain himself after Stalin's accord with Hitler led to his being eclipsed in Union Seminary's history and in the history of the church in general. Reinhold Niebuhr, who shared Ward's early Social Gospel optimism, evolved in his thinking over the course of the 1930s, adopting a theological ethic ("Christian Realism") that made him more acceptable to the mainstream. Unlike Ward, Niebuhr would become one of the most widely known and influential American theologians and public intellectuals of the twentieth century.

44. For more on his distinguished career, see John M. Swomley Jr. Papers, 1940–2002, DG 226, SCPC.

45. Joelle Farrell, "In Memory of Franklin Littell," Council on Centers of Jewish-Christian Relations, accessed February 24, 2013, http://www.ccjr.us/news /in-memoriam/littell; Christine McLaughlin, "Gift of a Lifetime," *Temple Review* 65, no. 2 (Fall 2011): 32–35.

2

1. For Henry Emerson Fosdick, see Robert Moats Miller, *Harry Emerson Fosdick: Preacher, Pastor, Prophet* (New York: Oxford University Press, 1985).

2. Niebuhr argued that the idealism and utopianism that characterized many of the early Social Gospelers was a form of self-love or the self-delusion of innocence. Such self-love could infect nations as well as individuals, resulting in a kind of Manicheanism that could cause collectivities to do evil things. His "Christian Realism" contributed not only to Christian ethical thought but also to international relations theory. His beliefs led him to support the US entry into World War II, to adopt a Cold War anti-Communism stance, and—ironically—to support the use of nuclear weapons.

3. The Religion and Labor Foundation had been founded by Willard Uphaus, a radical Methodist layman and pacifist who had taught at Yale Divinity School.

During the McCarthy era he spent nearly a year in jail for refusing to divulge the names of people who attended World Fellowship, which was the summer retreat center he ran in Conway, New Hampshire. See Josh Barnabel, "Dr. Willard Uphaus: Leader of Pacifist Causes in the 50s," *New York Times*, October 11, 1983, http://www.nytimes.com/1983/10/11/obituaries/dr-willard-uphaus-leader-of-pacifist-causes-in-the-50-s.html.

4. FOR Statement of Purpose, accessed January 26, 2016, http://forusa.org/about/sop.

5. Jennifer Bleyer, "Like a Tree with Many Rings, a Building with Many Lives," *New York Times*, April 24, 2005, http://www.nytimes.com/2005/04/24/nyregion/thecity/24eleg.html?_r=1&.

6. Houser to Walline, February 18, 1941, GMH PP.

7. Houser, interview by the author, September 27, 2011.

8. Houser, interview by the author, August 2008.

9. George M. Houser, "Diary September 14," *Union Review* 2, no. 1 (November 1940): 13, Series 10D, Box 1, Folder 4, UTS2, Union Records, The Burke Library, UTS.

10. David M. Kennedy, *Freedom from Fear: The American People in Depression and War, 1929–1945* (New York: Oxford University Press, 1999), 393.

11. Franklin D. Roosevelt, "Fireside Chat on the War in Europe," in *The Essential Franklin Delano Roosevelt: FDR's Greatest Speeches, Fireside Chats, Messages and Proclamations*, ed. John Gabriel Hunt (New York: Random House, 1995), 169–70.

12. George M. Houser, "Resisting the Draft," *Christian Century* 112, no. 24 (August 16–23, 1995): 775.

13. Kennedy, *Freedom from Fear*, 451, quoting from Maurice Matloff and Edwin M. Snell, *Strategic Planning for Coalition Warfare, 1941–1942* (Washington, DC: Department of the Army, 1953), 14.

14. Houser, "Diary, September 14."

15. Houser, "Diary, September 14."

16. Houser, "Diary, September 14."

17. Donald Benedict, *Born Again Radical* (New York: Pilgrim, 1982), 30–31.

18. George M. Houser, "Diary, October 3," *Union Review* 2, no. 1 (November 1940): 13, Series 10D, Box 1, Folder 4, UTS2, Union Records, The Burke Library, UTS.

19. Houser, "Diary, October 3."

20. This is the account Houser provided of how the group came together; but in an interview with this author, Don Benedict gave major credit to Dellinger and Houser for pulling the group together. Don Benedict, interview by the author, July 13, 2008.

21. In addition to the drafters, the statement was signed by Sheldon L. Rahn, Eldon Durham, James Glyer, Tom Keehn, Perry H. Hultin, William H. Lovell, Houser W. Burroughs Jr., James W. Orser, Ted Thornton, John H. Burrowes, Walter H. Jackson, Richard J. Wichlei, J. Herbert Brautigam Jr., and Joseph J. Bevilacqua.

22. Dellinger's own account of his colorful life is contained in his autobiography, *From Yale to Jail: The Life Story of a Moral Dissenter* (Marion, SD: Rose Hill, 1993).

23. Benedict, interview by the author; Benedict, *Born Again Radical*.

24. "Obituary: Meredith Dallas," accessed April 4, 2014, http://antiochcollege .org/news/obituaries/meredith_dallas.html.

25. "A Christian Conviction on Conscription and Registration," October 10, 1940 (unpublished manuscript), GMH PP.

26. The peace churches and other organizations like the ACLU had lobbied the government for CO status that could be carried out in Civilian Public Service (CPS) camps run by the churches. They were reacting to the disastrous situation during World War I when COs were sent to military camps where they were often abused by draftees or were jailed and often physically brutalized. But as the CPS was implemented it became apparent that the military was the stronger influence in the camps. Moreover, the work was often meaningless; working without pay, the men had to finance their own stays, and many were even used as guinea pigs to test a variety of warfare methods. For more on this, see *The Good War and Those Who Refused to Fight It*, produced by Judith Ehrlich and Rick Tejada-Flores, available from Bullfrog Films, http://www.bullfrogfilms.com/catalog/gwar.html.

27. "A Christian Conviction."

28. William H. Lovell, "Conscientious Objection in 1940—Reminiscences." Statement to Presbyterian Peace Committee at General Assembly, 1990 (unpublished manuscript), GMH PP.

29. Because they were the first to boldly defy the draft, the Union Eight got national publicity out of all proportion to their numbers. In 1942, A. J. Muste, Richard Gregg, and several older FOR leaders refused to register when the draft was extended, but the government elected not to prosecute them. See Joseph Kip Kosek, *Acts of Conscience: Christian Nonviolence and Modern American Democracy* (New York: Columbia University Press, 2009), 165.

30. McDermott, quoted in "Divinity Students Face Jail on Draft," *New York Times*, October 12, 1940, https://www.nytimes.com/1940/10/13/archives/divinitystudents-face-jail-on-draft-mcdermott-threatens-to-crack.html.

31. Students quoted in *New York World-Telegram*, October 12, 1940, GMH PP.

32. Houser, "Diary," October 12–13, 14.

33. Robert T. Handy, *A History of Union Theological Seminary in New York* (New York: Columbia University Press, 1987), 180–82.

34. Handy, *A History*, 186–87. "Union Seminary to Curb Radicals," *New York Times*, May 23, 1934, https://www.nytimes.com/1934/05/23/archives/union-seminary-to -curb-radicals-dr-coffin-tells-alumni-he-will-not.html?searchResultPosition=1.

35. "Dykstra Says Objectors Must Register," *New York Post*, October 12, 1940, GMH PP.

36. "20 Theological Students United to Defy Draft," *Herald Tribune*, October 12, 1940, GMH PP.

37. Reinhold Niebuhr to Mr. Wyckoff, GMH PP.

38. Press Release from Union Theological Seminary Faculty, October 14, 1940, Roger L. Shinn Papers, Series 3, Subseries 3D, Box 1, Folder 1, The Burke Library, UTS; "Seminary Scores Draft Objectors," *New York Times*, October 15, 1940, https:// www.nytimes.com/1940/10/15/archives/seminary-scores-draft-objectors-faculty -of-union-theological.html.

39. Resolution passed unanimously by the Student Cabinet, October 11, 1940, Roger Shinn Papers, Series 3, Subseries 3D, Box 1, Folder 1, The Burke Library, UTS.

40. Otto Houser quoted in "Denver Man Thought He'd Get the Limit," *Rocky Mountain News*, November 15, 1940, GMH PP.

41. Ethel Houser to Houser, October 22, 1940, GMH PP.

42. Dellinger's father's threat is related in Benedict's *Born Again Radical* and by Houser in an interview with the author, July 2011. The suicide never happened.

43. George M. Houser, "Reflections of a Religious War Objector," in *A Few Small Candles: War Resisters of World War II Tell Their Stories*, ed. Larry Gara and Lenna Mae Gara (Kent, OH: Kent State University Press, 1999), 135–36.

44. Muste and Thomas quoted in Houser, "Reflections," 136; Dellinger, *From Yale to Jail*, 79.

45. Margaret [Houser] to Houser, October 20, 1940, GMH PP. Margaret's husband was drafted and would later see service in China.

46. Martha [Houser] to Houser, October 28, 1940, GMH PP.

47. Glenn Young to Houser, n.d., GMH PP.

48. George M. Houser, "Diary October 14," *Union Review* 2, no. 1 (November 1940): 15, Series 10D, Box 1, Folder 4, UTS2, Union Records, The Burke Library, UTS, 15.

49. Houser, "Reflections," 135.

50. Houser, "Reflections," 136–37; Houser interviewed by Philip Greenspan, July 21, 2006, for *Men of Peace: World War II Conscientious Objectors*, ed. Mary R. Hopkins (Belize: Producionnes de la Hamaca, Caye Caulker, 2010), Kindle, GMH PP.

51. The US District Court, *The United States of America vs. George M. Houser, Defendant. Indictment*, GMH PP.

52. George M. Houser, "Diary, November 10," *Union Review* 2, no. 1 (November 1940): 16, Series 10D, Box 1, Folder 4, UTS2, Union Records, The Burke Library, UTS.

53. David Dellinger, "Why I Refused to Register in the October 1940 Draft and a Little of What It Led To," in Gara and Gara, *A Few Small Candles*, 30.

54. *United States District Court Southern District of New York vs. Richard J. Wichlei, William N. Lovell, Donald Benedict, David Dellinger, Meredith Dallas, George M. Houser, Joseph G. Bevilacqua and Howard E. Spragg before Hon.* Samuel Mandelbaum, District Judge, November 14, 1940, GMH PP.

55. "8 Draft Resisters Get Prison Terms," *New York Times*, November 15, 1940, https://www.nytimes.com/1940/11/15/archives/8-draft-objectors-get-prison-terms-divinity-students-sentenced-to.html.

56. Houser, "Reflections," 138–39.

57. Warren Hall, "8 Divinity Students Who Defied Draft Get Year in Prison," GMH PP.

58. Eugene V. Debs, "Statement to the Court Upon Being Convicted of Violating the Sedition Act," September 18, 1918, accessed June 17, 2020, https://www.marxists.org/archive/debs/works/1918/court.htm.

59. Dellinger, "Why I Refused to Register," 32.

60. Rev. Mr. Marble quoted in "Denver Man Thought He'd Get Limit," *Rocky Mountain News*, November 15, 1940, GMH PP.

61. "For Religious C.O.'s and Others," n.d., GMH PP.

62. George M. Houser, *Erasing the Color Line* (New York: Fellowship, 1945), 52, CDGA CORE Collected Records, Box 2, SCPC.

63. Marian Mollin, *Radical Pacifism in Modern America: Egalitarianism and Protest* (Philadelphia: University of Pennsylvania Press, 2006), 18.

64. Roger Shinn to Houser, December 22, 1940, Roger L. Shinn Papers, Series 3, Subseries 3D, Box 1, Folder 1, Burke Library, UTS.

65. Houser to Shinn, December 26, 1940.

66. Houser to Shinn, January 31, 1941.

67. Shinn to Houser, February 9, 1941.

68. Houser to Shinn February 28, 1941.

69. Shinn to Houser, March 9, 1941.

70. Houser to Shinn, February 20, 1940.

71. The draft card burning was part of a campaign against the Truman administration's Universal Military Training proposal, which sought to replace the Selective Service Act. See Kosek, *Acts of Conscience*, 197.

72. Roger L. Shinn, *Wars and Rumors of Wars* (Nashville, TN: Abingdon, 1972).

73. When Union students again refused to register for the draft during the Vietnam War, Shinn was one of the faculty members who wrote a letter supporting them. He was also among members of the Union community who published a statement regarding apartheid in South Africa in 1967 and worked through the 1980s to divest the seminary's endowment of shares in companies profiting from apartheid. See Carolyn Klaasen, "Letters Between a Prisoner and a Soldier: The Houser-Shinn Correspondence from the Roger L. Shinn Collection," April 29, 2016, *The Burke Library Blog*, accessed April 18, 2018, https://blogs.cul.columbia.edu/burke/category/history/page/2/.

74. Houser to Roger Shinn, n.d., GMH PP.

75. Houser to A. J. Muste, June 11, 1941, DG13 FOR-USA, Section II, Series A-3, Box 11, SCPC.

76. A. J. Muste to Houser, June 25, 1941.

77. Mollin, *Radical Pacifism*, 21.

78. Houser, *Erasing the Color Line*, 47–53; Mollin, 20–21; James Robinson, "Chicago," 38 (unpublished manuscript), n.d., GMH PP.

79. Houser to Walline, December 26, 1940, GMH PP.

80. Houser to Walline, January 2, 1941, GMH PP.

81. Houser to Walline, February 2, 1941, GMH PP.

82. Walline, quoted in Houser to Walline, April 16, 2014, GMH PP.

83. Houser to Walline, April 21, 1941, GMH PP.

84. Houser to Walline, April 29, 1941, GMH PP.

85. Houser to Walline, October 3, 1941, GMH PP.

3

1. According to Houser, restrictive covenants covered 80 percent of the city's area. See George Houser, *Erasing the Color Line*, 3rd ed. (New York: Fellowship, 1951), 46; CORE Papers, Series 6, Reel 49-14.

2. Jacquelyn Dowd Hall, "The Long Civil Rights Movement and the Political Uses of the Past," *Journal of American History* 91, no. 4 (March 2005): 1240. For histories of racially discriminatory federal policy, see Ira Katznelson, *When Affirmative Action Was White* (New York: W. W. Norton, 2005); and Ira Katznelson, *Fear Itself: The New Deal and the Origins of Our Time* (New York: W. W. Norton, 2013).

3. Arnold R. Hirsch, *Making the Second Ghetto: Race and Housing in Chicago, 1940–1960* (Chicago: University of Chicago Press, 1998); Roger Biles, "Race and Housing in Chicago," *Journal of the Illinois State Historical Society (1998–)* 94, no. 1 (Spring 2001): 31–38, http://www.jstor.org/stable/40193533.

4. Homer A. Jack, "Chicago Has One More Chance," *Nation*, September 13, 1947.

5. John D'Emilio, *Lost Prophet: The Life and Times of Bayard Rustin* (New York: Free Press, 2003), 43–44.

6. Jervis Anderson, *Bayard Rustin: Troubles I've Seen* (New York: HarperCollins, 1997), 68.

7. For more on Farmer's life see his autobiography, James Farmer, *Lay Bare the Heart: An Autobiography of the Civil Rights Movement* (New York: Arbor House, 1985).

8. In a debate in the 1960s between Malcolm X and Rustin, Rustin stoutly defended integration over black nationalism.

9. Rustin's life has been covered in several biographies, collections of his writings, and a film: see D'Emilio, *Lost Prophet*; Daniel Levine, *Bayard Rustin and the Civil Rights Movement* (New Brunswick, NJ: Rutgers University Press, 2000); Anderson, *Bayard Rustin*; Michael G. Long, ed., *I Must Resist: Bayard Rustin's Life in Letters* (San Francisco: City Lights, 2012); Michael G. Long, ed., *Down the Line: The Collected Writings of Bayard Rustin* (Chicago: Quadrangle, 1971); Bennett Singer and Nancy Kates, *Brother Outsider: The Life of Bayard Rustin* (2003; New York: Question Why Films, 2010), DVD, http://www.amazon.com/gp/product/B003LR5BBC/ref=s9_psimh_gw_p14_do_i3?pf_rd_m=ATVPDKIKX0DER&pf_rd_s=desktop-1&pf_rd_r=0YKJFWYPX4QN7THQ27BR&pf_rd_t=36701&pf_rd_p=1970559082&pf_rd_i=desktop.

10. Bayard Rustin, "Memorandum: Program and Area Covered," September 12, 1942, in Long, *I Must Resist*, 5.

11. Houser, interview by Zac Peterson, May 3, 2012, used with permission.

12. Leilah Danielson, *American Gandhi: A. J. Muste and the History of Radicalism in the Twentieth Century* (Philadelphia: University of Pennsylvania Press, 2014), Kindle, loc. 4659 of 12060; George M. Houser, "Reflections on the Life and Times of James Farmer," 8, n.d. (unpublished review of Farmer's *Lay Bare the Heart*), GMH PP; Houser, interview by Philip Greenspan, July 21, 2006, GMH PP.

13. George M. Houser, "The Program for a Fellowship Group or Cell," n.d., GMH PP.

14. Houser, interview by the author, July 11, 2011.

15. Houser had not finished his thesis, which was required for graduation. After his retirement he wrote to the University of Chicago Seminary to ask if he could complete his dissertation. By this time, he had written reams of articles as well as the manuscript for a book. The seminary authorities agreed that the manuscript could

serve as the dissertation. In 1984, forty-four years after he had begun his academic work, Houser was awarded a master of divinity degree.

16. Jean Houser, interview by the author, July 11, 2011.

17. George M. Houser, "Reflections of a Religious War Objector," in *A Few Small Candles: War Resisters of World War II Tell Their Stories*, ed. Larry Gara and Lenna Mar Gara (Kent, OH: Kent State University Press, 1999), 150.

18. George Houser, "George Houser Memoir," interview by C. Arthur Bradley, World War II Conscientious Objectors Project, H817G, Norris L Brookens Library Archives/Special Collections, University of Illinois at Springfield, http://cdm16614 .contentdm.oclc.org/cdm/compoundobject/collection/uis/id/2492/rec/1; see Houser interviewed by Katherine M. Shannon, September 11, 1967, Ralph J. Bunche Oral History Collection, Moorland-Spingarn Research Center (RJB-39), Howard University.

19. August Meier and Elliott Rudwick, *CORE: A Study in the Civil Rights Movement 1942–1968* (New York: Oxford University Press, 1973), 5; "Homer Jack," CORE, accessed March 12, 2016, http://www.core-online.org/History/homer_jack.htm.

20. Meier and Rudwick, *CORE*, 5.

21. George M. Houser, "The Birth of CORE," draft of an article for *The CORE Guide to Negro History*, November 25, 1965, GMH PP.

22. James Farmer, "Memorandum to A. J. Muste on Provisional Plans for a Brotherhood Mobilization," February 19, 1942, and "Supplemental Memorandum on Brotherhood Mobilization," n.d.; Farmer, *Lay Bare the Heart*, Appendix A, 355–60; Section II FOR-USA, Box 2, Folder 1, SCPC. Houser's role in editing the memorandum is found in "James L. Farmer, Jr. Remembered," October 7, 1999, GMH PP. Houser agreed that the MOWM was not likely to pull off a mass civil disobedience campaign: "The negro masses are hardly ready for it." But there would be a unique place for an organization like CORE—a small, well-disciplined organization to take on the race issue. See Houser to Farmer, February 13, 1943, CORE Papers, microfilm Series 3, Reel 11-47, 00907.

23. For Farmer's recollections of this meeting, see *Lay Bare the Heart*, 102–3.

24. John Swomley, "F.O.R.'s Early Efforts for Racial Equality," *Fellowship* 56, nos. 7–8 (July–August 1990): 7; Minutes, FOR National Council, April 10, 1942, DG 13, Section II FOR-USA, Series A, Subseries A-2, Box 3, SCPC.

25. James (Jimmy) Robinson in *The Civic Knowledge Project Remembers, 1942–3*, University of Chicago, https://www.youtube.com/watch?v=DukoUsonM1A, 54 mins.

26. George Houser, CORE *A Brief History* pamphlet prepared for CORE, July 1949, DG 13 Section II FOR-USA, Series E, Box 19.

27. Houser, CORE *A Brief History*, 3. There has been some controversy in the literature over who was actually responsible for founding CORE. Sometimes Farmer alone is given the credit, while at other times Farmer and Houser are mentioned together. In his autobiography and in a 1992 interview in *Fellowship*, Farmer thought of his memo to the National Council as the gestation of the organization. See Farmer, *Lay Bare the Heart*, 194. Also see "James Farmer on the Beginnings and End of the Congress of Racial Equality 50 Years Later," an interview by Robin Washington, *Fellowship* 58, nos. 4–5 (April–May 1992): 6–8. Houser wrote to the editor of *Fellowship* shortly after to try to set the record straight, declaring that while Farmer had indeed

proposed the idea of a national mobilization, the actual formation of CORE was a collective process. See George Houser, "To the Editor," *Fellowship* 58, nos. 4–5 (April–May 1992): 2. Both can be credited but in different ways. Farmer's memo generated the vision, while Houser's organizational skills at the local level enabled this vision to be carried out. The FOR's role was also controversial. It is clear that the FOR did not formally sponsor CORE. In a review of Farmer's autobiography Houser insisted that "the FOR provided sympathetic ground on which organizational efforts like CORE could be conceived and activated" but that it was not a FOR "baby." See Houser, "Reflections on the Life and Times."

28. James Robinson, "Chicago," n.d. (unpublished manuscript), GMH PP. This is a personal memoir of his Chicago years.

29. Houser's recollection in *The Civic Knowledge Project Remembers*; Farmer, *Lay Bare the Heart*, 105–6.

30. Meier and Rudwick, *CORE*, 14–15.

31. Houser, interview by Katherine M. Shannon, September 11, 1967.

32. Robinson, "Chicago," 27.

33. Houser, interview by Katherine M. Shannon, September 11, 1967.

34. Houser, *Erasing the Color Line*, 34–36.

35. Houser's recollection in *The Civic Knowledge Project*.

36. Farmer, *Lay Bare the Heart*, 108–9.

37. Houser, *Erasing the Color Line*, 5.

38. Meier and Rudwick, *CORE*, 8.

39. *CORE Action Discipline*, mimeographed pamphlet as amended by the National Convention of the Congress of Racial Equality, June 1946, CORE Papers, Microfilm Series 6, Reel 49-8, 00343.

40. James Robinson, "Personal Memoir," n.d. (unpublished manuscript), GMH PP.

41. Houser, *Erasing the Color Line*, 46; Farmer, *Lay Bare the Heart*, 114–15.

42. Houser, *Erasing the Color Line*, 22; Farmer, *Lay Bare the Heart*, 113; Houser, "Dinner at Stoner's," reprinted in James Peck, *Cracking the Color Line*, pamphlet published by CORE, 1960, CORE Papers, Microfilm Series 6, Reel 49-18; "History of the Stoner's Case," 1942, CORE Papers, Microfilm Series 3, Reel 8-12.

43. Robinson, "Personal Memoir," 32, GMH PP.

44. Meier and Rudwick, *CORE*, 15.

45. Minutes, First Annual Meeting, Chicago Committee of Racial Equality, June 4–6, 1943, CDG-A CORE Collected Records, Box 1, SCPC.

46. Farmer, *Lay Bare the Heart*, 112–13.

47. Muste to Houser and Farmer, June 4, 1943, DG 13 Section II FOR-USA, Series A-3, Box 2, SCPC.

48. CORE, Minutes, First Annual Meeting, Committee of Racial Equality, June 4–6, 1943, CDG-A CORE Collected Records, Box 1, SCPC. Leilah Danielson has pointed out that such a strict set of rules for personal conduct had not been successful with the MOWM, which had at first toyed with the idea of a national civil disobedience campaign and then abandoned it. While the civil rights movement of the late 1950s and 1960s had used Gandhian techniques, they were used tactically, not

out of some deep personal commitment on the part of the masses to nonviolence as a "way of life." See Danielson, *American Gandhi*.

49. CORE, Minutes, First Annual Meeting.

50. Farmer, *Lay Bare the Heart*, 113.

51. All active CORE members were required to serve on at least one committee or in one of three action units: a public places unit, a schools and hospitals unit, and an education unit.

52. Houser, interview by Katherine M. Shannon, September 11, 1967.

53. This story is recounted in Farmer, *Lay Bare the Heart*, 114.

54. Houser, *CORE: A Brief History*, 7–8; CORE, Minutes, First Annual Meeting; Houser, *Erasing the Color Line*, 21–24; Houser, "Dinner at Stoner's"; Farmer, *Lay Bare the Heart*, 113–14.

55. *Discrimination at the University of Chicago: Background for Action*, pamphlet no. 2, 1943, GMH PP.

56. Muste to Houser and Farmer, June 4, 1943.

57. Houser to John M. Swomley, July 1, 1943, DG 13 FOR-USA, Series A-2, Box 3, SCPC.

58. Houser to Muste, June 8, 1943, DG 13 Section II FOR-USA, Series A-2, Box 3, SCPC.

59. Farmer, *Lay Bare the Heart*, 111.

60. Swomley to Houser, April 10, 1985, GMH PP.

61. Farmer, *Lay Bare the Heart*, 111. According to Farmer, Muste had told him that Bayard Rustin agreed with Muste on this matter.

62. Houser, interview by Lisa Brock, No Easy Victories (website), http://www.noeasyvictories.org/interviews/into2_houser.php.

63. Houser to Muste, December 6, 1943, DG 13, Section II FOR-USA, Series A-3, Box 2, SCPC.

64. Muste to Houser, December 10, 1943, DG 13, Section II FOR-USA, Series A-3, Box 2, SCPC.

65. Houser, "Needed—Unity on Pacifist Policy," n.d., GMH PP.

66. Muste to Houser, January 11, 1944, DG 13 Section II FOR-USA, Series A-2, Box 3, SCPC.

67. Muste to Houser, January 11, 1944, DG 13 Section II FOR-USA, Series A-2, Box 3, SCPC.

68. Muste to Houser, January 11, 1944.

69. Houser to Muste, February 23, 1944, DG 13 Section II FOR-USA, Series A-2, Box 3, SCPC; Muste to Houser, February 25, 1944, DG 13 Section II FOR-USA, Series A-3, Box 2, SCPC.

70. Farmer, *Lay Bare the Heart*, 116.

71. Houser, "Reflections on the Life."

72. For Farmer's problems as an organizer, see Rustin to Muste, October 7, 1943, DG 13 Section II FOR-USA, Series A-2, Box 4, Folder 7; Muste to Swomley, February 1, 1945, and Muste to Swomley, Sayre, and Irene Ford, May 7, 1945, A. J. Muste, Correspondence 1940–1947, DG 13 Section II FOR-USA, Series A-3, Box 2, Folder 1, SCPC.

73. Bayard Rustin, "The Negro and Nonviolence," in *Down the Line: The Collected Writings of Bayard Rustin* (Chicago: Quadrangle, 1971), 10.

74. George M. Houser, "Memo on a Mass Non-Violent Interracial Movement," 1945, CORE Papers, Microfilm Series 3, Reel 11-47.

75. Houser, "Memo."

76. Meier and Rudwick, *CORE*, 19.

77. Muste to Houser, April 12, 1944, DG 13, Section II FOR-USA, Series A-3, Box 2, SCPC.

78. Provisional Statement on Program for George Houser's Work, n.d., DG 13, Section II FOR-USA, Series A-3, Box 2, SCPC.

79. For example, Houser was involved in trying to get Truman to grant amnesty for all the imprisoned COs, carried on a correspondence with many imprisoned COs, and visited many of them in CO camps and in prison.

80. Farmer, *Lay Bare the Heart*, 160.

81. When Farmer died on July 9, 1999, Houser was one of the invited speakers at a celebration of Farmer's life held at the Kennedy Center in Washington, DC, and later he was one of three featured speakers, in addition to Reverend James Lawson and Julian Bond, at a memorial service in New York City hosted by the FOR.

82. Houser had secured from the FOR a statement reiterating the FOR's position that it "in no sense seeks to control C.O.R.E. groups." Thus, the FOR was subsidizing CORE without controlling it. See "Memo on CORE and Relation to F.O.R., July 21, 1944," DG 13 Section II FOR-USA, Series E, Box 19, SCPC.

83. Muste to Swomley and Sayre, August 13, 1946, DG 226, Box 14, SCPC.

84. For more on this racial violence see Jack, "Chicago Has One More Chance," 250–52; Hirsch, *Making the Second Ghetto*.

85. Meier and Rudwick, *CORE*, 20.

86. George M. Houser, Letter Accompanying Report on Third Annual Convention of CORE, July 1945, CDG-A, CORE Collected Records, Box 2, SCPC.

87. Houser, *Erasing the Color Line*, 34.

88. *Report to the FOR National Council about the Racial Industrial Work*, May 30, 1947, DG 13 Section II FOR-USA, Series A-2, Box 4, SCPC.

89. George M. Houser, "Memo on the Year-Round Project," 1945, GMH PP.

90. "Interracial Workshop Progress Report," July 1947, 1, CORE Papers, Microfilm Series 3, Reel 13-53.

91. Houser, interview by the author, July 13, 2009.

92. "Interracial Workshop Progress Report," July 1947, CORE Papers; Houser, "Project Brotherhood," reprinted from *Fellowship* by CORE, Spring 1952, CDG-A CORE Collected Records, Box 1, SCPC; "Bulletin: Summer Interracial Workshop," July 30, 1949, CORE Papers Series 3, Reel 13-53.

93. Raymond Arsenault, in *Freedom Riders: 1961 and the Struggle for Racial Justice* (New York: Oxford University Press, 2006), 1, note 1. A file in Box 51 of the Rustin Papers in the CORE Archives credits Rustin, Johnny Carr, Donald Coan, Doreen Curtis, and A. C. Thompson with writing the lyrics; but Robin Washington, who was in the room when Rustin and Houser were discussing the song, claims that

Houser also had a hand in writing the lyrics. See Robin Washington, email message to author, September 20, 2015.

94. "Euclid Beach Incident," 1946, 3, CORE Papers, Microfilm Series 3, Reel 9-16.

95. "Euclid Beach Incident," 1946.

96. Houser, *Erasing the Color Line*, 1951, 34; James Peck, "The Proof of the Pudding," reprinted from *Crisis*, November 1949, CDG-A CORE Collected Records Box 1, SCPC.

97. *Report of the Interracial Workshop*, Washington, DC, July 31, 1951, CDG-A CORE Collected Records, Box 2, SCPC.

98. Statement on the Communist Issue Adopted by the Convention of the Congress of Racial Equality, June 1948, CORE Papers, Microfilm Series 4, Reel 16-1.

99. Houser, interview by Zac Peterson, May 3, 2012. The extent of Communist influence in the ANC is contested in the literature. Steven Ellis claims that the post-1952 SACP controlled *Umkhonto we Sizwe*, the armed wing of the ANC, and even the entire ANC, over several decades of exile. See Steven Ellis, *External Mission: The ANC in Exile, 1960–1990* (New York: Oxford University Press, 2013). Paul S. Landau agrees with this assessment but critiques some of Ellis's analysis of the particulars of the SACP involvement, among them that the ANC was controlled by the SAPC. See Paul S. Landau, "Controlled by Communists? (Re)Assessing the ANC in Its Exilic Decades," *South African Historical Journal* 67, no. 2 (2015): 222–41, http://dx.doi.org/10.1080/02582473.2015.1031818. After Mandela's death, Martin Plaut reported that Mandela himself had been a member of the SACP's Central Committee. See Martin Plaut, "Why Mandela's Communist Party Membership Is Important," *New Statesman*, December 10, 2013, http://www.newstatesman.com/world-affairs/2013/12/why-mandelas-communist-party-membership-important. Landau also supports this but says Mandela's joining the Central Committee was a strategic act. Others, however, have disputed this. Philip Bonner contends that until 1951 Mandela opposed an alliance with the SACP and that he did so later only because he decided to accept the decision of the collective. See Philip Bonner, "The Antinomies of Nelson Mandela," in *The Cambridge Companion to Nelson Mandela*, ed. Rita Barnard (Cambridge: Cambridge University Press, 2014), 29–49, http://doi.org/10.1017/CCO9781139003766.003.38. In several later speeches Mandela credited the SACP with being an ally in the struggle for freedom and argued that the government's banning of the party in 1950, "was but a prelude to the suppression of all democratic opinion in our country." See Nelson Mandela, "Speech of the Deputy President of the African National Congress, Nelson Mandela, at the Rally to Relaunch the South African Communist Party," July 29, 1990, Nelson Mandela Foundation, http://db.nelsonmandela.org/speeches/pub_view.asp?pg=item&ItemID=NMS049.

100. Louise S. Robbins, *The Dismissal of Miss Ruth Brown: Civil Rights, Censorship, and the American Library* (Norman: University of Oklahoma Press, 2000), 169.

101. Brown to Houser, May 22, 1950, quoted in Robbins, *The Dismissal of Miss Ruth Brown*, chap. 2, note 46.

102. George M. Houser, "A Personal Retrospective on the 1947 Journey of Reconciliation" (typescript of a paper given at Bluffington College, September 1992), CORE Collected Records, CDG-A FOR-USA, Section II, Box 1, SCPC.

103. Irene Morgan was not the first person to challenge segregation in public carriers. Rustin himself had challenged Jim Crow on a bus in Louisville in 1942 and was dragged off and beaten by the police.

104. *Morgan v. Commonwealth of Virginia* 328 U.S. 373 (1946).

105. Houser, "A Personal Retrospective," 3–4.

106. The Fellowship of Southern Churchmen was an interracial, interdenominational group of clergy and laypeople who from 1934 through 1986 worked on issues concerning race relations, anti-Semitism, rural dependency, labor conditions, and other social problems. Fellowship of Southern Churchmen Records, 1937–1986, Collection No. 03479, Southern Historical Collection at the Louis Round Wilson Special Collections Library, University of North Carolina.

107. Ella Baker and Pauli Murray's reactions are recorded in Arsenault, *Freedom Riders*, 35. Juanita Nelson's reaction was recalled by Houser, interview by Zac Peterson, May 3, 2012, and in *You Don't Have to Ride Jim Crow*, produced and directed by Robin Washington (Durham: New Hampshire Public Television, 1995), http://www.robinwashington.com/jimcrow/.

108. Thurgood Marshall quoted in George Streator, "Negroes Cautioned in Resistance Idea," *New York Times*, November 23, 1946, https://www.nytimes.com/1946/11/23/archives/negroes-cautioned-on-resistance-idea-nonviolent-disobedience-as.html.

109. Homer A. Jack, "The Journey of Reconciliation," *Common Ground* (Autumn 1947): 22, CDG-A CORE Collected Records, Box 2; Houser, interview in *You Don't Have to Ride Jim Crow*.

110. Houser, "A Personal Retrospective," 7.

111. Peck would be severely beaten in the 1961 Freedom Ride.

112. Felmet was arrested several times in connection with his opposition to the war. He later ran for the US House in 1974 and the US Senate in 1978.

113. Among the radical activists Lynn defended in the 1960s were H. Rap Brown, the Black Panther; Robert F. Williams, who fled to Cuba to escape prosecution in the United States for a kidnapping charge; the Puerto Rican "independistas"; several draft resisters during the Vietnam War; and two Black Panthers in cases the NAACP refused to take. For more about these cases see Conrad Lynn, *There Is a Fountain: The Autobiography of Conrad Lynn* (Brooklyn, NY: Lawrence Hill, 1993), 141–57; 208–20.

114. Nishani Frazier, *Harambee City: The Congress of Racial Equality in Cleveland and the Rise of Black Power Populism* (Fayetteville: University of Arkansas Press, 2017), 44. In 1956–1957, William Worthy, who espoused black internationalism, defied the US government's travel ban to Communist nations and spent forty-one days reporting in China, Hungary, and the Soviet Union and subsequently had his passport revoked. Continuing to defy the law he visited Communist Cuba four times, for which he was indicted for violating the Immigration and Nationality Act (INA) of 1952. He also served as a confidant to both Robert Williams and Malcolm X. See Timothy H. Lovelace Jr., "Cold War Stories: William Worthy, the Right to Travel, and Afro-American Reporting on the Cuban Revolution," n.d., https://web.law.columbia.edu/sites/default/files/microsites/gender-sexuality/lovelace-cold_war_stories.pdf. Reverend Dr. Nathan Wright would chair the 1967 Black Power conference

when the tactics of the civil rights movement changed from the demand for individual rights to demands for group rights.

115. One southern FBI agent wrote that "it is thought that the instant organization is either communist dominated or infiltrated." But a special agent in New York took a different tone. "These people honestly believe that they will save the world by peaceful methods," he wrote. George M. Houser, "What the Watchers Saw," *Fellowship* 71, no. 9–10 (September–October 2005): 7–8, SCPC.

116. Houser, "A Personal Retrospective," 7.

117. Houser, 8.

118. FOR, DG 13 Section II FOR-USA, Series E, Box 19, SCPC.

119. George M. Houser and Bayard Rustin, *We Challenged Jim Crow! A Report on the Journey of Reconciliation, April 9–23, 1947* (New York: Fellowship of Reconciliation and the Congress of Racial Equality), 10; CDG-A Core Collected Records, Box 1, SCPC.

120. Lynn, *There Is a Fountain*, 111; Houser, "A Personal Retrospective."

121. Ollie Stewart, "Journey of Reconciliation Knocks Props from Under Weak J.C. System," *Baltimore Afro-American*, April 26, 1947, ProQuest.

122. Houser, "A Personal Retrospective."

123. Lynn, *There Is a Fountain*, 112.

124. Lynn, 112.

125. See note 126.

126. This account of the scene in Chapel Hill is taken from various versions contained in Arsenault, *Freedom Riders*, 45–47; Houser, "A Personal Retrospective"; Houser, interview by Katherine M. Shannon, September 11, 1967; Washington, *You Don't Have to Ride*; Lynn, *There is a Fountain*, 108–12.

127. Houser, "A Personal Retrospective."

128. Houser, interview by Katherine M. Shannon, September 11, 1967.

129. Arsenault, *Freedom Riders*, 48.

130. Stewart, "Journey of Reconciliation Knocks Props."

131. Homer A. Jack, "The Journey of Reconciliation," *Common Ground*, n.d., 23, CDG-A Core Collected Records, Box 2, SCPC.

132. Arsenault, *Freedom Riders*, 48.

133. James Peck, *Freedom Ride* (New York: Grove, 1962), 24–26, quoted in Arsenault, 49.

134. Arsenault, 55; Washington, *You Don't Have to Ride*.

135. These accounts are collected in CDG-A Core Collected Records, Box 2, SCPC.

136. Houser and Rustin, *We Challenged*, 11–12.

137. Houser, "A Personal Retrospective," 17–18.

138. Houser, "A Personal Retrospective."

139. Houser, 28–30.

140. Memo from John Nevin Sayre to Muste, August 6, 1946, George Houser Collected Papers, CDG-A Box 7, SCPC.

141. "Report of the Summer Interracial Workshop, Washington, DC, July 1954," CDG-A CORE Collected Records, Box 1, SCPC.

142. Hall, "The Long Civil Rights Movement," 1242.

143. Robert R. Taylor to Houser, September 29, 1945, Chicago Summer Workshop 1945–46, CORE Papers, Microfilm Reel 8-13.

144. J. L. Krug to Houser, August 15, 1949, DG 13 FOR-USA, Series E, Box 19, SCPC.

145. Thomas J. Sugrue, *Sweet Land of Liberty: The Forgotten Struggle for Civil Rights in the North* (New York: Random House, 2009, 149–50).

146. Houser, "A Personal Retrospective," 18–20.

147. Stewart, "Journey of Reconciliation Knocks Props."

148. Jefferson Award for Advancement of Democracy to Houser, February 11, 1948, GMH PP.

149. Cynthia Gebauer, "A Workshop—The Inside Story," CDG-A Core Collected Records, Box 1, SCPC.

150. Kajikawa, quoted in "Interracial Workshop Progress Report," July 1947.

151. Helen D. Oerkvitz to Houser, June 25, 2000, GMH PP.

4

1. For more on Dr. Lawrence, see "Changing the Face of Medicine: Dr. Margaret Morgan Lawrence," National Institutes of Health (website), accessed May 21, 2017, https://www.nlm.nih.gov/changingthefaceofmedicine/physicians/biography_195 .html.

2. Information about Skyview Acres is related in several interviews with the Housers as well as the author's visit to the site: see Houser, interview by the author, February 13, 2009; Houser, interview by the author, March 19, 2009; Houser, interview by Zac Peterson, May 4, 2012, used with permission.

3. Wally Nelson, interview by Sheila B. Michaels, November 27, 1999, Columbia University Oral History Collection SCSB-6065086; August Meier and Elliott Rudwick, *CORE: A Study in the Civil Rights Movement 1942–1968* (New York: Oxford University Press, 1973), 66–69.

4. Meier and Rudwick, *CORE*, 61.

5. Meier and Rudwick, 62.

6. Meier and Rudwick, 64–65.

7. Minutes, FOR Executive Committee Meeting, April 5, 1954, DG 13, FOR-USA Section II, Series A-2, Box 4, SCPC.

8. Houser, interview by Zac Peterson, May 3, 2012, used with permission.

9. David Dellinger, *From Yale to Jail: The Life Story of a Moral Dissenter* (Marion, SD: Rose Hill, 1996), 158.

10. Bill Sutherland, interview by Prexy Nesbitt and Mimi Edmunds, No Easy Victories (website), July 19, 2003, http://www.noeasyvictories.org/interviews /into1_sutherland.php.

11. Bill Sutherland and Matt Meyer, *Guns and Gandhi in Africa: Pan African Insights on Nonviolence, Armed Struggle and Liberation in Africa* (Trenton, NJ: Africa World, 2000), 5.

12. The word "propaganda" is Sisulu's. See Sisulu to Houser, March 26, 1952, ACOA Records, Series 3, Subseries 40: South Africa, Box 100, Folder 1, ARC.

13. Houser, interview by Lisa Brock, No Easy Victories (website), July 19, 2004, http://www.noeasyvictories.org/interviews/into2_houser.php.

14. Matthews was already familiar with the United States, as he had done graduate work at Yale in 1933–34. See William Minter and Sylvia Hill, "Anti-Apartheid Solidarity in the United States-South Africa Relations: From the Margins to the Mainstream," in The Road to Democracy in South Africa: International Solidarity, vol. 3, part 2 (Pretoria: Unisa, 2008), 758.

15. Sisulu had written to Houser: "Your letter of the 17th of March has been a source of great inspiration to me. I am very delighted to learn that your organization [CORE] has taken such a great interest in the struggle for fundamental human rights by my organization." See Sisulu to Houser, March 26, 1952.

16. Manilal Gandhi to Houser, March 10, 1952, ACOA Records, Series 3, Subseries 40: South Africa, South African Correspondence June–December 1952, Box 100, Folder 1, ARC.

17. E. E. Mahabane to Houser, March 18, 1952, ACOA Records, Series 3, Subseries 40: South Africa, South African Correspondence June–December 1952, Box 100, Folder 1, ARC.

18. George M. Houser, No One Can Stop the Rain: Glimpses of Africa's Liberation Struggle (New York: Pilgrim, 1989), 13. Sisulu had written, "We have made emphasis on a nonviolent approach; having judged my people from the strike of 1950, they will certainly behave well." Z. K. Matthews had told Houser that "we take great comfort from the fact that Gandhism was born on South African soil. Through these same means India was able to achieve a tremendous upsurge of consciousness of destiny among the people of India." See Sisulu to Houser, March 26, 1952. Also see Matthews to Houser, March 18, 1952, ACOA Records, Series 3, Subseries 40: South Africa, Box 100, Folder 1, ARC; George M. Houser, "American Supporters of the Defiance Campaign" (presentation to the UN Special Committee on Apartheid, June 25, 1982), 2, AAA, http://africanactivist.msu.edu/document_metadata.php?objectid=32-130-38C.

19. Uma Dhupelia-Mesthrie, Gandhi's Prisoner? The Life of Gandhi's Son Manilal (Cape Town: Kwela, 2004), 343, 354. Gandhi eventually allied himself with the liberals and joined the Liberal Party in 1954.

20. Houser, interview by Zac Peterson, May 7, 2012, used with permission.

21. The CAA was founded by Paul Robeson and Max Yergan, a YMCA secretary assigned to South Africa. Although many of its members had Communist leanings, not all of them toed the Communist line. Several tendencies within African American culture were included. The CAA developed close ties with leaders of the African National Congress and attended international Pan-Africanist meetings. Before its demise, it boasted such well-known African Americans as Paul Robeson, W. E. B. Du Bois, Ralph Bunche, Alphaeus Hunton, Adam Clayton Powell Jr., Mordecai Johnson, E. Franklin Frazier, A. Philip Randolph, and Mary McLeod Bethune. For more on the CAA see Hollis Ralph Lynch, Black American Radicals and the Liberation of Africa, 1937–1955, Monograph Series no. 5 (Ithaca, NY: Africana Studies and Research Center, Cornell University, 1978); Charles Denton Johnson, "Re-Thinking the Emergence of the Struggle for South African Liberation in the United States: Max

Yergan and the Council on African Affairs, 1922–1946," *Journal of Southern African Studies* 39, no. 1 (2013): 171–92, https://doi.org/10.1080/03057070.2013.768448; Alhaji Conteh, "Forging a New Africa: Black Internationalism and the Council on African Affairs, 1937–1955" (PhD diss., Howard University, 2016), ProQuest (10190725).

22. Johnson, "Re-Thinking the Emergence."

23. Francis Njubi Nesbitt, *Race for Sanctions: African Americans against Apartheid, 1946–1994* (Bloomington: Indiana University Press, 2004), 6.

24. Thomas Borstelmann, *Apartheid's Reluctant Uncle: The United States and Southern Africa in the Early Cold War* (New York: Oxford University Press, 1993), 67.

25. Gerald Horne, *White Supremacy Confronted: U.S. Imperialism and Anti-Communism vs. the Liberation of Southern Africa, from Rhodes to Mandela* (New York: International Publishers, 2019), 172.

26. Manning Marable, *Race, Reform and Rebellion: The Second Reconstruction in Black America, 1945–1990* (Jackson: University Press of Mississippi, 2007), 26, 30.

27. See, for example, Marable, *Race, Reform,* 26–32; Gerald Horne, "Commentary: Who Lost the Cold War? Africans and African Americans," *Diplomatic History* 20 (Fall 1996): 613–26; Brenda Gayle Plummer, *Rising Wind: Black Americans and U.S. Foreign Affairs, 1935–1960* (Chapel Hill: University of North Carolina Press, 1996); Penny M. Von Eschen, *Race against Empire: Black Americans and Anticolonialism, 1937–1957* (Ithaca, NY: Cornell University Press, 1997); Nesbitt, *Race for Sanctions,* 10–11; Borstelmann, *Apartheid's Reluctant Uncle,* 67; Manfred Berg, "Black Civil Rights and Liberal Anticommunism: The NAACP in the Early Cold War," *Journal of American History* 94, no. 1 (June 2007): 84. According to Nesbitt, the Cold War also resulted in black newspapers like the *Chicago Defender* and *Amsterdam News* toning down the anti-imperialist rhetoric they had formerly espoused. See Nesbitt, *Race for Sanctions,* 11.

28. Carol Anderson, *Bourgeois Radicals: The NAACP and the Struggle for Colonial Liberation, 1941–1960* (New York: Cambridge University Press, 2015). See also Carol Anderson, "International Conscience, the Cold War, and Apartheid: The NAACP's Alliance with the Reverend Michael Scott for South West Africa's Liberation, 1946–1951," *Journal of World History* 19, no. 3 (2008): 297–325.

29. After his ouster Yergan worked with the FBI in the persecution of his former colleagues, became a spokesman for the State Department, and traveled to South Africa where he spoke in favor of apartheid. See David Henry Anthony III, *Max Yergan: Race Man, Internationalist, Cold Warrior* (New York: New York University Press, 2006); Lynch, *Black American Radicals,* 39.

30. For more on the demise of the CAA and its aftereffects see Mary L. Dudziak, *Cold War Civil Rights: Race and the Image of American Democracy* (Princeton, NJ: Princeton University Press, 2000); Horne, *White Supremacy Confronted,* 159–207; Von Eschen, *Race against Empire;* Conteh, "Forging A New Africa."

31. See, for example, Von Eschen, *Race against Empire,* 143; Horne, *White Supremacy Confronted,* 238–39; Nesbitt, *Race for Sanctions,* 25–26.

32. For a description of this rift see Jervis Anderson, *A. Philip Randolph: A Biographical Portrait* (New York: Harcourt, Brace Jovanovich, 1973), 236–37.

33. Y. A. Cachalia to the General Secretary, Congress of Racial Equality, March 15, 1952, ACOA Records, Series 3, Subseries 40, Box 100, Folder 1, ARC.

34. Alphaeus Hunton to Rev. Donald Harrington, March 21, 1952; Houser to Mr. W. A. Hunton, March 28, 1952, William Alphaeus Hunton Papers, Box 1, Folder 16, ScMicro R-5003. R. 1, Schomburg Center for Research in Black Culture, New York Public Library.

35. Houser, interview by Lisa Brock, July 19, 2004, note 6.

36. Houser had written to Homer Jack, who had traveled to South Africa in summer 1952 wanting to know what his impressions were of the strength of Communist influence in the ANC. Jack replied that he was worried about Communist influence but was nevertheless impressed with the Defiance Campaign and that if he were in South Africa he would participate in the campaign's activities and work to oust the Communists. He admitted, however, that the Communists had so far been restrained. See Houser to Homer Jack, September 9, 1952, and Homer Jack to Houser, September 12, 1952, ACOA Records, Series 1, Box 1, Folder 3, ARC; Houser, *No One Can Stop*, 13–14; Telegram from FOR leader, John Nevin Sayre, advising against the demonstration, March 13, 1952, ACOA Records, Series 2, Box 8, Folder 1, ARC.

37. Houser, *No One Can Stop*, 15.

38. Houser, interview by Lisa Brock, July 19, 2004.

39. For descriptions of the CAA event see Nesbitt, *Race for Sanctions*, 19–24.

40. Houser, "American Supporters of the Defiance Campaign," 3.

41. Houser, interview by Lisa Brock, July 19, 2004.

42. Walter Sisulu and Y. A. Cachalia to Houser, June 18, 1952, ACOA Records, Series 2, Box 8, Folder 2, ARC.

43. Houser, interview by Lisa Brock, July 19, 2004. Between 1952 and 1953 AFSAR produced eighteen to twenty bulletins. See Houser, "American Supporters of the Defiance Campaign," 5.

44. George M. Houser, *Nonviolent Revolution in South Africa* (New York: Fellowship, 1953), mentioned in "Bulletin 10, Americans for South African Resistance," January 14, 1953, 5, https://africanactivist.msu.edu/document_metadata.php?objectid=32-130-6BA.

45. Houser, interview by Lisa Brock, July 19, 2004.

46. Houser, "American Supporters of the Defiance Campaign," 6.

47. A. W. Blaxall to Houser, February 28, 1953, and press clipping, ACOA Records, Series 3, Subseries 40, Box 100, Folder 3, ARC; Houser, "American Supporters of the Defiance Campaign," 8.

48. George M. Houser, "Assessing Africa's Liberation Struggle," *Africa Today* 34, no. 4 (1987): 19, http://www.jstor.org/stable/4186444.

49. "Report of the Meeting of the American Committee on Africa," May 14, 1953; "ACOA Statement of Purpose," 1953, ACOA Records Series 1, Box 3, Folder 29, ARC; "ACOA Executive Committee Minutes," August 13, 1953, ACOA Records Series 1, Box 2, Folder 8, ARC. According to George Shepherd, "George Houser was the primary moving spirit in the formation of the American Committee on Africa." See George W. Shepherd Jr., *They Are Us: Fifty Years of Human Rights Advocacy* (Bloomington, IN: Xlibris, 2002), 149.

50. "Prospectus of the American Committee on Africa," November 1953, ACOA Records Series 1, Box 2, Folder 8, ARC. Absent from this group was Bayard Rustin.

He had traveled to Africa in 1952 and had proposed a shift that would have committed the FOR to an African program with Rustin as the leader, but his January 1953 arrest on the charge of "lewd vagrancy," which resulted in a jail term and termination from the FOR, dashed any hope of getting this program off the ground. See John D'Emilio, *Lost Prophet: The Life and Times of Bayard Rustin* (New York: Free Press, 2003), 191–92.

51. John Gunther, *Inside Africa* (New York: Harper & Brothers, 1953); Vernon Bartlett, *Struggle for Africa* (New York: Frederick A. Praeger, 1953).

52. Shepherd, *They Are Us*, 96.

53. George M. Houser, "Meeting Africa's Challenge: The Story of the American Committee on Africa," *Issue: A Journal of Opinion, Africanist Studies 1955–1975* 6, nos. 2–3 (Summer–Autumn 1976): 1, https://doi.org/10.2307/1166441.

54. Ministry of Foreign Affairs, *Final Communiqué of the Asian-African Conference of Bandung (24 April 1955)* (Jakarta: Indonesia, Ministry of Foreign Affairs, 1955), 5, https://www.cvce.eu/en/obj/final_communique_of_the_asian_african_conference_of_bandung_24_april_1955-en-676237bd-72f7-471f-949a-88b6ae513585.html. For more on the significance of Bandung see Christopher J. Lee, ed., *Making a World after Empire: The Bandung Moment and Its Political Afterlives* (Athens: Ohio University Press, 2010).

55. John Gunther had also recognized the gathering momentum for independence, writing the following in the first chapter of his book: "While partaking with confused zeal of much that the western world has to offer many parts of Africa are at the same time attempting to throw off the political shackles of the West. Africans want our education and techniques, our mode of life and standard of living, but not our domination or exploitation." See Gunther, *Inside Africa*, 3.

56. Shepherd, *They Are Us*, 138–41.

57. Shepherd, 144.

58. Shepherd, 155. The John Haynes Holmes Building was a natural setting for the first office of the ACOA. John Haynes Holmes, a former minister of the Community Church from the early part of the twentieth century, had embraced Mohandas Gandhi's militant nonviolence in numerous sermons and publications. The church provided ongoing support for the ACOA and the South African struggle in the decades that followed, including office space for the ANC in the 1970s. See Bruce Southworth, "Mohandas Gandhi, The Community Church of New York and the American Committee on Africa," AAA, http://africanactivist.msu.edu/document_metadata.php?objectid=32-130-370.

59. Shepherd, *They Are Us*, 155.

60. George Shepherd, Executive Secretary, press release, April 28, 1954, ACOA Records, Box 43, Folder 46, ARC.

61. A mandate was an authorization granted by the League of Nations to allied victors to govern former German or Turkish colonies after World War I. Those in Africa included South West Africa, Somaliland, French Togoland, the Cameroons, and Ruanda-Urundi.

62. For differing views on the relationship between collective and individual rights and their history, see Roland Burke, *Decolonization and the Evolution of*

International Human Rights (Philadelphia: University of Pennsylvania Press, 2010); Samuel Moyn, *The Last Utopia: Human Rights in History* (Cambridge, MA: Belknap Press of Harvard University Press, 2010).

63. William Korey, *NGOs and the Universal Declaration of Human Rights* (New York: St. Martin's Press, 1998), 2–9.

64. Sisulu to Houser, March 26, 1952.

65. George M. Houser, "Human Rights and the Liberation Struggle . . . The Importance of Creative Tension," *Africa Today* 39, no. 4 (1992): 9, https://www.jstor.org/stable/4186859.

66. Houser, "Human Rights and the Liberation Struggle."

67. For more on the struggle for the right to petition, see Burke, *Decolonization and the Evolution*, 59–91.

5

1. Houser to James R. Robinson, n.d., GMH PP.

2. George M. Houser, *No One Can Stop the Rain: Glimpses of Africa's Liberation Struggle* (New York: Pilgrim, 1989), 21.

3. As early as 1900 the first Pan-African Conference was held at Westminster Town Hall in London where delegates made speeches calling for legislation to ensure racial equality, and after 1913 the ANC made contacts in Britain. The ANC at this time also communicated with W. E. B. Du Bois and Marcus Garvey. See Gregory Houston, "International Solidarity: Introduction," in *The Road to Democracy in South Africa: International Solidarity*, vol. 3, part 1 (Pretoria: Unisa, 2008), 2.

4. Rob Skinner, *The Foundations of Anti-Apartheid: Liberal Humanitarians and Transnational Activists in Britain and the United States, c. 1919–64* (New York: Palgrave Macmillan, 2010), 93.

5. Hatch's *The Dilemma of South Africa* had appeared in 1952 and *The Intelligent Socialist's Guide to Africa* in 1953.

6. "Michael Guthrie Scott," *South Africa History Online*, https://www.sahistory.org.za/people/michael-guthrie-scott.

7. Skinner, *The Foundations*, 100.

8. George Houser, Africa Journal 1954, bk. 1, May 30, original handwritten manuscript, GMH PP.

9. For details on the political crisis caused by the marriage see Skinner, *The Foundations*, 93–96. For more on Seretse Khama's life, see Susan Williams, *Colour Bar: The Triumph of Seretse Khama and His Nation* (London: Penguin, 2007).

10. Ehiedu E. G. Iweriebor, "The Colonization of Africa." *Africana Age: African and African Diasporan Transformations in the 20th Century* (New York: Schomburg Center for Research in Black Culture, New York Public Library), http://exhibitions.nypl.org/africanaage/essay-colonization-of-africa.html.

11. Michael Collins, "Nation, State and Agency: Evolving Historiographies of African Decolonization," in *Britain, France and the Decolonization of Africa: Future Imperfect?*, ed. Andrew W. M. Smith and Chris Jeppesen (London: UCL Press, 2017), 17–42.

12. On this point see Larry Grubbs, *Secular Missionaries: Americans and African Development in the 1960s* (Amherst: University of Massachusetts Press, 2010).

13. These included what are now Senegal, the Cote d'Ivoire (Ivory Coast), Mauritania, French Sudan (now Mali), Upper Volta (now Burkina Faso), Niger, and Dahomey (now Benin).

14. Iweriebor, "The Colonization of Africa."

15. Lisa Brock, "The 1950s: Africa Solidarity Rising," in *No Easy Victories: African Liberation and American Activists over a Half Century, 1950–2000*, ed. William Minter, Gail Hovey, and Charles Cobb Jr. (Trenton, NJ: Africa World, 2008), 69.

16. Houser, Africa Journal 1954, bk. 2.

17. Houser, Africa Journal 1954.

18. Houser, "Assessing Africa's Liberation Struggle," 20.

19. George M. Houser, "Human Rights and the Liberation Struggle . . . The Importance of Creative Tension," *Africa Today* 39, no. 4 (1992): 8, http://www.jstor.org/stable/4186859.

20. Martin Plaut, "The Africans Who Fought in WWII," BBC News, November 9, 2009, http://news.bbc.co.uk/2/hi/africa/8344170.stm.

21. Houser, Africa Journal 1954, bk. 1, GMH PP.

22. Houser, Africa Journal 1954.

23. Houser, Africa Journal 1954.

24. Houser, Africa Journal 1954, bk. 2.

25. Houser, Africa Journal 1954, bk. 1.

26. Houser, Africa Journal 1954.

27. Houser, Africa Journal 1954, bk. 2.

28. Houser, Africa Journal 1954.

29. Gunther, *Inside Africa*, 715–34.

30. See, for example, Gerald McKnight, *Verdict on Schweitzer: The Man Behind the Legend of Lambaréné* (New York: John Day, 1964).

31. Houser, Africa Journal 1954, bk. 2.

32. Houser, Africa Journal 1954.

33. Houser, Africa Journal 1954, bk. 2.

34. Houser, Africa Journal 1954.

35. For a history of Leopold's reign, the colonialism that led up to it, and the human rights movement that finally brought his crimes to light, see Adam Hochschild, *King Leopold's Ghost: A Story of Greed, Terror, and Heroism in Colonial Africa* (New York: Houghton Mifflin, 1998); Tim Stanley, "Belgium's Heart of Darkness," *History Today* 62, no. 10 (October 10, 2012), http://www.historytoday.com/tim-stanley/belgiums-heart-darkness.

36. Houser, Africa Journal 1954, bk. 2.

37. Houser, Africa Journal 1954.

38. Houser, Africa Journal 1954.

39. Houser, Africa Journal 1954.

40. Houser, Africa Journal 1954, bk. 3.

41. Gunther, *Inside Africa*, 586. For a history of Angola see Lawrence W. Henderson, *Angola: Five Centuries of Conflict* (Ithaca, NY: Cornell University Press, 1979).

42. Houser, *No One Can Stop*, 45.

43. This was a relatively new development, dating from constitutional changes in 1951, in which Portugal became an "Afro-European" power. See Gunther, *Inside Africa*, 586.

44. While most of the Angolan missionaries appeared to accept the status of the colonial state, the Portuguese had always feared that foreign missions might bring foreign governments in their wake, and they tended to see any uprising as fomented by the missionaries. See David Birmingham, *Portugal and Africa* (New York: Palgrave, 1999), 74–78.

45. Houser, Africa Journal 1954, bk. 2.

46. Houser, Africa Journal 1954.

47. Houser, Africa Journal 1954.

48. To be "employed" meant receiving a wage. Thus, subsistence farmers could be picked up as "unemployed." According to one colonial administrator, the tax, imposed in 1920, was a mechanism to control how the African fulfilled his labor obligation. See Jeremy Ball, "Colonial Labor in Twentieth-Century Angola," *History Compass* 3 (December 21, 2005), https://doi.org/10.1111/j.1478-0542.2005.00168.x.

49. Houser, *No One Can Stop*, 46.

50. Houser, Africa Journal 1954, bk. 2.

51. Houser, Africa Journal, 1954.

52. Houser, Africa Journal 1954.

53. Houser, *No One Can Stop*, 48.

54. Houser, Africa Journal 1954, bk. 3.

55. Houser, Africa Journal 1954.

56. Houser, Africa Journal 1954.

57. Gunther, *Inside Africa*, 449.

58. Gunther, 453.

59. Houser, *No One Can Stop*, 50.

60. Houser, 51.

61. Houser, 52.

62. The Freedom Charter was an alliance of all the liberation forces in the country at that time, including the ANC, the South African Indian Congress, the South African Coloured People's Congress, the South African Congress of Democrats, and the South African Congress of Trade Unions (SACTU). Its vision of an alternative social order served to strengthen the antiapartheid movement after the defeat of the Defiance Campaign and to raise the consciousness of the masses.

63. George M. Houser, "Indomitable Spirit of Optimism," in *Oliver Tambo Remembered*, ed. Z. Pallo Jordan (Johannesburg: Pan Macmillan South Africa, 2007), 398.

64. Houser, *No One Can Stop*, 55–57.

65. Houser, 57.

66. Houser, 57.

67. Report by George M. Houser, October 1, 1954, RACOA, Microfilm Reel 1, Part 2, Frame 233.

6

1. George M. Houser, *No One Can Stop the Rain: Glimpses of Africa's Liberation Struggle* (New York: Pilgrim), 64.

2. "Memorandum, American Committee on Africa: Aims and Structure," September 15, 1954, ACOA Records, Series 1, Box 1, Folder 1, ARC.

3. Donald Harrington, "Memorandum to Executive Committee and Advisory Board," May 12, 1955, ACOA Records, Series 1, Box 1, Folder 1, ARC.

4. George Houser, "Memoir," transcript of an interview conducted by C. Arthur Bradley, 1988, 65–66, Oral History Collection, H817G, University of Illinois at Springfield, http://www.idaillinois.org/cdm/compoundobject/collection/uis/id/2492; Roger Baldwin had tried to discourage Houser from taking the job. See Roger Baldwin to Fenner Brockway, March 2, 1955, ACOA Records, Series 2, Box 8, Folder 14, ARC. Houser responded that the ACOA had not been given a fair trial and that organizations do not spring up automatically without somebody putting terrific effort into it. See Houser to Baldwin, May 9, 1955, ACOA Records, Series 2, Box 8, Folder 15, ARC.

5. Houser, interview by Celeste Wallin, December 10, 1968, 2, GMH PP.

6. Houser, "Memoir," 65.

7. During the early years there was not a single US publication outside of occasional *New York Times* reports that carried informed interpretations. These were, for the most part, considered to be biased against the democratic movements and generally censored. *Africa Today* was banned in South Africa until 1965. See George W. Shepherd, "*Africa Today* in the Early Years: The Debate over Strategy for the Liberation of South Africa," *Africa Today* 41, no. 1 (1994), 11–12, 14, http://www.jstor.org/stable/4186959.

8. George M. Houser, "Outline of Prospectus for American Committee on Africa, April 21, 1955," ACOA Records, Series 1, Box 1, Folder 1, ARC.

9. Houser to Homer Jack, September 5, 1955, ACOA Records, Series 2, Box 8, Folder 25, ARC.

10. Huddleston's private school was defying the Bantu Education Act, which mandated an apartheid education. He was also involved in protesting the forced removal of blacks from Sophiatown, a township outside Johannesburg under the Group Areas Act of 1950. He was recalled to England in December 1955 over increasing fears for his safety but continued to write and speak out passionately about the oppression in South Africa.

11. In June 1955, the Congress passed an almost unanimous resolution in support of decolonization. Unlike its European allies, it didn't hold that mere discussion by the United Nations constituted the forbidden intervention in domestic affairs, but neither did it support calls for freedom. See Roger N. Baldwin, "U.S. Policy Towards Africa," *Africa Today* 2, no. 5 (November–December 1955): 9–10, https://www.jstor.org/stable/i388853.

12. Robert J. McMahon, "Eisenhower and Third World Nationalism: A Critique of the Revisionists," *Political Science Quarterly* 101, no. 3 (Fall 1986): 470, http://www.jstor.org/stable/2151625.

13. Prior to the establishment of the Bureau of African Affairs, Africa had been subsumed under bureaus that dealt with either Europe or Asia.

14. Robert Coughlan, "First of Two Parts Black Africa Surges to Independence," *Life*, January 26, 1959, 100–110; Robert Coughlan, "Stormy Future for Africa," *Life*, February 2, 1959), 82–95.

15. George M. Houser, *Annual Report of the Executive Director*, March 9, 1959, AAA, http://africanactivist.msu.edu/document_metadata.php?objectid=32-130-23FE.

16. "Appeal Letter from Donald Harrington," November 23, 1955, ACOA Records, Series 2, Box 8, Folder 37, ARC.

17. For more on Nyerere see Chambi Chachge and Annar Cassam, eds., *The Liberation of Africa: The Legacy of Nyerere* (Cape Town: Pambazuka, 2010); Paul Bjerk, *Julius Nyerere* (Athens: Ohio University Press, 2017); Julius Nyerere, *Freedom and Unity-Uhuru na Umoja: A Selection from Writings and Speeches, 1952–1965* (London: Oxford University Press, 1967).

18. Houser, *No One Can Stop*, 66; Houser, "Memoir," 68.

19. Houser, *No One Can Stop*, 66.

20. Olympio was assassinated in a military coup by demobilized soldiers from the French colonial army who were angry that he had refused them service in the new Togo army. Though events surrounding the assassination remain cloudy, the French government may also have had reason to fear Olympio, as he was steering his country away from the French orbit. See Christophe Boisbouvier, "Togo: Qui a tué l'ancien président Sylvanus Olympio?," *Jeune Afrique*, January 18, 2013, http://www.jeuneafrique .com/138661/politique/togo-qui-a-tu-l-ancien-pr-sident-sylvanus-olympio/.

21. Jennifer Davis, interview by Zac Peterson, November 8, 2014, used with permission; "ACOA Activities," *Africa Today* 2, no. 3 (July–August 1955): 22, http://www .jstor.org/stable/4183727.

22. The Congress of Democrats had been initiated largely by the ANC as a white affiliate of the Congress Alliance, an antiapartheid coalition that had been formed by the ANC, since at the time the ANC was not open to whites.

23. Frieda Matthews to Houser, December 10, 1956, in Houser, *No One Can Stop*, 117.

24. "Freedom Charter 1955," *South African History Online*, http://www.sahistory.org .za/article/freedom-charter.

25. ACOA, "ACOA Notes," *Africa Today* 4, no. 4 (July–August 1957): 2, http:// www.jstor.org/stable/4183881.

26. The ACOA was not the only organization raising funds for the prisoners. For instance, Christian Action, a British antiapartheid organization, gave more. See Houser, *No One Can Stop*, 121.

27. For more on Sudan's conflicts see Somini Sengupta, "In South Sudan, Mass Killings, Rapes and the Limits of U.S. Diplomacy," *New York Times*, January 18, 2017, https://www.nytimes.com/2017/01/18/world/africa/south-sudan-united-nations .html; Jeffrey Gettleman, "After Years of Struggle, South Sudan Becomes a New Nation," *New York Times*, July 9, 2011, http://www.nytimes.com/2011/07/10/world /africa/10sudan.html?smid=pl-share; Jeffrey Gettleman, "Quandary in South Sudan: Should It Lose Its Hard-Won Independence?," *New York Times*, January 23, 2017, https://www.nytimes.com/2017/01/23/world/africa/quandary-in -south-sudan-should-it-lose-its-hard-won-independence.html?rref=collection%2 Ftimestopic%2FSudan&action=click&contentCollection=world&region=stream&- module=stream_unit&version=latest&contentPlacement=4&pgtype=collection.

28. Caroline Elkins, *Imperial Reckoning: The Untold Story of Britain's Gulag in Kenya* (New York: Henry Holt, 2005), xi.

29. David Anderson, *Histories of the Hanged: The Dirty War in Kenya and the End of Empire* (New York: W. W. Norton, 2005), 1.

30. David Goldsworthy, *Tom Mboya: The Man Kenya Wanted to Forget* (Nairobi: Africana, 1982), ix.

31. For Mboya, the grant of $35,000 was a widely acknowledged personal triumph. For the AFL-CIO, support of Mboya may have been motivated by the opportunity for American labor to establish an influence in Africa independent of Communist attempts to corral Africa's independence movements. See Goldsworthy, *Tom Mboya*, 62.

32. One example that Mboya gave in his speeches was that in Tanganyika there were only eighteen Africans with college degrees, and there were no medical doctors or lawyers after eighty years of British rule. Similar conditions existed in other British colonies.

33. George M. Houser, "Meeting Africa's Challenge: The Story of the American Committee on Africa," *Issue: A Journal of Opinion, Africanist Studies 1955–1975* 6, nos. 2–3 (Summer–Autumn 1976): 17, https://www.jstor.org/stable/1166441.

34. Harold L. Oram was a major fundraiser for humanitarian causes. Among his other clients were the NAACP Legal Defense and Educational Fund, the World Wildlife Fund, the Natural Resources Defense Council, the ACLU, the Fund for Peace, and the World Population Emergency Campaign, which eventually merged with Planned Parenthood.

35. Houser, "Meeting Africa's Challenge," 19.

36. George Houser, "Africa Revisited," *Africa Today* 4, no. 5 (September–October 1957): 6, https://www.jstor.org/stable/i388864; George Houser, Africa Journal 1957, original handwritten manuscript, GMH PP.

37. Houser, "Africa Revisited," 3; Houser, Africa Journal 1957.

38. The source of the alienation between Gbedemah and Nkrumah was Gbedemah's belief that Nkrumah was mismanaging Ghana's finances, especially with his grandiose seven-year plan and the cult of personality he was developing. See "Summary of Letter from A. K. Gbedemah to Kwame Nkrumah," February 24, 2016, accessed October 15, 2018, https://www.modernghana.com/news/676875/summary-of-letter-from-ka-gbedemah-to-president-kwame-nkru.html.

39. Houser, "Africa Revisited," 7.

40. In 1953 the Central African Federation comprised the British protectorates of Northern Rhodesia and Nyasaland and the self-governing colony of Southern Rhodesia. It was governed by a white minority, and to the Africans this represented a means of extending European influence, which dominated Southern Rhodesia, into the northern territories of Northern Rhodesia and Nyasaland. This would have created another apartheid society like the one in South Africa. See ACOA, *Statement on Crisis in Central African Federation* (New York: American Committee on Africa, 1959), AAA, http://africanactivist.msu.edu/document_metadata.php?objectid=32-130-D87; Channing B. Richardson et al., *The Federation of Rhodesia and Nyasaland: The Future of a Dilemma, Africa Today Pamphlet* (New York: American Committee on Africa), AAA, http://africanactivist.msu.edu/document_metadata.php?objectid=32-130-B60; Houser, *No One Can Stop*, 99–109.

41. John Hughes, "Ban on Visit to Rhodesia Questioned," *Christian Science Monitor*, August 12, 1957, 10; ACOA, "ACOA Notes," *Africa Today* 4, no. 5 (September–October 1957): 2, https://www.jstor.org/stable/i388864.

42. Minutes, Annual Meeting of the Executive Board of the American Committee on Africa, March 9, 1959, ACOA Records, Series 1, Box 2, Folder 12, ARC.

43. ACOA Executive Board Minutes, January 6, 1958, ACOA Records, Series 1, Box 2, Folder 11, ARC.

44. "Declaration of Conscience," *Africa Today* 4, no. 6 (November–December 1957): 31–34, http://www.jstor.org/stable/4183905; also available at AAA, http://africanactivist.msu.edu/document_metadata.php?objectid=32-130-FBA.

45. ACOA, *Report on Declaration of Conscience Campaign* (New York: American Committee on Africa, n.d.), AAA, http://africanactivist.msu.edu/document_metadata.php?objectid=32-130-FF0.

46. Nesbitt, *Race for Sanctions*, 32.

47. George M. Houser, "Mr. Louw and the Declaration," *Africa Today* 5, no. 1 (January–February 1958): 3–4, http://www.jstor.org/stable/4183926; John Hughes, "South Africa Retorts to Racial Critics: Controls to Stay Restrictions Defended," *Christian Science Monitor*, December 13, 1957, 16.

48. ACOA, *Report on Declaration of Conscience*.

49. For more on Dennis Brutus see "Dennis Brutus," *South African History Online*, https://www.sahistory.org.za/people/dennis-brutus; Dennis Brutus, *Poetry and Protest: A Dennis Brutus Reader*, ed. Lee Sustar and Aisha Karim (Chicago: Haymarket, 2006); Dennis Brutus, *The Dennis Brutus Tapes: Essays at Autobiography*, ed. Bernth Lindors (Woodbridge, UK: Boydell and Brewer, 2011).

50. In a speech on July 2, 1957, Kennedy had called on the US administration to stop supporting France and to start working for Algerian independence. See "Eisenhower Wary on Algeria Policy," *New York Times*, July 4, 1957, https://www.nytimes.com/1957/07/04/archives/eisenhower-wary-on-algeria-policy-us-is-trying-to-be-fair-and.html. Press reports of Kennedy's speech came up in many meetings Houser had with African nationalists during his travels at this time. See Houser, *No One Can Stop*, 95.

51. Houser, *No One Can Stop*, 91–92.

52. Memorandum, "Gilbert Jonas to Donald Harrington, Chairman of the American Committee on Africa and All Members of the Steering Committee," October 9, 1958, ACOA Records, Series 1, Box 1, Folder 3, ARC.

53. Memorandum, "George Houser to the Steering Committee," October 13, 1958, ACOA Records, Series 1, Box 1, Folder 3, ARC.

54. For more on the trial, see Thomas G. Karis, "The South African Treason Trial," *Political Science Quarterly* 76, no. 2 (June 1961): 222, http://www.jstor/stable/2146218.

55. Houser, *No One Can Stop*, 122.

56. Houser, *No One Can Stop*, 123.

57. In January 1958, sixty-five of the defendants, including Chief Luthuli and Oliver Tambo, were released while the others were accused of high treason. The trial lasted four years, ending in the acquittal of all remaining defendants. In the end, the

government failed to prove its charge that the charter represented a "conspiracy to use violence to overthrow the present government and replace it with a Communist state." In the meantime, however, by keeping the leadership of the movement out of circulation and scrambling for money for both legal defense and support for families left without breadwinners, the state had effectively muzzled the antiapartheid movement. Silencing the movement was probably their intention, as they had allowed the Congress of the People (in violation of their own banning order) to proceed before moving with the arrests.

58. Nkrumah quoted in Houser, *Annual Report*, March 9, 1959.

59. Five previous Pan-African conferences had been held outside Africa.

60. Accompanying Houser to the conference were Homer Jack, his longtime colleague; Frank Montero, a member of the ACOA board and associate vice president of the Urban League; board member William X. Scheinman; and John Marcum, a professor of political science at Lincoln University. See Houser, *No One Can Stop*, 72.

61. Ama Biney, "The Legacy of Kwame Nkrumah in Retrospect," *Journal of Pan African Studies* 2, no. 3 (March 2008): 129–59.

62. George M. Houser, *A Report on the All-African People's Conference Held in Accra, Ghana, December 8–13, 1958* (New York: American Committee on Africa, n.d.) AAA, http://africanactivist.msu.edu/document_metadata.php?objectid=32-130-D84; Kwame Nkrumah, "Speech by the Prime Minister of Ghana at the Opening Session of the All-African People's Conference, Accra, Ghana" (speech, December 8, 1958), http://www.columbia.edu/itc/history/mann/w3005/nkrumba.html.

63. Nkomo, founder of the Zimbabwe African People's Union (ZAPU), would later have a falling out with Mugabe and would be forced into exile.

64. Manuel Necaca to George Padmore, May 10, 1958 in Houser, *No One Can Stop*, 77; Houser, interview by Lisa Brock, No Easy Victories (website), http://www.noeasyvictories.org/interviews/into2_houser.php.

65. Homer A. Jack, "Ideological Conflicts: Russia and the West, Cairo vs. Accra," *Africa Today* 6, no. 1 (1959): 12, http://www.jstor.org/stable/4183991.

66. Houser, *A Report*.

67. Houser, *A Report*.

68. Memorandum, "George Houser to the Steering Committee," October 13, 1958.

69. Gilbert Jonas was a public relations specialist and fundraiser. From 1956 to 1969 he held various positions in organizations concentrating on international affairs, particularly Vietnam. In 1956 he became vice president of Harold Oram's public relations firm. For more on Jonas, see Gilbert Jonas Biography, Gilbert Jonas Collection, 00166, Michigan State University Archives and Historical Collections, http://archives.msu.edu/findaid/166.html#ref2; Margalit Fox, "Gilbert Jonas, 76, N.A.A.C.P. Fundraiser Dies," *New York Times*, September 27, 2006, https://www.nytimes.com/2006/09/27/obituaries/27jonas.html.

70. George M. Houser (unpublished manuscript), GMH PP.

71. Lisa Brock, "The 1950s: Africa Solidarity Rising," in *No Easy Victories: African Liberation and American Activists over a Half Century, 1950–2000*, ed. William Minter, Gail Hovey, and Charles Cobb Jr. (Trenton, NJ: Africa World, 2008), 66. Cites the unpublished handwritten manuscript by George M. Houser for *No One Can Stop*.

72. George M. Houser, *A Report on George Houser's Trip to Africa, March 1960* (New York: American Committee on Africa, 1960), AAA, http://africanactivist.msu.edu /document_metadata.php?objectid=32-130-FA6.

73. "The History of African Liberation Day," The Talking Drum (website), accessed October 17, 2019, http://www.thetalkingdrum.com/ald.html.

74. "Africa Speaks at Carnegie Hall," *Africa Today* 6, no. 3 (1959): 17–19, http:// www.jstor.org/stable/4184014.

75. Olympio quoted in *Who Speaks for Africa? A Report on the Activities of the American Committee on Africa* (New York: American Committee on Africa, n.d.), AAA, http://africanactivist.msu.edu/document_metadata.php?objectid=32-130-D86.

76. *ACOA Annual Report*, June 1, 1960, to May 31, 1961, AAA, http://africanactivist .msu.edu/document_metadata.php?objectid=32-130-D89.

77. George M. Houser, *Annual Report of the Executive Director* (New York: American Committee on Africa, 1960), AAA, http://africanactivist.msu.edu/document _metadata.php?objectid=32-130-23F6.

78. ACOA, *Statement on Crisis in Central African Federation* (New York: American Committee on Africa, 1959), AAA, http://africanactivist.msu.edu/document_metadata .php?objectid=32-130-D87. Houser's relationship to the four African leaders and their tour of the United States is recounted in Houser, *No One Can Stop*, 99–109.

79. ACOA Executive Board Minutes, June 29, 1959, ACOA Records, Series 1, Box 2, Folder 12, ARC.

80. ACOA Executive Board Minutes, November 9, 1959, ACOA Records, Series 1, Box 2, Folder 12, ARC. By summer 1959, the ACOA office had moved to its third location since its beginnings in 1954. It was now renting space at 801 Second Avenue, just a block from UN headquarters, making it easier for staff to monitor events at the UN. For each move (and there would be several more) Houser and his staff did the moving themselves, lifting heavy file cabinets and desks, boxes of papers, telephones, lamps, and other paraphernalia down flights of stairs, over curbs, and into rented U-Haul trucks. Karen Rothmyer, who served on the staff during one of these moves, recalled her amazement at Houser, a man who knew everyone there is to know in Africa, pitching in with his woolen cap over his ears looking like any common laborer. See Karen Rothmyer, interview by the author, November 18, 2015.

81. Coughlan, "Stormy Future for Africa," 89. Shortly after the AAPC, however, relations between Nkrumah and Mboya cooled over the ICFTU's orientation to the West and Nkrumah's stance of neutralism between East and West. Mboya's reputation within Kenya was also becoming controversial.

82. *Meet the Press*, "Tom Mboya, Kenyan Political Leader," NBC News Productions, April 12, 1959, https://www.youtube.com/watch?v=djx6Oop81m4. The questions raised by American journalists during this interview are interesting in that they reveal the prejudices within the American public about Africa; these prejudices had been shaped by the legacy of colonialism and were now being influenced by the Cold War environment. Mboya's diplomatic replies indicate the brilliant political instincts of this young politician.

83. George M. Houser, "Mboya Visits the U.S.," *Africa Today* 6, no. 3 (May–June 1959): 9–11, http://www.jstor.org/stable/4184012.

84. Shachtman describes Scheinman as "young, tough, idealistic, and . . . wealthy, willing to put his money in the service of his ideals." See Thomas Shachtman, *Airlift to America: How Barack Obama, Sr., John F. Kennedy, Tom Mboya and 800 East African Students Changed Their World and Ours* (New York: St. Martin's Press, 2009), 21.

85. So close were Scheinman and Mboya that after his death in 1999, Scheinman's ashes were taken to Kenya to be buried beside the grave of Tom Mboya. See Joseph B. Treaster, "W. X. Scheinman, 72, Broker and Friend of Kenyan Leader," *New York Times*, July 25, 1999, http://www.nytimes.com/1999/07/25/business/w-x-scheinman-72-broker-and-friend-of-kenyan-leader.html.

86. An interesting part of the airlift story is that the fundraising letters were carried by Cora Weiss and Frank Montero to the UN post office so that they could be stamped with a UN stamp. There were no stick-on stamps then, so the hundreds of envelopes and stamps had to be licked by the two of them. In the absence of computers, the records of those who donated were kept in pencil by a Japanese-American woman who had grown up in an internment camp in California. See Cora Weiss, interview by the author, June 23, 2015.

87. Cora Weiss, interview by the author, June 23, 2015. Cora Weiss's papers are held in the Swarthmore Peace Collection archives, https://www.swarthmore.edu/library/peace/DG201-225/dg222cweiss.htm. For more on Cora Weiss see "Cora Weiss Oral History Project," Columbia Center for Oral History, 2014, https://static1.squarespace.com/static/575a10ba27d4bd5d7300a207/t/57601b8d9f7266ebae932dbc/1465916301804/Weiss_Cora_2014.pdf.

88. Cora Weiss, interview by the author, June 23, 2015. Peter and Cora Weiss were longtime supporters of the ACOA, Peter serving for many years as its president and Cora providing many hours of volunteer time helping to organize its major events. They were a powerhouse couple, active in many other peace and justice causes. Peter Weiss's papers are held in the Swarthmore Peace Collection archives, https://www.swarthmore.edu/library/peace/CDGA.S-Z/WeissPeter.htm. The *New York Times* described Frank Montero as "a racial pioneer who in his various guises as political gadfly, government official, foundation executive and real estate developer devoted his life to smoothing the way toward an integrated society." See Robert Mcg. Thomas Jr., "Frank C. Montero, Racial Pioneer, Dies at 89," *New York Times*, May 25, 1998, https://www.nytimes.com/search?endDate=19980526&query=Frank%20C.%20Montero%2C%20Racial%20Pioneer%2C%20Dies%20at%2089&sort=best&startDate=19980525.

89. Shachtman, *Airlift*, 7.

90. For more about African students' experiences in the USSR, see Maxim Matusevich, "Probing the Limits of Internationalism: African Students Confront Soviet Ritual," *Anthropology of East Europe Review* 27, no. 2 (Fall 2009): 19–39, https://scholarworks.iu.edu/journals/index.php/aeer/article/download/166/259.

91. Cora Weiss, interview by the author, June 23, 2015.

92. Shachtman, *Airlift*, 7.

93. In the half-dozen states critical to Kennedy's Electoral College victory, the black press had been reporting positively for months on Kennedy's involvement with the airlifts. See Shachtman, *Airlift*, 185–86.

94. Shachtman, 242–43.

95. Shachtman, 236–44.

96. Cora Weiss, interview by the author, June 23, 2015; Brock, "The 1950s," 66.

97. Brock, 66. For more about Jay Lovestone, see Ted Morgan, *Jay Lovestone: A Covert Life* (New York: Random House, 1999).

98. Houser, *Annual Report*, 1960.

7

1. For more on this, see Walter Rodney, *How Europe Underdeveloped Africa* (London: Verso, 2018).

2. Harold Macmillan, "Address to South African Parliament," February 3, 1960, https://web-archives.univ-pau.fr/english/TD2doc1.pdf. South African officials reacted with outrage to the speech and were determined to dig in their heels. But it served to bring opposition to apartheid out into the open and marked the beginning of South Africa's increasing international isolation.

3. United Nations, "Declaration on the Granting of Independence to Colonial Countries and Peoples," adopted December 14, 1960, https://www.un.org/ga/search/view_doc.asp?symbol=A/RES/1514(XV). The colonial countries refused to support the resolution and the United States abstained.

4. Ali A. Mazrui, "The Independent African States and the Struggle for Southern Africa," in *The Decolonization of Africa: Southern Africa and the Horn of Africa, Working Documents and Report of the Meeting of Experts Held in Warsaw, Poland, from 9 to 13 October, 1978* (Paris: UNESCO, 1981), 13, https://unesdoc.unesco.org/ark:/48223/pf0000045919.

5. George M. Houser, *Executive Director's Report to the Executive Board at the Annual Meeting*, April 26, 1966, ACOA Records, Series I, Box 2, Folder 20, ARC.

6. George M. Houser, *No One Can Stop the Rain: Glimpses of Africa's Liberation Struggle* (New York: Pilgrim, 1989), 188.

7. George M. Houser, *Observations on Trends in Non-Independent Africa's Struggle for Freedom: A Report to the Executive Board of the American Committee on Africa* (New York: American Committee on Africa, n.d.), AAA, http://africanactivist.msu.edu/document_metadata.php?objectid=32-130-2542.

8. Piero Gleijeses, *Conflicting Missions: Havana, Washington, and Africa, 1959–1976* (Chapel Hill: University of North Carolina Press, 2002), 5.

9. Figures on the numbers of educated and trained Congolese differ slightly. Both, however, attest to the paucity of educated personnel to run the country after independence. See Houser, *No One Can Stop*, 139; Adam Hochschild, *King Leopold's Ghost: A Story of Greed, Terror, and Heroism in Colonial Africa* (Boston: Houghton Mifflin, 1998), 301.

10. The Belgian government supported the secession as a way of maintaining access for their industry to the region. White extremists in South Africa also supported it as did then Vice President Nixon of the United States, who praised Tshombe as a staunch anti-Communist Christian. See Sandra W. Meditz and Tim Merrill, *Zaire: A Country Study*, 4th ed. (Washington, DC: Library of Congress, Federal Research Division, 1994), 33–35; Guy Vanthemsche, *Belgium and the Congo, 1885–1980* (Cambridge: Cambridge University Press, 2012), 202, http://doi.org/10.1017/CBO9781139043038.

11. George M. Houser, *Meeting Africa's Challenge: The Story of the American Committee on Africa* (New York: American Committee on Africa, n.d.), 5, AAA, http://africanactivist.msu.edu/document_metadata.php?objectid=32-130-C2B.

12. ACOA, "American Citizens Welcome Prime Minister Lumumba of Congo," press release, July 26, 1960, http://africanactivist.msu.edu/asearch2.php?keyword=Lumumba&keywordmode=all; ACOA, "An Open Letter of Welcome to Prime Minister Patrice Lumumba of the Republic of the Congo on His Arrival in the U.S.A.," AAA, http://africanactivist.msu.edu/document_metadata.php?objectid=32-130-1011; Houser, *No One Can Stop*, 140, 361.

13. Madeleine G. Kalb, *The Congo Cables: The Cold War in Africa—from Eisenhower to Kennedy* (New York: Macmillan, 1982), 128–29. Prominent members of Congress were also painting the Katanga secession as a pro-Western rebellion against native savagery and Lumumba's leftist tyranny. See Robert Kinloch Massie, *Loosing the Bonds: The United States and South Africa in the Apartheid Years* (New York: Doubleday, 1997), 108.

14. For CIA complicity see *The CIA Family Jewels*, National Security Archives, https://nsarchive2.gwu.edu/NSAEBB/NSAEBB222/index.htm; Scott Shane, "Memories of a C.I.A. Officer Resonate in a New Era," *New York Times*, February 24, 2008, http://www.nytimes.com/2008/02/24/world/africa/24congo.html; Houser, *No One Can Stop*, 143–44; Hochschild, *King Leopold's Ghost*, 302–3; Stephen Kinzer, *The Brothers: John Foster Dulles, Allen Dulles, and Their Secret World War* (New York: Henry Holt, 2013), 248–50, 257–73, 277–85; David Talbot, *The Devil's Chessboard: Allen Dulles, the CIA, and the Rise of America's Secret Government* (New York: HarperCollins, 2015), 375–89. The Belgian involvement is detailed in Ludo De Witte, *The Assassination of Lumumba*, trans. Ann Wright and Renée Fenby (London: Verso, 2001).

15. John Stockwell, *In Search of Enemies: A CIA Story* (New York: W. W. Norton, 1978), 237.

16. After Mobutu's overthrow in 1997, the new president, Laurent Désiré Kabila, changed the name of the country back to the Democratic Republic of the Congo.

17. George M. Houser, "Letter to the Editor," *New York Times*, December 12, 1964, https://timesmachine.nytimes.com/timesmachine/1964/12/12/issue.html.

18. William Minter, *Apartheid's Contras: An Inquiry into the Roots of War in Angola and Mozambique* (London: Zed, 1994), 13–14.

19. Minter, *Apartheid's Contras*, 89–90. For a more detailed understanding of the relationship between the various nationalist factions, see John Marcum, *The Angolan Revolution*, vol. 2, *Exile Politics and Guerrilla Warfare 1982–1976* (Cambridge, MA: MIT Press, 1978).

20. Houser, *No One Can Stop*, 177.

21. George M. Houser, "Assessing Africa's Liberation Struggle," *Africa Today* 34, no. 4 (1987): 25, http://www.jstor.org/stable/4186444.

22. Houser, *No One Can Stop*, 177.

23. Marcum, *The Angolan Revolution*, 2:46–58.

24. Marcum, 14–15.

25. Minter, *Apartheid's Contras*, 19.

26. Minter, 18.

27. Houser, *No One Can Stop*, 199–200.

28. Houser, 200.

29. Council for the Development of Social Science Research in Africa, "Amilcar Cabral's Assassination," CODESRIA (Dakar, Senegal: CODESRIA), http://www.codesria.org/spip.php?article576.

30. Houser, *No One Can Stop*, 227.

31. Lloyd Sachikonye, *Zimbabwe's Lost Decade: Politics, Development and Society* (Harare: Weaver, 2011), 6.

32. The terms "multiracial," "nonracial," and "interracial" have often been used interchangeably, but in the South African context there have been some distinctions between them. For more on this see David Everatt, *The Origins of Non-Racialism: White Opposition to Apartheid in the 1950s* (Johannesburg: Witwatersrand University Press, 2009); Gerhart Mare, "'Non-Racialism' in the Struggle Against Apartheid," *Society in Transition* 34, no. 1 (2003), 1,; "Origins: Formation, Sharpeville and Banning," *South African History Online*, http://www.sahistory.org.za/article/origins-formation-sharpeville-and-banning-1959-1960; Daily Vox, "A Lesson in the History of the ANC's Multiracialism and Non-Racialism," February 4, 2017, accessed April 7, 2018, https://www.thedailyvox.co.za/anc-multiracialism-nonracialism-history/.

33. "Sharpeville Massacre, 21 March, 1960," *South African History Online*, March 31, 2011, https://www.sahistory.org.za/article/sharpeville-massacre-21-march-1960.

34. "Talking Drums: Boycott?," *Africa Today* 7, no. 1 (March 1960): 3, http://www.jstor.org/stable/4184057.

35. ACOA, memorandum on an American Boycott of South African Goods, January 6, 1960, AAA, http://africanactivist.msu.edu/document_metadata.php?objectid=32-130-23F8; Executive Board Minutes, January 6, 1960, ACOA Records, Series 1, Box 2, Folder 13, ARC.

36. Executive Board Minutes, March 14, 1960, ACOA Records, Series 1, Box 2, Folder 34, ARC.

37. ACOA, "Oliver Tambo, Top South African, Refused U.S. Visa," press release, June 4, 1960, RACOA Microfilm Part 2, Reel 7, Frames 00759-60, University Publications of America.

38. ACOA, *24 Recommendations to Help End Apartheid in South Africa* (New York: American Committee on Africa, 1960), AAA, http://africanactivist.msu.edu/document_metadata.php?objectid=32-130-234E.

39. ACOA, *Action Against Apartheid: What You Can Do About Racial Discrimination in South Africa* (New York: American Committee on Africa, 1960), AAA, http://africanactivist.msu.edu/document_metadata.php?objectid=32-130-B67.

40. Enuga S. Reddy, "The United Nations and the Struggle for Liberation in South Africa," in *The Road to Democracy in South Africa: International Solidarity*, vol. 3, part 1, ed. South African Democracy Education Trust (Pretoria: Unisa, 2008), 41–139.

41. E. S. Reddy, interview by Lisa Brock, No Easy Victories (website), July 20, 2004, http://www.noeasyvictories.org/interviews/into3_reddy.php.

42. George M. Houser, "Statement by George M. Houser, Executive Director Emeritus of the American Committee on Africa at the Twenty-Fifth Anniversary of the Special Committee against Apartheid, May 6, 1988," GMH PP.

43. George M. Houser, "United States Policy and Southern Africa" (paper commissioned by the Phelps-Stokes Fund for its seminar on US Policy Towards Africa, Africa Fund, March 28–30, 1974), 5, AAA, http://africanactivist.msu.edu/document _metadata.php?objectid=32-130-F08.

44. Massie, *Loosing the Bonds*, 130. Massie maintains that Kennedy was uncomfortable with the perception that he owed his job to the votes of African Americans and didn't want to reinforce it. This may partially explain his reluctance to give more than token support to the anticolonial and antiapartheid movements.

45. See letter from African leaders quoted in Gleijeses, *Conflicting Missions*, 6.

46. Chester Bowles, a civil rights advocate, had as early as 1956 written *Africa's Challenge to America* (Berkeley: University of California Press, 1957). His tenure as undersecretary of state, however, was cut short when he was removed in 1961 ostensibly because he had failed to carry out key duties as an administrator in the Department of State and because he leaked his opposition to the Bay of Pigs invasion.

47. Members of the Advisory Council included a broad range of scholars, lawyers, activists, businesspeople, foundation executives, and other institutional leaders. See Massie, *Loosing the Bonds*, 132. Houser and John Marcum's tenure on the council, however, was cut short after the European division of the State Department learned that he and Marcum had traveled with UPA guerrillas in Angola. See Robert Zebulun Larson, "The Transnational and Local Dimensions of the Anti-Apartheid Movement" (PhD diss., Ohio State University, 2019), 93, ProQuest (27602960).

48. Arthur M. Schlesinger Jr., *A Thousand Days: John F. Kennedy in the White House* (Boston: Houghton Mifflin, 1965), 581–83.

49. David A. Dickson, "U.S. Foreign Policy toward Southern and Central Africa: The Kennedy and Johnson Years," *Presidential Studies Quarterly* 23, no. 2 (1993): 303, http://www.jstor.org/stable/27532280.

50. Massie, *Loosing the Bonds*, 127.

51. The weapons that had been used in Portugal had come through a secret agreement the United States had made with Portugal in 1951. When they learned of this agreement, the Kennedy administration tightened the flow of these weapons to Portugal but kept silent about it. See Massie, *Loosing the Bonds*, 124–25.

52. John Marcum, *The Angolan Revolution: The Anatomy of an Explosion*, vol. 1 (Cambridge, MA: MIT Press, 1969), 184; George M. Houser, "This Far and No Further," *Africa Today* 10, no. 2 (February 1963): 6–7, http://www.jstor.org/stable/4184386.

53. Houser, *No One Can Stop*, 268–69.

54. The Lyndon B. Johnson National Security Files: Africa National Security Files, 1963–1969, ix–x, http://cisupa.proquest.com/ksc_assets/catalog/3365.pdf.

55. George M. Houser, "The Changing Face of African Nationalism," *Africa Today* 7, no. 2 (April 1960): 9–10, http://www.jstor.org/stable/4184074; George M. Houser, *A Report on George Houser's Trip to Africa* (New York: American Committee on Africa, 1960), AAA, http://africanactivist.msu.edu/document_metadata.php ?objectid=32-130-FA6; George M. Houser, Africa Journal, February 1960, GMH PP.

56. Leilah Danielson, *American Gandhi: A. J. Muste and the History of Radicalism in the Twentieth Century* (Philadelphia: University of Pennsylvania Press, 2014), Kindle, loc 4439 of 2064.

57. Houser, *No One Can Stop*, 228.

58. Agostinho Neto had traveled to the United States with the hope of dispelling the taint of Communism associated with the MPLA, but Washington had remained wary of him. See Marcum, *The Angolan Revolution*, 2:14.

59. From 1962 to 1969, Washington funneled a modest supply of money and arms to Roberto through Congolese and other channels in case of a Portuguese defeat. Nixon's election in 1968 "deactivated" Roberto but left him on a yearly $10,000 retainer for intelligence information. See Marcum, *The Angolan Revolution*, 2:237. The taint of CIA collaboration must have traveled widely through the world of leftist intellectuals. Houser's son Steven related a story to the author that a Marxist professor he had in college tried to tell him that his father was a front for the CIA. The professor had simply read the accusation somewhere; however, nothing Steven could do would dissuade the professor of the unreliability of that accusation.

60. Houser, interview by Lisa Brock, No Easy Victories (website), http://www.noeasyvictories.org/interviews/into2_houser.php.

61. The Portuguese-American Committee on Foreign Affairs was a lobbying and propaganda group for the Portuguese government composed of about seventy New Englanders of Portuguese descent headed by a Boston-based lawyer. For more on this committee and its attacks on the ACOA see "Statement Made by George M. Houser Executive Director of the American Committee on Africa on the Charge Made by the Portuguese-American Committee on Foreign Affairs," press release, November 17, 1961, AAA, http://africanactivist.msu.edu/document_metadata.php?objectid=32-130-D8E; Houser to National Committee Members, memorandum, February 15, 1962, GMH PP; Associated Press, November 16, 1961, GMH PP; Houser, interview by Zac Peterson, Session 6, May 7, 2012, interview used with permission; Houser, *Meeting Africa's Challenge*, 5.

62. In a letter to Oleg Ignatief, editor of Progress Publishers in Moscow, Houser sought to refute the many false accusations that had appeared in papers throughout Europe, Africa, and the Soviet Union over the course of two decades. See Houser to Ignatief, April 5, 1979, GMH PP. He also wrote a lengthy statement on the history of his relationship with Holden Roberto, again in an attempt to quell the rumors. See George M. Houser, "A Footnote on the Relationship of ACOA to UPA-FNLA-GRAE," n.d., ACOA Records, Series 3, Box 79, Folder 66, ARC.

63. Welensky's comments cited in "Dear Friend" letter from George M. Houser, February 10, 1960, AAA, http://africanactivist.msu.edu/document_metadata.php?objectid=32-130-FA6.

64. George M. Houser, "Statement to Executive Board," December 6, 1960, ACOA Records, Series 1, Box 2, Folder 13, ARC; George M. Houser, Africa Journal, November 1960, GMH PP.

65. George M. Houser, *The Congo Revisited* (New York: American Committee on Africa, 1960), AAA, http://africanactivist.msu.edu/document_metadata.php?objectid=32-130-100F.

66. George M. Houser, "Statement to Executive Board," December 6, 1960, ACOA Records, Series 1, Box 2, Folder 13, ARC.

67. For stories about these groups see William Minter, Charles Hovey Jr., and Gail Cobb, eds., *No Easy Victories: African Liberation and American Activists over a Half Century, 1950–2000* (Trenton, NJ: Africa World, 2008).

68. In an interview later in his life, Houser expressed great respect for Malcolm X. "If he had lived, who knows what our relationship might have been?" he told an interviewer. It is curious that Houser did not agree with the Panthers' policy of armed self-defense, yet Houser was willing to countenance it in Africa. See Houser, interview by Zac Peterson, May 7, 2012, used with permission. Toward the end of his life, Houser became good friends with Albert "Big Man" Howard, a former Black Panther who spoke at Houser's memorial service in California.

69. For more on this history see Clayborne Carson, *In Struggle: SNCC and the Black Awakening of the 1960s* (Cambridge, MA: Harvard University Press, 1981); Peniel E. Joseph, *Stokely: A Life* (New York: Basic/Civitas, 2014).

70. Houser, *No One Can Stop*, 267.

71. The ACOA's attempt to prevent Carlos Cook, a Black Nationalist, from speaking at a Harlem rally in October 1960—one in which Prime Minister Kwame Nkrumah addressed a crowd of thousands—was surely seen in that light. See Foster Hailey, "Nkrumah Tells Rally in Harlem Negroes Form U.S.-Africa Bond," *New York Times*, October 6, 1960. Despite Houser's attempt to prevent Cook from speaking, Nkrumah invited him to come to the podium where he also joined Malcolm X, Adam Clayton Powell Jr., and others. See Brenda Gayle Plummer, *In Search of Power: African Americans in the Era of Decolonization, 1956–1974* (New York: Cambridge University Press, 2013), 48.

72. E. S. Reddy, interview by Gail Hovey, No Easy Victories (website), http://www.noeasyvictories.org/interviews/int03_reddy.php.

73. E. S. Reddy, interview by Gail Hovey.

74. Steven Houser in email to author, October 17, 2019.

75. Houser to E. S. Reddy, January 14, 1969, ACOA Records, Series 1, Box 1, Folder 37, Inter-Office Memoranda, January–May 1969.

76. George M. Houser, "Statement to Executive Board, December 6, 1960," ACOA Records, Series 1, Box 2, Folder 13, ARC.

77. See, for example, "Jim Forman Delivers Black Manifesto at Riverside Church," accessed April 9, 2018, https://snccdigital.org/events/jim-forman-delivers-black-manifesto-at-riverside-church/.

78. George W. Shepherd Jr., *Anti-Apartheid: Transnational Conflict and Western Policy in the Liberation of South Africa* (Westport, CT: Greenwood, 1977), 41. For more about this controversy see the following articles: Jason Mosley, "Academe and Africa," *Africa Today* 18, no. 1 (January 1971): 1–3; Ronald H. Chilcote and Martin Legassick, "The African Challenge to American Scholarship in Africa," *Africa Today* 18, no. 1 (January 1971): 4–11; Margaret L. Bates, "Some Thoughts on Research," *Africa Today* 18, no. 1 (January 1971): 14–17; Philip W. Bell et al., "Letter to the President," *Africa Today* 18, no. 1 (January 1971): 28.

79. Francis Njubi Nesbitt, *Race for Sanctions: African Americans against Apartheid, 1946–1994* (Bloomington: Indiana University Press, 2004), 35–36. W. E. B. Du Bois had earlier sought to convince the NAACP to institutionalize an organizational

framework for black American interest in Africa but had found it reluctant to do so. In 1956, in a letter to a friend, he criticized the ACOA as "naturally, . . . doing some good work and publishing some facts about the present situation" but called it fundamentally "reactionary" and unable to present the full African story. Du Bois may have been miffed at not being consulted or given a place in the ACOA. He was probably also stung by Houser's refusal to work with the CAA. See James H. Meriwether, "The American Negro Leadership Conference on Africa and its Arden House Conference: Politicizing & Institutionalizing the Relationship with Africa," *Afro-Americans in New York Life and History* 21, no. 2 (July 1997): 39.

80. Steering Committee Minutes, May 9, 1965, ACOA, AAA, http://africanactivist .msu.edu/document_metadata.php?objectid=32-130-23A9.

81. Although it seems clear from ACOA records that Houser was intimately involved in the creation of the ANLCA, some scholars who had not consulted the ACOA archives have sought to distance him from the organization's origins. See, for example, Ehimika A. Ifidon and Edward O. Erhagbe, "The Making of an African American Foreign Policy Lobby: The American Negro Leadership Conference on Africa," *Lagos Historical Review* 11 (July 2011): 93–112, https://doi.org/10.4314/lhr .v11i1.6.

82. Nesbitt, *Race for Sanctions*, 45; Plummer, *In Search of Power*, 122.

83. Lewis Baldwin, "Martin Luther King, Jr., a 'Coalition of Conscience,' and Freedom in South Africa," in *Freedom's Distant Shores: American Protestants and Post-Colonial Alliances with Africa*, ed. R. Drew Smith (Waco, TX: Baylor University Press, 2006), 63.

84. For details on the problems leading to the demise of the ANLCA see Meriwether, "The American Negro Leadership Council"; Ifidon and Eerhagbe, "The Making of an African American Foreign Policy"; and Randolph Stakeman, "The American Negro Leadership Conference on Africa" (paper presented at the African Studies Association Annual Meeting, December, 1993), GMH PP.

85. Memorandum by George M. Houser to the Unofficial Commission on Angola, December 21, 1961, AAA, http://africanactivist.msu.edu/document_metadata .php?objectid=32-130-2352.

86. George Houser, Africa Journal, January 1961, original handwritten manuscript, GMH PP.

87. Accounts of this trip with the UPA rebels are found in Houser, Africa Journal January 1962, GMH PP; Houser, *No One Can Stop*, 155–56; George M. Houser, *A Report on a Journey through Rebel Angola* (New York: American Committee on Africa, n.d.), AAA, http://africanactivist.msu.edu /document_metadata.php?objectid=32-130-B71; George M. Houser, "Journey to Rebel Angola," *Africa Today* 9, no. 2 (March 1962): 4–7, http://www.jstor.org /stable/27821932.

88. George M. Houser, *Draft Report on the Third All African People's Conference Held in Cairo from March 25 to 30, 1961* (New York: American Committee on Africa, 1961), AAA, http://africanactivist.msu.edu/document_metadata.php?objectid=32-130-FBD; George M. Houser, "At Cairo: The Third All-African People's Conference," *Africa Today* 8, no. 4 (April 1961): 11–13, http://www.jstor.org/stable/4184206.

89. Houser, *No One Can Stop*, 156.

90. Houser, "Assessing," 31.

91. Houser, "Journey to Rebel Angola," 7.

92. Houser, *A Report on a Journey*.

93. ACOA Steering Committee Minutes, May 9, 1962, AAA, http://africanactivist.msu.edu/document_metadata.php?objectid=32-130-23A9.

94. For a detailed history of the relationships between the liberation movements in Angola, see Marcum, *The Angolan Revolution* 2:100–240. See especially chapters 3–5.

95. ACOA, "American Labor Gives Support," *Face to Africa: Bulletin of the American Committee on Africa* 1, no. 1 (May 1962): 2, AAA, http://africanactivist.msu.edu/document_metadata.php?objectid=32-130-6DD.

96. Ian Gilchrist in email to author, November 24, 2019.

97. Houser, *No One Can Stop*, 162.

98. ACOA, *A Brief Review of Action Taken on and around Human Rights Day, December 10, in Connection with the Appeal for Action against Apartheid Campaign* (New York: American Committee on Africa, n.d.), AAA, http://africanactivist.msu.edu/document_metadata.php?objectid=32-130-657.

99. George M. Houser, "Architects of New Africa," *Africa Today* 10, no. 6 (June 1963): 4, https://www.jstor.org/stable/i388910.

100. George M. Houser, *Report on a Trip to Africa, May–June 1963* (New York: American Committee on Africa, 1963), AAA, http://africanactivist.msu.edu/document_metadata.php?objectid=32-130-B77.

101. Houser's discussions with the various nationalists on this trip are recorded in his Africa Journal, May–June 1963, GMH PP.

102. Houser, *No One Can Stop*, 167–68; Ian Gilchrist, *A Report on the Gilchrist Withdrawal from Leopoldville* (New York: American Committee on Africa, n.d.), AAA, http://africanactivist.msu.edu/document_metadata.php?objectid=32-130-2351; Gilchrist to Miss Deborah Kallen, American Committee on Africa, July 26, 1964; Gilchrist to Houser, July 31, 1964, ACOA Records, Series 3, Box 79, Folder 13; Gilchrist in email to author, November 24, 2019.

103. Gilchrist to Houser, August 8, 1964; Houser to Gilchrist, August 10, 1964, ACOA Records, Series 3, Box 79, Folder 13, ARC.

104. Gilchrist email to author, November 24, 2019.

105. Houser, "A Footnote on the Relationship."

106. Gilchrist email to author, November 24, 2019. Gilchrist went on to say, "It was, in my view, simply a tragedy that Roberto ultimately did not succeed in achieving more of the courage and idealism that he had initially shown."

107. For more about the Rivonia Trial, see Joel Joffe, *The State vs. Nelson Mandela: The Trial That Changed South Africa* (Oxford: Oneworld, 2007).

108. "Staff Report" to Executive Board Annual Meeting, n.d., Garlick and Hoffman, Certified Public Accountants, American Committee on Africa Report of Examination, 1963, ACOA Records Addendum, Box 6, Folder 4, ARC.

109. Tambo quoted in "Greetings," *Africa Today* 10, no. 9 (November 1963): 9–11, http://www.jstor.org/stable/4184463.

110. Cabral and Mondlane quoted in "Greetings."

111. George M. Houser, *African Dynamics and ACOA Direction, Report to the Executive Board*, March 16, 1964, ACOA Records, Series 1, Box 2, Folder 18, ARC.

112. George M. Houser, *Executive Director's Report, Annual Meeting of the Executive Board, American Committee on Africa* (New York: American Committee on Africa, 1965), AAA, http://africanactivist.msu.edu/document_metadata.php?objectid=32-130-23C1.

113. Houser, *African Dynamics and ACOA Direction*, 3.

114. George M. Houser, *Observations on Trends in Non-Independent Africa's Struggle for Freedom* (New York: American Committee on Africa, n.d.), AAA, http://africanactivist.msu.edu/document_metadata.php?objectid=32-130-2542.

115. George M. Houser, *Executive Director's Report to the Executive Board at the Annual Meeting*, April 26, 1966, ACOA Records, Executive Committee Minutes, January–May 1966, Series 1, Box 2, Folder 20, ARC.

116. ACOA, "Partners in Apartheid: U.S. Policy on South Africa," *Africa Today* 11, no. 3 (March 1964): 2–17, http://www.jstor.org/stable/4187823.

117. George M. Houser, *Executive Director's Report to the Annual Meeting, American Committee on Africa Executive Board* (New York: American Committee on Africa, 1965), ACOA, AAA, http://africanactivist.msu.edu/document_metadata.php?objectid=32-130-23C1; Program, National Conference on South African Crisis and American Action, March 21–23, 1965, Washington, DC, AAA, http://africanactivist.msu.edu/document_metadata.php?objectid=32-130-132E.

118. See ACOA, "A Special Report on American Involvement in the South African Economy," *Africa Today* 13, no. 1 (January 1966): 1–40, http://www.jstor.org/stable/4184684.

119. Gail Hovey, "Jennifer Davis: Clarity, Determination, and Coalition Building," in *African Liberation and American Activists Over a Half Century, 1950–2000* (Trenton, NJ: Africa World, 2008), 169–72; Jennifer Davis, interview by Zac Peterson, January 8, 2014, used with permission.

120. Robinson, whose prior education had provided him with little knowledge about Africa, recalled in his memoir that sometime in the 1960s he wrote to "a newly discovered organization in New York, the American Committee on Africa" to obtain information about the wars in Portuguese Africa and was sent "reams" of material. See Randall Robinson, *Defending the Spirit: A Black Life in America* (New York: Penguin, 1999), 94.

121. In 1978 Foster became the first black elected from the Bronx to the New York City Council. He remained on the council for twenty-four years.

122. Human Rights Day Rally, flyer, December 10, 1965, AAA, http://africanactivist.msu.edu/document_metadata.php?objectid=32-130-111C; Martin Luther King Jr., "Address to the South Africa Benefit of the American Committee on Africa at Hunter College, New York City" (speech, December 10, 1965), AAA, http://africanactivist.msu.edu/document_metadata.php?objectid=32-130-112I.

123. Massie, *Loosing the Bonds*, 212–13.

124. Bernard Rivers, interview by the author, November 18, 2015. The story first aired in a report entitled *The Oil Conspiracy* (Washington, DC: Center for Social Action, United Church of Christ, 1976), see http://africanactivist.msu.edu

/document_metadata.php?objectid=32-130-32F. It was subsequently expanded and published as a book that won Britain's equivalent of the Pulitzer Prize. See Martin Bailey, *Oilgate: The Sanctions Scandal* (London: Coronet, 1979).

125. Rivers, interview; Bailey, *Oilgate*, 7; *The Oil Conspiracy;* Bernard Rivers, "Testimony Regarding the Supply of Oil to Southern Rhodesia Made Before the Fourth Committee of the United Nations General Assembly" (speech, UN General Assembly, November 30, 1977), AAA, http://africanactivist.msu.edu/document_metadata.php?objectid=32-130-8C.

126. The extent of the oil giants' influence on the American government was revealed when this author, who was involved in the effort to get the story out, approached Brady Tyson, who was then on the staff of the US mission to the UN with a portfolio for human rights. It was 1977, ten years after sanctions had been imposed, and Ian Smith's government was still going strong. Those of us who met with Tyson asked him why the Carter administration had done nothing to curtail Mobil Oil's complicity in the oil conspiracy. Tyson had been an ardent civil rights activist who had served on the board of the Southern Christian Leadership Conference. Thus, we were shocked by his answer: were Carter to move against the oil companies, he explained, there would be an immediate military coup in the United States.

127. ACOA, "Proposal for a Campaign on First National City and Chase Manhattan Banks in New York," 1966, ACOA Records, Series 3, Box 100, Folder 47.

128. Massie, *Loosing the Bonds*, 218; George M. Houser, "A Rationale for the Protest against Banks Doing Business with South Africa," 1966, ACOA Records, Series 3, Box 100, Folder 46, ARC.

129. In addition to Chase and First National City, the other banks were Bank of America, Manufacturers Hanover Trust, Morgan Guaranty Trust, Irving Trust, Continental Illinois National Bank and Trust, and First National Bank of Chicago. See Houser, *No One Can Stop*, 270 (specifically see asterisked note on this page).

130. The press reported that the two banks denied the validity of the $23 million, but Randolph's figure was based on the amounts of withdrawal pledges the committee had received from individuals, organizations, and institutions. Some withdrawals occurred without informing the banks of the specific reason for withdrawal, and some institutions wanted to withhold identification for fear of reprisals. See A. Philip Randolph, "Statement by A. Philip Randolph on Progress of Bank Campaign," press release, December 7, 1966, http://africanactivist.msu.edu/document_metadata.php?objectid=32-130-1035.

131. Houser, *No One Can Stop*, 271.

132. Houser, 271.

133. George M. Houser, "African Liberation Movements: Report on a Trip to Africa, Spring 1967," *Africa Today* 14, no. 4 (August 1967): 11–13, http://www.jstor.org/stable/4184811.

134. George M. Houser, "A Report on a Trip to Africa, May 11–June 10, 1967," 11, GMH PP.

135. "Festus Isaac, Toivo Ja-Toivo, D. D. Shoombe to the Secretary, Mr. B. I. Miller, Committee on South West Africa, United Nations Organization, RE: Petition, 29, 1958," ACOA Records, Series 3, Box 94, Folder 8, ARC.

136. ACOA, "Statement by the American Committee on Africa on the Taped Message Received from a Petitioner in South West Africa," October 7, 1958, ACOA Records, Series 3, Box 94, Folder 37, ARC.

137. Chief Hosea Kutako, Chief Samuel Witbooi, and Mr. Sam Nujoma, president of the Ovamboland People's Organization to Houser, November 19, 1959, ACOA Records, Series 3, Box 94, Folder 8.

138. Sam Nujoma, Chief Hosea Kutako, and Chief Samuel Witbooi to ACOA, November 19, 1959, Series 3, Box 94, ACOA Records Addendum, ARC.

139. UN General Assembly Twenty-first Session, Res. 2145 (XXI) Question of South West Africa, October 27, 1966, http://www.worldlii.org/int/other/UNGA /1966/13.pdf; UN General Assembly Fifth Special Session, Res. 2248 Question of South West Africa, May 19, 1967, http://www.refworld.org/docid/3b00f048c .html.

140. George M. Houser, "Observations on the Current African Situation and the Direction of the American Committee on Africa," n.d., ACOA Records Addendum, Box 6, Folder 9, ARC.

141. Houser, Africa Journal South West Africa Trip 1967, GMH PP.

142. See note 143.

143. Accounts of the attempted flight into South West Africa are found in Houser, Africa Journal, South West Africa Trip and Houser, *No One Can Stop*, 243–46, as well as in several post-trip reports. See Ad Hoc Committee for the Development of an Independent South West Africa, *Statement by the Ad Hoc Committee for the Development of an Independent South West Africa* (New York: American Committee on Africa, n.d.), AAA, http://africanactivist.msu.edu/document_metadata.php ?objectid=32-130-131F; Samuel F. Ashelman et al., *Report to the United Nations Council on South West Africa from the Ad Hoc Committee for the Development of an Independent South West Africa* (New York: American Committee on Africa, 1968), AAA, http:// africanactivist.msu.edu/document_metadata.php?objectid=32-130-BA0; Lyle Tatum, *Confrontation Above South West Africa*, January 22, 1968, AAA, http://africanactivist .msu.edu/document_metadata.php?objectid=32-130-1323.

144. There is a discrepancy between which engines went out in Houser's two accounts of the incident—the one in his journal and the other in the book published many years later. This account is from the journal written much closer to the time the incident occurred.

145. Houser, *No One Can Stop*, 245–46.

146. Ad Hoc Committee for the Development of an Independent South West Africa, *Statement*.

147. "Protest 'Fly-in' to S-W. Africa Blocked," *Washington Post*, December 7, 1967; "South Africans Foil Trip by Five," *New York Times*, December 7, 1967; "Facing Reality Over S.W.A.," *Times of Zambia*, December 7, 1967; "US Group Is Refused S.W.A. Rights," *Cape Times*, December 7, 1967.

148. Vorster quoted in *Die Transvaler*, December 7, 1967; Houser, *No One Can Stop*, 246.

149. Ad Hoc Committee for the Development of an Independent South West Africa, *Statement*.

Notes to Pages 187–192

150. "Testimony to Be Given to the United Nations Council for South West Africa by George M. Houser, the Ad Hoc Committee for the Development of an Independent South West Africa" (speech, UN Council for South West Africa, n.d.), ACOA Records, Series 1, Box 2, Folder 22, ARC.

8

1. Robert Kinloch Massie, *Loosing the Bonds: The United States and South Africa in the Apartheid Years* (New York: Doubleday, 1997), 362.

2. Massie, *Loosing the Bonds*, 362. It was a similar analysis, delivered by Martin Luther King Jr. at the Riverside Church in 1967, that many believe led to his assassination. See M. L. King Jr., "Beyond Vietnam: A Time to Break Silence," American Rhetoric Online Speech Bank (website), https://www.americanrhetoric.com/speeches/mlkatimetobreaksilence.htm.

3. "1968 Democratic Party Platform, August 26, 1968," American Presidency Project (website), http://www.presidency.ucsb.edu/ws/index.php?pid=29604.

4. The World Council of Churches, like the UN, was a product of the surge in global political cooperation and focus on human rights following World War II. The WCC's headquarters were established in Geneva, Switzerland, strategically sited as the locus of the European headquarters of the UN and of numerous international organizations. The Programme to Combat Racism was born at a time of deep political crisis and increasing racial polarization. For more on this see Claude E. Welch Jr., "Mobilizing Morality: The World Council of Churches and Its Program to Combat Racism, 1969–1994," *Human Rights Quarterly* 23, no. 4 (November 2001): 863–910, https://www.jstor.org/stable/4489365.

5. Houser, interview by Celeste Wallin, December 10, 1986, GMH PP, 13.

6. George M. Houser, "Response," *Christianity and Crisis* 32, no. 12 (July 10, 1972): 165–66.

7. Prexy Nesbitt, interview by the author, February 21, 2016.

8. United States Interdepartmental Group for Africa, *The Kissinger Study of Southern Africa: National Security Study Memorandum 39 (Secret)*, ed. Mohamed A. El-Khawas and Barry Cohen (Westport, CT: Lawrence Hill, 1976).

9. As National Security staff member Roger Morris would reveal in later years, the discussions about Africa policy within the NSC had unfolded under a persistent "pall of racism"; Massie, *Loosing the Bonds*, 234–27.

10. Massie, 301–2.

11. Edgar Lockwood and Christine Root, *We Take Pleasure in Announcing the Opening of the Washington Office on Africa* (Washington, DC: Washington Office on Africa), AAA, http://africanactivist.msu.edu/document_metadata.php?objectid=32-130-14AA.

12. Reverend William Wipfler in conversation with the author, May 19, 2014. Wipfler was the human rights officer for the National Council of Churches.

13. Charles C. Diggs Jr. to Houser, November 22, 1977, ACOA Records Addendum, Box 13, Folder 8, ARC.

14. George M. Houser, "What the U.S. Can Do about Apartheid, Excerpts from Testimony Given before the House Sub-committee on Africa, March 15, 1966," *Africa Today* 13, no. 3 (March 1966): 4, http://www.jstor.org/stable/4184699.

15. For more on Dennis Brutus see: Dennis Brutus, *The Dennis Brutus Tapes: Essays at Autobiography*, ed. Bernth Lindors (Woodbridge, UK: Boydell and Brewer, 2011); Dennis Brutus, *Poetry and Protest: A Dennis Brutus Reader*, ed. Lee Sustar and Aisha Karim (Chicago: Haymarket, 2006).

16. ACOA, "South Africa and the Olympics," n.d., ACOA Records, Series 1, Box 2, Folder 23, ARC.

17. Jim Bouton, *Report on Mexico Trip* (New York: American Committee on Africa, 1968), AAA, http://africanactivist.msu.edu/document_metadata.php?objectid =32-130-10Co/.

18. Richard Lapchick, interview by the author, July 7, 2015. For a history of the role of sports in South Africa's politics and the boycott tactic, see Richard E. Lapchick, *The Politics of Race and International Sport: The Case of South Africa* (Westport, CT: Greenwood, 1975); *Sports Boycott in the International Campaign against Apartheid* (New York: United Nations Centre Against Apartheid, 1977), AAA, http:// africanactivist.msu.edu/document_metadata.php?objectid=32-130-2F3.

19. Although the ACOA was an early proponent of the cultural boycott, it was not the first. See Gregory Houston, "International Solidarity: Introduction," in *The Road to Democracy in South Africa: International Solidarity*, vol. 3, ed. South African Democracy Education Trust (Pretoria: Unisa, 2008), 30.

20. ACOA, *We Say NO to Apartheid: A Declaration of American Artists* (New York: American Committee on Africa, n.d.), AAA, http://africanactivist.msu.edu /document_metadata.php?objectid=32-130-FC3. Among the signers were Henry Fonda, Tallulah Bankhead, Harry Belafonte, Leonard Bernstein, Victor Borge, Carol Burnett, Diahann Carroll, Sammy Davis Jr., Ossie Davis, Ruby Dee, Julie Harris, Van Heflin, Lena Horne, Langston Hughes, Eartha Kitt, Johnny Mathis, Burgess Meredith, Arthur Miller, Edmond O'Brien, Sidney Poitier, Paul Robeson, Nina Simone, Ed Sullivan, and Eli Wallach.

21. This tactic was not exactly new with Houser. Chicago organizer Saul Alinsky had led protests at Kodak's shareholder meeting in 1967 to demand minority hiring policies. See his interview in *Playboy* magazine at http://www.bahaistudies.net /neurelitism/library/alinsky_interview_1967.pdf; and in 1968 Students for a Democratic Society led demonstrations at Dow Chemical's meetings to protest its manufacture of napalm that was being used in Vietnam. See "Resistance and Revolution: The Anti-War Movement at the University of Michigan, 1965–1972," Michigan in the World (website), http://michiganintheworld.history.lsa.umich .edu/antivietnamwar/exhibits/show/exhibit/military_and_the_university /dow_chemical.

22. Jennifer Davis, interview by Zac Peterson, January 8, 2014, used with permission.

23. The Sullivan Principles were enunciated in 1977 with an additional principle added in 1984. They became a benchmark against which companies could measure their corporate hiring practices in South Africa. By 1986, 160 of the 244 American companies doing business in South Africa had adopted the Sullivan Principles, but in 1977 the ACOA held a press conference in which it severely criticized these principles, sending its scathing critique to the corporations that claimed they were making

changes in South Africa. See "ACOA Press Release on the Sullivan Principles," press release, April 18, 1977, AAA, http://africanactivist.msu.edu/document_metadata .php?objectid=32-130-C31.

24. Houser, *No One Can Stop*, 350.

25. George M. Houser, "Memorandum to the Executive Board RE the Changing Situation in South Africa and Our Response to It," October 1971, ACOA Records, Series 1, Box 2, Folder 28, ARC. By 1987, with apartheid still in place, Sullivan reversed himself, calling for corporations to withdraw altogether from South Africa and for the United States to impose trade and investment sanctions on the regime.

26. Corporate Information Center, *The Frankfort Documents: Secret Bank Loans to the South African Government* (New York: Corporate Information Center, 1973), AAA, http://africanactivist.msu.edu/document_metadata.php?objectid=32-130-D2; *ACOA Annual Report 1973*, AAA, http://africanactivist.msu.edu/document_metadata .php?objectid=32-130-AC4.

27. "Black Group Seeks Halt to S. African Air Route," *Evening Star*, May 27, 1969; Warren Hoge, "Rip S. African Flights to JFK," *New York Post*, May 27, 1969; Naomi S. Rovner, "Ban Proposed on Biased Foreign Airlines," *Baltimore Sun*, May 28, 1969, ACOA Records, Series 1, Box 2, Folder 25, ARC.

28. ACOA, "American Involvement in the South African Economy," *Africa Today* 13, no. 1 (January 1966): 2–40, https://www.jstor.org/stable/4184685; Blyden B. Jackson, "Apartheid and Imperialism: A Study of U.S. Corporate Involvement in South Africa," *Africa Today* 17, no. 5 (1970): 1–39, www.jstor.org/stable/4185114.

29. George M. Houser, "The Polaroid Approach to South Africa," *Christian Century* 88, no. 8 (February 24, 1971): 249–52; George M. Houser, "U.S. Business Should Leave South Africa," *New York Times*, April 18, 1971, https://www.nytimes.com/1971/04/18 /archives/us-business-should-leave-south-africa-investment-dollars-bolster.html.

30. Massie, *Loosing the Bonds*, 273.

31. George M. Houser, "Polaroid's Dramatic Withdrawal from South Africa," *Christian Century* 95, no. 13 (April 12, 1978): 392–93.

32. George M. Houser, *Report on Africa Trip: November 18 to December 9, 1968* (New York: American Committee on Africa, n.d.), AAA, http://africanactivist.msu.edu /document_metadata.php?objectid=32-130-BAA.

33. Houser, *Report on Africa Trip*.

34. Houser to Peter Weiss, November 24, 1968, GMH PP.

35. Houser to Peter Weiss, November 24, 1968.

36. George M. Houser, "Eduardo Chivambo Mondlane: Memorial Service," February 13, 1969, AAA, http://africanactivist.msu.edu/document_metadata.php?-objectid=32-130-11A7. The opening remarks at the memorial service for Eduardo Chivambo Mondlane.

37. "Gulf Oil Earnings Skidded 15% in Quarter; Protesters Set Off Uproar at Meeting," *Wall Street Journal*, April 29, 1970, 4.

38. "ACOA Notes #2," May 21, 1971, AAA, http://africanactivist.msu.edu /document_metadata.php?objectid=32-130-BD2.

39. Gulf had become not only a financial ally of Portugal, paying more than $61 million in taxes and royalties to Portugal in 1972 alone, but it was also a public

apologist for Portuguese colonialism. See ACOA, *Annual Report 1973*, AAA, http://
africanactivist.msu.edu/document_metadata.php?objectid=32-130-AC4.

40. Executive Board Meeting, April 20, 1970, ACOA Records, Series 1, Box 2,
Folder 26, ARC.

41. Jennifer Davis, "Allies in Empire: The U.S. and Portugal in Africa Part I: U. S.
Economic Involvement," *Africa Today* 17, no. 4 (1970): 1–15, https://www.jstor
.org/stable/4185103; William Minter, "Allies in Empire Part II: Military Involvement,"
Africa Today 17, no. 4 (1970): 28–32, https://www.jstor.org/stable/4185103; William
Minter, "Allies in Empire Part III: American Foreign Policy and Colonialism," *Africa
Today* 17, no. 4 (July–August 1970): 34–36, https://www.jstor.org/stable/4185103.

42. Like so many other promising African leaders, Dialo Telli was betrayed by
Sékou Touré, in whose government he had served. Arrested and imprisoned, Telli
would die of torture and deliberate starvation.

43. Harry Belafonte, *My Song: A Memoir* (New York: Alfred A. Knopf, 2011), 341,
quoted in Peniel E. Joseph, *Stokely: A Life* (New York: Basics/Civitas, 2014), 309.

44. Houser, Africa Journal 1970. GMH PP.

45. Houser claims that he became aware of Roberto's authoritarian tendencies
as early as 1963 at the OAU conference in Addis Ababa. Houser noticed this again
when he came to the UN later that year and the following year when he was in
Léopoldville. The incident with Dr. Gilchrist's having to flee must have also shaken
Houser's confidence in Roberto. See George M. Houser, *No One Can Stop the Rain:
Glimpses of Africa's Liberation Struggle* (New York: Pilgrim, 1989), 162–71.

46. Horne makes the point that Houser's hands were tied by his determination
to keep the AFL-CIO on board. See Horne, *White Supremacy Confronted: U.S. Imperialism and Anti-Communism vs. the Liberation of Southern Africa from Rhodes to Mandela*
(New York: International Publishers, 2019), 369.

47. After returning from a year abroad at the University College of Dar es Salaam,
Tanzania, Nesbitt and Houser's daughter, Martie, both students at Antioch College,
began one of the first college divestment campaigns in the country. Nesbitt was a
founder of the Mozambique Support Network and ran the Mozambique Solidarity Office on behalf of the Mozambique government. He later worked for the Interreligious
Foundation for Community Organization (IFCO) running a training institute named
after Amílcar Cabral and for the Washington-based Institute for Policy Studies. Nesbitt
also worked as a program officer for the MacArthur Foundation and as program director for the WCC's Programme to Combat Racism. With Bob van Lierop, he founded
the Africa Information Service, worked as an aide to Chicago's black mayor, Harold
Washington, and as a union organizer. He has devoted his life to connecting Americans with Africans and Africa through teaching, writing, and organizing study tours
to Africa. See Prexy Nesbitt, interview by the author, February 10, 2016; Prexy Nesbitt,
interview by William Minter, No Easy Victories (website), http://www.noeasyvicto-
ries.org/interviews/int08_nesbitt.php; Prexy Nesbitt, interview by Zac Peterson, November 22, 2015, used with permission; Prexy Nesbitt, interview by Julie Frederikse,
October 12, 2004, AAA, http://africanactivist.msu.edu/video.php?objectid=32-12F-2.

48. ACOA Executive Board Meeting, April 20, 1970, ACOA Records, Series 1, Box
2, Folder 26, ARC.

49. "Anti-apartheid Split," *Washington Star*, August 8, 1970, ACOA Records, Series 2, Box 41, Folder 16, ARC.

50. "An Appeal by Black Americans for United States Support to Israel," *New York Times*, June 28, 1970, ACOA Records, Series 2, Box 41, Folder 16, ARC.

51. Black power activists saw similarities between their own struggle for freedom and that of the Palestinians, another people of color. For more on this controversy, see Michael R. Fischbach, *Black Power and Palestine: Transnational Countries of Color* (Redwood City, CA: Stanford University Press, 2018); Marjorie N. Feld, *Nations Divided: American Jews and the Struggle over Apartheid* (New York: Palgrave Macmillan, 2014), 53–70. Other reasons some African Americans found for opposing aid to Israel included the processing of South African diamonds by Israel, South African contributions to Israel during the Six-Day War, the visits of an Israeli defense official to South Africa allegedly to discuss counterinsurgency methods, and the economic ties being set up between the two countries by Israel's Foreign Trade bank.

52. "Policy Statement," 1970, ACOA Records, Series 2, Box 41, Folder 16, ARC.

53. Nesbitt recalled that most of the staff favored supporting the MPLA. See Nesbitt, interview by Zac Peterson, November 11, 2015, used with permission.

54. ACOA Executive Board Meeting, September 14, 1970, ACOA Records, Series 1, Box 2, Folder 27, ARC; Nesbitt, interview by the author, February 10, 2016.

55. George M. Houser, *Report*, September 5, 1972, Box 1, George Houser Papers, quoted in Horne, *White Supremacy Confronted*, 519.

56. George M. Houser, "Comment on Prexy's Report to the Board," September 25, 1970, ACOA Records, Series 1, Box 2, Folder 27, ARC.

57. Special Executive Board Meeting, October 8, 1970, ACOA Records, Series 1, Box 2, Folder 27, ARC.

58. ACOA Executive Board Meeting, December 3, 1970, ACOA Records, Series 1, Box 2, Folder 27, ARC.

59. Summary of Special Board Meeting Held February 26, 1971, ACOA Records, Series 1, Box 2, Folder 28, ARC. In his book, Houser dates this special board meeting to spring 1969, but the records indicate that it was 1971. See Houser, *No One Can Stop*, 173.

60. Executive Board Meeting, July 8, 1971, ACOA Records, Series 1, Box 2, Folder 28, ARC.

61. Nesbitt, telephone call with the author, June 18, 2020.

62. According to Nesbitt, "George was not comfortable working with organizations where he didn't know exactly who was going to run it, exactly what the agenda was going to be and that he would not have to worry about a lot of extraneous political pressures like FBI surveillance." See Nesbitt, interview by the author, February 10, 2016; Nesbitt, interview by the author, February 21, 2016.

63. Executive Board Minutes, December 3, 1970, ACOA Records, Series 1, Box 2, Folder 27, ARC.

64. Nesbitt, interview by the author, February 10, 2016.

65. Minutes, Special Executive Board Meeting, March 21, 1972, ACOA Records, Series 1, Box 2, Folder 29, ARC.

66. ACOA, *The Status of the Liberation Struggle in Africa: A Midyear Report from the American Committee on Africa* (New York: American Committee on Africa, 1971), AAA, http://africanactivist.msu.edu/document_metadata.php?objectid=32-130-6E7.

67. George M. Houser, "Memo to Executive Board, American Committee on Africa, Re Summer 1972 Trip to Africa," September 5, 1972, AAA, http://africanactivist.msu.edu/document_metadata.php?objectid=32-130-FDD.

68. American Committee on Africa, "South African Joins Black Leaders in Backing Demand for U.N. Authority in Namibia," press release, February 4, 1972, AAA, http://africanactivist.msu.edu/document_metadata.php?objectid=32-130-131B.

69. Winifred Courtney and Jennifer Davis, *Namibia: U.S. Corporate Involvement* (New York: The Africa Fund, 1972), AAA, http://africanactivist.msu.edu/document_metadata.php?objectid=32-130-F05.

70. *Zambia Times*, June 20, 1972, reproduced in "Dear Friend" letter from Houser, September 1972, AAA, http://africanactivist.msu.edu/document_metadata.php?objectid=32-130-BE4.

71. George M. Houser, *A Report to the United Nations Council for Namibia on an Attempt to Enter Namibia with a U.N. Visa* (New York: Africa Fund, 1972), AAA, http://africanactivist.msu.edu/document_metadata.php?objectid=32-130-BE2.

72. Among the newspapers containing articles about the aborted visit that Houser was able to collect were the *Johannesburg Star*, *Rand Daily Mail*, *Zambia Daily Mail*, *Zambia Times*, *Dar es Salaam Daily News*, and *Sunday News*, GMH PP.

73. "American in SWA Gate-Crash Bid No Wild-Eyed Fanatic," *Johannesburg Star*, July 8, 1972, GMH PP.

74. According to Houser's sources, the traitorous liberation fighters were promised high positions in Guinea-Bissau in return for the elimination of PAIGC leaders and the abandonment of the Cape Verde islands. See George M. Houser, *A Report on My 17th Trip to Africa* (New York: American Committee on Africa, 1973), AAA, http://africanactivist.msu.edu/document_metadata.php?objectid=32-130-BF5.

75. Houser, *A Report on My 17th Trip*.

76. Amilcar Cabral, "A Report to Our Friends," *Africa Today* 20, no. 1 (Winter 1973): 7–13, https://www.jstor.org/stable/4185278.

77. George M. Houser and Lawrence W. Henderson, "In Memory of Amilcar Cabral: Two Statements," *Africa Today* 20, no. 1 (1973): 3–6, http://www.jstor.org/stable/4185277.

78. George M. Houser, "Assessing Africa's Liberation Struggle," *Africa Today* 34, no. 4 (1987): 26, https://www.jstor.org/stable/4186444.

79. Houser, Africa Journal 1973, GMH PP; Houser, *A Report on My 17th Trip*.

9

1. The Portuguese coup, known as the "Carnation Revolution," is celebrated as a national holiday in Portugal. The coup was carried out by a group of midlevel army officers who chose to put their command under that of General Spinoza who had promised to work toward the early establishment of constitutionality and free elections. Spinoza had written a book arguing that a military solution to the insurgency in the colonies was not viable and that a political solution would have to be

found. See "CIA Intelligence Memorandum: The Coup in Portugal," April 27, 1974, US Central Intelligence Agency, https://www.cia.gov/library/readingroom/docs /CIA-RDP85T00353R000100040012-9.pdf.

2. George M. Houser, "Memo to Executive Board, National Committee re Portugal's Coup, African Colonies (and ACOA)," May 28, 1974, AAA, http:// africanactivist.msu.edu/document_metadata.php?objectid=32-130-11F1.

3. ACOA, "U.S. Citizens to Recognize the Newly Formed Republic of Guinea Bissau," mailing, n.d., AAA, http://africanactivist.msu.edu/document_metadata .php?objectid=32-130-12E8.

4. George M. Houser, *Observation Growing Out of Trip to Africa, October 17– November 7, 1974* (New York: American Committee on Africa), AAA, http:// africanactivist.msu.edu/document_metadata.php?objectid=32-130-C05; George M. Houser, "Re: Trip to Africa October 17, 1974–November 5, 1974," AAA, http:// africanactivist.msu.edu/document_metadata.php?objectid=32-130-1E1D.

5. George M. Houser, *No One Can Stop the Rain: Glimpses of Africa's Liberation Struggle* (New York: Pilgrim, 1989), 192.

6. Houser, *No One Can Stop*, 192.

7. Houser, "Re: Trip to Africa-October 17, 1974-November 5, 1974."

8. George M. Houser and Herb Shore, *Mozambique: The Size of Freedom* (New York: Africa Fund, 1975), AAA, http://africanactivist.msu.edu/document_metadata .php?objectid=32-130-F0C.

9. Lynne Bethke and Scott Braunschweig, *Global Survey on Education in Emergencies: Angola Country Report* (New York: Women's Commission for Refugee Women and Children, 2003), 4, accessed April 15, 2018, http://www.refworld.org /pdfid/48aa82edo.pdf.

10. After the mid-1980s, however, the continuing war and devastation in Mozambique began to reduce the literacy rate. See Mario Mouzinho and Debora Nandja, *Literacy in Mozambique: Education for All Challenges: EFA Global Monitoring Report 2006* (New York: UNESCO, 2006), 3, accessed April 15, 2018, http://unesdoc.unesco.org /images/0014/001462/146284e.pdf.

11. Jamie Miller, "In Search of Détente," in *An African Volk: The Apartheid Regime and Its Search for Survival* (New York: Oxford University Press, 2016), 3–16, http://doi .org/ 10.1093/acprof:oso/9780190274832.001.0001.

12. George M. Houser, "Southern Africa: Détente or Prologue to Struggle?," *Christianity and Crisis* 34, no. 24 (January 20, 1975): 318.

13. Allen Isaacman and Jennifer Davis, "United States Policy toward Mozambique since 1945: 'The Defense of Colonialism and Regional Stability,'" *Africa Today* 25, no. 1 (January–March 1978): 29–55, http://www.jstor.org/stable/4185751.

14. Houser, *No One Can Stop*, 295.

15. Samora Machel's inaugural speech, quoted in Gail Gerhart, "Independence Comes to Mozambique," *Africa Today* 22, no. 3 (July–September 1975): 12, http:// www.jstor.org/stable/4185517.

16. George Houser, Africa Journal October 1975. GMH PP.

17. George M. Houser, *Report on a Visit to Mozambique, October 1975* (New York: American Committee on Africa, 1976), AAA, http://africanactivist.msu.edu/ document_metadata.php?objectid=32-130-C1E.

18. George M. Houser, *Report on Guinea-Bissau, Cape Verde and Angola Part I* (New York: American Committee on Africa, 1975), AAA, http://africanactivist.msu.edu /document_metadata.php?objectid=32-130-C09.

19. Houser, *Report on Guinea-Bissau Part I.*

20. George M. Houser, *Report on Guinea-Bissau, Cape Verde and Angola, Part III* (New York: American Committee on Africa), https://africanactivist.msu.edu /document_metadata.php?objectid=32-130-C0B.

21. The desire of the United States and Europe to protect their economic interests in Angola's resources was an important factor in leading to their intervention. An additional factor beyond the Cold War motivation was the US concern for the continued stability of South Africa. Angola shares a common border with Namibia, which was then under South African control. The Benguela Railroad, which runs through Angola to the Atlantic, was a critical lifeline for the export of copper from landlocked Zaire and Zambia, two countries with which South Africa was trying to forge "friendly" relations. See George M. Houser, Jennifer Davis, Susan Rogers, and Herb Shore, *No One Can Stop the Rain: Angola and the MPLA* (New York: Africa Fund, 1976–1977).

22. According to Prexy Nesbitt, the Ford administration and the South African government knew that the amount of aid they were willing to allot UNITA was insufficient to defeat the MPLA. The Ford administration simply wanted to punish the MPLA for winning the civil war. The South African government was not interested in putting Savimbi in power; they just wanted to destabilize the Angolan government and prevent it from offering assistance to either the African National Congress or Namibia's South West Africa People's Organization. See Prexy Nesbitt, "U.S. Foreign Policy: Lessons from the Angola Conflict," *Africa Today* 39, nos. 1–2 (1992): 62, http://www.jstor.org/stable/4186803.

23. According to Sean Gervasi, the characterization of the aid as "the largest" appears to have come from "highly placed officials within the U.S. Department of Defense who are opposed to U.S. policy in Angola." See Sean Gervasi, *Continuing Escalation in the Angola Crisis* (New York: Africa Fund, 1975), AAA, http://africanactivist .msu.edu/document_metadata.php?objectid=32-130-F10; John Stockwell, chief of the Angola Task Force, had been told the money was to "prevent an easy victory" for the MPLA. See John Stockwell, *In Search of Enemies: A CIA Story* (New York: W. W. Norton, 1978), 45.

24. William Minter, "U.S. Policy in Angola and Mozambique," *Africa Today* 23, no. 3 (July–September 1976): 56, http://www.jstor.org/stable/4185618. For a thorough analysis of the complex wars in Angola and Mozambique, see William Minter, *Apartheid's Contras: An Inquiry into the Roots of War in Angola and Mozambique* (London: Zed, 1994).

25. Even after the FNLA's defeat and the OAU's recognition of the MPLA as Angola's government, Holden Roberto continued to press Congress to recognize the legitimacy of his side. In a long letter to the US Congress written in February 1978, he averred that he had become the tool of rabid anti-Communist forces in the United States. See Holden Roberto, "To the Honourable Members of Congress," February 20, 1978, ACOA Records, Series 3, Box 79, Folder 27, ARC.

26. Kathleen Telsch, "U.S. Vetoes Entry of Angola in U.N.," *New York Times*, June 24, 1976, https://www.nytimes.com/1976/06/24/archives/us-vetoes-entry-of-angola-in-un-cites-presence-of-a-large-cuban.html.

27. The Tunney Amendment was triggered when leaks to the press revealed that the CIA was prepared to spend at least $50 million in Angola. At that time, congressional liberals discovered that there was money for CIA operations in Angola hidden in the Department of Defense appropriations bill. See Washington Office on Africa, *Ford and Congress Clash Over Angola* (Washington, DC: Washington Office on Africa, 1976), AAA, http://africanactivist.msu.edu/document_metadata.php?objectid=32-130-108A.

28. The Clark Amendment resulted from hearings on Angola held by Senator Richard Clark and Congressman Charles Diggs after their discovery of the secret war being waged by the CIA in 1975. Shortly after the public airing of the details, the Senate voted to cut off funding for CIA operations in Angola. The Tunney and Clark amendments, coming on the heels of the Vietnam debacle, represented the high point of a congressional revolt against the anti-Communist ethos of the Cold War and executive prerogative in foreign policy. For more on this legislation see "Clark Amendment Article," accessed January 19, 2019, academic.brooklyn.cuny.edu/history/johnson/clark.htm; Ronald W. Walters, "The Clark Amendment: Analysis of U.S. Policy Choices in Angola," *Black Scholar* 12, no. 4 (July–August, 1981): 2–12, http://www.jstor.org/stable/41066776. In addition to the CIA discovery, it is likely that Senator Clark's progressive stand on southern Africa (he also introduced the Senate bill to repeal the Byrd Amendment) was influenced by his relationship with Houser. The two had had a long relationship and were on a first-name basis with each other.

29. Kissinger memo cited by Stockwell, *In Search of Enemies*, 234. According to William Minter, the primary motivation for US intervention against the MPLA resulted from feelings of vulnerability among US Cold Warriors who were facing defeat in Vietnam, the Watergate scandal at home, and a popular revolution in Angola with ties to Moscow that threatened a NATO ally, Portugal. The United States had to show the Soviets that it could still defend its turf. Minter, *Apartheid's Contras*, 145.

30. Nesbitt, "U.S. Foreign Policy," 57.

31. George M. Houser, "Communism and the War in Angola," *New York Times*, December 14, 1975, https://www.nytimes.com/1975/12/14/archives/commmunism-and-the-way-in-angola.html.

32. Houser, "Communism and the War in Angola."

33. Houser, "Communism and the War in Angola."

34. George M. Houser, "Needed: An Africa-Centered Angola Policy" (statement by George M. Houser, Executive Director of the American Committee on Africa, to the Subcommittee on African Affairs of the Senate Committee on Foreign Relations on February 4, 1976), AAA, http://africanactivist.msu.edu/document_metadata.php?objectid=32-130-C16. The ACOA had received reports from many sources that the recruiting of mercenaries began in earnest right after both houses of Congress passed the Clark Amendment. See ACOA, "CIA-Supplied Mercenaries Fight in Angola," mailing, n.d., AAA, http://africanactivist.msu.edu/document_metadata.

php?objectid=32-130-1177; see David Anable, "U.S. Role in Angola Grows Despite Denial," *Christian Science Monitor*, January 2, 1976, AAA, http://africanactivist.msu .edu/document_metadata.php?objectid=32-130-1177.

35. Houser, "Needed: An Africa-Centered Angola Policy."

36. Paul Irish, *For the Coalition for the Liberation of Southern Africa* (New York: American Committee on Africa, 1976), AAA, http://africanactivist.msu.edu/document _metadata.php?objectid=32-130-C24.

37. Houser, Africa Journal, Cuba 1976, GMH PP; George M. Houser, *Report of the Havana Seminar (February 25–29, 1976)* (New York: American Committee on Africa), AAA, http://africanactivist.msu.edu/document_metadata.php?objectid=32-130-C17; James E. Bristol, *Report on Seminar on Angola, Havana, Cuba, February 26–29, 1976* (Philadelphia: American Friends Service Committee, 1976), AAA, http://africanactivist.msu.edu/document_metadata.php?objectid=32-130-130A.

38. Minutes, ACOA Executive Board Meeting, March 11, 1976, AAA, http://africanactivist.msu.edu/document_metadata.php?objectid=32-130-244E.

39. George M. Houser, "Statement of George M. Houser, Executive Director American Committee on Africa for the Seminar of the United Nations Special Committee on Policies of Apartheid, Havana, April 24–28, 1976" (presentation at the International Seminar on the Eradication of Apartheid and in Support of the Struggle for Liberation of South Africa, United Nations Special Committee, May 1976), AAA, http://africanactivist.msu.edu/document_metadata.php?objectid=32-130-C20.

40. Houser, Africa Journal, Cuba, 1976.

41. George M. Houser, "Testimony before the Democratic Party Platform Committee, May 19, 1976," AAA, http://africanactivist.msu.edu/document_metadata .php?objectid=32-130-C1F.

42. *1976 Democratic Party Platform*, American Presidency Project, http://www .presidency.ucsb.edu/ws/index.php?pid=29606.

43. Houser, Africa Journal 1976: Guinea-Bissau, GMH PP; George M. Houser, *A Report on Guinea-Bissau* (New York: American Committee on Africa, 1976), AAA, http://africanactivist.msu.edu/document_metadata.php?objectid=32-130-FC8.

44. Evidence of violations of the arms embargo is detailed in Jennifer Davis and Richard Leonard, "U.S. Implementation of the Arms Embargo Against South Africa: A Review of National Legislation and Enforcement Procedures" (speech prepared for the International Seminar on the Implementation and Reinforcement of the Arms Embargo Against South Africa held under the auspices of the Special Committee against Apartheid, April 1–3, 1981), AAA, http://africanactivist .msu.edu/document_metadata.php?objectid=32-130-1E19. See also Tim Weiner, "A Nominee's Withdrawal; Inman Faced Scrutiny on Jailed Arms Dealer," *New York Times*, January 20, 1994, http://www.nytimes.com/1994/01/20/us/a-nominee-s -withdrawal-inman-faced-scrutiny-on-jailed-arms-dealer.html; Richard Knight, "Letter to the Editor," *New York Times*, January 28, 1994, http://richardknight.homestead .com/inman.html.

45. George M. Houser, "Carter's African Policy," *Southern Africa Perspectives* 2 (New York: Africa Fund, 1979), AAA, http://africanactivist.msu.edu/document _metadata.php?objectid=32-130-E88.

46. George M. Houser, "An Assessment of the Carter Administration's Policy on Southern Africa," *ACOA Action News*, no. 1 (July–August 1977): 2, AAA, http://africanactivist.msu.edu/document_metadata.php?objectid=32-130-A9F.

47. ACOA, "Leader of Soweto (South Africa) Uprising to Speak," press release, n.d., AAA, http://africanactivist.msu.edu/document_metadata.php?objectid=32-130-C2F.

48. ACOA, *Successful Actions against the Krugerrand, March 1978* (New York: American Committee on Africa, 1978), AAA, http://africanactivist.msu.edu/document_metadata.php?objectid=32-130-C4D.

49. ACOA, "Press Release on the Sullivan Principles," press release, April 18, 1977, AAA, http://africanactivist.msu.edu/document_metadata.php?objectid=32-130-C31; Jennifer Davis, "Too Little, Too Late," *Southern Africa Perspectives* 3, no. 77 (April 1977), AAA, http://africanactivist.msu.edu/document_metadata.php?objectid=32-130-E7D.

50. Truman Dunn, "ACOA Forges Links with Energy Groups," *ACOA Action News* 6 (Fall 1979), AAA, http://africanactivist.msu.edu/document_metadata.php?objectid=32-130-AA3.

51. South Africa at the time was facing an economic crisis. The price of gold had slumped from $175 per ounce in April 1975 to $123 in November 1976. Unemployment was rising, and the rate of inflation was estimated at 11.5 percent with a no-growth economy. South Africa was also facing a balance of payments deficit estimated at $1.7 billion for 1976. This economic crisis was compounded by greatly increased defense spending, up 42 percent from the previous year. Hence the need for outside loans. See ACOA, "Call to Protest Bank Loans to South Africa," policy document, n.d., AAA, http://africanactivist.msu.edu/document_metadata.php?objectid=32-130-C36.

52. Prexy Nesbitt, interview by Zac Peterson, used with permission; George M. Houser, "The Church and American Investment in South Africa" (lecture as part of the Christianity, Imperialism, and Africa lecture series, Northwestern University, November 14, 1977), GMH PP.

53. Prexy Nesbitt, *Anti-Apartheid Activities in the United States of America: A Rising Tide* (New York: United Nations, 1977), AAA, http://africanactivist.msu.edu/document_metadata.php?objectid=32-130-C46; "SA-US Corporate Ties Assailed," *ACOA Action News*, no. 3 (Spring 1978), 1, AAA, http://africanactivist.msu.edu/document_metadata.php?objectid=32-130-AA1.

54. Derek Reveron, "Pamphlet Power: Small Group of Activists Puts Pressure on Big Firms to Get Out of South Africa," *Wall Street Journal*, February 23, 1978, 48.

55. Massie, *Loosing the Bonds*, 378.

56. Josh Nessen, *Student Anti-Apartheid Newsletter*, December 1979, AAA, http://africanactivist.msu.edu/document_metadata.php?objectid=32-130-ADF.

57. Dumisani S. Kumalo, *Report on 10-Week Tour of the United States* (New York: American Committee on Africa, 1979), AAA, http://africanactivist.msu.edu/document_metadata.php?objectid=32-130-C67.

58. Maida Springer-Kemp to Houser, July 18, 1978, ACOA Records Addendum, Box 10, Folder 7, ARC.

59. Richard Knight, "Documenting the U.S. Solidarity Movement—with Reflections on the Sanctions and Divestment Campaigns" (paper presented at the conference "A Decade of Freedom: Celebrating the Role of the International Anti-Apartheid in South Africa's Freedom Struggle," Durban, South Africa, October 10–13, 2004), AAA, http://africanactivist.msu.edu/document_metadata.php?objectid=32-130-372.

60. William Minter, "An Unfinished Journey," in *No Easy Victories: African Liberation and American Activists over a Half Century, 1950–2000*, ed. William Minter, Gail Hovey, and Charles Cobb Jr. (Trenton, NJ: Africa World, 2008), 41.

61. A detailed study of this period in Namibia's history and the diplomatic attempts to find a resolution is found in Piero Gleijeses, "A Test of Wills: Jimmy Carter, South Africa and the Independence of Namibia," *Diplomatic History* 34, no. 5 (November 2010): 853–91, http://www.jstor.org/stable/24916462.

62. Gleijeses, "A Test of Wills," 883.

63. *ACOA Action News*, no. 5 (Spring 1979), AAA, http://africanactivist.msu.edu/document_metadata.php?objectid=32-130-D9C. Houser to President Carter, telegram, September 24, 1979: "Urge you to make public statement opposing lifting sanctions against Zimbabwe/Rhodesia . . .," ACOA Records Addendum, Box 10, Folder 1, ARC.

64. American Committee on Africa, *A Tribute to George Houser* (New York: American Committee on Africa and the Africa Fund, 1981), AAA, http://africanactivist.msu.edu/document_metadata.php?objectid=32-130-132B.

65. Nick Ryan, "North Africa's Forgotten War," *Mother Jones*, March 2, 1999, https://www.motherjones.com/politics/1999/03/north-africas-forgotten-war/.

66. Anne Lippert, "Statement by Professor Anne Lippert, Ohio Northern University [to the U.S. House of Representatives Subcommittee on Africa Hearings on the Conflict in Western Sahara and U.S. Policy]," testimony, July 23, 1979, AAA, http://africanactivist.msu.edu/document_metadata.php?objectid=32-130-2010.

67. United Nations General Assembly 75th Plenary Meeting, November 21, 1979, *Resolution 34/37, Question of Western Sahara*, https://undocs.org/A/RES/34/37.

68. George M. Houser, *With Polisario in Western Sahara* (New York: American Committee on Africa, 1979), AAA, http://africanactivist.msu.edu/document_metadata.php?objectid=32-130-1CB0. Other reports about the Western Sahara can be found in Houser, Africa Journal, POLISARIO May 5–21, 1979, GMH PP; Houser, *No One Can Stop*, 312–15; Richard Knight, *Report on a Visit to the Democratic Arab Saharawi Republic and Algeria* (New York: American Committee on Africa, 1979), AAA, http://africanactivist.msu.edu/document_metadata.php?objectid=32-130-1084; George M. Houser, "Statement on Western Sahara before the Subcommittee on Africa of the Committee on Foreign Affairs, U.S. House of Representatives," testimony, July 23, 1979, AAA, http://africanactivist.msu.edu/document_metadata.php?objectid=32-130-10A3; Houser, "Blood on the Sahara: America Is Fighting King Hassan's War," *Progressive* (December 1980): 48–50; Lippert, "Statement by Professor Anne Lippert."

69. *Annual Report of the Executive Secretary of the Africa Fund*, April 24, 1980, AAA, http://africanactivist.msu.edu/document_metadata.php?objectid=32-130-F2A.

70. Houser, *No One Can Stop*, 315.

71. José Artajo quoted by Houser in *No One Can Stop*, 315.

72. In *No One Can Stop*, Houser refers to Palumbo as a "metallurgist," while in a report made shortly after his return he is referred to as an "economist."

73. Knight, *Report on a Visit*.

74. Houser, *No One Can Stop*, 319.

75. Early on, the United States played a key role in pressing Spain to accept the Madrid Treaty in which Spain ceded the Sahara to Morocco in 1975, but when rebellion broke out in Western Sahara the United States tried to remain neutral. In 1978 the Carter administration froze arms sales to Morocco but resumed them in 1979 after the administration received pressure from some members of Congress who considered Morocco a strategic Cold War ally. See Abdel-Rahim Al-Manar Slimi, "The United States, Morocco and the Western Sahara Dispute," Carnegie Endowment for International Peace (website), accessed April 17, 2018, http://carnegieendowment .org/2009/06/17/united-states-morocco-and-western-sahara-dispute-pub-23275.

76. Houser, *No One Can Stop*, 320; Houser, *With Polisario in Western Sahara*.

77. Houser, *No One Can Stop*, 321.

78. Houser, 3.

79. Houser, *No One Can Stop*, 322.

80. Houser, 322.

81. Ban Ki-Moon quoted in Conor Gaffey, "Western Sahara: What Is the 40-Year Dispute All About?," *Newsweek*, March 9, 1916, http://www.newsweek.com /western-sahara-morocco-algeria-polisario-front-435170.

82. Dumisani Kumalo in message read at a memorial service for George Houser, New York City, November 6, 2015.

83. George M. Houser, "Rebuilding the 'House of Stones,'" draft of article written for *The Progressive*, n.d., GMH PP.

84. George M. Houser, "The Zimbabwe Miracle: An Observer's Report on the Rhodesian Elections Feb. 27–29, 1980" (New York: American Committee on Africa, 1980), AAA, http://africanactivist.msu.edu/document_metadata.php?objectid =32-130-C77. Other accounts of Houser's delegation can be found in Houser, *No One Can Stop*, 337–43; Houser, Africa Journal, Zimbabwe February 1980, GMH PP; Tilden J. LeMelle, "Zimbabwe: Parliamentary Election of 1980: A Personal Recollection," July 2008, AAA, https://africanactivist.msu.edu/document_metadata.php?objec-tid=32-130-472; Tilden J. LeMelle, "Winning against a Stacked Deck: The Election in Zimbabwe," *Africa Today* 27, no. 1 (1980): 5–16.

85. Washington Office on Africa, "American Observers Call on British to End Bias in Zimbabwe," mailing, February 26, 1980, AAA, http://africanactivist.msu .edu/document_metadata.php?objectid=32-130-106E.

86. Aida Parker, "Rabid Anti-White in a 'Warehouse of Radicals,'" *Citizen*, February 22, 1980, GMH PP.

87. For purposes of the electoral campaign, officially Rhodesia had reverted to its colonial status as a British colony and the British governor, Lord Christopher Soames, was in charge. See LeMelle, "Zimbabwe: Parliamentary Election."

88. Houser, *No One Can Stop*, 339–40.

89. Houser, "The Zimbabwe Miracle."

90. Houser, "The Zimbabwe Miracle."

91. Tilden Lemelle, interview by the author, June 29, 2015.

92. Washington Office on Africa, "American Observers Call on British to End Bias."

93. *First Report of the Rhodesian General Election of 1980 by an Independent American Observer Delegation* (New York: American Committee on Africa, 1980), AAA, http:// africanactivist.msu.edu/document_metadata.php?objectid=32-130-14D6.

94. Houser, *The Zimbabwe Miracle.*

95. George M. Houser, *Report on a Trip to Africa—1978* (New York: American Committee on Africa, n.d.), AAA, http://africanactivist.msu.edu/document_metadata .php?objectid=32-130-C56.

96. For an explanation of why ZANU-PF won, see LeMelle, "Winning against a Stacked Deck."

97. George M. Houser, "Zimbabwe's Gifted Leader Faces Manifold Problems," *Christianity and Crisis* 40, no. 14 (September 15, 1980): 235–38, .

98. Robert Mugabe, "Prime Minister of the Republic of Zimbabwe" (speech, August 26, 1980), AAA, http://africanactivist.msu.edu/document_metadata.php?objectid =32-130-C82.

10

1. Dumisani Kumalo in a letter to Jennifer Davis written from Harare, Zimbabwe, in December 1982. ACOA Records Addendum, Box 58, Folder 2, ARC.

2. Among the African leaders sending tributes were President Julius K. Nyerere of Tanzania; Prime Minister Robert Mugabe of Zimbabwe; President Kenneth Kaunda of Zambia; President Sam Nujoma of SWAPO; Acting President-General Oliver Tambo of the African National Congress; Director of Foreign Affairs Henry Isaacs of the Pan African Congress; Minister of Foreign Affairs Adel Hakim of the Sahrawi Arab Democratic Republic; ANC Chief Representative to the UN Johnny Makatini; National Director of International Cooperation Janet Mondlane of Mozambique; M. N. Pather, secretary general of the South African Council on Sport; Minister of Information and Tourism N. M. Shamuyaria of Zimbabwe; and Mohamed Sahnoun, Algerian ambassador to France.

3. Statement by E. J. M. Zvobgo, *A Tribute to George Houser*, Special Supplement, June 17, 1981, GMH PP.

4. William Booth, "A Quarter Century of Struggle," *ACOA Action News*, no. 9 (Spring 1981): 1, AAA, http://africanactivist.msu.edu/document_metadata.php?objectid=32-130-AA6.

5. Message from President Julius K. Nyerere of Tanzania, *A Tribute to George Houser* (New York: American Committee on Africa, 1981), AAA, http://africanactivist .msu.edu/document_metadata.php?objectid=32-130-132B.

6. This account of Houser's trip and his discussion with Chissano were taken from George Houser, Africa Journal 1981, original handwritten manuscript, GMH PP; George Houser, "Memo to a Few Friends," May 1981, GMH PP; Houser, *No One Can Stop the Rain: Glimpses of Africa's Liberation Struggle* (New York: Pilgrim, 1989), 308.

7. Houser, Africa Journal 1981; Houser, "Memo to a Few Friends," May 1981, GMH PP. More on Crocker's mission to broker a solution can be found in Robert Kinloch Massie, *Loosing the Bonds: The United States and South Africa in the Apartheid*

Years (New York: Doubleday, 1997), 487–96. Crocker's own self-serving account, in which he credits his own diplomacy for the defeat of apartheid, can be found in Chester A. Crocker, *High Noon in Southern Africa: Making Peace in a Rough Neighborhood* (New York: W. W. Norton, 1992).

8. William Minter, *Apartheid's Contras: An Inquiry into the Roots of War in Angola and Mozambique* (London: Zed, 1994), 152.

9. George M. Houser, "Relations between the United States of America and South Africa" (paper prepared for the North American Regional Conference for Action Against Apartheid, United Nations, June 18–21, 1984), AAA, http://africanactivist .msu.edu/document_metadata.php?objectid=32-130-CCD, 6.

10. Houser, "Relations between the United States"; Sanford J. Ungar and Peter Vale, "South Africa: Why Constructive Engagement Failed," *Foreign Affairs* 64, no. 2 (1985): 234–58, http://www.jstor.org/stable/20042571. For more on the policy of constructive engagement see J. E. Davies, *Constructive Engagement? Chester Crocker & American Policy in South Africa, Namibia & Angola* (Athens: Ohio University Press, 2007).

11. Pressure came not just from conservative Republicans but also from some Democrats with large conservative Cuban constituencies or from those who were vulnerable to well- organized far-right constituencies. See Prexy Nesbitt, "U.S. Foreign Policy: Lessons from the Angola Conflict," *Africa Today* 39, nos. 1–2 (1992): 59, http://www.jstor.org/stable/4186803; 59; Minter, *Apartheid's Contras*, 152–53.

12. Prexy Nesbitt described the devastation wrought by American support for UNITA and South Africa in Mozambique and Angola as an "unrecorded holocaust." See Prexy Nesbitt, "Guest Editor's Introduction," *Africa Today* 39, nos. 1–2 (1992): 6, http://www.jstor.org/stable/4186799. See also William Minter, "The U.S. and the War in Angola," *Review of African Political Economy* 50 (March 1991): 135–44, http://www.jstor.org/stable/4005928; World Peace Foundation, "Mass Atrocity Endings: Angola Civil War," accessed April 2, 2018, https://sites.tufts.edu /atrocityendings/2015/08/07/angola-civil-war/.

13. Robert Zebulun Larson, "The Transnational and Local Dimensions of the Anti-Apartheid Movement" (PhD diss., Ohio State University), ProQuest (27602960).

14. The UDF was composed of a wide array of civic organizations, including churches, labor unions, civic organizations, women's organizations, student organizations, cultural workers, and sports bodies. It was for a nonracial South Africa but eschewed the violent tactics that the ANC had turned to. See J. Brooks Specter, "The UDF at 30: An Organization That Shook Apartheid's Foundation," *Daily Maverick*, August 22, 2013, accessed December 19, 2018, https://www .dailymaverick.co.za/article/2013-08-22-the-udf-at-30-an-organisation-that-shook -apartheids-foundation.

15. Massie, *Loosing the Bonds*, 560, 584. Houser was arrested in one of these campaigns. Working closely with the Congressional Black Caucus, TransAfrica assisted in devising legislative strategy for the Comprehensive Anti-Apartheid Act of 1986, which imposed sanctions against South Africa leading eventually to the end of apartheid in 1991. For more on Robinson and TransAfrica see Robinson, *Defending the Spirit: A Black Life in America* (New York: Penguin, 1999).

16. Richard Knight, "Sanctions, Disinvestment, and U.S. Corporations in South Africa," in *Sanctioning Apartheid*, ed. Robert E. Edgar (Trenton, NJ: Africa World, 1990), 67.

17. The ACOA documents, now housed at the Amistad Research Center of Tulane University, are among the center's largest deposits.

18. Steven Houser email to the author, September 9, 2018.

19. Houser, Africa Journal, Algeria 1984, 1987, GMH PP.

20. By 1989, the Africa Fund had a budget of over $1 million. See *The Africa Fund Report 1989*, AAA, http://africanactivist.msu.edu/document_metadata.php?objectid=32-130-EB2.

21. George Houser, "Memo to Jennifer Davis RE Trip to Namibia for Election Watch," memorandum, November 9, 1989, AAA, http://africanactivist.msu.edu/document_metadata.php?objectid=32-130-F6A.

22. Transcript of handwritten report from George Houser, faxed to New York on October 9, 1989, October 10, 1989, AAA, http://africanactivist.msu.edu/document_metadata.php?objectid=32-130-20BA.

23. Houser, Africa Journal, Namibia, Zimbabwe 1989, GMH PP; John A. Marcum, "Africa's Liberation Struggle: Memoirs of a Participant Observer," *Africa Today* 37, no. 2 (1990), 99. This is a review of Houser's *No One Can Stop the Rain*.

24. Houser, Africa Journal, Namibia March 1990, GMH PP.

25. Houser, Africa Journal, South Africa 1991, GMH PP. Joe Slovo was a member of the Communist Party, a drafter of the Freedom Charter, one of the defendants in the Treason Trial, and chief of staff of *Umkhonto we Sizwe*, the ANC's military wing and the first white member of the ANC's National Executive Council. Helen Suzman was an antiapartheid activist and opposition member of parliament for thirty-six years.

26. George Houser, "Reports from South Africa," *Christianity and Crisis* 51, no. 8 (May 27, 1991): 166–68.

27. George M. Houser, *Observations after Revisiting South Africa* (New York: American Committee on Africa, 1991), 6, AAA, http://africanactivist.msu.edu/document_metadata.php?objectid=32-130-1A2A.

28. Houser, Africa Journal, South Africa 1991.

29. Houser, *Observations after Revisiting*, 10.

30. Houser, Africa Journal, South Africa 1991.

31. William Minter and Sylvia Hill, "Anti-apartheid Solidarity in the United States–South Africa Relations: From the Margins to the Mainstream," in *The Road to Democracy in South Africa: International Solidarity*, vol. 3, part 2 (Pretoria: Unisa, 2008), 819.

32. For more on this political violence see Southern Africa Project of the Lawyers' Committee for Civil Rights Under Law, "Political Violence in South Africa," n.d., AAA, http://africanactivist.msu.edu/document_metadata.php?objectid=32-130-1C85. According to the South African Institute of Race Relations, more than ten thousand people died in political violence between January 1989 and December 1992; see Massie, *Loosing the Bonds*, 674.

33. Houser, Africa Journal, South Africa 1992, GMH PP.

34. Information about the caravan can be found in George Houser's Cuba Journal 1992, original handwritten manuscript, GMH PP. Also see George M. Houser, "Cuba: Trading with the Enemy," *Christianity and Crisis* 53, no. 3 (March 1, 1993): 54–57.

35. The embargo had driven Cuba to rely on the Soviet Union as its primary trading partner. When the Soviet Union collapsed in the early 1990s, the Cuban economy quickly tanked, causing shortages of food, medicine, and other important supplies for more than eleven million people.

36. See Trading with the Enemy Act, Title 50, Appendix—War and National Defense, Sec. 16(a) (b) (1), 30, https://www.treasury.gov/resource-center/sanctions/Documents/twea.pdf; Cuban Democracy Act, Title 22, Section 6001, https://www.treasury.gov/resource-center/sanctions/Documents/cda.pdf.

37. Houser reported in his journal that over the last three years, 19,400 children from Russia, Belorussia, and Ukraine had been treated at the facility; see George Houser's Cuba Journal 1992, original handwritten manuscript.

38. Houser's Cuba Journal.

39. Houser's Cuba Journal.

40. Houser, "Cuba: Trading with the Enemy," 57.

41. Houser, private message, August 25–September 3, 1993, GMH PP. These were longhand notes written while in the hospital.

42. Minter and Hill, "Anti-apartheid Solidarity," 822.

43. Emily Leys, remarks at the memorial service for George Houser, New York City, November 6, 2015.

44. Walter Sisulu, *I Will Go Singing: Walter Sisulu Speaks of His Life and the Struggle for Freedom in South Africa* (Ndabeni, South Africa: Robben Island Museum in association with the Africa Fund, 2001).

45. George Houser, "South Africa's Walter Sisulu," September 12, 1997 (unpublished manuscript), GMH PP; Sisulu, *I Will Go Singing*, viii.

46. Houser, "South Africa's Walter Sisulu."

47. George Houser, "2009—The Year of Change" (unpublished letter to friends, February 2010), GMH PP.

48. On her release in 2003, Kathy Boudin became an adjunct professor at Columbia University's School of Social Work. In 2016, New York Governor Cuomo commuted Judith Clark's sentence, making her eligible for parole. However, stiff opposition from the law enforcement community prevented the parole board from acting on the commutation. She was finally paroled in April 2019 after the New York State Supreme Court ruled that the parole board had acted "arbitrarily and capriciously" in denying her parole.

49. Steve Lieberman, "Vigil Set to Fight Brinks Parole," *Journal News*, July 10, 2001, 15–16.

50. Peter Applebome, "Following a Kindly Light and Casting One," *New York Times*, December 2, 2007, https://www.nytimes.com/2007/12/02/nyregion/02towns.html.

51. For a description of this award and its significance see "The Order of the Companions of O. R. Tambo," https://web.archive.org/web/20131105165927/http://www.thepresidency.gov.za/pebble.asp?relid=7672.

52. Hema Easley, "Rockland's George Houser Honored by South Africa," *Journal News*, May 13, 2010, http://www.lohud.com/article/20100513/NEWS03/5130302/1019/Rockland-s-George-Houser-honored-by-South-Africa.

53. Houser, interview by the author, May 3, 2010.

54. Suzan Clarke, "Activist Couple Leaving Rockland," *Journal News*, June 12, 2009, 4A.

55. Email announcement from Ethan Vesley-Flad, Communications Director, Fellowship of Reconciliation, August 20, 2015.

56. Margalit Fox, "George Houser, Freedom Rides Pioneer and Founder of CORE Dies at 99," *New York Times*, August 20, 2015; Emily Langer, "George M. Houser, Organizer of an Early Freedom Ride, Dies at 99," *Washington Post*, August 22, 2015.

57. Recollections at memorial service for George Houser, New York City, November 6, 2015.

58. Houser, email to author, March 20, 2009.

59. Nelson Mandela in conversation with Richard Lapchick, as reported by Lapchick at the memorial service for George Houser, Santa Rosa, California, September 19, 2015.

60. Massie, *Loosing the Bonds*, 433–34.

61. The occasion for the speech was Houser's receipt of the Peace and Justice Award from the Westchester People's Action Committee Foundation in 2006. See Steven Houser, email to author, September 15, 2018.

62. George M. Houser, "Human Rights and the Liberation Struggle . . . The Importance of Creative Tension," *Africa Today* 39, no. 4 (1992): 12–13, 17, https://www.jstor.org/stable/4186859. Sentences in quotation marks taken from Houser, *No One Can Stop*, 366.

63. "Lead Kindly Light" was written in 1833 by the British poet and theologian John Henry Newman as a poem titled "The Pillar and the Cloud." It was the favorite hymn of Houser's mother, and he adopted the words as a kind of motto for his life.

64. Applebome, "Following a Kindly Light."

Selected Bibliography

The following abbreviations are used for frequently cited archival sources. Complete citations for individual documents drawn from these archives are found in the notes and are not listed here. They include CORE and ACOA organizational minutes, memoranda, correspondence, reports, financial statements, government and UN testimony, newspaper clippings, and articles written by staff of both organizations.

ARC
> Amistad Research Center, Tulane University. American Committee on Africa Records, 1948–1987. American Committee on Africa Records Addendum.

RACOA
> Records of the American Committee on Africa (Microform), Bethesda, MD: University Publications of America, 1992.

AAA
> African Activists Archive (online), Michigan State University. A partial collection of American Committee on Africa Records (and other selected documents). http://africanactivist.msu.edu/index.php.

CORE Papers
> Papers of the Congress of Racial Equality, 1941–1967. Stanford, NC: Microfilming Corp. of America.
> Papers of the Congress of Racial Equality, Addendum, 1944–1968. Stanford, NC: Microfilming Corp. of America.

SCPC
> Swarthmore Peace Collection, Swarthmore College.
> CORE Collected Records, 1942–1972. CDG-A.
> Fellowship of Reconciliation Records-USA, 1915–current. DG13.
> George Houser Collected Papers. CDG-A.
> A. J. Muste Papers, 1920–1967. DG50.
> Complete chronological archive of *Fellowship*, the official publication of the Fellowship of Reconciliation.

UTS
> Union Theological Seminary Special Collections, Burke Library.
> Roger L. Shinn Papers, 1920–2010, Series 3, Subseries 3D.
> *Union Review.*

GMH PP

George M. Houser's personal papers (in author's possession). Family correspondence, miscellaneous correspondence, photographs, awards, newspaper clippings, articles, pamphlets, and letters to the editor by George M. Houser, UN and congressional testimony, miscellaneous reports on Africa, handwritten journals from his trips to Africa and Cuba. Complete citations are found in the notes.

INTERVIEWS

Benedict, Donald. Interview by C. Arthur Bradley, 1988, transcript, Oral History Collection, B434D, Norris L. Brookens Library Archives, University of Illinois at Springfield. http://www.idaillinois.org/cdm/fullbrowser/collection/uis/id/5278/rv/compoundobject/cpd/1000.

Davis, Jennifer. Interview by Zac Peterson. Tapes in author's possession courtesy of Peterson.

"George Houser Memoir." Interview by C. Arthur Bradley, 1988, transcript, Oral History Collection, H817G, Norris L. Brookens, Library Archives, University of Illinois at Springfield. http://www.idaillinois.org/cdm/compoundobject/collection/uis/id/2492.

"George Houser Memoir." Interview by C. Arthur Bradley, 1988, transcript, World War II Conscientious Objectors Project, H817G, Norris L Brookens Library Archives/Special Collections, University of Illinois at Springfield, http://cdm16614.contentdm.oclc.org/cdm/compoundobject/collection/uis/id/2492/rec/1.

Houser, George. Interview by Kathryn M. Shannon, September 11, 1967, Ralph J. Bunche Oral History Collection, Moorland-Spingarn Research Center (RJB-39), Howard University.

———. Interview by Brenda B. Square. ARC

———. Interview by Celeste Wallin, December 10, 1986. GMH PP

———. Interview by Philip Greenspan, July 21, 2016, for the book *Men of Peace: World War II Conscientious Objectors*, edited by Mary R. Hopkins. Belize: Producionnes de la Hamaca, 2010. GMH PP.

———. Interview by Sheila B. Michaels, April 29, 1999. Columbia University Oral History Collection SCSB-6065086.

———. Interview by Zac Peterson. Tapes in author's possession courtesy of Peterson.

Nelson, Wally. Interviewed by Sheila B. Michaels, November 27, 1999. Columbia University Oral History Collection SCSB-6065086.

Nesbitt, Prexy. Interview by Zac Peterson. Tape in author's possession courtesy of Peterson.

Robinson, James. Interviewed by Sheila B. Michaels, January 12, 15, 20; February 3, 5, 12, 17, 19, 26; March 5, 8, 25. Columbia University Oral History Collection SCSB-6065086.

Roodenko, Igal. Interview, April 11, 1974. Southern Oral History Program Collection. Interview B-0010. https://dc.lib.unc.edu/cdm/search/collection/sohp/searchterm/Roodenko%2C+Igal./field/creato/mode/exact/conn/and/order/title/ad/asc/cosuppress/0.

BOOKS AND BOOK CHAPTERS

Anderson, Carol. *Bourgeois Radicals: The NAACP and the Struggle for Colonial Liberation, 1941–1960*. New York: Cambridge University Press, 2015.

———. *Eyes Off the Prize: The United Nations and the African American Struggle for Human Rights, 1944–1955*. Cambridge: Cambridge University Press, 2003.

Anderson, David. *Histories of the Hanged: The Dirty War in Kenya and the End of Empire*. New York: W. W. Norton, 2005.

Anderson, Jervis. *A. Philip Randolph: A Biographical Portrait*. New York: Harcourt, Brace Jovanovich, 1973.

———. *Bayard Rustin: Troubles I've Seen*. New York: HarperCollins, 1997.

Anthony, David Henry, III. *Max Yergan: Race Man, Internationalist, Cold Warrior*. New York: New York University Press, 2006.

Arsenault, Raymond. *Freedom Riders: 1961 and the Struggle for Racial Justice*. New York: Oxford University Press, 2006.

Bailey, Martin. *Oilgate: The Sanctions Scandal*. London: Coronet, 1979.

Baldwin, Lewis. "Martin Luther King, Jr., a 'Coalition of Conscience,' and Freedom in South Africa." In *Freedom's Distant Shores: American Protestants and Post-Colonial Alliances with Africa*, edited by R. Drew Smith, 53–82. Waco, TX: Baylor University Press, 2006.

Baldwin, Lewis V. *Toward the Beloved Community: Martin Luther King, Jr. and South Africa*. Cleveland, OH: Pilgrim, 1995.

Bartlett, Vernon. *Struggle for Africa*. New York: Frederick A. Praeger, 1953.

Benedict, Donald. *Born Again Radical*. New York: Pilgrim, 1982.

Birmingham, David. *The Decolonization of Africa*. 1st ed. London: Routledge, 1995.

———. *Portugal and Africa*. New York: Palgrave, 1999.

Bonner, Philip. "The Antinomies of Nelson Mandela." In *The Cambridge Companion to Nelson Mandela*, edited by Rita Barnard, 29–49. Cambridge: Cambridge University Press, 2014. https://doi.org/10.1017/CCO9781139003766.003.

Borstelmann, Thomas. *Apartheid's Reluctant Uncle: The United States and Southern Africa in the Early Cold War*. New York: Oxford University Press, 1993.

———. *The Cold War and the Color Line: American Race Relations in the Global Arena*. Cambridge, MA: Harvard University Press, 2003.

Bowles, Chester. *Africa's Challenge to America*. Berkeley: University of California Press, 1957.

Brock, Lisa. "The 1950s: Africa Solidarity Rising." In *No Easy Victories: African Liberation and American Activists over a Half Century, 1950–2000*, edited by William Minter, Gail Hovey, and Charles Cobb Jr., 5–72. Trenton, NJ: Africa World, 2008.

Brutus, Dennis. *The Dennis Brutus Tapes: Essays at Autobiography*. Edited by Bernth Lindors. Woodbridge, UK: Boydell and Brewer, 2011.

———. *Poetry and Protest: A Dennis Brutus Reader*. Edited by Lee Sustar and Aisha Karim. Chicago: Haymarket, 2006.

Burke, Roland. *Decolonization and the Evolution of International Human Rights*. Philadelphia: University of Pennsylvania Press, 2010.

Callinicos, Luli. *Oliver Tambo: Beyond the Engeli Mountains*. 2nd ed. Claremont, South Africa: David Phillips, 2004.

Carson, Clayborne. *In Struggle: SNCC and the Black Awakening of the 1960s*. Cambridge, MA: Harvard University Press, 1981.

Chachge, Chambi, and Annar Cassam, eds. *The Liberation of Africa: The Legacy of Nyerere* Cape Town: Pambazuka, 2010.

Clark, Elmer T., ed. *The Philippines and What the Methodists Are Doing There*. New York: Joint Division of Education and Cultivation, Board of Missions and Church Extension, 1941. Emory University Microfilm.

Cohen, Robert. *When the Old Left Was Young: Student Radicals and America's First Mass Student Movement, 1929–1941*. New York: Oxford University Press, 1993.

Coker, Christopher. *The United States and South Africa, 1968–1985: Constructive Engagement and Its Critics*. Durham, NC: Duke University Press, 1986.

Collins, Michael. "Nation, State and Agency: Evolving Historiographies of African Decolonization." In *Britain, France and the Decolonization of Africa: Future Imperfect?*, edited by Andrew W. M. Smith and Chris Jeppesen, 17–42. London: UCL Press, 2017.

Collins, Sheila D., and Gertrude Schaffner Goldberg, eds. *When Government Helped: Learning from the Successes and Failures of the New Deal*. New York: Oxford University Press, 2014.

Couper, Scott. *Albert Luthuli: Bound by Faith*. Pietermaritzburg: University of KwaZulu-Natal Press, 2010.

Crocker, Chester A. *High Noon in Southern Africa: Making Peace in a Rough Neighborhood*. New York: W. W. Norton, 1992.

Danielson, Leilah. *American Gandhi: A. J. Muste and the History of Radicalism in the Twentieth Century*. Philadelphia: University of Pennsylvania Press, 2014. Kindle.

Davies, J. E. *Constructive Engagement? Chester Crocker & American Policy in South Africa, Namibia & Angola*. Athens: Ohio University Press, 2007.

Dellinger, David. "Why I Refused to Register in the October 1940 Draft and a Little of What It Led To." In *A Few Small Candles: War Resisters of World War II Tell Their Stories*, edited by Larry Gara and Lenna Mae Gara, 20–37. Kent, OH: Kent State University Press, 1999.

———. *From Yale to Jail: The Life Story of a Moral Dissenter*. Marion, SD: Rose Hill, 1993.

D'Emilio, John. *Lost Prophet: The Life and Times of Bayard Rustin*. New York: Free Press, 2003.

De Villiers, Les. *In Sight of Surrender: The U.S. Sanctions Campaign against South Africa, 1946–1993*. Westport, CT: Praeger, 1995.

De Witte, Ludo. *The Assassination of Lumumba*. Translated by Ann Wright and Renée Fenby. London: Verso, 2001.

Dhupelia-Mesthrie, Uma. *Gandhi's Prisoner? The Life of Gandhi's Son Manilal*. Cape Town: Kwela, 2004.

Dorrien, Gary. *Social Ethics in the Making: Interpreting an American Tradition*. Oxford: Wiley-Blackwell, 2011.

Draper, Hal. "The Student Movement of the 1930s: A Political History." In *As We Saw the Thirties: Essays on Social and Political Movements of a Decade*, edited by Rita James Simon, 151–89. Urbana: University of Illinois Press, 1967.

Dudziak, Mary L. *Cold War Civil Rights: Race and the Image of American Democracy.* Princeton, NJ: Princeton University Press, 2000.

Eddy, Sherwood, and Kirby Page. *The Abolition of War: The Case against War and Questions and Answers Concerning War, Christianity and World Problems.* Christianity and World Problems Series no. 7. New York: George H. Doran, 1924.

Edgar, Robert E., ed. *Sanctioning Apartheid.* Trenton, NJ: Africa World, 1990.

Elkins, Caroline. *Imperial Reckoning: The Untold Story of Britain's Gulag in Kenya.* New York: Henry Holt, 2005.

Ellis, Steven. *External Mission: The ANC in Exile, 1960–1990.* New York: Oxford University Press, 2013.

Everatt, David. *The Origins of Non-Racialism: White Opposition to Apartheid in the 1950s.* Johannesburg: Witwatersrand University Press, 2009.

Farmer, James. *Lay Bare the Heart: An Autobiography of the Civil Rights Movement.* New York: Arbor House, 1985.

Feld, Majorie N. *Nations Divided: American Jews and the Struggle over Apartheid.* New York: Palgrave Macmillan, 2014.

Fischbach, Michael R. *Black Power and Palestine: Transnational Countries of Color.* Redwood City, CA: Stanford University Press, 2018.

Frazier, Nishani. *Harambee City: The Congress of Racial Equality in Cleveland and the Rise of Black Power Populism.* Fayetteville: University of Arkansas Press, 2017. Kindle.

Gara, Larry, and Lenna Mae Gara, eds. *A Few Small Candles: War Resisters of World War II Tell Their Stories.* Kent, OH: Kent State University Press, 1999.

Gish, Steven D. *Desmond Tutu: A Biography.* Westport, CT: Greenwood, 2004.

Gladwell, Malcolm. *David and Goliath: Underdogs, Misfits, and the Art of Battling Giants.* New York: Little, Brown, 2013.

Gleijeses, Piero. *Conflicting Missions: Havana, Washington, and Africa, 1959–1976.* Chapel Hill: University of North Carolina Press, 2002.

Goldsworthy, David. *Tom Mboya: The Man Kenya Wanted to Forget.* Nairobi: Africana, 1982.

Grubbs, Larry. *Secular Missionaries: Americans and African Development in the 1960s.* Amherst: University of Massachusetts Press, 2010.

Gunther, John. *Inside Africa.* New York: Harper & Brothers, 1953.

Handy, Robert T. *A History of Union Theological Seminary in New York.* New York: Columbia University Press, 1987.

Henderson, Lawrence W. *Angola: Five Centuries of Conflict.* Ithaca, NY: Cornell University Press, 1979.

Hirsch, Arnold R. *Making the Second Ghetto: Race and Housing in Chicago, 1940–1960.* Chicago: University of Chicago Press, 1998.

Hochschild, Adam. *King Leopold's Ghost: A Story of Greed, Terror, and Heroism in Colonial Africa.* New York: Houghton Mifflin, 1998.

Hopkins, Mary R., ed. *Men of Peace: World War II Conscientious Objectors.* Belize: Producionnes de la Hamaca, Caye Caulker, 2010. Kindle.

Horne, Gerald. *White Supremacy Confronted: U.S. Imperialism and Anti-Communism vs. the Liberation of Southern Africa, from Rhodes to Mandela.* New York: International Publishers, 2019.

Hostetter, David L. *Movement Matters: American Antiapartheid Activism and the Rise of Multicultural Politics*. New York: Routledge, 2006.

Houser, George M. "Freedom's Struggle Crosses Oceans and Mountains: Martin Luther King, Jr., and the Liberation Struggles in Africa and America." In *We Shall Overcome: Martin Luther King, Jr., and the Black Freedom Struggle*, edited by Peter J. Albert and Ronald Hoffman, 169–96. New York: Pantheon in cooperation with the United States Capitol Historical Society, 1990.

———. "Indomitable Spirit of Optimism." In *Oliver Tambo Remembered*, edited by Z. Pallo Jordan, 397–400. Johannesburg: Pan Macmillan South Africa, 2007.

———. *No One Can Stop the Rain: Glimpses of Africa's Liberation Struggle*. New York: Pilgrim, 1989.

Houston, Gregory. "International Solidarity: Introduction." In Vol. 3, Part 1 of *The Road to Democracy: International Solidarity*, edited by South African Democracy Education Trust, 1–39. Pretoria: Unisa, 2008.

Hovey, Gail. "Jennifer Davis: Clarity, Determination, and Coalition Building." In *No Easy Victories: African Liberation and American Activists over a Half Century, 1950–2000*, edited by William Minter, Gail Hovey, and Charles Cobb Jr., 169–72. Trenton, NJ: Africa World, 2008.

Hunt, John Gabriel, ed. *The Essential Franklin Delano Roosevelt: FDR's Greatest Speeches, Fireside Chats, Messages and Proclamations*. New York: Random House, 1995.

Joffe, Joel. *The State vs. Nelson Mandela: The Trial That Changed South Africa*. Oxford: Oneworld, 2007.

Joseph, Peniel E. *Stokely: A Life*. New York: Basic/Civitas, 2014.

Kalb, Madeleine G. *The Congo Cables: The Cold War in Africa—from Eisenhower to Kennedy*. New York: Macmillan, 1982.

Katznelson, Ira. *Fear Itself: The New Deal and the Origins of Our Time*. New York: W. W. Norton, 2013.

———. *When Affirmative Action Was White*. New York: W. W. Norton, 2005.

Kennedy, David M. *Freedom from Fear: The American People in Depression and War, 1929–1945*. New York: Oxford University Press, 1999.

Kinzer, Stephen. *The Brothers: John Foster Dulles, Allen Dulles, and Their Secret World War*. New York: Henry Holt, 2013.

Korey, William. *NGOs and the Universal Declaration of Human Rights*. New York: St. Martin's Press, 1998.

Kosek, Joseph Kip. *Acts of Conscience: Christian Nonviolence and Modern American Democracy*. New York: Columbia University Press, 2009.

Lapchick, Richard E. *The Politics of Race and International Sport: The Case of South Africa*. Westport, CT: Greenwood, 1975.

Lee, Christopher J., ed. *Making a World after Empire: The Bandung Moment and Its Political Afterlives*. Athens: Ohio University Press, 2010.

Levine, Daniel. *Bayard Rustin and the Civil Rights Movement*. New Brunswick, NJ: Rutgers University Press, 2000.

Long, Michael G., ed. *Down the Line: The Collected Writings of Bayard Rustin*. Chicago: Quadrangle, 1971.

———, ed. *I Must Resist: Bayard Rustin's Life in Letters*. San Francisco: City Lights, 2012.

Lynn, Conrad. *There Is a Fountain: The Autobiography of Conrad Lynn.* Brooklyn, NY: Lawrence Hill, 1993.

Marable, Manning. *Race, Reform and Rebellion: The Second Reconstruction in Black America, 1945–1990.* Jackson: University Press of Mississippi, 2007.

Marcum, John A. *The Angolan Revolution,* Vol. 1, *The Anatomy of an Explosion.* Cambridge: MIT Press, 1969.

———. *The Angolan Revolution.* Vol. 2, *Exile Politics and Guerrilla Warfare 1982–1976.* Cambridge, MA: MIT Press, 1978.

Massie, Robert Kinloch. *Loosing the Bonds: The United States and South Africa in the Apartheid Years.* New York: Doubleday, 1997.

Mazrui, Ali A. "The Independent African States and the Struggle for Southern Africa." In *The Decolonization of Africa: Southern Africa and the Horn of Africa, Working Documents and Report of the Meeting of Experts Held in Warsaw, Poland, from 9 to 13 October 1978,* 13–23. Paris: UNESCO, 1981. https://unesdoc.unesco.org/ark:/48223/pf0000045919.

McKnight, Gerald. *Verdict on Schweitzer: The Man Behind the Legend of Lambaréné.* New York: John Day, 1964.

Meditz, Sandra W., and Tim Merrill. *Zaire: A Country Study.* 4th ed. Foreign Area Studies American University. Washington, DC: Library of Congress, Federal Research Division, 1994.

Meier, August, and Elliott Rudwick. *CORE: A Study in the Civil Rights Movement 1942–1968.* New York: Oxford University Press, 1973.

Miller, Jamie. "In Search of Détente." In *An African Volk: The Apartheid Regime and Its Search for Survival,* 3–78. New York: Oxford University Press, 2016.

Miller, Robert Moats. *Harry Emerson Fosdick: Preacher, Pastor, Prophet.* New York: Oxford University Press, 1985.

Minter, William. *Apartheid's Contras: An Inquiry into the Roots of War in Angola and Mozambique.* London: Zed, 1994.

———. "Wars of Liberation, Internal Conflicts, and Destabilisation." Aluka Collection, 2006–10. https://www.aluka.org/stable/10.5555/al.sff.document.ae000005?-searchUri=so%3Dps_collection_name_str%2Basc%26Query%3DWars%2Bof %2BLiberation%252C%2BInternal%2BConflicts%252C%2Band %2BDestabilisation.

Minter, William, and Sylvia Hill. "Anti-Apartheid Solidarity in the United States-South Africa Relations: From the Margins to the Mainstream." In Vol. 3, Part 2 of *The Road to Democracy in South Africa: International Solidarity,* 745–822. Pretoria: Unisa, 2008.

Minter, William, Gail Hovey, and Charles Cobb Jr., eds. *No Easy Victories: African Liberation and American Activists Over Half a Century, 1950–2000.* Trenton, NJ: Africa World, 2008.

Mollin, Marian. *Radical Pacifism in Modern America: Egalitarianism and Protest.* Philadelphia: University of Pennsylvania Press, 2006.

Morgan, Ted. *Jay Lovestone: A Covert Life.* New York: Random House, 1999.

Morris, Aldon D. *The Origins of the Civil Rights Movement: Black Communities Organizing for Change.* New York: Free Press, 1984.

Moyn, Samuel. *The Last Utopia: Human Rights in History.* Cambridge, MA: Belknap Press of Harvard University Press, 2010.

Nesbitt, Francis Njubi. *Race for Sanctions: African Americans against Apartheid, 1946–1994.* Bloomington: Indiana University Press, 2004.

Nutt, Rick L. *The Whole Gospel for the Whole World: Sherwood Eddy and the American Protestant Mission.* Macon, GA: Mercer University Press, 1997.

Pagan, Eileen. *Class, Culture and the Classroom: The Student Peace Movement of the 1930s.* Philadelphia: Temple University Press, 1982.

Plummer, Brenda Gayle. *In Search of Power: African Americans in the Era of Decolonization, 1956–1974.* New York: Cambridge University Press, 2013.

Reddy, Enuga S. "The United Nations and the Struggle for Liberation in South Africa." In Vol. 3, Part 1 of *The Road to Democracy: International Solidarity,* edited by South African Democracy Education Trust, 41–139. Pretoria: Unisa, 2008.

Robbins, Louise S. *The Dismissal of Miss Ruth Brown: Civil Rights, Censorship, and the American Library.* Norman: University of Oklahoma Press, 2000.

Robinson, Randall. *Defending the Spirit: A Black Life in America.* New York: Penguin, 1999.

Rodney, Walter. *How Europe Underdeveloped Africa.* London: Verso, 2018.

Rustin, Bayard. *Down the Line: The Collected Writings of Bayard Rustin.* Chicago: Quadrangle, 1971.

———. *The Bayard Rustin Papers.* Compiled by Nanette Dobrosky. Bethesda, MD: University Publishers of America, 1988.

———. "The Negro and Nonviolence." In *Down the Line: The Collected Writings of Bayard Rustin,* 6–10. Chicago: Quadrangle, 1971.

Sachikonye, Lloyd. *Zimbabwe's Lost Decade: Politics, Development and Society.* Harare: Weaver, 2012.

Schlesinger, Arthur M., Jr. *A Thousand Days: John F. Kennedy in the White House.* Boston: Houghton Mifflin, 1965.

Shachtman, Thomas. *Airlift to America: How Barack Obama, Sr., John F. Kennedy, Tom Mboya, and 800 East African Students Changed Their World and Ours.* New York: St. Martin's Press, 2009.

Shepherd, George W., Jr. *Anti-Apartheid: Transnational Conflict and Western Policy in the Liberation of South Africa.* Westport, CT: Greenwood, 1977.

———. *They Are Us: Fifty Years of Human Rights Advocacy.* Bloomington, IN: Xlibris, 2002.

Shinn, Roger L. *Wars and Rumors of Wars.* Nashville, TN: Abingdon, 1972.

Sisulu, Walter. *I Will Go Singing: Walter Sisulu Speaks of His Life and the Struggle for Freedom in South Africa,* edited by George M. Houser and Herbert Shore. Ndabeni, South Africa: Robben Island Museum in association with the Africa Fund, 2001.

Skinner, Rob. *The Foundations of Anti-Apartheid: Liberal Humanitarians and Transnational Activists in Britain and the United States, c. 1919–64.* New York: Palgrave Macmillan, 2010.

Smith, Andrew W. M., and Chris Jeppesen, eds. *Britain, France and the Decolonization of Africa.* London: UCL Press, 2017. https://www.jstor.org/stable/j.ctt1mtz521.6.

Smith, R. Drew, ed. *Freedom's Distant Shores: American Protestants and Post-colonial Alliances with Africa.* Waco, TX: Baylor University Press, 2006.

South African Democracy Education Trust. *The Road to Democracy in South Africa.* Vol. 3, Part 1 of *International Solidarity.* Pretoria: Unisa, 2008.

Stamatov, Peter. *The Origins of Global Humanitarianism: Religion, Empires, and Advocacy.* New York: Cambridge University Press, 2013.

Stockwell, John. *In Search of Enemies: A CIA Story.* New York: W. W. Norton, 1978.

Sugrue, Thomas J. *Sweet Land of Liberty: The Forgotten Struggle for Civil Rights in the North.* New York: Random House, 2009.

Sutherland, Bill, and Matt Meyer. *Guns and Gandhi in Africa: Pan African Insights on Nonviolence, Armed Struggle and Liberation in Africa.* Trenton, NJ: Africa World, 2000.

Swomley, John M. *Confronting Systems of Violence: Memoirs of a Peace Activist.* Nyack, NY: Fellowship Publications, 1998.

Talbot, David. *The Devil's Chessboard: Allen Dulles, the CIA, and the Rise of America's Secret Government.* New York: HarperCollins, 2015.

Thompson, Michael G. *For God and Globe: Christian Internationalism in the United States between the Great War and the Cold War.* Ithaca, NY: Cornell University Press, 2015.

Thomson, Alex. *U.S. Foreign Policy towards Apartheid South Africa, 1948–1994.* New York: Palgrave Macmillan, 2008.

Tracy, James. *Direct Action: Radical Pacifism from the Union Eight to the Chicago Seven.* Chicago: University of Chicago Press, 1996.

US Interdepartmental Group for Africa. *The Kissinger Study of Southern Africa: National Security Study Memorandum 39 (Secret).* Edited by Mohamed A. El-Khawas and Barry Cohen. Westport, CT: Lawrence Hill.

Vanthemsche, Guy. *Belgium and the Congo, 1885–1980.* Cambridge: Cambridge University Press, 2012. https://doi.org/10.1017/CBO9781139043038.

Von Eschen, Penny M. *Race against Empire: Black Americans and Anticolonialism, 1937–1957.* Ithaca, NY: Cornell University Press, 1997.

Wallis, Jill. *Mother of World Peace: The Life of Muriel Lester.* Enfield Lock, UK: Hisarlik, 1993.

Williams, Susan. *Colour Bar: The Triumph of Seretse Khama and His Nation.* London: Penguin, 2007.

Yoder, John Howard. *Nevertheless: Varieties of Religious Pacifism.* 2nd ed. Scottdale, PA: Herald, 1992.

DISSERTATIONS, MONOGRAPHS, UNPUBLISHED PAPERS

Conteh, Alhaji. "Forging a New Africa: Black Internationalism and the Council on African Affairs, 1937–1955." PhD diss., Howard University, 2016. ProQuest (10190725).

Desroches, Christian. *The Burdens of a World Power: The Eisenhower Administration and Decolonisation in Sub-Saharan Africa, 1955–1960.* PhD diss., Universite Laval (Canada), 2001. ProQuest (MQ57857).

Diamond, Sara. "Pen-Pals and Politics: Trans-Atlantic Liberalism and the Anti-Apartheid Movement During the Cold War." Paper for the completion of the American Political History Seminar taken with Professor David Oshinsky, Rutgers University, February 20, 1995. GMH PP.

Houser, George M. "Impressions of an American Exchange Student at Lingnan."
GMH PP.

———. "James L. Farmer, Jr. Remembered." October 7, 1999. GMH PP.

———. "Reflections on the Life and Times of James Farmer." n.d. Review of Farmer's autobiography, *Lay Bare the Heart*. Unpublished manuscript. GMH PP.

———. "The Birth of Core." *The CORE Guide to Negro History*. Unpublished manuscript. November 25, 1965, GMH PP.

———. "The Program for a Fellowship Group or Cell." n.d. Unpublished manuscript. GMH PP.

Larson, Robert Zebulun. "The Transnational and Local Dimensions of the Anti-Apartheid Movement." PhD diss., Ohio State University, 2019. ProQuest (27602960).

Lovell, William H. "Conscientious Objection in 1940—Reminiscences." Statement to Presbyterian Peace Committee at General Assembly, 1990. GMH PP.

Lynch, Hollis Ralph. *Black American Radicals and the Liberation of Africa, 1937–1955*. Monograph Series no. 5. Ithaca, NY: Africana Studies and Research Center, Cornell University, 1978.

Peterson, Patti McGill. "The Young Socialist Movement in America from 1905 to 1940: A Study of the Young People's Socialist League." PhD diss., University of Wisconsin–Madison, 1974. ProQuest (7430124).

Robinson, James. "Personal Memoir." Unpublished manuscript. GMH PP.

———. "Chicago." Unpublished manuscript. GMH PP.

CONFERENCE PAPERS AND PROCEEDINGS NOT FOUND IN LISTED ARCHIVES

Houser, George M. "The Church and American Investment in South Africa." Lecture in the Christianity, Imperialism, and Africa series. Northwestern University, November 14, 1977. GMH PP.

Mario, Mouzinho and Debora Nandja, "Literacy in Mozambique: Education for All Challenges." Paper commissioned for the EFA Global Monitoring Report 2006, *Literacy for Life*. New York: UNESCO. Accessed April 15, 2018. http://unesdoc.unesco.org/images/0014/001462/146284e.pdf.

Ministry of Foreign Affairs. *Final Communiqué of the Asian-African Conference of Bandung (24 April 1955)*. Jakarta: Ministry of Foreign Affairs, 1955. https://www.cvce.eu/en/obj/final_communique_of_the_asian_african_conference_of_bandung_24_april_1955-en-676237bd-72f7-471f-949a-88b6ae513585.html.

Nkrumah, Kwame. "Speech by the Prime Minister of Ghana at the Opening Session of the All-African People's Conference." All-African People's Conference, Accra, Ghana, December 8, 1958. http://www.columbia.edu/itc/history/mann/w3005/nkrumba.html.

Stakeman, Randolph. "The American Negro Leadership Conference on Africa." Paper presented at the African Studies Association Annual Meeting, December 1993. GMH PP.

JOURNAL AND MAGAZINE ARTICLES, MISCELLANEOUS DOCUMENTS

All articles and documents drawn from the above-listed archives, including minutes of meetings, staff memoranda, and other CORE and ACOA documents, are fully cited in the notes. Because George M. Houser and the American Committee on Africa appear as the authors of so many references, they are shortened here and in the notes to Houser and ACOA.

ACOA. "ACOA Activities." *Africa Today* 2, no. 3 (July–August 1955): 22. http://www
.jstor.org/stable/4183727.
———. "ACOA Notes." *Africa Today* 4, no. 4 (July–August 1957): 2 + 13. http://www
.jstor.org/stable/4183881.
———. "ACOA Notes." *Africa Today* 4, no. 5 (September–October 1957): 2, https://
www.jstor.org/stable/i388864.
———. "African Economy." *Africa Today* 13, no. 1 (January 1966): 1–40. http://www
.jstor.org/stable/4184684.
———. "Africa Speaks at Carnegie Hall." *Africa Today* 6, no. 3 (1959): 17–19. http://
www.jstor.org/stable/4184014.
———. "American Involvement in the South African Economy." *Africa Today* 13, no.
1 (January 1966): 2–40.
Anderson, Carol. "International Conscience, the Cold War, and Apartheid: The
NAACP's Alliance with the Reverend Michael Scott for South West Africa's
Liberation, 1946–1951." *Journal of World History* 19, no. 3 (2008): 297–325.
Baldwin, Roger N. "U.S. Policy Towards Africa." *Africa Today* 2, no. 5 (November–
December 1955): 9–10, 16. https://www.jstor.org/stable/i388853.
Ball, Jeremy. "Colonial Labor in Twentieth-Century Angola." *History Compass* 3 (De-
cember 21, 2005). https://doi.org/10.1111/j.1478-0542.2005.00168.x.
Berg, Manfred. "Black Civil Rights and Liberal Anticommunism: The NAACP in the
Early Cold War." *Journal of American History* 94, no. 1 (June 2007): 75–96. https://
www.jstor.org/stable/25094777.
Bethke, Lynne, and Scott Braunschweig. *Global Survey on Education in Emergencies:
Angola Country Report.* New York: Women's Commission for Refugee Women
and Children, 2003. Accessed April 15, 2018. http://www.refworld.org/pdfid
/48aa82edo.pdf.
Biles, Roger. "Race and Housing in Chicago." *Journal of the Illinois State Historical So-
ciety (1998–)* 94, no. 1 (Spring 2001): 31–38. https://www.jstor.org/stable/40193533.
Biney, Ama. "The Legacy of Kwame Nkrumah in Retrospect." *Journal of Pan African
Studies Online* 2, no. 3 (March 2008): 129–59.
Boisbouvier, Christophe. "Togo: Qui a tué l'ancien président Sylvanus Olympio?,"
Jeune Afrique, January 18, 2013. http://www.jeuneafrique.com/138661/politique
/togo-qui-a-tu-l-ancien-pr-sident-sylvanus-olympio/.
Bonner, Philip. "The Antinomies of Nelson Mandela." In *Cambridge Companion to
Nelson Mandela,* edited by Rita Barnard, 29–49. Cambridge: Cambridge Univer-
sity Press, 2014. https://doi.org/10.1017/CCO9781139003766.003.38.
Cabral, Amilcar. "A Report to our Friends." *Africa Today* 20, no. 1 (Winter 1973): 7–13.
http://www.jstor.org/stable/4185278.
Coughlan, Robert. "First of Two Parts Black Africa Surges to Independence." *Life,*
January 26, 1959, 100–110.

————. "Stormy Future for Africa." *Life*, February 2, 1959, 82–95.

Council for the Development of Social Science Research in Africa. *Amilcar Cabral's Assassination*. Dakar, Senegal: CODESRIA, 2010. http://www.codesria.org /spip.php?article576.

Daily Vox. "A Lesson in the History of the ANC's Multiracialism and Non-Racialism." February 4, 2017. Accessed April 7, 2018. https://www.thedailyvox.co.za/anc -multiracialism-nonracialism-history/.

Davis, Jennifer. "Allies in Empire: The U.S. and Portugal in Africa Part I: U.S. Economic Involvement." *Africa Today* 17, no. 4 (July–August 1970): 1–15. https:// www.jstor.org/stable/4185103.

"Declaration of Conscience." *Africa Today* 4, no. 6 (November–December 1957): 31– 34. http://www.jstor.org/stable/4183905.

Dickson, David A. "U.S. Foreign Policy toward Southern and Central Africa: The Kennedy and Johnson Years." *Presidential Studies Quarterly* 23, no. 2 (1993): 301–15. www.jstor.org/stable/27532280.

Farmer, James. "James Farmer on the Beginnings and End of the Congress of Racial Equality 50 Years Later." Interview by Robin Washington. *Fellowship* 58, nos. 4–5 (April–May 1992): 6–8, 17, SCPC.

Fellowship of Southern Churchmen Records, 1937–1986, Collection Number 03479, Southern Historical Collection at the Louis Round Wilson Special Collections Library, University of North Carolina.

Gaffey, Conor. "Western Sahara: What Is the 40-Year Dispute All About?" *Newsweek*, March 9, 2016. Accessed February 15, 2017. http://www.newsweek.com /western-sahara-morocco-algeria-polisario-front-435170.

Gerhart, Gail. "Independence Comes to Mozambique." *Africa Today* 22, no. 3 (July– September 1975): 11–14. http://www.jstor.org/stable/4185517.

Gleijeses, Piero. "Test of Wills: Jimmy Carter, South Africa and the Independence of Namibia, A." *Diplomatic History* 34, no. 5 (November 2010): 853–91. http://www .jstor.org/stable/24916462.

"Greetings." *Africa Today* 10, no. 9 (November 1963): 9–11. http://www.jstor.org /stable/4184463.

Hall, Jacquelyn Dowd. "The Long Civil Rights Movement and the Political Uses of the Past." *Journal of American History* 91, no. 4 (March 2005): 1233–63. https:// www.jstor.org/stable/3660172.

Hawley, Edward A., Mustapha K. Pasha, and George W. R. Kalule. "Africa Today's Yesterdays II." *Africa Today* 26, no. 1 (1979): 27–48. http://www.jstor.org /stable/4185826.

Horne, Gerald. "Commentary: Who Lost the Cold War? Africans and African Americans." *Diplomatic History* 20 (Fall 1996): 613–26. https://www.jstor.org /stable/24913321.

Houser, George M. "Africa Revisited." *Africa Today* 4, no. 5 (September–October 1957): 3–7. https://www.jstor.org/stable/i388864.

————. "African Liberation Movements: Report on a Trip to Africa, Spring 1967." *Africa Today* 14, no. 4 (August 1967): 11–13. https://www.jstor.org/stable /4184811.

———. "American Committee on Africa." *Journal of Modern African Studies* 1, no. 3 (1963): 387–88. https://www.jstor.org/stable/158920.

———. "Angola in Perspective." *Christianity and Crisis* 35, no. 17 (October 27, 1975): 246–51.

———. "Architects of New Africa." *Africa Today* 10, no. 6 (June 1963): 4–6. https://www.jstor.org/stable/i388910.

———. "Assessing Africa's Liberation Struggle." *Africa Today* 34, no. 4 (1987): 17–32. http://www.jstor.org/stable/4186444.

———. "At Cairo: The Third All-African People's Conference." *Africa Today* 8, no. 4 (April 1961): 11–13. https://www.jstor.org/stable/i388889.

———. "Blood on the Sahara: America Is Fighting King Hassan's War." *Progressive*, December 1980, 48–50. GMH PP.

———. "Book Review: *The Treason Cage* by Anthony Sampson." *Africa Today* 5, no. 4 (July–August 1958): 17–18: http://www.jstor.org/stable/4183963.

———. "Book Review: *The Tribe That Lost its Head* by Nicholas Monsarrat." *Africa Today* 4, no. 4 (July–August 1957): 14. http://www.jstor.org/stable/4183885.

———. "The Changing Face of African Nationalism." *Africa Today* 7, no. 2 (April 1960): 9–10. http://www.jstor.org/stable/418406.

———. "Cuba: Trading with the Enemy." *Christianity and Crisis* 53, no. 3 (March 1, 1993): 54–57.

———. "Diary." *Union Review* 2, no. 1 (November 1940): 13, Series 10D, Box 1, Folder 4, UTS2. Union Records, Burke Library, UTS.

———. "Elections in Namibia Prepare for Independence." *Christian Century* 107, no. 3 (January 24, 1990): 79–81.

———. "Freedom for Africa's Last Colony." *Christian Social Action* 3, no. 2 (February 1990): 8–13. GMH PP.

———. "Human Rights and the Liberation Struggle . . . The Importance of Creative Tension." *Africa Today* 39, no. 4 (1992): 5–17. https://www.jstor.org/stable/4186859.

———. "Journey to Rebel Angola." *Africa Today* 9, no. 2 (March 1962): 4–7. https://www.jstor.org/stable/27821932.

———. "Leopoldville Revisited." *Africa Today* 7, no. 8 (December 1960): 5–7. http://www.jstor.org/stable/4184155.

———. "Letters from Danbury, December 13, 1940." *Union Review* 2, no. 2 (March 1941): 13. Series 10D, Box 1, Folder 4, UTS2, Union Records, Burke Library, UTS.

———. "Mboya Visits the U.S." *Africa Today* 6, no. 3 (May–June 1959): 9–11. http://www.jstor.org/stable/4184008.

———. "Meeting Africa's Challenge: The Story of the American Committee on Africa." *Issue: A Journal of Opinion, Africanist Studies 1955–1975* 6, nos. 2–3 (Summer–Autumn 1976): 17. https://www.jstor.org/stable/1166441.

———. "Mr. Louw and the Declaration." *Africa Today* 5, no. 1 (January–February 1958): 3–4, 14. http://www.jstor.org/stable/4183926.

———. "Needed: A Change in U.S. Policy in Southern Africa." American Committee on Africa, New York, March 16, 1977, GMH PP.

———. "Observations after Visiting South Africa." *Africa Today* 38, no. 2 (1991): 82–92. http://www.jstor.org/stable/4186749.

———. "Our Faltering UN Strategy on Africa." *Christianity and Crisis* 21, no. 4 (March 20, 1961): 38–41.

———. "Pan-Africanism Enters a New Era." *Fellowship* 25, no. 5 (March 1, 1959): 15–16, 34. SCPC.

———. "The Polaroid Approach to South Africa." *Christian Century* 88, no. 8 (February 24, 1971): 249–52.

———. "Polaroid's Dramatic Withdrawal from South Africa." *Christian Century* 95, no. 13 (April 12, 1978): 392–93.

———. "Prelude to Revolution in South Africa." *Current History (Pre 1986)* 30, no. 000177 (May 1, 1956): 262–68.

———. "Relations between the United States and South Africa." *Black Scholar* 15, no. 6 (November–December 1984): 33–38. https://www.jstor.org/stable/41067116.

———. "Reports from South Africa." *Christianity and Crisis* 51, no. 8 (May 27, 1991): 166–68.

———. "Resisting the Draft." *Christian Century* 112, no. 24 (August 16–23, 1995): 774–77.

———. "Response." *Christianity and Crisis* 32, no. 12 (July 10, 1972): 165–66.

———. "The Situation in South Africa." *Crisis* 70, no. 10 (December 1963): 589–95. https://books-google-com.ezproxy.cul.columbia.edu/books?id=lFsEAAAAMBAJ.

———. "Southern Africa: Détente or Prologue to Struggle?" *Christianity and Crisis* 34, no. 24 (January 20, 1975): 315-20.

———. "Tackling Jim Crow Is a Dangerous Job." *Fellowship* 79, nos. 7–12 (September 1, 2015): 8–30. SCPC.

———. "This Far and No Further." *Africa Today* 10, no. 2 (February 1963): 6–7. http://www.jstor.org/stable/4184386.

———. "To Pretoria Forward March." *Africa Today* 11, no. 8 (October 1964): 4–6. https://www.jstor.org/stable/4184556.

———. "To the Editor," *Fellowship* 58, nos. 4–5 (April–May 1992): 2. SCPC

———. "Turning Point in Namibia." *Christian Century* 95, no. 43 (December 27, 1978): 1253–54.

———. "The US at the UN." *Africa Today* 11, no. 1 (January 1964): 6–7. https://www.jstor.org/stable/4184488.

———. "U.S. Business Should Leave South Africa." *New York Times*, April 18, 1971. https://www.nytimes.com/1971/04/18/archives/us-business-should-leave-south-africa-investment-dollars-bolster.html.

———. "What Americans Know about Africa." *Africa Today* 2, no. 3 (July–August 1955): 13–14. http://www.jstor.org/stable/4183720.

———. "Wally Nelson: An Appreciation." *Fellowship* 68, nos. 7–8 (August 31, 2002): 33. SCPC.

———. "What the Watchers Saw." *Fellowship* 71, no. 9–10 (September/October 2005): 7–8. SCPC.

———. "Zimbabwe's Gifted Leader Faces Manifold Problems." *Christianity and Crisis* 40, no. 14 (September 15, 1980): 235–238.

Houser, George M., and Lawrence W. Henderson. "In Memory of Amilcar Cabral: Two Statements." *Africa Today* 20, no. 1 (1973): http://www.jstor.org/stable/4185277.

Ifidon, Ehimika A., and Edward O. Erhagbe. "The Making of an African American Foreign Policy Lobby: The American Negro Leadership Conference on Africa." *Lagos Historical Review* (July 1, 2011): 93–112. https://doi.org/10.4314/lhr.v11i1.6

Isaacman, Allen, and Jennifer Davis. "United States Policy toward Mozambique since 1945: 'The Defense of Colonialism and Regional Stability.'" *Africa Today* 25, no. 1 (January–March 1978): 29–55. http://www.jstor.org/stable/4185751.

Iweriebor, Ehiedu E. G. "The Colonization of Africa." *Africana Age: African and African Diasporan Transformations in the 20th Century.* New York: Schomburg Center for Research in Black Culture, New York Public Library. http://exhibitions.nypl.org/africanaage/essay-colonization-of-africa.html.

Jack, Homer A. "Chicago Has One More Chance." *Nation*, September 13, 1947, 250–252.

———. "Ideological Conflicts: Russia and the West, Cairo vs. Accra." *Africa Today* 6, no. 1 (1959): 11–17. http://www.jstor.org/stable/4183991.

———. "The Cairo Conference." *Africa Today* 5, no. 2 (March–April 1958): 3–9. http://www.jstor.org/stable/4183936.

Jackson, Blyden B. "Apartheid and Imperialism: A Study of U.S. Corporate Involvement in South Africa." *Africa Today* 17, no. 5 (September–October 1970): 1–39. www.jstor.org/stable/4185114.

Jefferson Award for Advancement of Democracy to Houser, February 11, 1948. GMH PP.

Johnson, Charles Denton. "Re-Thinking the Emergence of the Struggle for South African Liberation in the United States: Max Yergan and the Council on African Affairs, 1922–1946." *Journal of Southern African Studies* 39, no. 1 (2013): 171–92. https://doi.org/10.1080/03057070.2013.768448.

Karis, Thomas G. "The South African Treason Trial." *Political Science Quarterly* 76, no. 2 (June 1961): 217–40. http://www.jstor/stable/2146218.

Landau, Paul S. "Controlled by Communists? (Re)Assessing the ANC in Its Exilic Decades." *South African Historical Journal* 67, no. 2 (2015): 222–41. http://dx.doi.org/10.1080/02582473.2015.1031818.

LeMelle, Tilden J. "Winning against a Stacked Deck: The Election in Zimbabwe." *Africa Today* 27, no. 1 (1980): 5–16. https://www.jstor.org/stable/4185902.

Lovelace, Timothy H., Jr. "Cold War Stories: William Worthy, the Right to Travel, and Afro-American Reporting on the Cuban Revolution," n.d. Columbia Law (website). https://web.law.columbia.edu/sites/default/files/microsites/gender-sexuality/lovelace-cold_war_stories.pdf.

Mandela, Nelson. "Speech of the Deputy President of the African National Congress, Nelson Mandela, at the Rally to Relaunch the South African Communist Party." Speech at the Nelson Mandela Foundation, July 29, 1990. http://db.nelsonmandela.org/speeches/pub_view.asp?pg=item&ItemID=NMS049.

Marcum, John A. "Africa's Liberation Struggle: Memoirs of a Participant Observer." Review of *No One Can Stop the Rain. Africa Today* 37, no. 2 (1990): 99–100. https://www.jstor.org/stable/4186656.

Mare, Gerhard. "'Non-Racialism' in the Struggle against Apartheid." *Society in Tran-sition* 34, no. 1 (January 1, 2003): 13–37.

Matusevich, Maxim. "Probing the Limits of Internationalism: African Students Confront Soviet Ritual." *Anthropology of East Europe Review* 27, no. 2 (Fall 2009): 19–39. https://scholarworks.iu.edu/journals/index.php/aeer/article/download/166/259.

McMahon, Robert J. "Eisenhower and Third World Nationalism: A Critique of the Revisionists." *Political Science Quarterly* 101, no. 3 (Fall 1986): 453–73. http://www.jstor.org/stable/2151625.

"Memo from John Nevin Sayre to A. J. Muste." August 6, 1946. George Houser Col-lected Papers, CDG-A Box 7, SCPC.

"Memorandum, Mary Louis Hooper to George Houser." November 5, 1965. ACOA Records, Series I, Box 1, Folder 24, ARC.

Meriwether, James H. "The American Negro Leadership Conference on Africa and its Arden House Conference: Politicizing and Institutionalizing the Relationship with Africa." *Afro-Americans in New York Life and History* 21, no. 2 (July 31, 1997): 39.

Meyer, Matt. "A Luta Continua: 'Unstoppable George' Departs." *Fellowship* 79, nos. 7–12 (Autumn 2015): 22–23.

Miller, Jamie. "In Search of Détente." In *An African Volk: The Apartheid Regime and Its Search for Survival*. By Jamie Miller, 3–16. New York: Oxford University Press, 2016. https://doi.org/10.1093/acprof:oso/9780190274832.001.0001.

Minter, William. "Allies in Empire Part II: Military Involvement." *Africa Today* 17, no. 4 (July–August 1970): 28–32. https://www.jstor.org/stable/4185103.

———. "Allies in Empire Part III: American Foreign Policy and Colonialism." *Africa Today* 17, no. 4 (July–August 1970): 34–36. https://www.jstor.org/stable/4185103.

———. "The U.S. and the War in Angola." *Review of African Political Economy* 50 (March 1991): 135–44. https://www.jstor.org/stable/4005928.

———. "U.S. Policy in Angola and Mozambique." *Africa Today* 23, no. 3 (July–September 1976): 56. http://www.jstor.org/stable/4185618.

Mouzinho, Mario, and Debora Nandja. "Literacy in Mozambique: Education for All Challenges." Paper commissioned for the EFA Global Monitoring Report 2006, *Literacy for Life*. New York: UNESCO. Accessed April 15, 2018. http://unesdoc.unesco.org/images/0014/001462/146284e.pdf.

Nesbitt, Prexy. "US Foreign Policy: Lessons from the Angola Conflict." *Africa Today* 39, nos. 1–2 (1992): 53–71. http://www.jstor.org/stable/4186803.

———. "Guest Editor's Introduction." *Africa Today* 39, nos. 1–2 (1992): 6–8. http://www.jstor.org/stable/4186799.

New York Times. "8 Draft Resisters Get Prison Terms." November 15, 1940. https://www.nytimes.com/1940/11/15/archives/8-draft-objectors-get-prison-terms-divinity-students-sentenced-to.html.

New York Times. "20 Divinity Students Here Defy Draft Law as Enforcement Agency for City Is Set Up." *New York Times*, October 12, 1940. https://www.nytimes.com/1940/10/12/archives/20-divinity-students-here-defy-draft-law-as-enforcement-agency-for.html?searchResultPosition=1.

Nkrumah, Kwame. "Speech by the Prime Minister of Ghana at the Opening Session of the All-African People's Conference." Speech, December 8, All-African People's Conference. 1958. http://www.columbia.edu/itc/history/mann/w3005/nkrumba.html.

"Pan-Africanist Congress." *South African History Online*, August 27, 2019. Accessed June 19, 2019. https://www.sahistory.org.za/article/pan-africanist-congress-pac.

"Partners in Apartheid: U.S. Policy on South Africa." *Africa Today* 11, no. 3 (March 1964): 2–17. http://www.jstor.org/stable/4187823.

Plaut, Martin. "Why Mandela's Communist Party Membership Is Important." *New Statesman*, December 10, 2013. Accessed May 13, 2016. http://www.newstatesman.com/world-affairs/2013/12/why-mandelas-communist-party-membership-important.

"Press Release from Union Theological Seminary Faculty." Press Release, October 14, 1940, Roger L. Shinn Papers, Series 3, Subseries 3D, Box 1, Folder 1, Burke Library, UTS.

Reeves, Reverend Ambrose. "The Sharpeville Massacre—A Watershed in South Africa." *South African History Online.* March 21, 1960. http://www.sahistory.org.za/archive/sharpeville-massacre-watershed-south-africa-reverend-ambrose-reeves.

"Resolution Passed Unanimously by the Student Cabinet." October 11, 1940. Roger L. Shinn Papers, Series 3, Subseries 3D, Box 1, Folder 1, Burke Library, UTS.

Ryan, Nick. "North Africa's Forgotten War." *Mother Jones*, March 2, 1999. https://www.motherjones.com/politics/1999/03/north-africas-forgotten-war/.

Shepherd, George W. "*Africa Today* in the Early Years: The Debate over Strategy for the Liberation of South Africa." *Africa Today* 41, no. 1 (1994): 11–12, 14. http://www.jstor.org/stable/4186959.

Slimi, Abdel-Rahim Al-Manar. "The United States, Morocco and the Western Sahara Dispute." June 17, 2009. Carnegie Endowment for International Peace. Accessed April 17, 2018. http://carnegieendowment.org/2009/06/17/united-states-morocco-and-western-sahara-dispute-pub-23275.

"A Special Report on American Involvement in the South African Economy." *Africa Today* 13, no. 1 (January 1966): 2–40. http://www.jstor.org/stable/4184684.

Stanley, Tim. "Belgium's Heart of Darkness." *History Today* 62, no. 10 (October 10, 2012). http://www.historytoday.com/tim-stanley/belgiums-heart-darkness.

Swomley, John. "F.O.R.'s Early Efforts for Racial Equality." *Fellowship* 56, nos. 7–8 (July–August 1990): 7–8. SCPC.

"Talking Drums: Boycott?" *Africa Today* 7, no. 1 (March 1960): 3–4. http://www.jstor.org/stable/4184057.

Ungar, Sanford J., and Peter Vale. "South Africa: Why Constructive Engagement Failed." *Foreign Affairs* 64, no. 2 (Winter 1985): 234–58. http://www.jstor.org/stable/20042571.

Walters, Ronald W. "The Clark Amendment: Analysis of U.S. Policy Choices in Angola." *Black Scholar* 12, no. 4 (July–August 1981): 2–12. http://www.jstor.org/stable/41066776.

Warner, Harry S. "South Africa: Who Provoked the Riots?" *Nation*, February 1952, 167–169.

Welch, Claude E., Jr. "Mobilizing Morality: The World Council of Churches and its Program to Combat Racism, 1969–1994." *Human Rights Quarterly* 23, no. 4 (November 2001): 863–910. https://www.jstor.org/stable/4489365.

World Peace Foundation. "Mass Atrocity Endings: Angola Civil War." Mass Atrocity Endings (website). Accessed April 2, 2018. https://sites.tufts.edu /atrocityendings/2015/08/07/angola-civil-war/.

US GOVERNMENT AND UN DOCUMENTS

CIA Family Jewels. National Security Archives. https://nsarchive2.gwu.edu /NSAEBB/NSAEBB222/index.htm.

"CIA Intelligence Memorandum: The Coup in Portugal Approved for release 2004 /08/16." Central Intelligence Agency. https://www.cia.gov/library/readingroom /docs/CIA-RDP85T00353R000100040012-9.pdf.

Comprehensive Anti-Apartheid Act of 1986, Public Law No: 99–440. https://www .congress.gov/bill/99th-congress/house-bill/4868.

Cuban Democracy Act, Title 22, Section 6001. https://www.treasury.gov/resource -center/sanctions/Documents/cda.pdf.

Lapchick, Richard E. *Sports Boycott in the International Campaign against Apartheid.* Centre Against Apartheid, U.N. Department of Political and Security Council Affairs. New York, 1977. http://africanactivist.msu.edu/document_metadata .php?objectid=32-130-2F3.

Lyndon B. Johnson National Security Files: Africa National Security Files, 1963–1969. http://cisupa.proquest.com/ksc_assets/catalog/3365.pdf.

Morgan v. Commonwealth of Virginia, 328 U.S. 373 (1946).

"1968 Democratic Party Platform." August 26, 1968. American Presidency Project. http://www.presidency.ucsb.edu/ws/index.php?pid=29604.

"1976 Democratic Party Platform." American Presidency Project. July 12, 1976. http://www.presidency.ucsb.edu/ws/index.php?pid=29606.

Trading with the Enemy Act, Title 50, Appendix—War and National Defense, Sec. 16(a)(b)(1), 30. https://www.treasury.gov/resource-center/sanctions /Documents/twea.pdf.

United Nations. "Declaration on the Granting of Independence to Colonial Countries and Peoples." December 14, 1960. https://www.un.org/ga/search/view _doc.asp?symbol=A/RES/1514(XV).

United States District Court Southern District of New York vs. Richard J. Wichlei, William N. Lovell, Donald Benedict, David Dellinger, Meredith Dallas, George M. Houser, Joseph G. Bevilacqua and Howard E. Spragg before Hon. Samuel Mandelbaum, District Judge, November 14, 1940. GMH PP.

United States District Court. The United States of America v. George M. Houser, Defendant. Indictment. GMH PP.

United Nations General Assembly. Fifth Special Session, Res. 2248 Question of South West Africa. May 19, 1967. http://www.refworld.org/docid/3b00f048c.html.

———.75th Plenary Meeting, November 21, 1979. Resolution 34/37 Question of Western Sahara. https://undocs.org/pdf?symbol=en/A/RES/34/37.

———. 21st Session. Res. 2145 (XXI) Question of South West Africa, October 27, 1966. http://www.worldlii.org/int/other/UNGA/1966/13.pdf.

United States Interdepartmental Group for Africa. *The Kissinger Study of Southern Africa: National Security Study Memorandum 39 (secret)*. Edited and introduced by Mohamed A. El-Khawas and Barry Cohen. 1st ed. Westport, CT: Lawrence Hill, 1976.

TESTIMONY BEFORE GOVERNMENT AND UN AGENCIES

Houser, George M. "Statement by George M. Houser, Executive Director Emeritus of the American Committee on Africa at the Twenty-fifth Anniversary of the Special Committee against Apartheid." May 6, 1988. GMH PP.

———. "Statement by George M. Houser, Executive Director of the American Committee on Africa, to the Subcommittee on African Affairs of the Senate Committee on Foreign Relations on February 4, 1976." GMH PP.

———. "What the U.S. Can Do about Apartheid: Testimony before the House Sub-committee on Africa." *Africa Today* 13, no. 3 (March 1966): 4–6. http://www.jstor.org/stable/4184699.

VIDEO

Civic Knowledge Project Remembers, 1942–1943. An Interview with George M. Houser and James Robinson. YouTube video. August 25, 2015. University of Chicago. https://www.youtube.com/watch?v=DukoUsonMiA.

Ehrlich, Judith, dir. *The Good War and Those Who Refused to Fight It*. Oley, PA: Bullfrog Films, 2000. http://www.bullfrogfilms.com/catalog/gwar.html.

Field, Connie, dir. *Have You Heard from Johannesburg: Seven Stories of the Global Anti-Apartheid Movement*. Minneapolis: Clarity Films, 2010. http://www.clarityfilms.org/haveyouheardfromjohannesburg/.

Field, Connie, and Rick Tejada-Flores, dirs. *A Tribute to George Houser from Connie Field and Rick Tejada-Flores*. Minneapolis: Clarity Films, 2015. http://africanactivist.msu.edu/video.php?objectid=32-12F-8A.

Houser, George M. *New York War Stories: Your Memories, Your Words*. New York: WNET, 2007. Accessed March 30, 2014. http://www.thirteen.org/newyorkwarstories/story.php?id=340.

Houser, Steven. "George Houser Greeting." YouTube video. May 23, 2014. https://www.youtube.com/watch?v=KSYlnCDylzo.

Knight, Richard. "Interview with Richard Knight." By David Wiley. Durban, South Africa. October 12, 2004. AAA. http://africanactivist.msu.edu/video.php?objectid=32-12F-3.

Nesbitt, Prexy. "Interview with Prexy Nesbitt." By Julie Fredrikse. Durban, South Africa. October 12, 2004. http://africanactivist.msu.edu/video.php?objectid=32-12F-2.

Singer, Bennett, and Nancy Kates, dirs. *Brother Outsider: The Life of Bayard Rustin*. DVD. 2003; New York: Question Why Films, 2010.

Washington, Robin, dir. *You Don't Have to Ride Jim Crow*. Durham: New Hampshire Public Television, 1995. DVD. http://www.robinwashington.com/jimcrow/order/.

Index

Numbers in *italics* indicate pages with illustrations

347

South Africa (*cont.*)
  Defiance Campaign in, 83–85, 87–90, 94,
  113–15, 279n18, 281n36; destruction and
  death from political violence in, 251,
  319n32; divestment of investments in
  apartheid-related companies, *148*, 173–
  74, 181–82, 226–27, 228–29, 260, 269n73;
  economic crisis in, 314n51; economy
  of and US investments and business
  relations in, 178–82, 188, 194–98, 222,
  224, 226–27, 260, 305n21, 305–6n23,
  306n25; education in, 120, 286n10;
  elections and elections observers
  in, 255; employment discrimination
  in, 196–97; Freedom Charter in, 114,
  123, 285n62, 319n25; gold coin sales
  from, 225–26; Houser meeting with
  liberation movement leaders, 209;
  Houser visits to, 112–17, 250–51, 255–56,
  257–58; international isolation of,
  293n2; international recognition of
  independence movement in, 3; loans to
  government of, 195–96, 226–27, 314n51;
  multiracial, nonracial, and interracial
  labels and policies in, 160, 295n32;
  Namibia mandate status under, 182–84,
  186–87, 207–9, 229, 249, 282n61, 309n72;
  nonaggression pacts with other African
  states, 215–16; oil embargo against,
  226; Order of the Grand Companions
  of Oliver Tambo Award for Houser,
  115, *152*, 257–58, 320n51; public criticism
  and revolutionary ferment in, 113–14;
  refugees from, 225; repression and
  arrests in, 90, 188, 224–25, 245;
  Sabotage Act passage in, 173; sanctions
  against, 86, 161–62, 179, 246, 248, 260;
  Sharpeville Massacre, 160–61; Soweto
  uprising, 224–25; sports boycott against,
  130, 193–94, 259, 305n18; stability in, US
  concerns about, 311n21; study tours
  of, 251, 255; surveillance of Houser
  in, 115–17; treason trial in and ACOA
  legal observer at trial, 131, 289–90n57,
  319n25; Truth and Reconciliation
  Commission, 259–60; US policy toward
  and interventions in, 180–81, 192–98,
  222; visa to visit, 96, 97, 113
South Africa Defense Fund, 123, 138, 287n26
South African Airways (SAA), 196–97, 208
South African Communist Party (SACP), 68,
  275n99
South African Congress of Trade Unions
  (SACTU), 123, 285n62

South African Indian Congress (SAIC), 123,
  285n62
South African Pioneer, 147
Southern Rhodesia. *See* Zimbabwe
  (Southern Rhodesia)
South West Africa. *See* Namibia (South West
  Africa)
South West African People's Organization
  (SWAPO), 183, 184, 203, 207, 208, 229,
  245, 246, 249, 256
Soviet Union: Communist experiment in, 8;
  Cuban facility for treatment of children
  of the Chernobyl nuclear accident in,
  253, 320n37; Cuba trade with, 320n35;
  education of African students in, 140,
  292n90; influence in Africa of, 134, 136
Spain, 91–92
sports boycott, 130, 193–94, 259, 305n18
Spragg, Howard, 26–27
Stanley, Eugene, 71
State Department Advisory Council on
  African Affairs, 162–63
Stevenson, Adlai, 139, *146*
Stewart, Ollie, 72, 73, 75, 78
Stoner's Restaurant, 55–56, 57–58
Stony Point Conference Center, 248
Student Anti-Apartheid Newsletter, 228
Student Christian Movement (SCM), 8, 9,
  10, 18
student movements: bank divestment
  campaign and demonstrations against,
  173–74, 181–82, 260; economic crisis and
  growth of, 7; effectiveness of, 7; foreign
  policy and social and political influences
  on, 7–10; social and economic justice
  focus of, 7–10
Student Nonviolent Coordinating
  Committee (SNCC), 166–67
Students for a Democratic Society (SDS),
  178, 305n21
Sudan, 124, 136, 287n27
Sullivan Principles and Leon Sullivan, 195,
  226, 305–6n23, 306n25
Sutherland, Bill, 83–84, 101, 102, 120, 127, 201,
  241–42
Suzman, Helen, 250, 319n25
SWAPO. *See* South West African People's
  Organization (SWAPO)
Swomley, John N., Jr., 18–19, 59, 83
Syria, 136

Tabata, I. B., 116–17
Tambo, Oliver: ACOA reputation with, 176;
  ANC Youth League role of, 83; arrest